Confessions from the Left

Major Concepts in Politics
and Political Theory

Garrett Ward Sheldon
General Editor

Vol. 15

PETER LANG
New York • Washington, D.C./Baltimore • Boston
Bern • Frankfurt am Main • Berlin • Vienna • Paris

John D. Nagle

Confessions from the Left

On the Pain, Necessity, and Joys of Political Renewal

PETER LANG
New York • Washington, D.C./Baltimore • Boston
Bern • Frankfurt am Main • Berlin • Vienna • Paris

Library of Congress Cataloging-in-Publication Data

Nagle, John D. (John David)
Confessions from the left: on the pain, necessity, and
joys of political renewal / John D. Nagle.
p. cm. — (Major concepts in politics and political theory: vol. 15)
Includes bibliographical references and index.
1. Political science. 2. Right and left (Political science). I. Title. II. Series.
JA66.N34   320.51'3—dc21   97-26605
ISBN 0-8204-3913-4
ISSN 1059-3535

Die Deutsche Bibliothek-CIP-Einheitsaufnahme

Nagle, John D.:
Confessions from the left: on the pain, necessity, and
joys of political renewal / John D. Nagle.
-New York; Washington, D.C./Baltimore; Boston; Bern;
Frankfurt am Main; Berlin; Vienna; Paris: Lang.
(Major concepts in politics and political theory; Vol. 15)
ISBN 0-8204-3913-4

Cover design by James F. Brisson.

The paper in this book meets the guidelines for permanence and durability
of the Committee on Production Guidelines for Book Longevity
of the Council of Library Resources.

© 1998 Peter Lang Publishing, Inc., New York

Printed in the United States of America.

For Ann, Alexandra, James, and Marisa

Contents

Acknowledgments

This work has been a long time in gestation, and I have benefited along the way from the insights and commentary of many colleagues. Collegial advice and reading of drafts, which I believe to be in general decline in academia, are most vital aids for work in progress. In the preparation for this project, I held long interviews with a select group of academic friends to elicit their views on left rethinking and renewal, and to try out my own ideas on key themes and points of contention. Here at Syracuse University Lou Kriesberg, John Agnew, Mark Rupert, and Paul Christensen have served as sounding boards for my ideas and have given me useful feedback. In Marburg, Reinhard Kühnl, Wilfried von Bredow, and Frank Deppe have helped shape my understanding of German and European political thought, and were particularly generous with their time. Hans See in Frankfurt, Peter Schultze in Berlin, Bill LeoGrande in Washington, and Isidor Wallimann in Basel have been good friends and willing listeners to earlier versions of important themes of this work. Whether in agreement or collegial debate, others who have contributed in various capacities include Claus Leggewie, Rainer Rilling, Eizens Silins, Ting Gong, Feng Chen, Jin Young Kim, Jin Min Chung, Alfredo Robles, Sankaran Krishna, Shishir Jha, Gautam Basu, Bhavna Dave, Ferenc Zsigo, Joe Julian, Jonathan Bach, Katalin Fabian, Martina Klisperova, Andrei Zdravomyslov, Andrei Korneyev, Valery Tishkov, Bernd Löwe, Gesine Schwann, Alison Mahr, and Hermann Schunk. In the end of course, responsibility for this work rests with me.

Chapter I

An End Is a New Beginning

I offer this work and these thoughts as a personal political confession in both meanings of that word: first, as an admission and acknowledgment (of fault, or of sins); and second, as a declaration of faith and loyalty (to values or ideals). It is a confession of a left scholar and activist who has waited too long to voice his disagreements with a left politics in decline and disrepute—a fault of omission. It is a confession of firm and continued political commitment, to the struggle for social justice and to a vital left politics capable of stemming the rightward drift toward an even more unjust and inegalitarian order, and of turning that drift around. Through this double sense of "confession" I hope to add some momentum to the search for a renewed left politics designed for our times.

This work is based on my more than thirty years of political activism on the academic left. I address the tasks of rethinking a left politics, which means reckoning with the failings of an older left politics (failings for today and the future, not necessarily failings in an earlier era), and renewing a left politics on a different basis. My own formative political experience, which shaped my original commitment to a left politics, has now been reshaped to the point where I must break with that past in order to maintain and revitalize my commitment to a future-oriented left politics.

A. A Personal Political Journey: Confessions of the Once and Still Committed

I have wanted for some time, and have hesitated for some time, to put these thoughts in print, that is, unretrievably in public view, since I know that even now they will disappoint and dismay some long-standing friends and colleagues. This long delay itself was a mistake, and it is a mistake that characterizes much of the difficulty in rethinking and renewing a left politics for our times; the error of holding on to comfortable ideas with which one no longer agrees, but holding on in part because many good people and fine friends still presumably hold these views.

I was somewhat of a latecomer to the politics of the left. I was a "red diaper" baby but did not come from a family background of left intellectualism. My parents were Chicago New Deal Democrats, coming from one of the best New Deal political machines in the country. My mother, born in a small Jewish shtetl in tsarist Russia (western Siberia, the province of Tomsk), had emigrated to America along with a brother in 1913 (great timing there), leaving from Riga and coming through Ellis Island to join other family members already in Chicago. My father was born in the United States, but his father had emigrated from a German-speaking area of Bohemia in what was then the Austro Hungarian Empire. My parents' politics had been consolidated by the experience of the Great Depression and the struggle of new immigrants to enter mainstream America, middle class society. My father had moved to Cleveland to maintain his employment with a firm in the yarn business. By the 1950s, our family had moved out of the Hough inner-city neighborhood and into suburban Beachwood and then upper-middle-class and heavily Jewish Shaker Heights, where I went to high school. We were solidly middle-class, and my father had, with only a high-school education, worked his way up to secretary-treasurer of this major yarn company. In the mid-1950s, my experience of American life was really mainstream middle-class and socially conservative. I would be the first in my family to go to college; it was my firm expectation, and one which my parents strongly supported, since it also went along with arrival in the great new middle class. My parents could not agree on religious education for me and my brother, so we were raised largely outside of any faith. However, as with many Jewish families in suburban Cleveland, for business and social reasons I did participate in the local Unitarian Church youth group for a while, and Unitarianism was the most open and liberal experience of my teen years.

My thinking about the business world was, however, quite negative; my father's boss was an obnoxious character who had a fine luxurious office for himself, and who spent lots of time at the country-club and on the golf course, while my father put in long evening and weekend hours ambitiously working his way up in the company. My father was now a confident part of top management, and for nearly twenty years he had seen success in his career. My father's work seemed indispensable to the company's growth; he knew more about the inner workings of the company, I thought, than the boss or any of the other managers. At some point, he wanted to become a partner in the firm, to join the ownership; his boss refused, a bitter argument lasting several days followed, and my father was fired. I can remember seeing him come home that day, a very different man, visibly stunned and depressed. He seemed suddenly older, and over the next several years he seemed worn down by life. He was never the same person after this loss of a position he had worked many years to achieve, and a new bitterness grew within him. Although at the time I did not view these events from any political perspective, it was clear to me that the business world was full of injustice. Business life was something I never wanted to get into, and the role of the big business owner, the boss, was in my mind a thoroughly negative one, associated not with creative effort or friendship with employees but with capriciousness and potential power for doing real injury to employees.

My early thinking about politics was heavily influenced by the McCarthyism of the mid-1950s; I could not see why it was unreasonable, during the cold war against Soviet communism, to root out potentially disloyal people from government positions. Communism, as it was presented to me, clearly seemed a threat to the United States and its interests, and I believed, in my teen years, that the United States did in fact represent the values of freedom, democracy, and even social progress. Although in terms of the personalities, I was attracted to Kennedy rather than Nixon, I was really pretty conservative in my adolescent years. This began to change only when I left home and went to MIT to study, at least at first, physics and mathematics.

At MIT in the early 1960s an independent student politics was just barely beginning to develop. I joined a fraternity in which politics was overwhelmingly white Protestant Republicanism; I was one of the few members from a Democratic family background, and one of even fewer who celebrated Kennedy's victory in 1960. For this I spent much of election night shut out of the fraternity house on Bay State Road in Back Bay Boston. I was ambivalent about the civil rights movement: I supported it in principle but often did not support its tactics, which seemed to be progressing, with Martin Luther King's civil disobediance, beyond the political norms of the times. I can remember that I really disliked Malcolm X and his brand of "black power" activism, which seemed to me then to be really wrongheaded and threatening to the hopes for a more decent and more integrated society. (While I have learned a lot more about the reasons for Malcolm X and his politics of black separatism and confrontation, I have not changed my overall view of his politics, which now unfortunately has regained attractiveness in some black student groups, partly because of the growing bankruptcy of the old civil rights leadership after the breakthroughs of the 1960s and 1970s). In short, I was not on the left politically; rather I was in a state of rather cold war liberalism (which, in retrospect, matched Kennedy's approach pretty well).

The crucial issue for my conversion to a left politics in the mid-1960s was the Vietnam War. Some of my professors at MIT, in the political science department, were involved in research for the Defense Department sponsored by the Advanced Research Project Agency (ARPA). I worked for Professor Ithiel de Sola Pool as a computer programmer on his research team; Ithiel Pool was a decent and humane person, a friend to students, and willing to speak his views openly and honestly. (As the Vietnam War became more controversial, many professors at MIT, known superhawks, simply shut up or stopped talking to students, except perhaps those students whose views were also firmly pro-war—although one could never be sure, since conversions like my own were pretty common.) From Professor Pool and others I gathered an early impression in 1962 and 1963 that Vietnam was to be the place where the United States would draw the line—a test case to stop the expansion of Asian communism, which was still seen purely as an extension of Moscow's will to dominate. I was impressed by Pool's knowledge of international politics, and by his commitment to liberal causes in the United States; it was in part my contact with him, and a few other faculty in the MIT political science department, that increased my interest in political life generally, and, combined with my gradual retreat from physics (I hated lab work), led me to switch majors to political science. I sometimes wonder at the (often unrealized) power that one or two interesting and engaging teachers can have in shaping a student's career and life. It is, I think, very difficult for anybody to be able to critically evaluate ideas separated from the personality of the messenger; it is especially difficult for young students, often studying away from home and community for the first time, to be able to weigh the substance of an idea (or a whole field) apart from the personal appeal of a small number of professors. On the other hand, the chanciness of life itself—the influence of the events that, though not really random, are unexpected and unplanned, on an individual life course—is a factor which should not be underestimated (as it so often is by ideologues of all stripes). In the early years of the United States involvement in Vietnam, therefore, I was generally supportive of the effort to resist the Vietcong, to aid the South Vietnamese regime in the hope of promoting democracy there. Kennedy's policy seemed prudent, on the basis of analyses by people like Defense Secretary Robert McNamara, who had after all assembled some of the best minds to direct Pentagon policy in a more scientific, rational manner. The pride of possession of scientific credentials was understandably strong among the MIT faculty and students, and the Kennedy regime brought lots of these folks into the thick of Washington politics. Remember that Kennedy's policy of graduated response was, for me, the alternative to calls by Barry Goldwater and Curtis Lemay to "bomb the Vietnamese back to the Stone Age." In the wake of Kennedy's assassination in 1963, I was fearful that Goldwater would become the next president, and I worked for Johnson's election and trusted that his policies would be more progressive—meaning, for me, moderately liberal in domestic affairs and less interventionist in foreign matters. I really did believe in 1964 that Johnson would not get us involved in Vietnam.

In the course of my undergraduate years at MIT, my migration from physics and math into political science, which seemed wonderfully interesting, began to waken my consciousness to the larger world beyond the United States. Although I had never been out of the United States (except briefly to Canada), I was fascinated by international relations and comparative politics. Rather than pursue law studies, which my parents favored, I moved to Harvard's graduate program in government and studied there for the next four years. Harvard's government department was in fact not very interesting at that time; many courses were largely stories of "great men I once knew" told by veterans of an elite-level diplomatic and advisory political class. I chose to pursue my first real research project for my doctorate there under the guidance of Seymour Martin Lipset. Lipset, one of the most prominent scholars in comparative political sociology, was himself migrating politically from his earlier socialist views. In the mid-1960s he was probably a centrist social democrat, in European terms (he has since migrated farther to the right and has worked for many years out of the

Hoover Institute in Stanford). He had just come to Harvard when I was there, and he helped me secure a job for 1966–1967 with a German survey research institute, the Institut für angewandte Sozialwissenschaft (Infas) in Bad Godesburg (now part of Bonn). My dissertation was a study of right-radicalism in West Germany, the politics of the upstart National Democrats (NPD) in 1966–1967, their ideology, and their electoral base. I improved my skills in the German language and was able to do some interviews with NPD voters by the end of my research stay. I loved Bonn and the food, beer, wine and pastries, and made some lifelong friends at Infas. It was at Infas that I met my first democratic socialists and independent left socialists (the communist party of West Germany was at that time officially banned); Infas, run by its entrepreneurial director Klaus Liepelt, did survey research almost exclusively for the German Social Democrats. The politics of the institute were an eye-opening experience for me, and my new German colleagues and friends had many debates that first year, about the Vietnam War, about socialism, about Willy Brandt, about the new Grand Coalition of Social Democrats and Christian Democrats in West Germany. I became an opponent of Johnson's Vietnam War policies, and a general supporter of left social democracy in its German context. For the first time I understood and came to support a left politics outside of what the Democratic Party offered in the United States. It was my first real road map into a socialist politics and gave me my first conceptual understanding of Marx and Marxist thinking. In May of 1967, my wife and I took a two-week trip to Moscow and viewed the May Day celebrations there. It was a very mixed bag of impressions—on the one hand, people seemed to be generally optimistic and proud of their country and its achievements, and Moscow was an exotic place; but on the other hand, it was a pretty colorless and controlling political and social system, without any real attraction for me as a place to live. This was very different from my reactions to West Germany, which had developed a very generous welfare system and a prosperous social market economy. However, my visit to Moscow further whetted my appetite for comparative politics based on extensive travel and living in different countries, and solidified my ideas about the kind of academic work I wanted to pursue.

On my return to the United States in 1967, I became active in the antiwar movement, even getting involved in SDS-sponsored demonstrations and a sit-in against a Dow Chemical recruiter on the Harvard campus. I worked, along with my wife, for Eugene McCarthy, gathering petition signatures and mobilizing campaign workers in the Brookline neighborhood where we lived with our newborn child. I marched in demonstrations to Post Office Square, saw people get roughed up by police and pro-war construction workers (nothing deadly, but punches and pulled beards and long hair); these experiences only hardened my new political leftism, and served to push me somewhat further to the left.

When I had finished my dissertation, I got a faculty job in 1968 at Syracuse University and spent my first years there as a young radical professor, engaging in the biggest demos Syracuse had ever seen, and pushing the campus faculty at Maxwell meetings to oppose the war. Syracuse was a pretty conservative university, but it was growing and adding new young faculty members, and campus life was becoming rapidly politicized by the Vietnam War. I let my hair grow long, did not wear coat and tie for lectures, and associated with other young leftist instructors, some much more militant than myself. I was denounced by one dean as a "dupe of the communists," and a right-wing professor at another local college also publicly denounced my treasonous politics; but 1968 was indeed a watershed year, a breakthrough for free speech on the war and political debate in the nation, and my career was not destroyed by my antiwar politics and activism. I could even, for the first time in the postwar history of Syracuse University, design and offer a course on Marxist theory (supported by a student petition), which I then taught for more than twenty years. The course was a huge success for many years, and my most satisfying teaching experience generally.

So my thinking and activism have been defined by a left politics ever since my college days in the mid-1960s. They have stemmed from my choice of support for the civil rights and antiwar movements in the United States, and from my early conversations with young German left social democrats in 1966–1967. My politics has been self-defined as socialist or democratic left ever since, but I have always been uneasy about the pat formulations (dogma) of what I would call the sectarian left, the antidemocratic left, or the end-of-history left. I am also of a generation that straddles both the Old Left of trade unionism, working-class parties, and the social democratic welfare state, and the New Left of antiwar, environmental, feminist, human rights, and Third World solidarity politics. I never bought the entire New Left critique of the Old Left, nor could I share the Old Left's reactionary reflex against the student and youth culture movements of 1968. In this respect, I am a 1968er of sorts, but with conflicting commitments on both sides of 1968. This itself has meant that I never bought into any left sectarianism, and I have been turned off by all claims to have the complete truth. Since I myself had conflicting commitments that I could neither reconcile entirely nor abandon, I have assumed a skeptical attitude toward all fundamentalism, including any on the left. It has seemed perfectly natural to have conflicting values and orientations, and this is in fact what has made my work and teaching in comparative politics so interesting over the years. I have felt comfortable over the years as an independent left scholar, in good measure because I could understand and support various policies that could not be fit into any one narrow ideological package. I have now come to view this condition not as a weakness of my commitment but as a reflection of personal internally contending values, including conservative and liberal values, which I now believe may play a useful role in rethinking and renewing a left progressive politics.

As a academic at Syracuse University in the field of comparative politics, I had the chance to develop collegial and personal ties to left scholars and activists in Europe (mainly Germany, but also Western and Eastern Europe, and the former Soviet Union) and to broaden my American perspective, though not much beyond the Western left. I make no claims to special insight on the ideas of the nonwestern left, although I have worked with many scholars and graduate students, especially from South Asia and East Asia, whose ideas, whether socialist or other, were stimulating to my own political thinking. In what follows, the nonwestern left and its increasing importance will find its way into my discourse through indirect or secondhand sources.

B. Why Now? Confession and Renewal

Throughout the period of the cold war, I have stayed firm in my commitment to some vision of a socialist political agenda. This was easy enough in the 1960s and 1970s, when left political ideas were overcoming McCarthyite strictures in American colleges and academic circles and were growing in popularity. I even put together the first course at Syracuse University on Marxist theory, at the request (by petition) of over 60 students, and taught this subject for more than twenty years. Throughout this period my own appreciation of Marx's ideas deepened, but I also maintained a critical stance toward aspects of Marx's work (cf. Nagle, 1991). I joined Marxist reading circles out of growing interest and need to discuss his ideas, and quit these circles when some members began to traffic in heavy quotation-mongering as the weapon of choice. I think my experiences and travels on the Marxist left have not been so unusual, in that I saw great insights in Marx but was really turned off by attempts to make Marx the last word on socialist thinking, or to try to justify every paragraph the poor man ever wrote. Yet I was never interested in bolting the political left for another political standpoint. So I have been dismayed by those who have abandoned the left for neoconservative or neoliberal politics, especially when they suddenly became the newly annointed for their brilliant insight and intellectual depth and were amply funded in their new proselytizing, even though I have also shared almost all of their misgivings about and critiques of the left. The more militant left certainly has overfulfilled its quota of stupid, vapid, and self-congratulatory ideas and proposals, and God knows that someone from within the left itself would inevitably pick up on these obvious failings and decide to exit (often for another fundamentalist utopia). Ex-leftists have always been prized by conservative and liberal idea promoters as crown witnesses to the utter bankruptcy of socialism, communism, or left thinking of any variety. My own perspective was that the left, while guilty of many mistakes and excesses and wrongheaded ideas, could correct itself and could mature beyond its infantilism of idealist and often youthful rebellion. Even those, like the late Irving Howe, co-founder of *Dissent* magazine, who acted as an faithful critic of the left while remaining a self-defined socialist, seemed to me during the cold war to give too much aid and comfort to the conservatives and liberals in their crusade against any type of socialist politics. I preferred myself to continue to act within the left as an independent thinker, neither accepting proclaimed "leftist" notions that I felt to be harmful to the cause of socialism nor clearly denouncing or renouncing those whose "left" politics were so flawed. As long as there seemed to be hope for a broad-based democratic left politics that included protection for repressed minorities and the poor, social controls on capital and finance, opposition to American support for right-wing dictators in the third world, and opposition to covert action against "progressive" third world regimes (Fidel Castro's Cuba in the early years; later Salvador Allende's Popular Unity government in Chile and Sandinista Nicaragua), I was very reluctant to either leave the left or put myself in the position of spending most of my effort openly arguing against certain left ideas and positions which I actually felt were wrongheaded, simplistic, or outdated.

With the slow decline of the Keynesian welfare state in the West, and the collapse of communism and the Soviet Union in Europe, it is now clear that any attempt to renew and revive a left politics for a post-cold war era of global capitalism must begin with an intellectual break from the left agenda and practices of the past forty years. With the realistic possibilities of that era—which were considerable and which should not simply be written off—now gone, the need to critique those ideas is greater, and the costs and risks of giving aid and comfort to antileft forces are lessened. The end of the East-West confrontation in its cold war formulation has, as I have argued elsewhere (Nagle, 1992), emancipated the democratic left from the impossible task of resisting right-wing anti-communism (through a stance of anti-anticommunism) while at the same time providing its own opposition to Soviet communism (through various visions of socialism with a human face). There is now a greater space for new thinking, as well as greater need, with less consideration of the immediate chances for realizing a socialist political agenda, which are, if not nil, much reduced and improbable.

At the same time, I have been listening to my friends on the left, reading their writings, following their political activities these past several years for signs of revision and renewal of left politics. I would date this for myself, as a conscious effort, from the late 1970s, coinciding with the Reagan-Thatcher breakthroughs on the right and the stagnant era of the Brezhnev-Andropov-Chernenko gerontocracy in the Soviet Union. It has seemed so difficult for the left, and for many of my own friends and colleagues on the left, to rethink and renew their commitments. It has been difficult for me as well, because the positions of the various left politics in earlier years did, in the main, have a logic and an idealism that I still believe are essential to a socialist politics. Yet at the same time the left really needs to increase its learning capacity, and part of this at least must involve a more all-around confession of past failings, and a much expanded openness to rethinking and revising its political agenda. This manuscript is dedicated to aiding that task, by putting the current period of left political crisis in historical and comparative perspective, by examining a series of issues confronting the left in an open and critical light, and by sifting through the comments of colleagues and friends for clues as to where potential new socialist agendas are perhaps becoming visible.

I do not pretend, in this work, to put forward any definitive formulation of a new left project, although my preferences on particular points will be fairly clear; I think I have learned that my own perspective is limited by my own experiences, my own personal position (white, male, middle-aged and married with three grown children, professor from the northeast United States). I may try to empathize with the very different positions of others, and I certainly have changed my views on any number of issues as a result of both up-close and distant learning, but I also know that any one individual cannot reflect accurately for others their unique experiences or the originality of their own critical thinking.

What I am attempting to do is to marshal my own experience, as honestly and forthrightly as I can, to try to make sense out of the current crisis of left thinking, to gauge the prospects for a left renewal, and finally to try to describe the early and still potential beginnings of the new socialist agenda that is taking shape. This is my own personal political journey, my reflections on what I have learned along the way, and what I now think about the challenges the left faces. My own preferences in terms of a socialist political project are pretty clearly stated along the way, but they are just my own choices, put forward here to further discussion and debate. My thought is that much more dialogue among those still committed or newly committed to the left is needed, on the widest-ranging array of ideas. My hope is that an openness in debate, an honesty of purpose, and a confession of limited knowledge and insight on the left will, in an environment of growing social polarization—the glaring new age of inequality—also be attractive to some parts of the youth now turning away from political life and civil society, and may offer a new rationale for democratic involvement and meaningful engagement.

References

Nagle, John (1991). *Looking at Marx*. Syracuse, NY: Center for Instructional Development.

———— (1992). "Befreiung vom Kommunismus: Denkanstöße aus dem amerikanischen Sozialismus" *Sozialismus* 18:10 (October) 64–69.

Chapter II

An End to Endism— There Are No Ends to History

A. Three Classic Western Value Systems: Progress through Conflict

At least since the French Revolution, Western politics has maintained three distinctive political value systems—conservatism, liberalism, and socialism—whose leading proponents have viewed their own value system as a complete worldview, standing alone and separate, and in steady conflict with wrongheaded or false competitors.

In the Western tradition at least, these three basic ideologies continue to shape political discourse in the modern era. Each of these grand perspectives offers a coherent worldview or *Weltanschauung*, a set of values or priorities for human society, and its own image of the good society. Each has demonstrated its capacity to motivate citizens, to legitimatize or to challenge regimes, to inspire new beginnings for nations. Each ideology leaves out or minimizes values other than its own, and is therefore incomplete as a description of what human beings desire or how they relate to society; each, pushed to its own extreme or utopian end, contains the seeds of dystopia and catastrophe.

No matter what some ideologues may claim, there exist several contradictory value systems rather than one because the human condition itself is full of contradictions. If there were in fact one unified ideology that could capture the essence of the human condition, then it would by now have become apparent, and alternative competing ideologies would have died out. Instead there has been a continuing clash of values, which must, I believe, be rooted in the deep contradictions of life itself as experienced by most people. I think that the most basic contradictions of the human condition are three, each related to one of the great value systems which have marked Western political cultures:

1. Human beings are mortal, and they know it. They feel at various times a need to identify a larger spiritual meaning for this earthly existence. They find daily comfort and in crises, crucial support in a sense of belonging that transcends their own individual life and certainly its material trappings.
2. Human beings are individuals. Each person is consciously separate from the collectivity and seeks freedom to develop his or her own personality, at times in discord with current community norms. The endless differentiation of individuals is the expression of the inventiveness of the species, contributed person by person despite conformist norms.
3. Human beings are social. They choose to live together, they feel a need for social interaction, and they care about the kind of society they live in. There is a sense of social conscience for most people, an idea of when a society has gone bad, or has failed to provide some minimum of social justice. Most people do have some compassion for others in society, even when they have no direct stake in others' well-being. Margaret Thatcher's famous quip, "There is no such thing as society" is nonsensical though politically effective as a modern media soundbite.

There may be a fourth contradiction, which is just now reaching popular consciousness: that the human species lives in a complex ecological system with all other species, and that this system can be threatened by human activity. It remains to be seen whether this quandary is subsumable under one or more competing value systems, or whether environmentalism represents a new qualitative dilemma of the human condition not reducible to other ideologies (cf. Craig Murphy's project for a global ecological Keynesianism, 1994; or Heilbroner's notions of a future ecological socialism, 1990.)

It may well be that conservatism, liberalism, and socialism draw their respective strengths (and weaknesses) from their ability to articulate primarily one (but not all) of these conditions which define the human experience. This would mean that until and unless these key quandaries somehow disappear, a single value system by itself will be unable to address the needs and desires of all people regardless of stage of life, economic situation, or cultural background.

Conservatism refers here to the classic and generic wisdom of people like Edmund Burke, Gustav le Bon, and Joseph le Maistre (or perhaps Confucius, from a nonwestern setting). The conservative values the stability of tradition, the proper or natural ordering of society and social relations, the spiritual and religious meaning of human exist-ence, and loyalty to one's land and people (cf. McClelland, 1970). In Western feudal society, this meant upholding the true faith of the coun-try, accepting one's born and natural place in the social hierarchy, and defending the homeland and people against outsiders. The conserva-tive value system is cautious about human nature and individual ratio-nality. It rests upon the assumption of limited possibilities for most, and the acceptance of an inevitable hierarchy in human society. It sees spiritual faith as offering fulfillment, and consolation for the suf-ferings and tragedies of earthly existence. It finds value in a moral order for the soul. The individual needs a transcendent identity, as a member of the larger tradition, whether religious, ethnic, kinship, lin-guistic, cultural, or national, which survives beyond any lifetime. The watchwords of conservatism are: *faith, tradition, country.* Conserva-tism is the politics of human identity.

Liberalism is meant here as the principled belief in the individual, in his or her rationality, and in the liberty to choose one's own path to self-improvement. Liberalism in the western tradition is identified with the thinking of Adam Smith, John Locke, Emanuel Kant, and John Stuart Mill. Liberalism is optimistic about individuals, who have com-mon sense and can reason for themselves. Liberalism values the free-ing of human reason from constraints—including religion, tradition, or government—in favor of enterprise and innovation, which are seen as the engines of progress for humankind. Efficiency in the economy depends on freeing individual opportunity. It is up to individuals to make their own way, to succeed or fail, and to decide on the meaning of life. For liberalism, the individual comes before society, self-interest before the collective welfare, and personal choice before community norms. The watchwords of liberalism are: *liberty, reason, individual-ism.* Liberalism embraces the politics of individual freedom.

Socialism covers the broad tradition including Robert Owen, Charles Fourier, Pierre-Joseph Proudhon, and Karl Marx (see Laidler, 1968). Socialism places its priorities on the idea of social justice, which means a society committed to meeting the basic human needs of the whole population. Socialism seeks some greater degree of social equality, to achieve what would be widely recognized as fairness or equity, and it promotes solidarity among groups to achieve solutions to problems.

Socialism argues for a social responsibility for the material well-being (welfare) of the poor and disadvantaged as more important than the maximum opportunity for individual wealth. Socialism emphasizes basic economic security rather than unlimited economic risk-taking. It puts the common good above the rights of self-centered individualism. Socialism reminds us that no man (or woman) is an island, that each individual depends on the larger society, and that solidarity among people is what holds the good society together. The watchwords of socialism are: *equality, security, solidarity.* Socialism demands a politics of social justice..

At various times, liberals and socialists have pronounced conservatism dead (one need only recall a slogan of the 1960s, "God is dead"); socialists or communists have relegated liberalism to the "trash-bin of history" (during the Great Depression, for example); and most recently, liberals and conservatives have claimed that socialism is an idea with no future. A more realistic, less dogmatic perspective recognizes that no historic value system is without lasting attraction, because each speaks to certain deeply felt human desires and needs. Likewise, a broad comparative perspective, which is the view of this text, also must recognize that no one value system by itself provides a complete and adequate understanding of the individual and of society, that each system is subject to continuing challenges. Moreover, in a complex dialectical process, each value system in fact needs the others for its own further evolution, since in isolation each becomes sterile dogma.

In fact, each value system has undergone periods of questioning and has shown a capacity to adapt to historical experience and changing socioeconomic and political structures (Rejai, 1984). Classic conservatism and the political conservatism of the Catholic church, at least in the West, have overcome their earlier opposition to political democracy; in good measure this is a lesson drawn from their collaboration with fascism in the 1920s and 1930s. In the United States, conservative thinking has generally repudiated its earlier support for racial segregation and its ideas of a natural racial hierarchy. Western liberalism has also learned from the class struggles and women's struggles in the nineteenth and early twentieth century, for equal rights for all citizens. Today, liberalism could not conceive of excluding any group from full citizenship status on the basis of either property requirements or gender disqualification. And (Western) liberalism, from the challenges of the Great Depression, has modified its position on the role of the state in economic matters, generally becoming more agreeable to expanded regulation and social service. Socialism was modernized in the nineteenth century through the works of Proudhon, Owens, and Marx. What had been, in the feudal period, a predominantly agrarian and craft guild socialism, hostile to modern urban industrial development, now welcomed modern science and industry as a new opportunity for fulfilling socialist goals. Socialism may now also be learning from the collapse of communism and the negative features of the Western welfare state, as well as from the "new social movements" for peace, environment, and women, which may produce a renewed socialist agenda compatible with postindustrial, environmental, and global market requirements.

This description of conservative, liberal and socialist value systems and their evolving competition has centered on the Western experience and has not attempted to include the social and political value systems associated with Confucianism, Buddhism, Hinduism, and Islam. Nor does it touch on the political thinking of the Arab historian Ibn Khaldun (1332–1406), the Indian theorist of nonviolence Mohandas K. (Mahatma) Gandhi (1869–1948), the theory of Sun Yat-sen (1867–1925), about the "Three Principles of the People," the popular socialist thought of the Cuban José Martí, or the African socialism of Leopold Senghor and Julius Nyerere (see Sigmund, 1967). Nonwestern or non-European value systems may contain different emphases or syntheses of the values expressed in Western conservative, liberal, and socialist thought, but the contradictions of competing values cannot be avoided in any system. The predominantly conservative cast of Confucian thought on proper government, morals, and ethics is at odds with the values of individualism and equality. Sun Yat-sen attempted to combine nationalism, democracy, and socialism in his theoretical framework, thereby tolerating internal contradictions within his overall system. Much of modern nonwestern political theory has been heavily influenced, either in acceptance and assimilation or rejection, by Western thought, and this has produced new variants and hybrid theories.

B. Consequences of Endism: Searching for Final Solutions

The Western political preoccupation with conflicts among the three classic value systems has obscured another side of the process of historical evolution of Western societies: that despite periods of triumph and triumphalism of one or another contending school of thought, or of defeat and humiliation of another, the competition of basic values has in fact constantly renewed itself. There are signs that even in the current period of tremendous crisis in socialist political thought and vision, some observers take a longer-term perspective and suggest that the contending schools of thought in fact must continue to engage each other, not as enemies searching for a final victory or a final solution, but as necessary complements in a complex and contradictory world of human existence.

Eberhard Puntsch is a deeply committed German liberal and former deputy in the Bavarian parliament. He studied philosophy and wrote for many years on issues of modern industry, human dignity, and politics. He is president of the liberal Thomas-Dehler Foundation in Munich. In a recent slender volume (1994) Puntsch presents an argument that the political spectrum is not bipolar, running from socialism on the left through liberalism in the middle to conservatism on the right, but rather has a different topography, in which liberalism, conservatism, and socialism each have independent standpoints on a triangle of core principles, from which they can critique and yet also complement each other. Puntsch (16–18) traces the history of the left-middle-right conceptualization to the middle of the nineteenth century, when in the Frankfurt Pauls-Church parliament of 1848, which attempted to draw up a new democratic constitution for a unified Germany, the seating arrangement (viewed from the speaker's podium) reflected a left faction composed of more radical democrats, a middle of liberal constitutionalists, and a right of monarchists. What Puntsch describes is the historical connection in the West more generally of socialist, liberal, and conservative viewpoints in the struggles over the formation of the modern nation-state and the domination of its politics. This time- and task-bound connection in itself should indicate that with time and transformation of society, economy, and culture, this left-middle-right concept of political alternatives would outlive its relevance. Clearly, in Puntsch's view, the time has come to recognize the need for a different conceptualization. He points to the many convergences in the party programs of the Social Democrats, Liberals, and Christian Democrats in contemporary Germany, with only shadings of differentiation. Yet Puntsch wants to retain the central values of socialism, liberalism, conservatism, because as he sees it, they are each and all essential components of a desired political project:

A state that can be considered humane must fulfill three principles: it must have order; its order must be just, or at least be seen as just, by the majority of its citizens; and it must be free. In other words, a humane state is built from the interaction of three principles—the principle of order, the principle of justice, and the principle of freedom (1994: 41, my translation).

Puntsch views these three principles as both "equally valid" and "indispensable" (56–57). From a German liberal perspective—which has drawn on the traumatic experiences of German politics, war, the holocaust of the first half of this century; and then the amazing rebirth of democracy, economic prosperity, and social welfare of the second half—Puntsch outlines what he sees in each of these three principles that is absolutely essential, and absolutely necessary as a complement to the others. At the same time, he devotes far more space to the liberal perspective and therefore does not at all surrender his own standpoint as a liberal. These three principles have been represented in the postwar (West) German party system by the Social Democrats, the Free Democrats, and the Christian Democrats, which continue to have different essential orientations and views on these principles and their relative importance.

For Puntsch, the great success of postwar German politics has been the emergence of a basic consensus on a representation of all three principles within the democratic political system. Like so many German political thinkers within the broad (corporatist) consensus, Puntsch contrasts the postwar consensus with the inhumane and anti-democratic outcomes of ideological infighting of the Weimar period, giving rise to the Nazi dictatorship of 1933–1945 and its tragedies for Germany and the world. As Puntsch recounts, rather fairly, the relative importance of each principle for each party, he connects his own liberal preference to his experiences as a nineteen-year old at the end of World War II, and his determination that nothing like the German dictatorship should ever happen again. For him, the liberal concept of freedom of the individual from dictatorship became a leading principle, yet at the same time he emphasizes the recognition of other principles held equally strongly by other citizens. This recognition and respect of one's own values and the values of others is the cement of the successful German democracy.

Is this too much relativism? Is it tied just to the searing experience of German fascism and its horrible consequences? Or is Puntsch reflecting on more basic lessons, which German liberals (as well as social democrats and conservatives) brought to the longer-term evolution of German society and which now form part of its democratic civic culture and its newer traditions? Is one of the great lessons of

Germany's history in this century, in fact, the need (in the West at least) to reconceptualize ideological positions in a new framework, in which a plurality of valid principles continue to contend, but in a mutually constructive framework of democracy (with no modifiers)?

Puntsch's reflections have their limitations, of course. He does not discuss the phenomenon of "mixed feelings" within individuals or their shifts with time and experience; rather, he speaks of the clarification of basic value orientation which "affords the possibility of gathering up people in their perspectives and positions and leading them to loyalty and cooperative work" (58–59). This, I think, neglects the value mixing and internal struggle (cf. also Tucker, 1961, on the internally divided psyche and alienation) which can turn thoughtful citizens off to politics. On the other hand, a clarification of values might mobilize precisely those individuals with more simplistic and dogmatic loyalties to one single principle. Nonetheless, Puntsch sees a more self-conscious effort to understand one's own standpoint and its origins as fostering greater tolerance for others, even within one's own general principled orientation (83–84).

Karl Mannheim in 1929 had accused German intellectuals of mistaking their ideas for eternal truths when they were just rationalizing particular social interests, and in so doing adding to the polarization of modern society; for this he was roundly denounced by his colleagues. He saw the misuse of intellectual work as ideological weaponry in the hands of political parties as a sign of the coming political civil war in Germany. But could it be that after the Nazi experience, at least for some time, German intellectuals had learned the lessons of modesty and tolerance (cf. Engler, 1991)? If so, does this mean that the lessons could be forgotten over time, or are they specific to just the immediate postwar generations? Can intellectuals really overcome the tendency to create ideology out of social science, or is this a temptation that they will, professionally, succumb to again and again? This theme will need to be addressed further, but the German experience after World War II is a profound test of Mannheim's thesis, though perhaps such an extreme case that generalization is not possible.

Puntsch's reflections come at the end of the cold war era, to whose political traditions he is paying homage. But in Germany today, liberals, in the Free Democratic Party at least, are facing an existential crisis of their own. Younger Germans with left-liberal views coming from the new social movements of the 1970s and 1980s are working with the Greens, the party of environmentalism, feminism, antibureaucracy, and peace. Puntsch treats the Greens as one of many "nonclassic" parties and advises liberals to pursue a fair (and therefore effective) battle to represent their issues; in this sense he still has the general concept that with an effective effort the Green voters can be absorbed into the "classic" parties again, as the "refugees and emigrants" from the East were absorbed in the 1950s (95–96). So while his reflections are telling for the old West Germany in its prime, German politics in the 1990s is undergoing a transformation in its political landscape that complicates his basic schematic topography but represents another stage in the democratic synthesis of conflicting and complementary principles.

Daniel Bell is one of the most prominent critics of Western societies of the postwar period. In the latter 1970s, Bell proclaimed a cultural crisis of modern capitalist, bourgeois society, and elaborated the decline of its ethical and moral underpinnings. Rejecting both antimodernist and postmodernist critiques, he spelled out the reasons that give rise to opposition to modern bourgeois society, and to the erosion of the very social norms and traditions that were necessary for the further viability of liberal democracy and market capitalism. Liberalism had basically taken these norms for granted, as free goods that did not have to be worked on in any organized fashion. In a more recent German-language edition of this work, Bell appended a new epilogue, which contains some telling updates and which put Bell's entire critique into a framework of value systems that compete and conflict but at the same time are absolutely necessary and complementary to each other. Throughout this new epilogue, Bell is at pains to demonstrate the sterility of all ideological purisms. In his section on the end of communism and the presumed victory of market capitalism, he warns:

> If there should be a market economy, then social justice demands a just, even distribution of income, so that individuals can strive for their desired goods from the same starting point. . . . Therefore, if we want to have a market economy, we need also a definition of "citizenship" (what I have called the "public budget") which permits individuals, unhindered, to participate in the market as in politics, as members of civil society (1991: 337–338).

Bell, like Puntsch, sees the old "left" and "right" labels as obsolete and misleading in the current situation, but at the same time he defends their core values, no matter how mistaken the "means" used to achieve their ideals (343). He sees some hope in the new debate in political philosophy which will, he hopes, question everything again, without all the old and now outdated ideological baggage (343). This hope, however, must be measured against the evidence of how hard it is to simply "forget" what was done in the name of what and why for so long. And I doubt that Bell means to suggest that the whole former history of Western social thinking is irrelevant to a renewal of Western social thought; after all, whence come the lessons to be learned except from a clear and honest appraisal of the past record that has led to the current crisis? Bell's insight is that in the current philosophical debate, the old questions and positions would not still dominate and would not suffocate the chance for a fresh appreciation of where the Western societies are now. Old perspectives should not put rigid boundaries around the present critiques and should not limit possible new syntheses, new ideas for reform, or a future political agenda.

Tellingly, Bell pleads for a renewal of a "normative public philosophy and the differing perspectives which provide the ethical basis for the polis, since every viable society is fundamentally a moral order, in which people share a ready respect for each other and for the common good" (344):

> I write, as I once described myself, in economics as a social democrat, in politics as a liberal, and in culture as a conservative. I don't see any contradiction in this, since the sphere of economics is not an end in itself, but rather an instrument, a means, to create prosperity and to find a just distribution within the "public budget." I am convinced that in the economic sphere the claims of the community come before those of the individual, since the good society is defined as one that provides everyone a living standard which makes possible dignity and participation in society. In culture I am a conservative, because I believe in continuity and tradition, and that this sphere of the aesthetic also has to subordinate itself to moral judgments (344, my translation).

Bell regrets that the old concepts of liberal, conservative, and socialist have become a hindrance to the debate, filled with old meanings and associations with old battles. Here again, however, there is as yet no new vocabulary, and one might take this as another sign of the openness of the current crisis and the uncertainty about how to define a renewal. So Bell continues, "My argument states that these three positions in fact are joined together on account of the normative view of society as a 'public budget,' in contrast to the lack of connection among moral viewpoints as represented by reactionary conservatives, who support an unfettered individualism in economics, and a moral censorship in social and cultural affairs" (344).

Andrew Schotter is chairman of the economics department at New York University. Western economists are overwhelmingly favorable to market capitalism, and have, among social scientists, been the most consistent critics of socialism as an economic alternative. Yet Schotter offers a critique of capitalism (1992) which recommends using "some socialism" as a needed antidote to capitalism. Schotter argues that with the demise of communism, which clouded all American political thinking about measures to improve capitalism and make it more humane, we can now begin to rethink measures that would especially give incentives to the poor and marginalized within our society, without seeing these as part of some socialist challenge to the entire system. His argument is in fact the old argument that to save capitalism from itself, some of the ideas or demands of socialism must be coopted. Schotter makes the case that this is necessary in order to give incentives to the poor and marginalized, especially youth, to change their behavior so as to better promote the maintenance of the market system itself: "When tax rates for the wealthy are low and social programs are small, this creates the incentive for antisocial behavior by the poor that decreases everyone's quality of life. When tax systems for the rich are higher and social programs are large, the poor have incentives to behave less destructively to themselves and others." For Schotter, the adoption of socialist measures is "the price capitalism pays for its failure to provide proper incentives to the underclass," and not some inherent superiority of socialism as a value system itself. Schotter's perspective is that of a defender of a preferred system—which, however, on practical grounds must reform itself using opposing and yet ultimately complementary principles for its long-term best interests. The key here is that Schotter, like many others when they get down to practical policy-making, conceptualize their favored value system (in this case economic liberalism, which Schotter describes as "the most productive system known to man") as flawed, incomplete, and in need of alternatives. A dogmatic position on this might be to accept these flaws, and to argue that trying to fix them using other value principles would only create worse effects, including the undermining of the ideological dominance of economic liberalism. More often, the true believer is likely to argue that any current failings are the result of existing imperfections in the capitalist market economy, and therefore that the only real cure is the promotion of a purer capitalism. Schotter, however, accepts that his own preferred system has its own inherent defects, which are not remediable within its own logic, but which can be ameliorated through an opposing principle, which he names as socialism. Along with Bell and Puntsch, Schotter would like, in the post-cold war era, to abandon the old hostility to policies that could be labeled "socialist," and he hopes that such policies might be discussed without the cold war polemics against communism.

C. Marxism as Critical Method and as Dogma: Dealing with the Legacy of Official Marxism

One of the features of socialism in the twentieth century has been the dominance of Marxist thought as the core of an industrial-age socialism. In the competition among various strands of socialism within the broadest definition of the term, Marxism emerged as the clear winner and soon became the "official" source of socialist inspiration and analysis, both in the Western socialist and social democratic parties and later in the Leninist revolutionary vanguard parties of Eastern Europe and the developing world. This intellectual victory of Marxism soon became worrisome, even to Marx in his own lifetime. (Marx once said, in exasperation over the misrepresentation of his ideas within the German Social Democratic Party, that "if this was Marxism, then he was not a Marxist.") Almost from the beginning of the rise of Marxism, therefore, the danger of its becoming an official party ideology, and later a party-state ideology in Marxist-Leninist regimes, became apparent to some socialists, Marxists, and anti-Marxists. On the other hand, no intellectual challenger to Marxist thought, whether from anarchist, peasant, syndicalist, communitarian, Christian, or Fabian roots, was able to match the Marxist critique of capitalism for analytic power and comprehensiveness. Marxism did not win the intellectual competition among socialists for nothing, and the continued attractiveness of Marxism for more than a century indicates the original and continuing power of Marx's ideas, not just their later status as official party and state ideologies. Even in the 1950s and 1960s, the ideas of the young Marx, widely publicized in the West for the first time in comprehensive form, inspired a new generation of left intellectuals to critique "official Marxism" of both East and West, and to reinterpret Marx as a humanist socialist. The debates over the "young Marx" versus the "elder Marx" which engaged so many left intellectuals during this period are an indication of the complexity and critical capacity of Marxism, even with regard to institutionally proclaimed communist truths or dogma.

The problem with the domination of socialist thought by Marxism, however, is not limited to its installation as an official ideology or to the bureaucratization and ossification of its critical capacities under party and state supervision. Marx did see history as reaching an end stage, the stage of communism, which would in his terms be the end of pre-history and the beginning of a true human history. In any case, the dialectic of class struggle, the struggle to emancipate humankind, the battle with liberalism and conservatism, would end, as a final solution to the problematic of human essence had been achieved. "Communism is the answer to the riddle of history and knows itself to be that answer" (Marx, 1978). Marx's vision is also a form of endism, in which the historical conflict among value systems has a final and liberating ending.

Marx's optimism on the time-frame for socialist advances was one of the weaknesses of his analysis which Marxists were most likely to admit. It was patent that despite the growth of industry and the urban working class in Europe and the United States, socialist consciousness among workers was at best partial and a politics of socialist reform was preferred over revolution by both leaders and the rank-and-file. In Germany, Eduard Bernstein undertook a major revision of Marx's concept of socialist transformation, to bring it into line with the realities of a splintered and nonrevolutionary proletariat, using the opportunities of liberal (bourgeois) democracy to politically educate workers and to produce a slower, piecemeal movement toward socialism. Bernstein was of course viciously attacked by "orthodox" official Marxists for "revisionism" and "selling out" the cause of revolution and socialist principles. Indeed, however, Bernstein was a forerunner of many attempts to demystify "official" Marxism by making it subject to critique and revision. His revision of Marx's political project rested on many of Marx's own insights and used many of Marx's methods of analysis, but it also developed a new synthesis of social democracy that borrowed heavily from the more emancipatory ideals of liberalism, creating a liberal-socialist synthesis which has marked Western democratic socialism in this century. Bernstein's famous phrase about social democracy as "liberalism for the working class" is indicative of his willingness to synthesize ideas from competing value systems, for the sake of developing new and, in his view, more practical socialist politics.

Other socialist thinkers in different settings have attempted to challenge Marxism for its "endist" concept of human social evolution. In Italy in 1930, Carlo Rosselli published his vision of "liberal socialism," a critique of Marxist "endism" and a call for combining the best values from both liberal and socialist traditions. Rosselli, coming from a bourgeois background of a liberal antifascist Jewish family, wanted to dethrone Marxism as a requisite to offering an alternative ethical socialism based on liberty for the individual:

> It is time to throw off the absurd reverential awe that surrounds everything having to do with Marx. We have to dissociate socialism from Marxism, or at any rate to concede that they might be dissociated, and recognize Marxism as one of the many transitory theorizations of the socialist movement—a movement that affirms itself spontaneously and independently of any theory and that is based on elementary motives and needs.
>
> Here I touch on a point that I believe is fundamental. We talk about liberty, we fight for liberty, but the first liberty we have to put in place is liberty within the movement itself, and that means breaking up these hardened layers of dogma and grotesque monopolies. The socialist movement has to be coherent enough to apply to itself the ideal rules that inspire its attempt to reform all society. Discipline is essential for action, but it is a mistake to impose it in the domain of ideas and ideologies" (Rosselli, 1994: 116–117).

Rosselli's boldness in borrowing from the treasure chest of liberalism was clearly ahead of its time. His formulations employed a methodological individualism as the basis for socialism, and this makes it difficult to have a direct commitment to community values, solidarity, and distributional justice. Yet Rosselli saw both liberalism and socialism as heirs of the Enlightenment, both doing battle with church and monarchy, as Marx sometimes did himself. Roselli saw liberalism and socialism, in longer historical perspective, as usefully complementary as well as often competitive, whereas Marx saw their temporary alliances as overshadowed by a historical necessity for socialism to vanquish liberalism, the "endist" prospect.

D. Living with Complexity and Ongoing Uncertainty

The view that basic value systems are necessary complements to each other, which provide a dynamic and presumably ongoing competition without end, is in fact quite widespread. This is, I believe, because very few people are "ideologues" or "true believers" in a single value system. Life and its complexities give rise to a variety of circumstances that cannot be covered by just one value, whether it be individual freedom, social justice, or a collective identity. As elaborated above, most people, even if they describe themselves as liberals, socialists, or conservatives, recognize implicitly or explicitly that there is a plurality of values, which they also share—at least in some circumstances and at some times in their own lives.

Most people, at different times, feel the values of each of these great ideological traditions, even if they do not label them conservative, liberal, or socialist. Especially in the United States, many ideas that we connect with American conservatism are in fact classic liberalism in the European context, and many ideas that we associate with American liberalism would be called social democratic or socialist in Europe.

So, for example, many people who do not go to church or belong to any religious group, and do not think of themselves as especially religious, feel the need for a spiritual interpretation of life at times of family tragedy, or in times of personal danger (war, natural disaster). As people age, they often find that they have developed a sense of tradition about their neighborhood, town, favorite sports team, or nation, and they feel offended by changes, innovations, even "improvements" that wipe away the familiar, the comfortable, the "natural" elements of their earlier years. On the other hand, even many quite "liberal" or "socially progressive" citizens feel annoyed at government bureaucracy when they face it themselves, or at paying higher taxes even for worthwhile programs. And who does not at some time, very often in youth, feel the need to just do something different, something adventurous, something he or she hasn't done before, to break out of the mold of conformity, to express individuality? Who, finally, is not at some time affected by personal encounters with the homeless and the down-and-out amidst our affluence, or even by television coverage of the social tragedy of plant closings which devastate communities? Who at times does not feel that there is too much unfairness in our society, that ordinary people don't get a fair break, that those at the top get away with breaking the law? Do these different feelings, and the values that they reflect, mean that people are simply confused, or can't get their values straight? Perhaps to an ideologue that would be one answer; people should choose one clear and coherent ideology and stick to it no matter what happens. But that is fortunately a minority opinion, not shared by most people, who have a sense, common sense, that life is contradictory, that sometimes we identify with a value strongly for certain circumstances, but not for others, and not blindly for all cases. Most people are therefore not ideologues, because they recognize the contradictory complexity of the human condition, which calls for hard choices among competing values in varying circumstances.

Each of the great value systems contains elements that are in conflict with the other two, and none can encompass all the value priorities of human society. In trying to increase the attention and resources given to any one value, a political system will increase the contradictions with other values. Only ideologues claim that one value system can meet all human needs, without sacrifice and without internal contradiction. For example, if a political system tries to improve its performance in economic growth by promoting greater material rewards for business entrepreneurship (a liberal economic value), it will decrease its commitment to the goals of social equality and solidarity, at least in the short term. In this age of global corporations, whose activities go far beyond the nation-state, greater freedom of business activity may conflict with conservative values of loyalty to one's own country and one's own people. If a political system tries to crack down on crime, to improve the quality of life in neighborhoods, in schools, and for families, it comes into conflict with aspects of personal liberty such as right of privacy, freedom of movement, presumption of innocence, or the right to own a handgun or a semi-automatic rifle. Massive spending for police, courts, and prisons also comes into conflict with spending priorities favoring education, health care, and day-care for children. If the political system tries to increase equality—for example, to redistribute income more evenly through progressive taxation or closing tax loopholes for the rich—conflicts will develop both with conservative distaste for a leveling of social classes and with liberal support for clear market incentives needed to promote individual effort and economic efficiency. Many issues produce conflicts within as well as between value systems. Population control policies in many developing nations especially, are seen as desirable by some conservatives, some liberals, and some socialists, for the survival and strength of the nation, for providing greater individual opportunities through smaller families, and for maintaining basic human welfare. On the other hand, these same measures may be opposed by other conservatives (for contradicting religious values against family planning), by liberals (for restricting personal choice through government power), and by socialists (for discriminating against the poor as a class, while the rich have as many children as they want). Much depends on how an issue is defined and how a policy to deal with that issue is to be carried out; the point remains that politics in all systems faces conflicting values and will have to make policy decisions that prefer some values over others. Politics therefore involves trade-offs among competing choices; different systems develop their own pattern of policy priorities which reflect the trade-offs their regimes support.

Trade-offs abound between environment and economic growth, between government regulation and the private marketplace, between community standards of decency and artistic and commercial freedoms. Such trade-offs ensure that politics is never simple, and that most solutions to existing problems involve some "side-effect" costs (foreseen or surprising) or new problems caused by the "solution." Partial coalitions of value systems are possible, and they often determine the broad outline of political preferences in a given nation during a given political era. In schematic terms, which are always muddled in actual practice, liberals and socialists, both of whom hold humanist, secular values, may combine against conservatives on issues of separation of church and state, and against the imposition of religious doctrine on the citizen. On the other hand, conservatives and liberals may combine against socialists on the need for greater social inequality either as an economic incentive or as the natural state of affairs. Finally, conservatives and socialists may agree (though for different reasons) on the need for social limits to materialistic greed and individual egoism, a stance that contradicts liberal values.

These struggles over value priorities in practical politics may be productive or destructive of political development. Conflicts among competing goals may give rise to new syntheses in which progress may be made on several value positions, but with new conflicts arising out of the new higher-level synthesis. For example, the new (Keynesian) welfare state programs that developed out of the Great Depression of the 1930s in the Western democracies certainly provided a higher level of both social equity and economic growth for several decades after World War II, and few would want to return to pre-Depression conditions. Yet the new bureaucratism of the welfare state and governmental interventions into economic life and the life of every family have also produced new conflicts and problems peculiar to this higher synthesis. Thus the struggle among values may bring progress, but no once-and-for-all equilibrium, harmony, or balance. On the other hand, value conflict may, in some societies, result in a failure to find new syntheses, and may harden competing positions into sterile combat, resulting in short-term ideological victories that guarantee long-term failure. An ideological regime that tries to permanently ignore competing values and their (partial) validity deprives itself of the dynamic for system learning. Openness of political debate (this was Gorbachev's idea of *glasnost*) and civility in political struggle may facilitate a higher learning curve for the system, but there are no guarantees. In the United States, one of the world's most stable democracies, the elimination of slavery as a legal institution could not be settled without a bloody civil war. Unpredictability is what makes politics so interesting and makes glib extrapolations of current trends or "success" formulas unconvincing.

Isaiah Berlin was the classic defender in the 1950s of liberalism—of its tolerance, freedom of choice, and "negative" liberty versus "positive" freedom. Berlin's chief insight was precisely his sense that even his most preferred value principle, that of liberalism, must remain limited in its ultimate claims on insight into the human condition. Berlin represented and defended a pretriumphalist liberalism, just recovering from its own period of ideological uncertainties and rethinking after two horrible wars, defeats at the hands of European fascism, and the economic failures of the Great Depression. His view of liberalism was more modest, yet still firm in conviction, and it rested upon just the sense of self-limitation that most people understand from the complexities and internal contradictions of their own experience. For him, it was a lack of readiness to recognize pluralism of values and grant opposing values their due that had in great measure led to the tragedies of humankind:

> One belief, more than any other, in responsible for the slaughter of individuals on the altars of the great historical ideals—justice or progress or the happiness of future generations, or the sacred mission of emancipation of a nation or race or class, or even liberty itself, which demands the sacrifice of individuals for the freedom of society. This is the belief that somewhere, in the past, of in the future, in divine revelation, or in the mind of an individual thinker, in the pronouncements of history or science, or in the simple heart of an uncorrupted good man, there is a final solution. This ancient faith rests on the conviction that all the positive values in which men have believed must, in the end, be compatible, and perhaps even entail one another (1958: 52).

Berlin, as a principled liberal, was willing to accept a respectful plurality of competing human values ("ends"), which could never be reduced through history or struggle to just one value principle that would assimilate or eliminate all the rest:

> "If, as I believe, the ends of man are many, and not all of them are in principle compatible with each other, then the possibility of conflict—and of tragedy— can never wholly be eliminated from human life, either personal or social.

The necessity of choosing between absolute claims is then an inescapable characteristic of the human condition" (54).

This is a major concession, of course, since it implies that one's vision of the good society must inherently still contain conflicts and difficult choices. Berlin is clear in the limitations of liberalism as an historic contender among values systems:

> I do not wish to say that individual freedom is, even in the most liberal societies, the sole, or even the dominant, criterion of social action. . . . The extent of a man's or a people's liberty to choose to live as they desire must be weighed against the claims of many other values, of which equality, or justice, or happiness, or security, or public order are perhaps the most obvious examples For this reason, it cannot be unlimited. We are rightly reminded by Mr. Tawney that the liberty of the strong, whether their strength is physical or economic, must be restrained. This maxim claims respect, not as a consequence of some a priori rule, whereby the respect for the liberty of one man logically entails respect for the liberty of others like him; but simply because respect for the principles of justice, or shame at gross inequality of treatment, is as basic in men as the desire for liberty (54–55).

Berlin feared, however, that there would be a temptation toward "monism," which would be especially strong because of the seeming certainty it conferred on the faithful, the true believers. He, of course, in his time saw such monism as situated mainly among socialists and conservatives, but his general point is still the same: "There is little need to stress the fact that monism, and faith in a single criterion, has always proved a deep source of satisfaction both to the intellect and to the emotions. . . . it is an attitude found in equal measure on the right and left wings in our days, and is not reconcilable with the principles accepted by those who respect the facts" (56).

Berlin's insights reflected a chastened but renewing liberalism of the postwar era, which included a liberal skepticism about final solutions, final purposes or states, or any endism. Unfortunately, many leading thinkers of liberalism would themselves succumb to "monism" and proclaim an end of history (Fukuyama, 1992) of their own. Bruce Douglass (1992) provides a good account of how liberal intellectuals gathered greater confidence in the finality and universality of liberalism as the answer to history's riddles, and were thus swept away with the heady events of the 1980s (the democratic trend in Latin America) and the stunning collapse of European communism in 1989–1991 to assert a new "end of history" confirmed by these events, implying a universal end state which all societies must reach, if they are to avoid simply being left behind forever in history.

What does this mean for a renewal of a left political agenda in the post-cold war era? First and foremost, it means that while the politics and policies of the left are currently in crisis, there is no good reason to believe that the left, or the idea of socialism, has forever vanished from contention in political life. Even now, at a low point in the political effectiveness of the left, there are many political thinkers who see the contribution of the left as essential to social progress and complementary to the value principles put forward by liberals and conservatives. Most people are not ideologues and therefore are open to a plurality of value principles in their lives and their political commitments. The future is still wide open for the values of socialism; there has been no "end of history"; there is no cause for defeatism.

Second, with the recognition of the continued viability of socialism as a political organizing principle for human society should come a readiness of socialists to accept the limitations of a left political agenda. If the left is to revive, it must also get over its own history of "endism" and "final solutions." That means acceptance of the validity of liberal and conservative perspectives, and the expectation that these competing value principles will continue to have a strong resonance within the citizenry. The left, in my opinion, should abandon any illusions of eventual but complete triumph over its complementary competitors. The left can best overcome its many failings from the era of welfare state democracy and Leninist communism by breaking from the belief (some would call it millenarianism; many would call it historical determinism) that only the left can lead the way into a better future. Even now, many on the left continue to put forward a grim choice between socialism and barbarism as the only two options for human society. Samir Amin, for example, writing on "The Future of Socialism" (1990), says that "More than ever, I would argue that the choice lies between socialism and barbarism" (106). Amin, one of the most prolific authors of the "dependency school," argues for a left project of a new "polycentric world" in which the dependent poor nations (the "South" in the North-South conflict) would have a much greater influence, overcoming centuries of Eurocentrism, but he insists that the future must be seen in terms of either a triumph by the left or barbaric, capitalistic world disorder. No doubt Amin believes that he is offering, from the perspective of the insurgent "South," an alternative to the old East-West conflict and an alternative socialist project, but he remains clearly wedded to the idea that for mankind to be saved, the left must simply triumph over its ideological competitors. Nothing less will do, if history is to achieve a humane end. This prematurely triumphal "endism" has played a role in mobilizing people, often idealistic young people, to sacrifice and steady commitment, but on the other hand it has set up innumerable unrealistic expectations which were later smashed, and has also led many to justify violent and antidemocratic means for the cause of eventual socialist victory. Are left intellectuals incapable, even now in defeat, of learning something of the lesson that Karl Mannheim once warned about—the tragedy of intellectual "endism," the temptation to make out of one's politics much more than can be empirically justified, a kind of self-aggrandizement (Engler, 1991)? Or is it now just necessary, and more timely, to openly and bluntly criticize Samir Amin's ideas as futile "endist" ideology that cannot lead to a renewed socialist politics but rather looks back to a clearly failed strategy?

Even as talented and sophisticated a thinker as Michael Harrington, one of the leading renewers of socialist thought in the 1980s until his death, argued that the ultimate success of socialism was the main hope for humankind. At the beginning of his tour de force, *Socialism: Past and Future*, Harrington posits that even in an era of retreat and defeat, "the political impulse and movement represented by those bewildered, half-exhausted democratic-socialist parties continue to be the major hope for freedom and justice" (1989: 2). For Harrington, despite the obvious setbacks of the present, the hopes of human society rested with a socialist triumph: "There is no guarantee that socialism will triumph—or that freedom and justice, even to the limited degree that they have been achieved until now—will survive the next century. All I claim here is that, if they are to survive, the socialist movement will be a critical factor" (3). In Harrington's long-term view, socialism had become, after the period of liberal progress, the carrier for the values of freedom and justice, and if socialism should fail, the outlook for humankind would indeed be dark. In this sense, then Harrington too wants to maintain a clear, if much drawn out, progression from conservative authoritarianism through capitalist liberalism to a democratic socialist future. For Harrington, the successful conservative politics of Reagan, Thatcher, and Kohl "proved again that their ideology is a contradiction in terms. It provides eighteenth-century rationales for twenty-first-century authoritarianism, myths of the invisible hand that justify the elitist maneuvers of the visible hand. . . ."

(278) Harrington does not perceive conservatism as capable of modernization or of rethinking its political aims, but rather sees the current conservative success as more of a return to the past. On the other hand, Harrington does see socialism as capable of such modernization, based on "its own profound truths," and then of moving on to an improved version of socialist politics. Harrington's vision of what is needed is far more flexible and less dogmatic than Amin's vision, and yet the concept of ideological "endism" is still deeply embedded, still a part of the Western concept of ideological struggle leading to final resolution (or final catastrophe).

A third point is that the left can and should look to coalitions with liberals and conservatives to advance its political agenda. A democratic, pluralist left, in recognition of its own limitations, needs to be open to coalition-building with nonsocialists, with those who hold other value principles. It should seek out areas where philosophical liberalism or conservatism comes together with socialist principles, where critical issues of the current era of great transitions allow for common ground from more than one perspective. Does this mean abandoning its own principles? Of course not, although it does mean abandoning useless and harmful delusions about some ultimate victory of a purely socialist idea for all time and all nations. It seems to me perfectly possible for the left to advocate coalitions on a wide range of issues to advance its own values among people who have previously been alienated by left dogmatism and left barricade-building, but who might well over time come over to socialist perspectives through practical work in coalitions with socialists. The reverse would also be possible—that socialists might well be attracted to liberal or conservative principles through coalitional work. A confident and renewed left would not fear the balance of migration; a non-renewed left will probably continue to try to defend its remaining bastions of influence through isolationism and protectionist attitudes toward the larger society and the "other world."

Fortunately, there are signs that some thinkers are interested in borrowing from other philosophical traditions in order to refashion a left politics for our times. Anthony Giddens, in his thoughtful *Beyond Left and Right*, argues for large-scale borrowing from philosophical conservatism for a basic redefinition of a left-progressive alternative to the politics of economic development. In one key section, Giddens outlines an alternative development program that recognizes the limitations of the Western welfare state model in an era of globalizing capitalism, in which calls for addressing "third world" as well as "first world" concerns:

> Alternative development has *damage limitation* as a basic concern, whether this be in respect of local culture or of the environment. Modernization almost everywhere, together with its many benefits, has had harmful consequences; in many situations we cannot expect further modernization to cope with these, since it helped bring them about. This is one main point of connection of a radical politics of development with philosophic conservatism; conservatism should be understood as in many cases a rational response to the destructiveness of modernity (1994: 159).

In this area, as in many others, Giddens is willing to break with Old Left political norms, to exit from older visions of a socialist future, and to borrow from a variety of critical insights on the key issues for rethinking what he calls a radical politics, a "generative politics for positive welfare." Giddens's thinking is instructive in many respects, since he has long been a difficult figure for the traditional left, both sympathetic to its general goals and yet a skeptic about its political strategy and practice. Perhaps one cannot expect basic, bold rethinking from those most clearly identified with the former mainstream of left political thought. Surely many on the left will not regard Giddens as a reliable source for a renewed left politics, and yet who is most likely to engage in a major rethinking if not those who have developed and maintained an outsider, independent, or eclectic course over the years, clearly at odds with the mainstream or established left yet offering their ideas for a better alternative that is still identifiable as a left (nonliberal, non-conservative) politics? In my own search through the writings of those whose ideas I have found attractive for this project, most come from a nonconformist left or eclectic left position; some have broken with the traditional left politics, some more than once, but they have still found their way back to the left political discourse, in part because of their disdain for ideological liberalism and conservatism, and in part because they still maintain some self-identification with basic socialist values.

The reworking of a new progressive politics for our time will still, however, produce a new politics of the left; Giddens seems to want to transcend the longstanding left-right distinction, and here I must disagree with this concept. I am much more sympathetic to the Italian liberal socialist Norberto Bobbio, another maverick thinker on the left, who recently reaffirmed, against all prophesy and punditry on the end of a viable left politics, the continuing vitality of the left's emphasis on equality, or as I have asserted, social justice, as the critical core of left politics, old and new. Bobbio, in reponse to the varied claims that the left-right political distinction has lost its relevance in a new era, states:

> On the basis of my reflections so far, which, if nothing else, are, I believe, pertinent to our times, and a scrutiny of the papers over the last few years, I believe that the criterion most frequently used to distinguish between the left and the right is the attitude of real people in society to the ideal of equality. . . . The concept of equality is relative, not absolute. It is relative to at least three variables which have to be taken into account every time the desirability of equality or its practicability are discussed: (a) the individuals between whom benefits and obligations should be shared; (b) the benefits or obligations to be shared; (c) the criteria by which they should be shared (Bobbio, 1996: 61).

I share Bobbio's feeling that any reworked left politics will be, in the long tradition of the left, a politics based on social justice, on reflections about social equality, about social equity, and about the nature of inequalities of the contemporary social order. This focus on social justice (on the political question of social equality) must differentiate a rethought left politics from its liberal and conservative competitors. In this new era of growing inequalities, I have no doubt that any retivalized left politics will maintain this traditional "left" distinction which Bobbio also describes in personal terms over his long career (Bobbio was born in 1909):

> Let me conclude my arguments by giving a personal account. I have always considered myself a man of the left, and therefore, for me, the term "left" has always had a positive connotation, even now when it is under such attack, and the term "right", which is now being widely reassessed, a negative connotation. During my life I have on occasion shown some interest in politics; in other words, I have felt the need . . . to get involved in politics, and more rarely, to engage in some political activity. The fundamental reason for this has always been an uneasinesss over the spectacle of enormous, disproportionate, unjustified inequalities between rich and poor, between those at the top and those at the bottom of the social ladder, and between those with power—that is to say, the ability to determine the behaviour of others in the economic, political and ideological spheres—and those without power (1996: 82–83).

Bobbio has captured here the essential distintiveness of left politics, which may change in all its particulars from one era to another but remain faithful to the basic search for social justice. The reworking process will dismay many on the left whose understanding derives from an earlier era, but its product, a rethought and revived left politics, will still offer a sharp, classic contrast to the non-left politics of our time—and here I must emphasize, to both liberalism and conservatism.

As I will argue throughout this work, the qualitative rethinking and revival of any ideological tradition will come through the breaking down of old habits and barriers to innovation that have inevitably set in, and this process will mean that some cherished positions (though not core values) will be abandoned, overturned, even derided as "wrongheaded" for the new era. Some stalwarts of the left from the earlier period, champions who deserve much credit for what they accomplished over a long lifetime of often selfless commitment and struggle, will find at the end of their political lives a confusing and disillusioning environment on the left, with some considerable bitterness over the new criticisms directed at their politics and their intellectual leadership. This is a heavy price to pay for the necessary rethinking of a left politics, and I wish it could be avoided. The left has a sorry history of personal infighting, of charges of "sellout" and "dogmatist," "revisionist" and "blind ideologue." It would be so much better if all those on the left who wish to continue the struggle for a more just society could bring themselves to avoid such slurs and insults, which add nothing to the search for a new left agenda. This of course will not happen, and so in this period of gathering together new forces for progressive change, there will probably be much mudslinging, but this in itself will not prevent the rise of new ideas from entering the debate, nor will it much affect the course of the debate itself. Just as history has not ended, neither can any ideological tradition call a halt to its own internal debate for all time and all circumstances.

References

Amin, Samir (1990). "The Future of Socialism" in William Tabb, ed. *The Future of Socialism*. New York: Monthly Review Press.

Bell, Daniel (1991). *Die kulturellen Widersprüche des Kapitalismus*. Frankfurt: Campus.

Berlin, Isaiah (1958). *Two Concepts of Liberty*. Oxford: Clarendon.

Bobbio, Norberto (1996). *Left and Right: The Significance of a Political Distinction*. Chicago: University of Chicago Press.

Douglass, Bruce (1992). "Liberalism" in M. Hawksworth and M. Dogan, eds., *Encyclopedia of Government and Politics*. London: Routledge.

Engler, Wolfgang (1991). "Wächter in finsterer Nacht", *Zeit* 48 (November 29) 4–5.

Fukuyama, Francis (1992). *The End of History and the Last Man*. London: Hamilton.

Giddens, Anthony (1994). *Beyond Left and Right: The Future of Radical Politics*. Palo Alto, CA: Stanford University Press.

Harrington, Michael (1989). *Socialism: Past and Future*. New York: Arcade.

Heilbroner, Robert (1990). "Reflections: After Communism?" *New Yorker* (September 10) 91–100.

Laidler, Harvey (1968). *The History of Socialism*. New York: Crowell.

Marx, Karl (1978). "The 1844 Manuscripts" in Robert Tucker, ed., *The Marx-Engels Reader*. New York: Norton.

McClelland, J.S. (1970). *The French Right from de Maistre to Maurras*. New York: Harper.

Murphy, Craig (1994). *International Organization and Industrial Change*. New York: Oxford University Press.

Puntsch, Eberhard (1994). *Der Links-Mitte-Rechts Unfug: Die Welt ist nicht zweipolig*. Munich: Aktuell.

Rejai, Mostafa (1984). *Comparative Political Ideologies*. New York: St. Martin's.

Rosselli, Carlo (1994). *Liberal Socialism*. Princeton: Princeton University Press.

Schotter, Andrew (1992) "Improve Capitalism. Use Some Socialism," *New York Times* (February 29) 23.

——— (1985). *Free Market Economics: A Critical Appraisal*. New York: St. Martins.

Sigmund, Paul (1967). *The Ideologies of the Developing Nations*. New York: Praeger.

Tucker, Robert (1961). Philosophy and Myth in Karl Marx. Cambridge: Cambridge University Press.

Chapter III

Uplifting Stories of Confession, Rebirth, and Renewals in Other Times

A. Socialism Reinvented in the 19th Century

Socialism as a political project has already undergone one rebirth and renewal in modern European history. In the nineteenth century, during the industrial revolution in Europe and North America, socialism as a political value system underwent a dramatic transformation, which enabled it to play a major role in the politics of the industrial era. To achieve a new synthesis, older visions of socialism or communism stemming from rural village life and guild craftsmen, which had defined alternative images of a society of collective solidarity during the feudal era, were gradually consigned to the past, while newer and innovative approaches to achieving a more just society in the era of industrial capitalism competed before a shifting but broad audience of people who were appalled at the effects of the rising domination over society by capitalist interests. The result was the birth of an industrial age socialist politics which overcame, in great measure, the barriers to emancipation of the working class, and which then in the twentieth century became the dominant ideology of social change, against which both liberalism and conservatism had to contend. Whatever judgments may now be made about the state of socialist politics at the end of the twentieth century, it was precisely the socialist challenge which preoccupied modern liberalism and conservatism, and which (see below) helped rework their political agendas for most of this period. This is an enormous achievement, which even today, in another period of crisis of socialist political thinking, has shaped modern Western society in virtually every aspect. And yet, for a generation after the final victory of reaction over the French Revolution, this future prospect must have seemed an impossible dream, and its proponents utopian dreamers.

At the beginning of the nineteenth century, with the victory of monarchy and reaction over the revolutionary forces of the French Revolution, the prospects for socialism seemed hopeless. With the growing alliance between the new industrial elites and the ruling aristocracy, the voices of social opposition were in a weak and isolated, seemingly dead-end position. How could the values of solidarity, equality, and community welfare be addressed effectively from a politics of the left in the face of such a disparity of power? Yet socialists and communists engaged in a long-running debate among themselves, often very self-critical and often seemingly self-contradictory, from which emerged two left politics, one revolving around democratic socialism (based heavily on Marx as revised by Bernstein), and one revolving around communist revolution (based on Marx as revised by Lenin). Each in turn played an immense role (positive and negative) in shaping the politics of Europe and North America in the twentieth century, and each was able to mobilize both intellectual and popular support for its left agenda.

The failings of capitalism from the view of the growing working class in the cities were legion; critiques came from all sides, including parish priests (though not generally the higher clergy) and the aristocracy, which saw its own economic base of power in the countryside now overmatched by the urban bourgeoisie. Marx himself, in the first volume of *Capital*, draws much of his indictment against the "werewolves" of capital from reports by local clergy, and from public hearings before magistrates of the crown. But while the nobility and the church (remember that liberalism is also a doctrinal error for the Catholic church) opposed the abuses of wild laissez-faire capitalism, the political elites generally preferred to coopt a part of the new industrial elite, while the economic elite, already scared to death of revolutionary potential in the new industrial cities, looked to the forces of continental reaction, monarchy and its armies, to protect private property against the threat from the urban proletariat. The failure of the revolutions of 1848, which were mostly bourgeois liberal and nationalist in origin but which also began to show the first signs of developing a more radical agenda, were in part due to the fears of a significant faction of the new economic elite, and its abandonment of political liberalism (freedom of the press, parliamentary democracy, constitutional order), in order to secure its property rights through military suppression of popular participation.

The more lasting and telling critiques of early capitalism came from the direction of the socialists: from agrarian socialists, anarchists (Bakunin, Goldman), communitarians (Owen), early laborites (Chartists), and syndicalists (Proudhon); and from groupings of socialist thinkers who viewed the new and untested class, the urban industrial proletariat, as the focus for socialist politics. Each of these partial interests or factions within the umbrella of the socialist movement contributed its ideas and competed for influence in the reshaping of socialism for a new era. A telling feature of this period of rethinking of socialist politics is that there was a complete failure to renew peasant socialism as a viable alternative to the industrial revolution (that at to say, there was no going back to a socialist vision rooted in a previous economic order). There was, despite the Owenites' efforts, also no success in the attempt to "delink" small towns and communities from the larger economic dynamics of Western societies, to build isolated islands of communitarian socialism in the larger sea of industrial capitalism. The success of Marxism lay in good measure with its embrace of industrialism, its optimism about the ultimate social benefits of science and technology, and its comprehensive vision of revolutionizing the entire social order. These points may still have some application to the current period of rethinking and renewal on the left, although one could not say that they will simply be repeated in some mechanistic way. The experience of the "modern" and of the "scientific revolution" has given us a richer base on which to form our concepts of how science and economic progress can contribute, or not, to a socialist vision of the good society.

Although Marxism by the end of the century had gained a certain theoretical dominance, the practical application of Marx's ideas in different settings contributed to a rich variety within modern industrial-era socialist politics. Marx himself openly borrowed from other socialist thinkers (Saint-Simon, Proudhon, Owen), both for images of a socialist alternative and for his own critique of capitalism. Marx also leaned heavily on the liberal political economy of Smith, Ricardo, and Malthus and the liberal idealism of Kant, Feuerbach, and Hegel (though transformed, of course) in creating his own historical analysis of the industrial era, its meaning in human history, and its potential for revolutionary change. Indeed, as many have noted (cf. Tucker 1978), Marx's life work is an evolving synthesis of German idealist philosophy, British political economy, and continental (especially French) visions of socialism. The power of Marx's grand theory lies precisely in this synthesis, which represents his ability to borrow insights from both German idealism and British liberalism. Shlomo Avineri has argued, in the debate during the 1960s over the "young" versus the "elder" Marx, that Marx in fact never completely broke with a universal and emancipating liberalism, that his political project was, correctly read, an extension of liberal humanism to include the working class. This is, then, what Western socialists, foremost among them Eduard Bernstein, took to the be task of German socialism, the universalization of liberal emancipation, a classless liberalism. When I read a recent interview with Günter Verheugen on the dilemma of the German Social Democrats today, his solution revolves around a continuing vision of socialists' realizing the liberal vision of individual freedom not just for the propertied or the socially advantaged, but for all citizens (Verheugen, 1995).

Without going overboard in making Marx out to be (only) a radical liberal humanist, however, it is clear that Marx, working through a theory of human alienation created by a class-polarized social order, borrowed heavily from liberal notions of freedom as individual autonomy. Marx arrives at very different solutions to the social problem of capitalism, yet he cites Smith extensively on the alienation and degradation of the worker. Smith and others from the Manchester school of liberal political economy also realized the degrading effects of extreme division of labor on the human spirit, but they could not transcend the notion. As Smith says, "But in every improved and civilised society, this is the state into which the labouring poor, that is, the great body of the people, must necessarily fall" (Tucker, 1978: 399). Although Smith recommended partial remedies, including some rudimentary education, the strictly capitalist perspective could not conceive of universal emancipation, a universal citizenship, within its own liberal idealism. Later "social" liberals, like Dewey or Greene, or today Rawls and Dworkin, have wrestled with just this problem within liberalism, and have been instrumental in moving liberalism (insofar as is possible) away from its strictly bourgeois class attachments. Whatever one thinks of this progression—and it is a progression—Marx's image of human emancipation in a future socialist society owes much to liberal idealism, and his connection of this emancipatory idealism to the capitalist dynamic owes much to liberal political economy.

Other socialist thinkers, such as Fourier, owed at least some debt to conservative thought in working out their models of the socialist future. Fourier's elaborate plans rest, after all, on a notion of some natural balance or harmony among a still class-divided society, a notion uppermost in the priorities of political conservatism. Indeed, the

Fourier model aims at a certain stability and order that conservatives have generally proclaimed as a major goal of their politics. This goal of social security and stability crosses over the political boundaries of socialism and conservatism, as discussed above, and it is not surprising that some brands of socialist politics should, especially in times of technological change, converge with conservative politics in opposing the pace or social impact of technological change. Marx was not of this school of thought, and in this way Marx's ideas were, among the competitors within socialist thought, probably the most optimistic about technological change; it was, after all, Marx's key notion that human productivity had now, with the industrial revolution, reached a historic breakthrough of mastery over nature that would enable humankind to eliminate poverty and material want. Failure to achieve this would be due now only to the failing of a class-polarized social order, so that the socialist transformation of that order would in fact release the gains of modern industry to all citizens, not just the bourgeoisie. In this respect too, Marx's image of a new socialism rested upon his historical understanding of the technological progress of the social economy: it had gone through many stages and was now capable of finally overcoming earlier limitations on communism (primitive communism), which could, in the given circumstances of the forces of production, only provide for an equality of poverty.

It is wholly unsurprising, in historical retrospect, that in Western Europe, where liberal democracy had made its greatest strides, modern socialism derived in large measure from Marx's synthesis evolved into a politics of democratic socialism. The case of German Social Democracy is instructive, and it demonstrates the attraction of liberal ideas within the socialist movement even where parliamentary democracy had not yet been achieved, and where a German liberal elite had not had the boldness and confidence to push ahead with a classic bourgeois democratic political vision. The Social Democratic Party of Germany (SPD), the first party to adopt Marxism as an official theoretical foundation in 1875, and therefore to begin the unfortunate process of institutionalizing Marx's ideas, was much influenced by liberal ideals of parliamentary democracy. Despite the failures of the 1848 Frankfurt Parliament, and the turn of German liberalism toward German nationalism (thus the national-liberal synthesis of the Kaiserreich period), the Social Democrats continued to work independently toward a fully democratic parliamentary system. Their commitment to political democracy was in fact much more substantial than

the commitment of most German liberals, and it has been often remarked that the SPD had incorporated a good deal (the political heart)
of the liberal project into its own vision of an evolutionary, peaceful,
and democratic path of social transformation.

In the competition over the shape of an industrial socialist politics,
both inductive and deductive approaches were involved. Sometimes
the current debate over renewal of a left politics gets needlessly bogged
down over whether one needs to get the big picture (the grand theory
or vision) first, or whether through grassroots and specific-issue activism the larger project takes shape through practice. The question of
theory versus practice, and the goal of some unity between the two,
has vexed political thinkers of all camps. In the renewal of socialism in
the nineteenth century, there were specific points where the deductive
and inductive met. One such point was the founding (unity) congress
of German Social Democracy in Eisenach in 1875. This historic joining of an ongoing labor movement with a grand vision provided the
synthesis for a major political movement, which over the next century
had a profound impact on German politics in a progressive social and
democratic fashion.

In Eastern Europe, where the Reformation, the Enlightenment, and
classic liberalism had made little impact against political-religious autocracy, ideas of a modernized socialism (including but not limited to
Marxism) would also not be much affected by the liberal politics and
its ideas of democracy and individual freedom. Instead, Lenin, following concepts and practices evolved by the Russian radical intelligentsia during the nineteenth century, borrowed heavily from their ideas
(Tkachov, Nechaev, Chernyshevsky) of "revolutionary vanguard" of a
totally dedicated and self-sacrificing cadre, an elite which would, and
must, take the lead over an incapable mass of workers and peasants.
Much of his own conceptualization of the problems of an activist socialist politics stresses the backwardness of the Russian economy and
the backwardness of its laboring classes, requiring a tightly organized
and talented cadre of leaders to redress the imbalance in power between masses and autocratic state. Those Russian Marxists (the
Mensheviks) who were in favor of a more gradual approach, or supported liberal ideas as a prerequisite to a democratic socialism, were
defeated in the competition with Leninist concepts at the point where
the old regime began to crumble but the material basis for a liberal
democratic revolution was still terribly weak. In his attempt to fashion
a "theory of the party," Lenin had to match the capacity of the state

for violent repression with a paramilitary revolutionary structure capable of leading armed struggle. Clearly the Leninist project came to rest on organizational imperatives of effective violence, and thus imported the logic of military operations and violent suppression of opponents, a logic laden with conservative (and military) values of obedience, hierarchy, and patriotic sacrifice. Other socialists of his own time, in Russia and abroad, foresaw the potential for a new autocracy arising from Lenin's party structure and the leading role of its cadre over the course of the revolution.

Luxemburg especially warned against the rise of a new dictatorship from Leninist principles, which would give rise to a new ruling class and betray the basic emancipatory ideas of socialism. Lenin, too, in his "theory of imperialism," departs from Marx's scheme of historical stages to introduce the concept of national liberation for less developed nations against Western imperialism, and thus borrows from the vocabulary and mobilizing potential of nationalism. The greatest revolutionary successes of indigenous Leninist parties or movements have been precisely in those nations (Russia, China, Vietnam, Cuba, even Yugoslavia) where Leninist communism combined with nationalism to mobilize popular support. This point is underlined by the collapse of communist internationalism under Stalin and by the use of nationalism by communist regimes in power. Eventually, the possibility or reality of war between communist states (between China and Russia, China and Vietnam, Yugoslavia and Albania) strengthened the forces of nationalism as a last legitimization of these regimes. In the postcommunist transformations of Eastern Europe and the former Soviet Union, at least one path for ex-communist elites is that of national socialism (an ethnic-based semifascist or national populist politics) practiced by Milosevic in Serbia, Zyuganov in Russia, and the nomenklatura-based "parties of power" in central Asia. Fortunately, many of the postcommunist parties of the region have chosen another path, that of an authentic locally based democratic socialism (Hungarian Socialist Party, Democratic Left Alliance in Poland, Democratic Labor in Lithuania, perhaps even the Bulgarian Socialists), and have had electoral success which has strengthened a democratic reintegration of a postcommunist left into the political landscape (Mahr and Nagle, 1995).

The bifurcation or division of Europe existed before the industrial revolution, but it was sharpened with the advent of economic modernization in the West, which weakened the East and gave rise to a new challenge to its cultures, to adopt Western ways or to find another (competitive) path to modernity. In the West, the renewal of a socialist politics embraced the progressive gains of liberalism and was fundamentally based on the successes of liberalism in economics and politics as preconditions for a new socialist agenda. Western socialism could in fact succeed only where liberalism had fulfilled its goals of an effective bourgeois democratic parliament, and where capitalist modernization had built up a large urban working class. In the East, although there were Westernizers among the socialist contenders, the renewal of socialism was much more influenced by the still-dominant conservative ideology of the preindustrial social order. Lenin's politics (and the politics of most of the pre-Leninist radical intelligentsia) would not wait for a possible future breakthrough of liberalism in Russia but turned instead to the short-term question of revolutionary organizing under the given repressive environment: What's to be done? Lenin's renewal of a revolutionary politics had to be based on issues of cadre organization, secrecy, cohesion of leadership, and decisive boldness of armed action. Leninism became an organizational model for revolution from above, which could be adopted by nonsocialist parties in similarly repressive political environments (for example by the Kuomintang in China or by several of the mujahedeen groupings in Afghanistan). Its single-minded vision of conquering state power puts it closer to conservative (Machiavellian) concepts of statecraft, concerned with the necessary elite skills for effective governing.

The crisis facing socialists after the defeat of the French Revolution and the political consolidation of European reaction produced a multitude of new and old ideas for revival of the left. From this competition emerged not one but two socialist politics, each corresponding to the political environment in which key actors outlined what seemed reasonable and practical for their circumstances. It is part of the tragedy of democratic socialist politics that it was always burdened with the crimes of its distantly related Leninism, even though the two branches were mortal enemies and matured in totally different contexts. Perhaps one of the advantages of the collapse of Leninism is that socialist thinking generally is emancipated from this strategic disadvantage (Nagle, 1992) and no longer has to either defend the indefensible, or compete with liberals and conservatives in anticommunist demonizing.

This process of socialist renewal was enormously successful, and in the West it became the dominant force for social reform for a century.

Even the Leninist challenge from the East required some concessions to a democratic socialism to maintain working-class loyalties or passivity. At a time of socialist crisis at the end of the twentieth century, one should recall this history of political revival as an exemplar of what is possible. But then, I would argue, this is inherently possible for all three grand value systems of Western civilization, and so crisis is a normal and functional element of the ongoing dialectic of political rebirth, rise, and decline in the face of changing circumstances. "The coincidence of the changing of circumstances and of human activity can be conceived and rationally understood only as revolutionizing practice" (Marx, "Theses on Feuerbach," in Tucker, 1978: 144). What Marx conceived as revolutionizing practice in human activity in general is at the core of political reasoning and rethinking of politics.

B. Conservatism Recovers from Its Collaboration with Fascism; Learns to Live with and Even Enjoy Liberal Democracy

In the interwar period in Europe, political conservatism was wedded to aggressive nationalism and racism, and was extremely ambiguous about political democracy. This was a continuation of a reactionary conservative tradition formed in the wake of the Napoleonic Wars in the early nineteenth century. Joseph de Maistre (1753–1821) formulated a mixture of nationalism with Catholic social conservatism to arrive at a politics of reaction against both liberal and socialist tendencies (cf. Hoover, 1992: 144ff). This brand of Continental conservatism was virulently antidemocratic and hoped to save the aristocratic regime through widening its popular appeal with "Christian pessimism about human nature." (144) The optimism of both modern liberalism and, even more, socialism was contrasted with a view of human nature which required a strong authoritarian state, with due respect for social hierarchy, maintenance of order, reliance on faith, and explicit limitations on individual freedom. The collapse of monarchical regimes in Europe at the end of World War I, the breakup of the Austro-Hungarian Empire, and the birth of many new democracies did not quickly give rise to a new political conservatism; in many respects the conservative politics of much of Europe remained hostile to democracy and oriented toward collaboration with other antidemocratic elites in the military, the church, the civil service, and extremist movements. Charles Maurras (1868–1952) formulated an anti-Semitic protofascist movement in France; Houston Stewart Chamberlain linked British Aryan nationalism with its German and Austrian counterparts. According to Ken Hoover, "While fascism itself can be intellectually separated from conservatism, the early complicity of some conservative intellectuals, literati and politicians in its rise to power contributed to the decline in the crediblity of conservative parties" (148). In Spain the marriage of this reactionary conservatism with Franco's Falangists produced a durable "union of religion, nationalism and social conservatism" that lasted for over four decades. The intellectual basis for this marriage can be found in the writings of José Ortega y Gasset (1883–1955) writings, which combine a disdain for the "masses" with a call for hierarchy, order, and a strong leader (El Caudillo). While it may be argued that the fascist Franco regime (and its imitators in Latin America) went beyond what Ortega intended, this is an unconvincing argument, similar to the one used to exonerate Lenin from responsibility for the later Stalinist atrocities. Interwar political conservatism was no friend of democracy and was willing to play a key role in its overthrow by fascist or right-wing authoritarian elites. The classic elite theorists (the "Italian school" of Robert Michels, Gaetano Mosca, and Vilfredo Pareto) of the interwar years provided further intellectual backing for a new antidemocratic corporatism; although the founders of modern elite theory came from rather different political origins, they rallied to the antiliberal, antidemocratic, and of course anti-Marxist agenda in the volatile interwar years (cf. Nagle, 1992).

In Weimar Germany, in particular, the conservative Protestant parties—Deutsche Volkspartei (DVP) or German Peoples Party and the more extreme Deutschnationale Volkspartei (DNVP) or German National Peoples Party—were from the very start of the Weimar period hostile to the democratic constitution and to the "Weimar system." Their leaders were not radical or bold enough to organize a rebellion against the democratic system, but they were no friends of parliamentary democracy, and their political weight was a constant burden to democracy throughout the Weimar period. The DNVP leaders, in particular those around Alfred Hugenberg, distinguished themselves through their serial conspiracies against the Weimar democracy, beginning well before the rise of Hitler and the Nazis as a mass party, and culminating in the Hartzburg Front coalition to destroy German democracy.

The Zentrum (Z) or Catholic Centrum Party, on the other hand—the multi-class respresentative of the Catholic faithful in Germany—

had been one of the early supporters of Weimar democracy and one of the few Catholic parties in Europe to support a liberal parliamentary system, in part because in Germany Catholics were a distinct minority and had been abused under the Bismarckian Reich as a suspect minority. The Zentrum was a moderate conservative party, capable of forming coalitions with center-left or center-right to achieve governing majorities in Weimar politics. Political democracy was perceived as a useful protection against such abuse, and the Zentrum leaders worked relatively well with the Liberals (Deutsche Demokratische Partei, DDP) and the Social Democrats (SPD) through most of the 1920s. As a vital element of the Weimar system, the Zentrum generally was a key player in every government of that period and thus shared government power and responsibility. However, within the ranks of political Catholicism were leaders such as Franz von Papen, who loathed liberal democracy and who schemed to build a coalition of forces to bring German democracy down (cf. esp. Hörster-Philipps, 1983). Here again, Catholic political conservatism was still hostile to democracy, and in the late years of Weimar Germany played an unsavory role in the rise of German fascism, as it had earlier played a supportive role for Italian fascism, and would later play a key role in the victory of Franco and the Falangists in the Spanish civil war.

In the interwar period, political conservatism played a varying role, sometimes more direct and sometimes more subtle, in the undermining of democracy and the rise of fascist and authoritarian nationalist regimes throughout East Central and Eastern Europe, including not only Germany but also Austria (before the Nazi Anschluß), Poland, Hungary, the Baltics, Finland, Romania, and Bulgaria (cf. Hoover, 1992). Only Czechoslovakia maintained its democratic system up to its dismemberment in 1938 and 1939 by fascist Germany with the connivance of conservative British and French governments. Conservatism thus richly deserved its reputation as an antidemocratic politics which could not be trusted to support civil liberties and human rights, especially in times of crisis. Throughout the fascist period, despite some notable personal exceptions, political conservatism collaborated with fascist regimes and served these regimes as long as they promised not to touch vital interests of key conservative elites in the church, in the military, and in the economy (Schweitzer, 1964).

Again, this might well have been expected, given that political conservatism had been so closely connected to monarchy and that there had been a close relationship between church and state right up to (and beyond) the end of these regimes on the continent. In the rise of liberalism and socialism, and the emergence of a secular parliamentary democracy, conservatives feared for the future of their worldview. The overturning of social order, first by the dynamic but materialistic bourgeoisie, and then by the potentially revolutionary urban proletariat, was anathema to conservative sensibilities regarding a natural hierarchy or classes. The separation of church and state likewise could be seen only as a direct assault on the long-established position of a state-sponsored religion with direct access to the daily lives of the community of believers. The advance of modern urban society over traditional values would almost certainly draw a strong negative reaction from conservative political elites. If liberal democracy appeared weak or indecisive, as it did in the interwar period and especially once the Great Depression set in, conservative politics did not hesitate to call into question the whole democratic experiment, and to bolster the most antidemocratic forces offering a variety of authoritarian and dictatorial alternatives.

Moreover, throughout the period of fascist dictatorship in Germany, conservative political elites did not oppose the most brutal supression of minorities and dissent, nor did they resist the other gruesome features of the regime. Indeed, to a great extent the goals of German fascism matched those of conservative elites (cf. Schweitzer,1964; Kühnl, 1983; Hörster-Philipps, 1983); the use of violence domestically against any opponent of the regime, and the use of war against neighboring states were supported by conservative elites as legitimate means to their desired goals.

After the end of World War II, prewar political conservatism was a shambles. The taint of collaboration with fascist regimes had ruined the legitimacy of conservative parties as potential partners in newly reconstructed political democracies in Europe. Conservatism of the prewar variety could simply not be trusted for the task of democratic renewal.

Conservative politics of the prewar era were also discredited because of their nationalist orientation; their support for military mobilization, which served their economic interests in the 1930s, later came back to haunt them after the catastrophe of the war itself. Germany—destroyed, torn apart, occupied—was now seen as the paraiah of Europe, responsible for the worst atrocities of the modern era. And leading conservatives, Franz von Papen and Alfred Hugenberg, were sitting alongside leading German fascists in the docket of criminals at the

Nuremburg trials. Conservative leaders and conservative politics had led the nation not to greatness and glory but to the low point of 1945 (the Stunde Null or "zero hour").

Organized religion, which provided the mass base for a prewar conservative politics, had miserably failed the greatest moral test of the century. The Catholic church had provided no moral leadership against war, atrocity, and Holocaust. The church had not even tried to engage its moral authority against political repression, and against the fascist war mobilization, before 1939. During the war the church had at best turned a blind eye to the atrocities in Poland, the Soviet Union, and Yugoslavia; it had no intention of opposing the Holocaust. The political conservatism of both the Catholic and the Protestant relgious elites had failed in a historic fashion, bringing disgrace to its cause.

How could political conservatism ever recover from this historic failure? Wasn't this an end of history for conservatism, from which it could never recover, à la Fukuyama? Clearly not, although it certainly was the end of the prewar, nationalist, militarist, and antidemocratic conservatism. But in the early postwar years, out of the ashes of this historic conservative defeat—and it was of historic proportions, offering virtually no chance of resurrecting in the prewar format—a situation that was very different from the condition of political conservatism after World War I and the end of the Kaiserreich, which saw comparatively little self-critical rethinking of what a conservative value system might mean as a politcal project.

The rethinking of German political conservatism emerged as Christian Democracy, a successful reworking of conservative values around entirely new political priorities and practices. In a celebration of fifty years of German Christian Democracy, Jürgen Aretz (1995) notes (in very glossed-over terminology) how conservatives from both the old Zentrum and the prewar Christian Social Peoples Service (CSVD), a small splinter group of relatively more progressive Protestants, had come to the recognition of the need for an interdenominational conservative coalition, overcoming the political sectarianism of the Weimar period. A small group of democratic conservatives now had their chance to reconstruct German democratic conservatism, and to push forward their project for postwar Germany: European, Western, and democratic (for an historical appreciation of political task of then-young German conservatives, cf. Dettling, 1994). Uppermost for the young conservative thinkers was an escape from antidemocratic German nationalism. Already this toleration between Catholic and Protestant conservatives represented a major break with German history and tradition, and the long bitter struggles of the past. What had been unthinkable before the war, and before the rise of German fascism—that is, a Christian coalition under one political organization—now became a major source of political revival on the right. Of course this came out of new necessities, to oppose, as Aretz says, both restoration of Nazism on the right and the rise of socialism on the left. What Aretz does not mention explicitly is the sad role of the conservative parties in the Weimar period, and especially in the last years of the first German democracy, in the demonization of democracy and of moderate compromises to avoid both right and left extremism. Aretz does pay tribute to the acceptance within the new emerging Christian Democracy of both liberal and social (socialist) values as now compatible with a renewed conservative agenda. Liberals and Christian socialists, formerly anathema to mainstream German conservatism and very much marginalized before 1945, now added their influence to the emerging new synthesis. The Christian Democratic Union (CDU), by far the most creative political rethinking in German postwar history, was the prototype of the modern democratic Volkspartei, with elements borrowed from various ideological traditions, but bound together pragmatically in a new political agenda on the moderate right. Aretz says that at the beginning it was certainly a disadvantage that the founders of the CDU could not count on established organizational structures, since they came from very different political origins and very scattered local initiatives, but he then adds that this circumstance compelled the Christian Democratic Union to develop as something really new, a decisive break with the prewar past of German conservatism.

The breakthrough of conservative political thinking to a new and revived agenda for the postwar period meant a sharp turning away from past political traditions. German nationalism was really abandoned in favor of a policy of cooperation and integration of Germany (West) into the community of liberal democracies, and the West German leadership, which began under Konrad Adenauer and which continues under Helmut Kohl, was committed to European integration—economic, social, and political. Of course there is still some nationalist sentiment among Christian Democratic leaders, for example from Alfred Dregger, and the Bavarian (Christian Social Union, CSU) wing of German Christian Democracy has profited from its regional Bavarian nationalism (under Franz-Josef Strauß especially, but still today under his successors). The Bavarian conservatives and their "local national-ism" are somewhat like Texas conservatives (formerly conservative Democrats, today mostly conservative Republicans) and their Texan nationalism. These mild nationalist sentiments are worlds away from the militaristic nationalism of mainstream Weimar conservatives.

Christian Democracy represented a moderate conservatism com-mitted totally to operating within parliamentary democracy. Despite all the personal authoritarianism of leaders like Konrad Adenauer and Franz-Josef Strauß, there is no doubt that the mainstream of postwar German conservatism now represented a prodemocratic politics; al-though the CDU became the political home for many former NSDAP, DNVP, and DVP voters and party members who had not supported democracy in the Weimar period, there is no doubt that the CDU leadership provided the political vehicle for a reeducation and integra-tion of millions of conservatives into postwar democratic politics of the Bonn republic. Similarly, after the collapse of European commu-nism, some of the post-communist "successor" parties in Poland, Hungary, Lithuania, and Slovakia are now major vehicles for a demo-cratic reintegration of former communist party members and activists into a newly established democratic politics (cf. Mahr and Nagle, 1995).

In economic policy, the postwar Christian Democracy initially in-cluded a strong Christian socialist wing; in fact, the first 1947 Ahlen Program of the CDU called for nationalization of large-scale industry, and wide-ranging socialization of land and natural resources. This Christian socialist view was most pronounced in the Frankfurt, Co-logne, and Berlin organizations of the CDU, and it was clearly a meld-ing of socialist values with Christian social teachings that helped to shape the new CDU. With pressure from the United States against socialist economic planning, and with the initial success of the cur-rency reform of 1948, Ludwig Erhard's policy of a capitalist "social market economy" gained dominance, yet it would be a mistake to trivialize this social market concept as either mere rhetoric or electoral window-dressing. The conservative Adenauer governments of the first period of the *Wirtschaftswunder* or "economic miracle" also included the shaping of a very comprehensive and increasingly generous social welfare system; some on the left (most of my friends in Germany) see this mainly as a forced concession to the cold war threat of the East German or Soviet model, which also offered a comprehensive state-run welfare security. They now expect that after the collapse of the Soviet and East German alternative model, Western conservatives will accordingly, perhaps stepwise, cut back their welfare commitments. I think that this is correct to some degree; certainly it was foremost in the minds of German Christian Democrats that they had to offer some social policy to compete with both Social Democrats and the Soviet communist model. Yet, I think this attitude belittles the motives of the chief founders of Christian Democracy, since they were in fact opponents of the old nationalist, militarist, antidemocratic conservatism of the prewar period, with good track records of opposition. This is why they had been marginalized as conservatives during that era, and why they had the chance, after the catastrophe of the Third Reich, to reshape German political conservatism in their image. Their motives were of course conservative motives; they were indeed faithful to their core values as conservatives, as they saw them and felt them. But their rethinking came from a long history of debate within German conservatism, and it is too easy to dismiss their postwar achievement as simply an instrumentalization of American-sponsored cold war politics. Those on the left who hated to be caricatured as pawns of Soviet policy or dupes of communism should be cautious about impugning the motives of others, conservatives or liberals.

Christian Democracy in its German incarnation was born out of the collapse into illegitimacy of the traditional, elitist, antidemocratic, nationalist conservatism of the Weimar period. Its founders therefore clearly and consciously borrowed elements from both liberalism and social democracy while rejecting both of these opposing value systems. This has always given rise to claims that Christian Democracy is pragmatic and lacking a coherent ideology of its own, but this is in fact belied by an analysis of its own distinctive features which separate it from socialism and liberalism. Kersbergen (1994), in his analysis of German Christian Democracy summarizes as follows:

> Christian Democracy and conservatism may not be precisely identical, but they do share the conviction that private property constitutes an inviolable right, that communism is an abhorrent movement, and that the state should be confined and carefully watched in terms of its interventionist zeal. (33)

Nevertheless, it is clear that in rethinking political conservatism, the founders of Christian Democracy consciously "plagiarized elements of liberal, conservative and socialist thought at will" (ibid). But while accepting the modern market economy, they rejected the principled individualist stance of classic liberalism. While accepting the need for political solidarity with the weak and the need for the state to guide

the economy through extensive consensus among government, industry and labor, they reject the class struggle of classic socialist politics.
David Broughton notes the Christian Democrats' rejection of nationalism in favor of national cooperation and international integration,
its full acceptance of liberal democracy for better or worse, and its
strong commitment to social welfare as the hybrid mixture which most
characterizes this renewal of political conservatism after World War II:

> The CDU/CSU became the main political force for integrating the various
> groups on the right via a process of absorption and amalgamation in the early
> 1950s. The Christian Democrats openly supported the new liberal demo-
> cratic system (unlike the Catholics in the past) and they explicitly sought class
> reconciliation and solidarity between different groups. The CDU-CSU was
> also prominent in the initial moves towards European integration and
> transnational cooperation based on the acceptance of a capitalist framework
> for running the economy (1994:102).

In offering its own rethought political conservatism, Christian Democracy became the success vehicle for rebuilding from the ruins of the
defeated and discredited right in German politics. Stathis Kalyvas's
study of Christian Democracy in Europe emphasizes the element of
conscious choice within the evolution of this rethinking of a center-
right politics, and also the significant intellectual breaks it involved.
Most important was the break after the war with the strict political line
of the Catholic church itself, a kind of secularization within the politics of Catholic communities. Postwar Christian Democracy was twenty-
five years ahead of the church in Rome in its full integration of Catholic, Christian and even non-religious conservatives into democratic
politics:

> As they moved away from the church, confessional parties embraced demo-
> cratic politics: voters became these parties' paramount source of support and
> legitimacy. Hence the confessional parties integrated the masses of newly
> enfranchised voters into the democratic systems they were originally sup-
> posed to subvert and reinforced the parliamentary democratic regimes of their
> respective countries (Kalyvas, 1996: 261).

This transformation resulted from conscious choices made in response to the changed political environment after the war, and the
new politics of Christian Democracy then helped to consolidate its
own political environment. "By transforming themselves, they transformed their political and societal environment in ways that were hardly
anticipated: democracy in Europe was often expanded and consoli-

dated by its enemies" (Kalyvas: 264). The antithesis between organized religion and liberal democracy in Europe, which had existed before World War II was now undone, by the legitimation of democratic
politics in a rethought and revitalized conservatism. Broughton makes
much the same point in noting that Christian Democracy no longer
relies on any strictly religious doctrine, and that this is a feature of its
success despite major shifts in public belief and practice:

> In other words, Christian Democrats claim that the maturation of compassion
> in society is the actualisation of the spirit of Christianity. Therefore, those
> who are ready to defend and to help expand human dignity, human rights,
> compassion, public justice and morality are ready to defend and express the
> Christian message. They are, in fact, Christian Democrats, even if they do
> not believe in God. In the Christian Democratic image of society and human-
> kind, Christianity is universal even in the absence of religion (1994: 45).

But was the new Christian Democracy really a conservative political renewal? After being influenced by liberal and socialist values, was
this rethinking and revival still identifiably conservative? It appears
likely that a major political reworking of any value system will be regarded by many as outside the tradition of that value system; only
over time is such a reworking likely to gain wide acceptance as a legitimate renewal in the broad tradition of that value system. Wilfried von
Bredow has characterized the postwar German system as a liberal
model "established not through or by the small liberal party, but which
possessed its decisive powerful adherents above all in the CDU" (1987:
267). Yet Bredow chooses not to characterize the CDU at all; he leaves
open the question as to just what kind of politics Christian Democracy
represents. However, it seems likely that those most involved in the
renewal process, and the varied coalition of supporters and voters,
perceived Christian Democracy as the conservative response to both
a secular humanist liberalism and a secular collectivist socialism in the
postwar era. They drew lessons from the mistakes and tragedies of
the Weimar Republic and the Third Reich years to fashion a conservative response that would attract conservatives, especially the religious
faithful (as well as those who identified strongly with tradition, family,
and a proud ethnic identity as Germans). Christian Democracy was
still rooted in religious faith and practice; in this alone it was a quint-
essential conservative response, its creativity coming in the religious
issue from its transdenominational character, a true breakthrough in
German political history.

Christian Democracy honored ideas of cultural tradition, from the most localized to the national level, and provided an integrative process through which the many displaced and uprooted Germans could retain their local or regional traditions. This too is time-honored conservatism, with which neither German Social Democrats nor Free Democrats could compete in the reintegration process of postwar West Germany. The cultural conservatism of German Christian Democracy was also one of the features that resonated with an uprooted, traumatized population after the war, longing for some cultural or social continuity rather than new and uncharted experimentation. One of the CDU's most powerful slogans of the 1950s was "No experiments," even though the whole postwar German democracy and its social market economy were in fact a huge experiment.

Finally, German Christian Democracy preserved an ethnic, bloodline identity of the German people; for CDU leaders, from Adenauer to Kohl, the German people are defined by their ethnic heritage, not by virtue of their residence or even their place of birth. As Chancellor Helmut Kohl has often stated, "German is not a country of immigrants." In stark contrast to the United States and many other Western democracies, the "ius sanguinis" or "law of the blood" still defines who is German and who is not. So German-born Turks are not German, but foreigners, despite years and even decades, of living, studying, and working in Germany. This was also in line with the classic conservative position. Now, in the 1990s, this has become more debatable even within the CDU, but again the Christian Democracy has stayed with this clearly conservative understanding of Germanness.

So, it seems, German political conservatism (and postwar conservatism in Western Europe generally) underwent a major rethinking as a requisite for its reentry into the liberal democratic politics of the postwar era. By abandoning certain positions of long standing, and by opting for unambiguous support for parliamentary democracy, a new conservative political agenda was synthesized, which was at once politically practical and still clearly a conservative politics. Additionally, this new conservative politics, though qualitatively very different from the prewar version, was able to absorb and reintegrate most of the popular base from the older and middle generations of conservative followers and voters. The success story of Christian Democracy for the postwar period in Germany is strong evidence of a capacity, within the broad tradition of political conservatism, to rework, in very basic ways the practical agenda which stems from that classic value system. The resonance of value-conservatism among a broad segment of the populace, including those whose conservative leanings are mixed with some liberal or socialist attitudes, has continued throughout the cold war, and gives no evidence of withering away today.

Political conservatism in Germany faces new crises, with the eventual retirement of Helmut Kohl from politics, and with the splits between a more national-capitalist faction and a more Christian welfare faction over a future course for Christian Democracy. It is not at all clear that German Christian Democracy, despite its current dominance in German national politics, can long avoid the crisis of its Italian counterpart. Italian Christian Democracy exploded at the end of the cold war, and Italian political conservatism is now engaged in a confused struggle among three alternative politics of the right—the national-capitalist politics of Berlusconi's Forza Italia, the liberal separatist populism of Bossi's Northern League, and the nationalist populism of Fini's refurbished National Alliance (formerly the neofascist MSI). Despite the prospect of renewed divisions within political conservatism, however, there is little reason to doubt that this value system is capable of still another rethinking and renewal.

C. Liberalism Recovers from the Great Depression, the Collapse of Interwar Democracy, and Support for Imperialism

In the midst of the Great Depression,with faith in free market capitalism shattered and with weak liberal democracies tumbling to right-wing nationalist or fascist movements in Europe, Western liberalism seemed to be in terminal decline. It is important to remember, from the vantage point of the 1990s, that only sixty years ago laissez-faire liberal politics was generally in disgrace, liberals were demoralized, and many liberal thinkers had abandoned the liberal project in favor of either nationalist dictatorship or a socialist politics. The young intellectuals of that time leaned heavily to the left in the still democratic United States and Britain, and to the right in fascist Italy and Germany. In Germany, the Nazi student organization had great success in the universities even before the Nazis came to power, and in the first years of the Third Reich the young university generation was a strong supporter of fascist ideology. Only after a few years did the students' enthusiasm for Nazi authority wane (cf. Grüttner, 1995), and even then there was no strong resistance to antidemocratic ideology, nor any notable center of democratic resistance to Hitler; some clandestine circles and activist individuals did develop a democratic or Christian humanist counterideology, but their numbers were quite small (and their heroism in the face of general isolation is therefore all the more impressive).

Even after the defeat of European fascism and Japanese militarism, liberals' self-confidence was slow to recover; it did so on the basis of a rethought and reworked liberal politics which downgraded many seemingly immutable truths of pre-Depression liberalism, and which borrowed shamelessly from a socialist politics of justice, social solidarity, and the welfare state. The voices of an unregulated free market, antistatist liberalism (or libertarianism) like Friedrich von Hayek and Milton Friedman were marginalized; despite substantial funding for their writings, the prewar form of liberal ideology was definitely on the defensive, and in the minority among liberal thinkers, who took their main task to be a qualitative reshaping of modern liberalism in a Keynesian, activist-state mode. The activist state—a state with considerable regulatory power in economic practices and social outcomes— had been anathema to free market pre-Depression liberalism. The champion of this liberal rethinking and rebirth, John Maynard Keynes, had himself anticipated this evolution in his famous pronouncement in 1926 of the "end of laissez-faire" (Keynes, 1926). Bruce Douglass, in his review of the evolution of liberal political thought, argues that in this crisis period, "as it became evident that the continuing influence of liberal thinking was in large measure responsible for the societies in question finding it difficult to make the necessary adaptations, questions were inevitably raised about the continuing viability of liberalism even as a guide to the making of economic policy" (1992: 131). In other words, Depression-era liberalism seemed to many, including many liberals, an ideology whose time had passed. However, the end of laissez-faire liberalism did not mean the end of liberalism as a value system altogether; quite the contrary, although as Douglass (1992) and Isaiah Berlin (1958) point out, it took quite a while, even after the Allied victory over fascism, for liberal thinkers to rebuild their confidence. As noted earlier, Berlin, in his famous "Two Concepts of Liberty" lectures at Oxford in 1958, took great pains to stress the partial and incomplete description of the human condition covered by liberalism. He stressed at that time, when Western liberalism was still recovering from the double traumas of the Depression and popular antidemocratic nationalism, that other value systems—conservatism and socialism—also had valid claims and were as deeply rooted as the desire for individual liberty (Berlin, 1958: 55).

The "new liberalism" (Freeden, 1978) of the postwar period had its own considerable influence on both conservative and socialist parties in the West. Even as strictly "liberal" parties (in Britain the Liberals, in Germany the Free Democrats, in France the Republicans) declined to modest proportions (generally about 10 percent of the electorate, no longer capable of reaching mass party status), liberal politics were mainly incorporated into the postwar political landscape through conservative and socialist (laborite or social democratic) parties. Wilfried von Bredow (1987: 267), one of the most perceptive political theorists of German liberalism, argues that the postwar German democracy established a liberal model, not through the small liberal party but through liberal influences within the Christian Democratic Union. Bredow thus points to the extensive borrowing from liberalism by the founders of Christian Democracy, which cannot be identified as a liberal party. Implicitly, Bredow's account of liberalism's triumph in postwar Germany credits the notion of ideological renewal of German conservatism in a democratic framework, and a dramatic break with the hopelessly compromised prewar conservatism. In fact, in Bredow's view the renewed liberalism worked its influence in both the early years of the Adenauer government and the later Brandt-Schmidt years of social-liberal coalition; the return of the CDU to power under Helmut Kohl in 1982 was in Bredow's view not comparable to Reagan's or Thatcher's victory, although the values of conservatism were also on the rise in Germany. The United States has maintained the exceptional position of having two much more thoroughly "liberal" parties, with admixtures of conservatism on the Republican side and social democracy on the Democratic side.

It was part of the wisdom of the cold war era of Western democracy that some element of economic redistribution was necessary for democratic stability, and stability was a key priority in the West after the turmoil and destruction of the first half of the century. Turning away from the earlier liberal "benign neglect" of social justice issues, the new liberals, in a broad consensus with social democrats and moderate conservatives (Christian Democrats), wished to avoid the "class warfare" of the prewar years, and thus to secure, on a more long-term basis, the social peace that was to be the foundation for a mature capitalist marketplace. The new wisdom held that some much expanded "public household" role (Daniel Bell's terminology) was needed to balance the inclinations and volatility of the private sector, yet with the clear aim of preserving the dominance of private capital in the overall evolution of economic affairs. This public sector activism was in turn necessary to maintain the legitimacy of the liberal democratic state as the ultimate protector of individual property rights. In the absence of such effective legitimation, democratic stability, indeed democracy itself, could not be ensured. The volatility of pre-Depression unfettered capitalism had created too much social polarization and mass insecurity, which could not be effectively contained within the confines of parliamentary democracy. In the search for longer-term stability and security for both capital and labor, the democratic state had to demonstrate a higher capacity for management. This was seen to be achievable through a national-level system of state regulation, intervention, and monetary and fiscal policy steering.

Throughout most of the cold war era, "liberalism pure" (*Liberalismus pur*) was simply not politically viable, yet liberal acceptance of the welfare state democracy, and its growing responsibility for management, steering, and regulation of economic and social affairs, allowed liberal ideas to have their own impact on the way the welfare state evolved, with an increasing respect for human rights and individual liberty. It is fashionable in the 1990s to decry the intrusion of government bureaucracy and regulation into virtually every area of citizens' lives, and to argue that the state has grown too large and too powerful. (I agree with much of this concern, but I see an alternative different from the classic antistate liberal position.) Yet the historical record refutes the more sweeping claim of the abuse of power by the welfare state; in fact, individual liberty of racial, gender, and religious groups is expressed today in the expanded freedoms of daily life for women, gays, Latinos, African-Americans, Jews, and Jehovah's Witnesses, among many others. The welfare state democracies not only had the best record regarding personal liberty, but they reached new historic high-water marks in the 1970s and 1980s, just when state bureaucracies were at a peak of size and authority. Indeed, the achievements of the welfare state, I would argue, were so compatible with the "new liberalism" that liberals themselves began to take credit for this new postwar trend (Douglass, 1992: 132–133).

This new flexibility of postwar liberalism in the West, through the development of a new tolerance for competing values (previously vilified), in course of time became the backbone of a renewed sense of purpose and historic mission for the liberal project. For Bell it was the ability to transcend the old ideological conflicts, and in this sense alone to transcend "ideology" but not the competition of values. For John Rawls it was the ability of liberalism to take the lead in shaping a society in which all individuals could act as moral agents, choosing their own concept of the good life and having the ability to act on that choice (Rawls, 1971). Rawls in particular became the leading thinker of a renewed liberalism that could claim, through its promotion of tolerance and respect for pluralism, its role as the leading philosophy of Western society. One might well argue that one of the strengths of renewed liberalism was its (rediscovered) ability to respect and par- tially accommodate other values, in this way becoming the central force for an open and tolerant society. This reclaiming of the leading position in the West was strengthened in the 1980s with on the one hand a growing recognition of the fiscal crisis of the welfare state and the stagnation and collapse of European communism, and on the other hand a rejection of both revived local and international religious fun- damentalism. Neither "state plan" nor "God's will" can or should re- place individual liberty and individual responsibility. Rather ironically (or maybe not) liberalism's rethinking and modesty in the early post- war years gave it a (temporary) advantage of nondogmatism in critiqu- ing the public order, the state, and the economy. Liberalism thus won a credible position as the defender of individual rights within the demo- cratic welfare state, and the voice of liberty and tolerance against secular or religious dogma that threatened suppression of choice and limita- tion of liberty.

Indeed, it is only relatively recently—starting, perhaps, with the "de- mocracy trend" in Southern Europe (Spain, Greece, and Portugal) in the 1970s and in Latin America in the 1980s—that some liberal ide- ologists have once again begun to feel confident that history is on their side. The triumphalism of someone like Fukuyama is a short blip in the longer time frame of liberal thinking; even at the time of Fukuyama's initial burst of publicity, there were older and wiser heads who still had some memory of the fragility of triumph, or had some greater historical sense of the rise and decline of particular ideologies. Indeed, from the outset it seemed clear that liberals in particular had reason to disown or at least distance themselves from Fukuyama's thesis, since this sort of ideological oversell might, in only a few years, lead to another crisis of confidence, as soon as the new wave of "de- mocratization" ran out of steam, or was drowned in a bloodbath of ethnic nationalist conflict, or was confronted with renewed class warfare brought on by the soaring new inequalities of unbound global capitalism. Robert Leicht, a longtime editor of the leading liberal newsweekly *die Zeit* in Hamburg, saw 1989 as a moment of crisis for Western liberalism, which with the end of the East-West ideological conflict had no sense of future direction for the liberal project, was likely to undergo a period of indecision in the face of rising illiberal tendencies, and would face blame for the "unbounded individualism, purely materialist enrichment drive in a 'grab-society,' loss of community values and even to vandalism" (1994: 3). Leicht, in a sort of anti-Fukuyama polemic, sees a great conflict emerging within liberalism, between those who propose a strictly free market vision of the future, with whatever social outcomes that brings, and those who propose an open society, which maximizes individual freedom for all citizens.

Perhaps this is a normal part of the life cycle of value systems and their evolution, from crisis and beginnings of renewal through blossoming and finally to overbearing, stifling dogma. It would be a shame if Western liberalism, now at another peak of influence, became dominated by its most dogmatic interpretations, thus turning a previous strength into a crippling weakness. For every ideology, the thought of having achieved some historic victory, the idea of sole possession of the truth, not just for the moment but forever, has begun the process of institutionalization of thought, of self-satisfaction with the status quo, of inattention to the failings of the real world, that have sooner or later become blinders to vision, and barriers to new, creative thinking and action.

From the evolution of liberalism as a political project in just this century, we can see a pattern of growing influence, halted by crises in Western capitalism and the demise of several of the liberal democracies in the interwar period, and then followed by rethinking and renewal starting in the interwar period and reaching fruition in the postwar period. The success of the postwar liberal welfare state gave renewed confidence to proponents of the new liberalism, and gradually Western liberalism regained its self-confidence. Most recently, with the growing crisis of the welfare state and the collapse of communism, some liberal triumphalists have tried to take liberalism down another path, one which is again less self-critical and less tolerant of other value systems and their resonance for the human condition. As in the cases of conservatism after World War II, and socialism during the industrial revolution of the nineteenth century, it was a severe crisis of confidence, which gave an opening to critical thinkers to rework liberal politics to take account of the failures of the previous period. Liberalism, which had been so badly defeated in the interwar period as a politics in practice, required a change of direction in order to reenter the arena of postwar, post-Depression politics as a viable actor, and there were liberal thinkers willing and able to take this initiative. Those who had been marginalized before now became the innovators of new ideas. Those whose ideas and leadership had been unassailable or unshakably dominant before the Great Depression were now seen as retrograde, as fossils of an earlier time, and as representatives of ideas whose time had passed. With some historical perspective one quickly comes to the notion of fluidity in liberal thought, revolving around certain core principles—individual liberty above all—but with great latitude for reworking according to the specifics of the political era.

Since, at the end of the cold war, the politics of liberalism have veered toward a more universalistic and less tolerant mode—at least among some advocates—the question arises whether the compromises and syntheses of the "new liberalism" of the postwar period were just a temporary ploy, a necessary expedient in an era of liberal weakness. Now, in times of socialist unease and the presumed "end of socialism," liberal thinkers are returning to their true colors, ready to renounce any social welfare politics as a deviation from core liberal norms, which center on individual property rights as the antidote to state power, and individual responsibility as more efficient than collective paternalism for emancipating people from their ills. Is it in fact the case that liberalism is now again revealing its real political nature, after a period of deviation born of political necessity during the cold war?

This question, it seems to me, revolves around the issue of what tactics mean in the realm of political agendas. What is the meaning of tactics, and what relation do tactics have to core values (in this case, the values of liberalism)? On the one hand, it certainly is possible for political leaders, or political thinkers, to change their position for short-term tactical reasons without giving up their longer-term goals. And on this basis leaders who for a long time have been associated with certain positions, and then change those positions for what might clearly seem to be short-term gain or advantage, must be suspected of still harboring their original goals. Certainly someone like Franz von Papen or Alfred Hugenberg, after the end of World War II, would not be a credible "convert" to democracy, and protestations of commitment to democracy would justly be seen as pure "tactic." Likewise the conversion of longtime advocates of militarist nationalism, or authoritarianism, or racism, to a new democratic liberalism in the wake of World War II would appear as a matter of convenience. So it is perfectly appropriate to question whether a rethought liberalism is only short-term tactic designed to ward off further defeat until a more propitious time for a foreseen return to "pure liberalism." This question can and generally is asked of all late converts. (The conversion of some young affluent Maoists like Norman Podhoretz to neoconservatism in the United States is a different kettle of fish.)

But the transformation of Western liberalism was led not by latter-day converts but by those who had been working on ideas for a "new liberalism" before and during the Great Depression, and who as young challengers to established liberal orthodoxy got their chance as a result of transformed circumstances. There is no reason to doubt their sincerity or their lifetime commitment to a rethought and qualitatively different brand of liberalism. Indeed, although political thinkers and activists often distrust the deeper motives of their competitors, the real opportunists of politics are not responsible for basic changes in political agendas that have a longer shelf life than cottage cheese. Liberalism is not a living being but a political orientation made up through the efforts of real human beings, whose longer-term commitments should be judged just as we would like our own commitments to be judged. On these grounds alone, the "new liberalism" of the postwar welfare state democracy is certainly much more than just short-term tactical maneuvering.

However, it is clear that tactics, taken as political reasoning about what is practical in the current situation, were a major factor in the rethinking and reshaping of Western liberal politics after World War II. To say this, however, is only to say that all politics has some connection to political reasoning about the current situation. This leaves open a variety of responses, from which a dominant renewed political agenda might emerge. But in some sense all political agendas are then tactical responses, based on some value principles but requiring political reasoning to arrive at a specific project or agenda for the present. If there are large-scale changes in circumstances, especially changes that bring political defeat and humiliation to a certain type of politics, then a more basic rethinking of that politics is one expected response. It seems to me that in this sense the charge of "tactical ploy" or "tactical maneuver" which is sometimes thrown up against cold war liberalism by those on the left, is not a telling accusation but itself an all-too-easy tactic for demeaning an opponent's motives and presupposing a hidden and more sinister agenda. (This tactic is of course used by liberals and conservatives against socialists, who are routinely accused of harboring long-term visions of socialist revolution and dictatorship, despite a lifetime of service to freedom and democracy.) Of course, under changed circumstances liberal politics will also change, but does this mean that the "new liberals" of the postwar period were just waiting for this opportunity?

It would indeed be strange if—in the light of global capital; with revolutions in telecommunications, transport, and productive technology; with a growing discontent with welfare statism—some liberal thinkers did not propose still another version of liberal politics, which addressed these issues using basic liberal principles as a starting point. But, I would argue, this is just as true for the rethinking of conservative or socialist politics, and is neither merely a "tactical ploy" nor a hidden agenda. There may indeed be "hidden agendas" of particular politicians and parties, but over the long term these are not decisive factors in the evolution of a grand tradition of political liberalism.

From the liberal experience of renewal, we can see again how its basic values permit rethinking and revival, based on the ability of those values to speak to the concerns of citizens in a variety of life situations, to reformulate the ways in which a liberal politics addresses those concerns, and to make a fresh beginning in a new political climate. There is no doubt that the "new liberalism" of the postwar era was still a liberal response, a liberalism for a new post-Depression era, and therefore a rescue and not a betrayal of the liberal tradition. Just as the reinvention of socialism in the nineteenth century was still a socialist politics—a new and successful adaptation—and just as Christian democracy in Europe was an authentically conservative adaptation and rethinking for the postwar era, the new liberalism was evidence of the capacity of liberal values to remain relevant to new conditions, which had made impossible the competitive pursuit of an older, historically surpassed, free market and minimalist state liberalism.

D. Lessons from History Regarding Value System Renewal: Prospects for Left Revival

There are some broad similarities among the uplifting stories of renewal after defeat for the political left today. First and foremost is the message that precisely this sort of crisis has been experienced by each of the major Western ideological traditions in its past, and in every case the basic values of that tradition have been successfully reworked into a renewed and newly competitive politics. There is no end of history in Fukuyama's sense, only an end of a political era and an end of a politics specific to that era. This "end of an era" is indeed a time of crisis, a time of uncertainty and doubt, and a time of sharp controversy about where the future of socialism (or liberalism, or conservatism) lies. Any renewal of a left politics that is adequate to the new era will involve a painful but also exciting period of internal struggle between the innovators and traditionalists, between ideas and directions which veer sharply away from past practices, and ideas and practices which must be defended by seasoned stalwarts of the cold war left. This may indeed look like a crisis to many observers, but it is also, and more importantly, an open-ended rethinking process that has, in the past, made it possible for each of the great ideological traditions to continue its pursuit of a vision grounded in its own core values.

Each of the modern Western ideologies is an independent value core, which reaches an attentive audience because of its continuing relevance to the human experience, and each is at the same time a response to its ideological competitors. Modern socialism could not be conceived except as a response to liberal industrial capitalism; postwar conservatism cannot be understood except by reference to the need to respond differently to the liberal and socialist challenges; the new liberalism after the Great Depression doesn't make sense except in the context of a gaining socialist momentum to change capitalism. These competing politics and their evolution are indeed tied to each other, in an ongoing dialectic of progress through negation. But in the Hegelian "master-slave" sense of interacting opposites that can be understood only in ongoing relational terms, there are two elements, totally opposing and yet necessary for each other, and they are always in a hierarchical relation, whereas in my conception, the dialectic is a threefold contest, with shifting coalitions and multiple strategies for borrowing. Each "value pole" may be challenged from multiple directions and may find new syntheses from not one absolute opposite (or negation) but from two, corresponding to the multiple complexities of the human condition in society. In this conception, it is all the more unlikely that one "value pole" will win a final victory, but it is perfectly normal for each "value pole" to experience crises requiring a new synthesis to remain competitive in new circumstances.

It is necessary that now the politics of the left undergo just such a period of self-criticism, of a sort not seen during the cold war period, where new voices will need to be heard, and long-standing criticisms of the failings of the established left politics—its priorities, its methods, its strategies—will be given new weight. Without self-criticism, which will inevitably sound in good measure like liberal and conservative criticism from outside the value perspectives of socialism, a new beginning will be delayed. That is unlikely, however, since the established left is now so weakened and lacking in perspectives that criticism from within has a much greater chance of being taken seriously. The humbling experience of defeat, even massive defeat, brings at least the advantage of opening the debate to new ideas, or ideas previously thought to be marginal, and to some extent leveling the playing field. Gunter Hoffmann of *die Zeit* has perceptively noted that in Britain and Germany, the most creative ideas for a renewed left politics were coming from people like Anthony Giddens and Ulrich Beck, generally sympathetic thinkers with some Marxist intellectual heritage but willing and eager to challenge—even now offensively challenging—traditional left ideas and openly borrowing from conservative and liberal critiques (Hoffmann, 1997). Hoffmann concludes that if German social democracy has any chance of making a new leap into modernity, it will have to overcome its fear of coming into contact with neoliberal and conservative ideas.

Second, the renewal process probably will lose some adherents of the older tradition, those whose politics cannot change or whose understanding is indeed frozen in time; these factions may simply become sideline observers of the renewal effort, or they may become reactionary opponents of a modernized left politics. Some of this occurred in the renewal of German conservatism after World War II, when certain diehard nationalists could never accept the loss of the Eastern territories. They however became small splinter groups outside the mainstream of the Bonn democracy, and their adherents did in fact wither away with the passing of generations. Their brand of German conservatism did not reproduce itself, but rather became the last of its breed. Some German socialists likewise could not accept the modernization of social democracy undertaken at Godesberg in 1959, and they either left politics entirely or became part of a tiny left fringe.

Third, it is possible that more than one renewal strategy may prove viable for some period of time; although Leninism now seemed to have collapsed, its revolutionary socialism was for most of this century a very serious challenger in less developed nations, especially in combination with the politics of nationalism. Western democratic socialism, although now also in crisis, has proved more durable, and

probably more will remain from its industrial-era traditions in the renewal process. Here too one must recognize that the need for renewal
is great, and only a thorough renewal is likely to offer a viable basis for
a future left politics. Yet there is some chance that more than one
alternative for renewal may emerge with considerable support, in certain cultures, classes, or political environments. The split in modern
socialism between democratic and Leninist versions was a tremendous burden to democratic socialism, and socialists often fought each
other at critical times for the survival of democracy. One lesson from
this is that the relationship among contending socialist politics does
make a difference; if this lesson is given its due weight, perhaps the
current contention among left alternatives can produce and maintain
a socialist culture of greater factional toleration and common grounding in democratic principle than was the case in the past.

Finally, and most important, the renewal process of each of the
major value systems of Western society over the past two centuries
has involved heavy borrowing from the critiques of its competitors.
Industrial socialism borrowed heavily, shamelessly, from liberal political economy and secular materialism to achieve its new synthesis,
which nevertheless remained identifiably socialist. European postwar
conservatism borrowed both from social democracy's state welfare
project and from liberalism's ideals of representative democracy in
order to rebuild a successful conservative politics. Liberalism adapted
to the trend toward a much increased role for the state in the economy
and society, heavily influenced by democratic socialism, and gradually
saw this "discovery" as part of its own political triumph. In each renewal, fears were raised that significant borrowing from competing
politics, from competing value systems, would betray the mission of
the traditions of socialism, or conservatism, or liberalism. The idea of
adapting certain parts of the competitor's analysis of the current socioeconomic situation raises the specter of loss of clear identity, or of
being subsumed by the dominant ideological tide of the time. Fears of
betrayal and loss of political identity were common and could be overcome only by the force of necessity to change. Yet the fears were
always misplaced, and the renewal process always produced a revived
political agenda, which soon came to be accepted as authentic to its
tradition. The real fear should be that lack of borrowing, and reliance
on only minimal change, will fail to produce a suitable—that is successful—adaptation to qualitatively changed circumstances, and that
the failure to change will extend the period of political dominance of

the competition, needlessly prolonging a specific era (liberal, conservative, or socialist) into dogmatic and ideological excesses.

The lessons from past cases of ideological recovery through renewal cannot point the way for the current attempt to rethink a socialist politics for a new era; this process is open-ended and depends very much on a confluence of events and actors to give shape to a new successful formula. But these short histories do seem to indicate a need to undergo a period of extensive and difficult self-criticism both from within and from outside the value system. This period will be accompanied by many defections among those who have given up on the basic values at the core of liberalism, conservatism, or socialism. The process, as might have been expected, is unlikely to be well organized or predictable in advance, and initially many more ideas and paths of renewal are offered than can be accommodated. But a major feature of periods of ideological renewal has been the growth of a new discourse that goes against earlier principles and dogmas of the political agenda, and now embraces debate among alternative visions.

Renewal involves welcoming new groups into the political fold, groups that previously had been seen as adversaries or uncertain partners. It is likely that in the (standard) formulation of a political agenda, one of the advantages is an ability to identify friends and foes, to clearly mark out positions to attract and mobilize audiences, and to offer programmatic points to satisfy their main needs. It is only when this existing formulation breaks down and is no longer effective that an opening to basic reformulation becomes likely. There are certainly considerable political costs involved in breaking with an old and trusted political agenda. Old allies will be unsettled and may themselves disconnect from the (liberal, socialist, conservative) movement. Openings to a new array of potential audiences will bring new contradictions inside the movement, where they will wreak havoc—conflict and rivalry for dominance. The more comfortable and stable understandings of older and middle generations who stayed the course, actively engaged in the struggle, and perhaps suffered personal loss as a result, will to some degree be dishonored through harsh examination. This is risky ground, and only a clear-cut inability to continue on the old course can give rise to a calculation that these costs must be borne in order to do what is now necessary for rethinking and renewal.

For many, the risks of a comprehensive rethinking are too great; the confusion and loss of certain valued positions may bring a sense of futility, or a feeling that one will never live to see the real breakthrough that one has long expected. Indeed, for many there will be an easier road into noninvolvement in the political arena, which now looks strange and unfamiliar, especially to those of the middle and senior generations whose political education centered on very different issues, in different environments.

Yet socialists should have confidence that their basic values will not fade into political oblivion. Socialist politics is certainly on the agenda for the future. We are now twenty years into an era of increasing inequality, between classes and regions and nations, which calls for a politics of equity, a political challenge to an unfettered capitalist mentality increasingly able to subordinate the nation-state to its profit perspectives. More and more, a left politics is needed to push for democratic and social controls to redress this imbalance of the power of those with large capitalist interests over those who are largely without capital. While liberals may also criticize "wild" capitalism, their politics aim at a more mature and self-regulated market system, a perspective that by itself fails to address the source of power imbalance and the dynamics of inequalities in the new era. Conservatives, and especially religious conservatives (including, foremost, Pope John Paul II), condemn the excesses of secular materialism, the abuses of capitalist power, and the neglect of the poor, but, although they may well affect individual business owners, these admonitions by themselves will do nothing to change the trends of our times. Only socialists can and do bring the issue of conscious social control over the path of economic development to the highest priority. Only a renewed socialist politics can hope to build, in coalition with other critics of the present system, a new counterweight to current trends, and reshape the pattern of economic and social change along lines of greater justice, solidarity, and community welfare.

Socialists bring to a renewal project a long history of struggle, commitment, and achievement, which is accumulated political capital to build on. Given new ideas and a new approach, socialists can speak for a very large part of the population, which knows that political liberalism is inherently conflicted in its commitment to public interests and community values, and that political conservatism is confused in its economic critique of capitalism, unable to grasp the logic of capitalist evolution. Without a renewed socialist politics, no major reform of current trends is possible. Socialists should be encouraged in their activism, for without a doubt there is still a viable future for a left politics.

References

Aretz, Jürgen (1995). "Die Gründung der CDU," in *Die politische Meinung* 40:307 (June) 6–12.

Berlin, Isaiah (1958). *Two Concepts of Liberty.* Oxford: Clarendon Press.

Bredow, Wilfried von (1987). "Zur geistig-politischen Situation des Liberalismus in der Bundesrepublik Deutschland," in Hans Vorländer, ed., *Verfall oder Renaissance des Liberalismus?* Munich: Günter Olzog Verlag.

Broughton, David (1994). "The CDU-CSU in Germany: is there any alternative?" in David Hanley, ed. *Christian Democracy in Europe: A comparative perspective.* London: Pinter.

Dettling, Warnfried (1994). "Die sprachlose Disziplin," *die Zeit* 45 (November 11) 18. Douglass, R. Bruce (1992). "Liberalism" in M. Hawkesworth and M. Kogan, eds. *Encyclopedia of Government and Politics* London: Routledge.

Freeden, M. (1978). *The New Liberalism.* Oxford: Clarendon Press.

Fukuyama, Francis (1992). *The End of History and the Last Man.* London: Hamilton. Grüttner, Michael (1995) *Studenten im Dritten Reich.* Paderborn: Verlag F. Schöningh.

Hoffman, Gunter (1997). "Tony Blair, die SPD und die Moderne," *die Zeit* (May 16) 3.

Hörster-Philipps, Ulrike (1983). "Conservative Concepts of Dictatorship in the Final Phase of the Weimar Republic," in I. Wallimann and M. Dobkowski, eds. *Towards the Holocaust.* Westport. CT: Greenwood.

Hoover, Kenneth (1992). "Conservatism," in Mary Hawksworth and Maurice Kogan, eds., *Encyclopedia of Government and Politics.* London: Routledge.

Kalyvas, Stathis (1996). *The Rise of Christian Democracy in Europe.* Ithaca and London: Cornell University Press.

Kersbergen, Kees van (1994). "The distinctiveness of Christian Democracy," in David Hanley, ed. *Christian Democracy in Europe: A comparative perspective.* London: Pinter.

Keynes, John Maynard (1926). *The End of Laissez-Faire.* London: L. and Virginia Woolf.

Kühnl, Reinhard (1983). "The Rise of Fascism in Germany and Its Causes," in I. Wallimann and M. Dobkowski, eds. *Towards the Holocaust.* Westport. CT: Greenwood.

Leicht, Robert (1994). "Was heißt heute noch liberal?" *die Zeit* 23 (June 10) 3–4.

Mahr, Alison and John Nagle (1995). "Successor Parties and Democratization in East-Central Europe" *Communist and Post-Communist Studies*, 28:4 (December).

Nagle, John (1992a). "Elite Recruitment," in Mary Hawksworth and Maurice Kogan, eds., *Encyclopedia of Government and Politics*. London: Routledge.

————(1992b). "Befreiung vom Kommunismus" *Sozialismus* 18:10 (October). Rawls, John (1971). *A Theory of Justice*. Cambridge: Harvard University Press.

Schweitzer, Arthur (1964). *Big Business in the Third Reich*. Bloomington: University of Indiana Press.

Tucker, Robert (1978). *The Marx-Engels Reader*. New York: Norton.

Verheugen, Günter (1995) "Wir haben ein Projekt und dafür brauchen wir einen Partner," *Blätter für deutsche und internationale Politik*. 9:95 (September) 1049–1059.

Chapter IV

Learning New Lessons and Unlearning Old Lessons—Outstanding Issues

A. Difficulties of Political Learning, Generally and for the Left

The crisis of the left has been as overidentified as the many crises of capitalism. Year by year during the course of this century, new tonnage of ideological screed against socialism (Marxism, communism, the Left) has been produced. This anti-left activity was a pretty good-paying industry, especially for ex-leftists, who were always nicely rewarded for their defection, and given every conceivable opportunity to cash in on their wonderful "insights" or "moral rebirth" or political "awakening" from their past errors. Defectors from the left are in this sense different from defectors in the reverse direction, since they generally have profited from their change of heart or mind. Many of their criticisms of the left were accurate, though others were so bizarre or twisted that they represented mostly personal vendettas against former colleagues and allies, now deadly enemies (which were returned in kind, but with far fewer resources on the left). Most of these writings had little effect on the left and its internal dialogue, since it was so easy to write them off, and indeed they perhaps had the general effect of strengthening the left's affirmation in its own politics. Up to a certain point, defections of a few intellectuals or political activists could be accommodated, and given the horror stories told by the newly converted, the left was even reaffirmed in its power or potential as a real threat to capitalism.

The image of the left intellectuals isolated from the real world and dogmatic in their beliefs was always a caricature, but with enough truth to apply to a number of prominent left thinkers. Yet at the beginning of the century, this caricature did not carry as much weight with the broader public, since the resonance of the left's new ideas was in fact closer to the realities of daily life, especially for the urban worker, than the established wisdom of the conservative and liberal worldviews. Only with the rise of the Fordist model of organized capitalism, with a much more secure and consumerist working class (cf. esp. Knox and Agnew, 1993: chap. 6, for a good theoretical overview with empirical measures), did the left intellectual's insistence on orthodox tenets become more and more alienated from the working class and working middle class audience. The point is that the "dogmatism of the left," and its abstractions divorced from the real world, were increasingly an effective symbol of the left's failure to adapt its ideas to changing circumstances. Many a left intellectual in the 1970s and 1980s reacted to the increasing decline of left politics with even more jargon, obscure formulations, and abstractions without empirical basis. Sadly, much of the new theorizing of left intellectuals was so off-putting that even left activists were discouraged by it. Fortunately, there are now some strong signs that those on the left are now willing, even eager, to speak out bluntly and directly against those "dogmatists" of obscurantism and elitism who most fulfill the neoconservative's stereotype of the politically correct left intellectual, with all of its pomposity and dogmatic self-righteousness. Conant (1995), in a withering attack on dogmatic academic leftism, traces some of the attempts by the Teachers for a Democratic Culture to overcome this stereotyping, while at the same time falling back into similar bad habits, and trying to build an audience on a shoestring budget (always a problem on the left, never a problem on the right). Clancy Sigal, a longtime left activist in both Europe and America, sees the current political defeat as opening a gate for left thinkers, through which they can now exit into a freer world of intellectual renewal, but which also requires an ability to overcome a "fear of flying" and to risk thinking more independently: "It's called gate fever, and I know a lot of people on the left who have it now that the prison gates are unlocked forever" (1992: 651). Sigal, in an entertaining account of how "The Karma Ran Over My Dogma," is ultimately an optimist about renewal, but with this advice:

> After a respectable breather, no doubt we'll soon be up and at 'em again. But this time around, dear hearts, no bullshit. No blather or hyphenated, postmodern, Derridean-induced, M.L.A.-approved, Leninist-fathered, neo-Hegelian prisonhouse of abstractions ("the people," "progressive coalition," any words starting with "multi-"), soupy generalities ("forces of reaction")

and waffles that feel like iron bars around my sense of reasonable syntax, and that always—I repeat always—end up in an authoritarian mess. We now know, beyond a shadow of a doubt, that the impulse to use left rhetoric comes from the same primeval fear of reality, and down deep a hopelessness about the possibilities of changing our condition . . .(666).

Sigal has a good point, but the underlying reason for intellectual retreat into obscure phrasemaking is tied to the decline in the real-world left politics, after a long period of success. While this is understandable, it is just one more barrier to the clear and understandable language that is needed to reformulate a left politics, a politics which connects with the "common sense" of the broad public:

> . . . there is a long way to go before we free ourselves of the whining, sentimental, self-serving, martyred, declamatory, Prussian-descended narrow rhetoric that is as much my radical reflex as yours. My mother and father, both labor organizers, were astonishingly free of this bilge—so there's no excuse for me. Maybe it was because they never went to college. Or because they had to learn to speak basic Yiddish, Russian, Croat, Polish, Italian and some Spanish before they could hope to earn the ears of their largely illiterate clients (ibid).

Maybe the sons and daughters of the earlier generation of labor activists, having had the opportunity to go to college, were inevitably more distant from the working class and its political thinking; maybe the new ideas will have to come from those on the left who have maintained, or regained, an authentic closeness to workers and employees. Certainly the generation of left intellectuals (myself included) who have not held blue-collar jobs since their college days are not well placed for this. Of course the downsizing of higher education may remedy the problem of class distance for some of us. Our contributions to rethinking a left politics, however, must lie in other areas—for example, in reporting and analysis of empirical trends, and especially in the international realm.

The use of abstract language and obscure phrases was certainly an impediment to reaching a wider audience, but it was probably just as much a reflection of the diminishing effectiveness of the older, common-language left politics in an era of deindustrialization and growing fiscal crisis in the welfare state. Some of the rationale for the retreat into ever smaller and more theoretical circles of the like-minded can be traced to the mounting defeats of the common-language social democratic left, or its cooptation as a loyal part of the status quo. The two tendencies were probably mutually reinforcing and contributed ultimately, among many on the left, to a lack of interest to engaging in sterile theoretical disputations, with a practical payoff that was virtually nil. Throughout the 1980s and into the 1990s, I have been invited to take part in these self-styled left intellectual debates (at Syracuse University, conducted by the Alternative Orange, an occasional publication of faculty and students), and I have always refused, despite my own belief in the advantages of open discussion and argumentation. The main reason, in retrospect, is that these debates are intellectually debilitating, lead nowhere, and can, if one wants to remain engaged, take up inordinate amounts of time. The last Marxist reading circle I belonged to broke up precisely for this reason; endless theoretical criticism and quotation-mongering was a bore and seemed to have no prospect of useful results. In general terms, the language deformities on the left in the last twenty years were one of the signs of the downward slope of left political fortunes and now constitute a continuing barrier for left renewal. Jon Wiener, commenting on the failure of the campaigns led by *The New Republic* and FAIR to expose Rush Limbaugh's errors and lies, remarked, "The left has to do more than expose his errors; it has to challenge his ideas in a language ordinary people can understand and—equally important—a language they can enjoy"(1995: 161). Wiener's analysis of the Limbaugh and "right-wing talk radio" hits on a good point: that it is entertaining, with some real humor, while so much of the left's message is couched in boring and snobbish language. Although it may not be possible to resurrect a leftist Will Rogers in today's media culture, it should be possible to recover some humor and good-nature in the left's attempt to get its message out. Recovering a commonsense use of language as a natural and unaffected tool of reworking a left politics will take time, but I would argue that the signs of this trend are already present, and most likely represent progress in the work of the renewal process generally. One of the features of a newly competitive left politics will be precisely its ability to explain itself to its intended audience in plain, straightforward language. I hasten to add here that plain language does not mean inarticulate or scatological slang (as in some futile attempt to connect with average workers or the urban poor); rather it means a clear exposition of how a left politics hopes to change things for the better, and why it makes sense to support the left agenda.

Those who criticized the left from within, and who made it their major task to criticize the left as one of its own (for example Irving Howe and his journal *Dissent*), were given some credibility, but their overwhelmingly negative commentary on the left made them, over time, hard to take—hard to associate with and still retain one's own defense of the left against rightist attacks. As long as the left was, or felt that it was, in a competitive struggle against liberal and conservative politics during the cold war era, it could not afford to pay much attention to the internal criticism of the dissenting left. Besides, in the period of "high Keynesianism," the growth of the welfare state and regulatory state agencies gave the mainstream social democratic or laborite left continuing reaffirmation of its formula for success. Even liberals and conservatives declared themselves to be Keynesians, part of the postwar consensus politics. Michael Harrington notes, "When Richard Nixon said in 1971 that he was a 'Keynesian,' he was engaged in crass political opportunism designed to win him re-election the next year and was telling the truth. Similarly, President Giscard d'Estaing of France, having defeated the Socialists in 1974, proclaimed himself to be a 'social democrat' (1986: 179). Even in the mid-1980s, Jacques Chirac, a neo-Gaullist conservative, could still say that "the social democratic model of society . . . more or less inspired all of the governments of our country since the Liberation" (cited in Harrington, 1986:119). The broad public support for this consensus may need to be recalled, since it was a defining feature of the postwar era and was for so long the success formula for Western social democracy.

For a long time, then, political success itself became a barrier to new learning, and at the same time the ongoing battle against liberal and conservative opponents directed much of the left's political learning toward countering the tactics of these formidable foes. Given a politics which had some success, although very gradual and always difficult, the Western left concentrated its learning capabilities on winning the already-defined wars of the Keynesian state, rather than questioning the wisdom or shortcomings of that project. Even in the last twenty years, since the mid-1970s, with the gradual rise of a more offensive and successful antiwelfarist politics in the West, the left devoted much of its creative energies to surviving the Thatcher or Reagan regime, keeping the welfare state intact, and defending past gains. In fact, through the 1980s, one could say that the left did a pretty good job in its increasingly defensive strategy, since Reagan and Thatcher were not able to fulfill their projects, and the welfare state limped into the 1990s bloodied but unbowed. In much of continental Europe, under the French socialists, the German Christian Democrats, or the Italian Christian Democrat-Socialist coalition, the social welfare system even made some additional gains, such as the new program of long-term nursing care for the elderly in Germany, and the additional "social integration" funds in France. But in the 1990s, increasingly, the price paid for a purely defensive left politics is to be seen as an outdated politics, based on arguments related to circumstances of thirty or sixty years ago. Another price is the increasing reliance on gaining popular support based on mobilizing fears of the conservative agenda; this "politics of fear" is appropriate and useful in its focus on the real dangers still largely hidden in the conservative attack on public commitment to social welfare and solidarity, even in its most statist bureaucratic form. And let's remember that for decades in its battle against the Keynesian welfare state, the right utilized the "politics of fear" or the "politics of hysteria" (often using grotesque racial, cultural, and military scenarios—Willy Horton or "Invasion USA" are two common genres). But as a centerpiece of the left's politics, this only dramatizes the lack of a more positive, future-oriented set of ideas within the socialist coalition. As Norman Birnbaum has argued, the lack of basic rethinking in ideas is related to the long-term practical successes of the postwar era:

> The socialist parties are prisoners of their own past successes in modifying a capitalist model of consumption by adding social purposes. Having neglected both the pedagogic and social dimensions of solidarity, they face an onslaught on the welfare state from those who once joined them in a European consensus. The socialists' managerial habits of thought, in brief, are of little use to them. The European publics are angry and disoriented, unwilling to accept market models of society but unpersuaded that the socialists now have something productive to offer. The parties still command intellectual resources and residues of spiritual energy and moral tradition. It remains to be seen if they can activate them (1993: 212).

Even in decline and defeat, the left has often seemed determined to defend a smaller and smaller portion of the political terrain, as if that had any chance of success. And yet, it is not only the left that has now been decisively challenged to rethink itself in order to become once again relevant to the post-1989 world. Robert Leicht, a liberal thinker and editor of *die Zeit*, has argued that all value systems are still relevant, but their visions need to be updated:

> Certainly, the left paradigm has suffered damage. Even if democratic socialism had clearly distanced itself from real existing socialism: because communism has become obsolete, the clarity also diminishes along with the dis-

tance. But the joyful mood of the conservatives could also be short-lived. Their naive faith in the self-running of the market corresponds to the picture of a 'blooming landscape' which will decorate eastern Germany in four, five years, or calculated from today, in two years. The hangover on the right is scarcely less than on the left. And if the collapse of the communist dictatorships should mark the victory of the open, liberal societies, where are the pathblazing contributions of the liberals to overcoming of the postcommunist crises in East and West? (1993: 3).

Paul Kennedy, a thoughtful liberal historian who became prominent for his sweeping portraits of the rise and fall of great powers, has in a more recent work outlined the difficulties of introducing far-reaching reforms to deal with the multiple problems facing Europe and America in the next century; he especially concentrates on the population and demographics, the environment, and political stability. He argues that even when such issues are fully recognized, the chances for fundamental rethinking of government policy and action are still rather low, because great political change runs up against the reluctance of the people themselves: "Humankind's instinctive avoidance of uncomfortable change and its preference to make only minor ones is likely to prevail" (1993: 337). For Kennedy, only major defeat and catastrophe are likely to be strong enough to break through the barriers against basic political innovation and far-reaching change.

But, building on Kennedy's reasoning, perhaps the combination of political defeat for the left in the West and the disappearance of Leninism in the East, has freed the left from its defense of older positions, now either lost or increasingly untenable (Nagle, 1992). The left, among all the historic value systems of the West, is the one now best positioned to formulate its vision anew, making clear breaks with its previous thinking and practices, and taking intellectual risks for the sake of renewal. Perhaps also the changing political environment, not only on the left but throughout the post-cold war landscape, has provided an opening to new ideas and new ways of conceptualizing a socialist politics. Leicht is right to suggest that liberals and conservatives are also challenged, intellectually, yet their own politics are dominant now, and in circumstances that are not as likely to produce fundamental rethinking. The left's politics are most in need of revision from the perspective of competitiveness, and the intellectual resources of the left are now likely to be the most liberated from past practices. Of course, all of the defeats and disillusionment can also lead to political paralysis, or to an exit from political activism. In the effort to "re-

think DSA" (Democratic Socialists of America), Steve Tarzynski has
noted the personal and psychological difficulties for a middle generation of democratic socialists in overhauling their political perspectives:

> My starting point in this presentation is from a very personal place . . . I
> realized as I thought long and hard about the issues developed here that I am
> going through some kind of political mid-life crisis. When I look at who and
> where I expected to be politically by this time in my life, and who and where
> I actually am today I cannot but feel a great sense of despondency. After
> twenty eight years of hard work, what is there to show for all my efforts. Newt
> Gingrich and the Oklahoma City bombing. I am pursued by the gnawing
> realization that I am not achieving anything politically anymore, and worse
> that I no longer derive any pleasure from the work itself. . . (1995: 42).

I can appreciate this pessimism, which can easily turn into a fatalistic retreat from political life altogether. Those of us who joined a left
politics of some sort in the 1960s felt that we were part of a majority
(its left vanguard) that was able to change things and would change
things for the better. A quarter of a century later, we are now in our
fifties and our efforts have run aground—and worse, the enemies of
social justice have all the momentum. As Tarzynski and Riddiough
survey the condition of DSA (which has actually expanded its membership from the 1980s and is, by left standards, relatively stable in its
finances), the social composition is telling:

> Twenty one locals are on the verge of being dechartered at the September
> 1995 NPC meeting. Most of our national level committees and commissions
> are non-functional, at best a few manage to get out an occasional newsletter.
> Locals are for the most part stodgy and stagnant, not growing, not meeting
> regularly, or have quietly faded away not even missed by their surrounding
> political communities. The social composition of our locals in most cases
> makes it next to impossible for young people, women, and people of color to
> feel welcome much less to have a sense of ownership (1995: 43).

Despite this gloomy picture, Tarzynski and Riddiough plead for a
thorough renewal of DSA as the only way to move ahead, for to remain with the old left agenda would indeed represent political fatalism: "The process will involve letting go of old notions, old visions,
old habits and customs, and old ways of thinking and doing. Denial
must be confronted and transcended. The sea and the weather have
changed radically" (46). Like many of this middle generation, the left
was once sought out by idealistic young people, eager to engage themselves in the struggle for fairness and justice, which was associated

with left politics. The new social movements, as well as the older civil rights and union movements, were, for all their differences, self-identified with a left politics, for which even the American democratic left was the principled vanguard. Even if the democratic left was itself small and not socially representative of the larger progressive coalition, it operated as part of that broader culture and shared an optimism that time and history were on its side.

In my recent conversations with German, French, and Italian socialists, I find that this middle generation is in much the same quandary, and facing many of the same psychological difficulties about political change on the left. The recent defeat of the German social democrats in Frankfurt and later in Berlin, where they had been in the majority for so long, have shocked but not yet changed German social democracy. At an SPD election rally for the mayoral candidate in Frankfurt in the summer of 1995, only a small handful of middle-aged and elderly party members showed up, and despite good weather and decent advertising, absolutely no enthusiasm, no joy, no optimism at all was evident. In the fall of 1995, in discussions in Strasbourg, some French socialist colleagues were encouraged by the relatively good showing of Lionel Jospin in the spring presidential elections, and they said that there was some interest among the younger generation in socialist politics; yet they themselves were becoming less active, and had no idea where a renewed socialist party and politics might lead. Some Italian colleagues from the former PCI (the Italian Communist Party, now the Party of the Democratic Left) also from the older generation (nearing retirement), were unsettled by the sudden collapse of the old party system, in which the PCI had a considerable if unofficial share of power, and had little idea where the Italian left might be heading, although it was clear that a major realignment of parties, and therefore of political programs, was under way.

So it has become commonplace on the left to recognize the degree of change that is necessary, and yet it is emotionally and psychologically very hard for the middle (and older) generation to abandon precisely those views and causes that were their original motivations for choosing a left politics. Some are willing to do this, but many will simply become inactive, taking political retirement before occupational retirement. Perhaps this is natural self-selection favorable to political rethinking; however, those who persevere may be those who are most amenable to rethinking left politics, and most motivated. There are signs that this is the case, in the growing currents of thought devoted precisely to this political rethinking, as the primary task on the left today. The new competing ideas on the left have widened greatly, and this arena is in my opinion once again becoming intellectually exciting because of its openness to far-reaching innovation.

There is now a broadening current of thought on the left that welcomes this task of a fundamental rethinking of its politics. Andrei Markovits and Philip Gorski, sympathetic observers of both the "Red" and "Green" left in Germany, see a special need for the social democratic tradition to be completely reworked: "The social-democratic Left—very much a creation of the late nineteenth century—will have to rethink its relationship to the state, to culture, to the individual, to the collectives of class and nation, to Europe and the global economy" (1993: 284). For Markovits and Gorski, the challenge from the New Left and its Green successors has been a positive element in moving the renewal process along, to produce a more "multicolored" left, more pluralistic and more flexible. One might note, however, that one item Markovits and Gorski omit from their considerable list of requirements for rethinking is the relation of the political left to religion; here too it seems that substantial rethinking would be in order. The point is not, however, to determine in advance what areas of rethinking have top priority, but to get on with the process itself. While it is impossible and undesirable to totally change the politics of the left—since that would mean abandoning all of the lessons of previous generations without reasoned consideration of what might still be valid and valuable—it does seem that the left is now into an era of rethinking as its major theoretical activity. What follows is an examination of many areas that are ripe for rethinking, with commentary and analysis, but without any effort to produce a coherent synthesis. That synthesis has not yet appeared, and the active competition among alternatives has really just begun, but there are some signs that will be considered in the concluding chapter.

B. Socialism and Religion

Both religious conservative and secular socialist politics criticize the selfishness and amorality of capitalist economics. I have often been amazed at the similarity of moralizing from both value positions against liberal economics, the rule of the dollar, the chasing after material self-interest, the consumerist temptation, and the impersonal, antisocial mechanisms of the free market. Although some secular socialists may deny that their own critique of capitalism is moralizing or moralistic, it seems to me that socialists in particular have a strong sense of social morality, which underlies all their opposition and fuels their disgust at the inequities of modern capitalism. It is perhaps instructive that the Swedish model of the social welfare state—often (and rightly) seen as the most advanced achievement of Western socialism—was the work of a labor movement and Swedish social democrats who in the 1920s had already abandoned Marxism as their theoretical base and had opted instead for a secular morality of "our home," in which all member of society would be treated as family. Thus Rudolf Meidner, one of the leading radical architects of the Swedish model, now also in decline, hopes that "moral values" will provide a future socialist counterbalance to "inhuman market forces." (Meidner, 1993: 227) After all, how could socialists get all worked up over social injustice unless they had some strong sense of what is ethical or moral or right?

Stuart Hampshire, the British philosopher, has said that socialism is first and foremost a moral project:

> For me socialism is not so much a theory as a set of moral injunctions, which seem to me clearly right and rationally justifiable: first, that the elimination of poverty ought to be the first priority of government after defense; secondly, that as great inequalities in wealth between different social groups lead to inequalities in power and in freedom of action, they are generally unjust and need to be redressed by government action; thirdly, that democratically elected governments ought to ensure that primary and basic human needs are given priority within the economic system, even if this involves some loss in the aggregate of goods and services which would otherwise be available. How these moral requirements are best realized, at particular times and places . . . are matters for the social sciences and also for a critical reading of history; after them also for personal experience and for worldly insight (1974: 249).

Irving Howe, citing this passage, notes that while he is sympathetic, there is nothing so distinctively "socialist" about this formulation; well-meaning "liberals" (in the American sense) could just as well support these "moral injunctions" (Howe, 1994: 58). His worry is that "unless plausible social structures and agencies could be located for realizing the values that were now being placed at the center of socialist thought, we were finally left with little more than our good will" (58). Howe reveals here the long-established fear on the part of the secular left that goodwill or moral injunctions are not enough, are not reliable, or even can be used to deflect people from the "real" task of finding concrete ways to implement, on a systematic and durable

basis, the goals of these socialist values. Howe, like so many other of
the secular left tradition, even its most democratically and pluralisti-
cally oriented strain, has severe reservations (prejudices) about the
role of moral injunction in the socialist project. I believe that at the
bottom of these reservations is the notion of religious morality as a
strategic adversary from the conservative camp, even when that religious morality also acts as a severe critic of liberal capitalism. Individuals may support socialism on religious or moral grounds, but only
a secular socialist project has a chance of success.

Yet obviously it is classic liberalism as a value system which denies
any credence to concepts of social or collective justice, which pro-
claims a complete individualist relativism of purposes and ends as the
supreme priority for its politics, and which opposes any attempt to
impose social or traditional morality on the entrepreneurial spirit. Why,
then, has it been so difficult for religious and secular opponents of
capitalism to join forces under the banner of socialism? Why has modern socialism been so strictly a secular project, and religious socialism
so alienated from this project? In this section I want to suggest that
the time is ripe now for a rethinking of this past opposition, that
conditions may now, at least in the West, have changed sufficiently to
reconcile secular and religious socialists, and to put religious motivations on an equal footing with secular ethics in a renewed left agenda.

Once, back in the 1950s, the progressive Protestant bishop Dou-
glas Pike proclaimed that "socialists have stolen our stuff." He perceived that issues of social justice were dominated by socialists, and
he wanted the church to get involved in these struggles. Pike's view
has existed for the past two centuries; religious leaders and activists
have long developed their own critiques of modern capitalist society
and its failings. On the other side, socialist critiques of capitalism,
including Marx's, have been every bit as moralizing and preachy as
conservative religious critiques. Indeed, one can pick out whole sections of *Centesimus Annus* (1991) proclaimed by Pope John Paul II
and perceive that a socialist politics is being spelled out. Building on
the hundredth anniversary of the *Rerum Novarum* of Pope Leo XIII,
which first spelled out the Church's partial opposition to "unbridled
capitalism" and limited support for the "working-class" struggle for a
just society, Pope John Paul celebrates the collapse of European communism (which is wrongly equated with the defeat of Marxist thinking)
and expands the church's claim as a moral critic of modern capitalism
as well. In two important sections the pope seeks to characterize the

church as the defender of the working class against the abuses of modern consumerism and alienating capitalism:

> Returning now to the initial question: Can it perhaps be said that after the failure of communism capitalism is the victorious social system and that capitalism should be the goal of the countries now making efforts to rebuild their economy and society? Is this the model which ought to be proposed to the countries of the Third World, which are searching for the path to true economic and civil progress?
>
> The answer is obviously complex. If by *capitalism* is meant an economic system which recognizes the fundamental and positive role of business, the market, private property and the resulting responsibility for the means of production as well as free human creativity in the economic sector, then the answer is certainly in the affirmative even though it would perhaps be more appropriate to speak of a *business economy, market economy* or simply *free economy*. But if by capitalism is meant a system in which freedom in the economic sector is not circumscribed within a strong juridical framework which places it at the service of human freedom in its totality and which sees it as a particular aspect of that freedom, the core of which is ethical and religious, then the reply is certainly negative (1991: 17).
>
> Although the church has no particular economic model to offer, its social teaching: recognizes the legitimacy of workers' efforts to obtain full respect for their dignity and to gain broader areas of participation in the life of industrial enterprises so that , while cooperating with others and under the direction of others, they can in a certain sense 'work for themselves' through the exercise of their intelligence and freedom.
>
> The integral development of the human person through work does not impede but rather promotes the greater productivity and efficiency of work itself, even though it may weaken consolidated power structures. A business cannot be considered only as a 'society of capital goods'; it is also a 'society of persons' in which people participate in different ways and with specific responsibilities, whether they supply the necessary capital for the company's activities or take part in such activities through their labor. To achieve these goals there is still need for a broad associated workers' movement directed toward the liberation and promotion of the whole person."(ibid)

This pope obviously has read Marx on alienation and has understood what he read. The language of Marx on the full development of the individual for every individual as the goal of socialism runs as a central theme throughout *Centesimus Annus*, a core theme which always demands social responsibilities of private ownership, although also accepting the legitimacy of private ownership of the means of production. So, while rejecting Marx's socialist alternative to capitalism, the pope commits the church to stand in opposition to private capital's demand for freedom from social responsibility:

Ownership of the means of production, whether in industry or agriculture, is just and legitimate if it serves useful work. It becomes illegitimate, however, when it is not utilized or when it serves to impede the work of others in an effort to gain a profit which is not the result of the overall expansion of work and the wealth of society, but rather is the result of curbing them or of illicit exploitation, speculation or the breaking of solidarity among working people. Ownership of this kind has no justification and represents an abuse in the sight of God and man.

   The obligation to earn one's bread by the sweat of one's brow also presumes the right to do so. A society in which this right is systematically denied, in which economic policies do not allow workers to reach satisfactory levels of employment, cannot be justified from an ethical point of view nor can that society attain social peace. Just as the person fully realizes himself in the free gift of self, so too ownership morally justifies itself in the creation, at the proper time and in the proper way, of opportunities for work and human growth for all." (ibid)

In *Centesimus Annus*, the Catholic church reaffirms its support for a socially just order, in which private ownership of capital is justified, but conditionally, insofar as it meets the demands of a just society. A just society in the terms of *Centesimus Annus* has a great deal of overlap with a socialist agenda, at least with a socialist agenda which does not aim at an historical triumph over liberalism and conservatism once and for all time. In fact, in the eyes of Pope John Paul II the worst enemy of the post-cold war era is clearly liberalism, which leads in the rich nations to a spiritless and antisocial consumerism and in the third world to impoverishment and marginalization of the masses (cf. Szulc, 1995).

   Yet despite this seeming convergence of views on the abuses of capitalism, and the need for corrective action, socialist politics in the West have seen Christianity, the leading faith of the West, as an opponent, and have seen organized religion, as Marx once formulated it, as an "opium" for soothing and consoling the afflicted and alienated, while doing nothing to challenge the system. The church, for its part, saw modern socialism as a major competitor, along with liberalism, aiming to impose a secular humanist vision on human society, since both ideologies considered religion backward superstition or foolish self-enslavement. (The positivist philosophy of Ayn Rand fulfills for the church its image of capitalist ideology as one based on nothing better than selfishness and disregard for social solidarity, or community, and containing only fierce contempt for the spiritual. Most followers of Rand are indeed contemptuous of religion and see no need for any other-directed or "social" ethics.)

In the nineteenth century, the church in Europe still held fast to its alliance with the monarchical—late feudal—state. The feudal state prescribed a religious code for its subjects, and as long as the Holy Alliance maintained its dominance, the church hierarchy (as opposed to its parish priests in many working-class districts) saw no need to rethink its attitude toward either liberalism or socialism. Insofar as the church was in fact a part of the ancien regime and its apparatus of power, the rising new socialist movement of the urban working class correctly perceived organized religious as hostile, and as incapable of forming a coalition with the new socialist politics of the industrial age. At best, some "rebel" or "worker" priests and nuns could aid the workers' cause in specific locales or on issues, but since these progressive members of the clergy were themselves marginalized within their own church hierarchy, the role of the church as such was that of a constant opponent to the political left.

In the West, therefore, modern socialist politics became a very heavily secular politics, and socialist parties, even when they brought someof the Catholic faithful into their ranks as members or leaders, still viewed themselves as strictly secular organizations, which could tolerate religious believers, but could not bring religious viewpoints as such into their political agenda. I remember in West Germany in the 1960s, when the Social Democrats under Willy Brandt, Herbert Wehner, and Helmut Schmidt were modernizing the party in their rise to governmental power, there was a show of inclusion of modern economic technocrats (Karl Schiller), leading progressive capitalists (Philipp Rosenthal), and practicing Catholics (Georg Leber) in the new SPD leadership. This was a big deal, a demonstration of the opening of German Social Democracy to new social groups, an attempt to broaden the base of its following (and it worked, in terms of electoral results).

In the United States, which radically altered the political-religious landscape by refusing to establish any state church, a multitude of new entrepreneurial churches evolved alongside the more traditional Christian faiths. Presumably there would have been greater opportunity for some alliances between the secular left and some part of the dizzying array of religious communities. Yet the split between the secular left and religious political communities has, it seems, been just as fundamental and just as difficult to overcome as a sustained and firm basis for a progressive left politics. Harvey Cox, a theology professor at Harvard and a longtime political progressive in numerous causes, has recently reminded the secular left in the United States that there has been some history of coalition with religious progressives, and he laments that these coalitions either have split apart or have been allowed to lapse:

> During my adult life I have been involved in the civil rights movement, the protest against the Vietnam War, and the Central American sanctuary movement. Religious leaders were in the forefront (and in the trenches) of each of these movements. I doubt that I will ever forget Rabbi Abraham Joshua Heschel intoning the Kaddish for the American and Vietnamese dead at Arlington cemetery; or Martin Luther King Jr. citing Moses at Mason Temple during the garbage workers' strike on the night before his death in Memphis; or William Sloane Coffin praying during the draft-card-burning service at the Arlington Street church in Boston. And through it all, Dorothy Day was a beatific presence. These figures represent a sector of American religion that is still quite alive today, though badly disorganized, frustratingly outmaneuvered, annoyingly underreported and outrageously outspent (1995: 20).

The split between secular and religious left communities and loyalties was part of Cox's own early experience, but Cox has not given up on the possibility of renewed and rethought coalition:

> Over the next decades, out there in society, the tension between the camps that had once dueled for my late-adolescent allegiance hung on. To me the spat has always seemed pointless. Secular progressives tend to forget that there are at least two major traditions of Christian political activism in American history. One is the ugly know-nothing, anti-immigrant, frequently racist and often anti-Semitic strand. The other is the populist, anti-corporate, often pacifist and sometimes utopian one. Christians, on the other hand, tend to forget that the American progressive tradition, though it has sometimes had episodes of anti-religious bombast, draws on values of compassion, neighborliness, distributive justice and peace-seeking that are nourished by religious narratives and sustained in live congregations (1995: 20).

Cox notes with dismay that the rise of the Christian Coalition on the political right has pushed the secular left into "opposing virtually any religiously motivated effort to influence public policy simply because it is religious. Nothing delights the pooh-bahs of the Christian Coalition more than this mistaken equation" (1995:20). Cox calls for a new alliance of religious and secular progressives to meet the challenge of the religious right, by bringing religion into the public arena rather than trying to exclude it under "separation of state and church." He believes that the opening for this alliance has come from current political necessity:

> Progressives have begun to realize that to purge the public square of religion is to cut the roots of the values that nourish our fondest causes. To stifle

religious dissent would muffle one of the few remaining institutions that mediate between individuals and the towering, impersonal structures that envelop them. To rule out religious imagery is to ignore a discourse that at its best can speak out powerfully against greed, ennui and coldness of heart (1995: 22–23).

Cox also noted the huge gap between the social policy pronouncements of the pope (presumably a good conservative) and the American religious right:

> When Pope John Paul II visited America in October, I carefully monitored the response of the religious right, for whom the Pope has often been depicted as a hero. The response was a breathtaking silence. The Pope told Americans they should not slam the door on immigrants. Was Bill Buckley listening? The Pope said they should support the United Nations. Did Pat Robertson, who sat on the stage with him in Central Park, retract the paranoid isolationism of his *The New World Order?* And the Pope warned that we should not dismantle the welfare net. Ralph Reed, call your office: it's about the 'Catholic Alliance' you are trying to organize as a wing of the coalition (1995: 23).

Yet although Cox's call for a new (or as he would see it, renewed) alliance of the secular and religious left seems eminently reasonable and productive, he does not talk about the deeper and longer-term reasons for the split, nor does he address the reasons why a new progressive left coalition might be more durable and broader-based than in the past. Only if some of the basic factors that have separated secular and religious left have fundamentally changed is there a possibility for a new alliance which might last beyond a specific issue or cause, to endure for the long-term political struggle as a real foundation of a rethought left politics.

Leo Ribuffo has argued that the left still responds to anything religious "with reflexive anticlericalism and willful ignorance. . . . Although the left has ostentatiously reconsidered many subjects in the last few years, religion has not been one of them" (1995: 175). In my own experience, I have found that secular left intellectuals are still overwhelmingly unwilling to contemplate religion and religious organization as a (note: *a* not *the*) coherent basis for a socialist politics. They still view organized religion, and individual religious faith, as an opposing viewpoint which can only distract from an effective commitment to a socialist political agenda. They choose to see mainly those issues—such as abortion or the place of religion in education and public life—where left ideas of separation of church and state, stemming from the long history of secular left struggle against state-imposed religion, still seem to be most important and still define a basic political chasm between religion and the left. While abortion is indeed an important issue in terms of women's self-determination and emancipation from paternalism, this issue alone is not sufficient to rule out consideration of religious motivation as a foundation for socialist political commitment. The left, in defending the right of a woman to choose abortion, does not at the same time have to cut itself off from all the other areas where secular and religious socialists may agree. Yet often, on the secular left, religion is still viewed as premodern, backward, or superstitious submission. Concepts like "family values," which should be a gold mine for a socialist politics, are abandoned to conservative politics, which then fills the void with its own traditional conservative and paternalist definition of family and associated values, which resonate broadly and effectively throughout the population. On the other hand, socialists could themselves become the defenders of "family values," for a left politics aimed at providing all families access to decent income, housing, health care, education, retirement, and personal security. Yet in some discussion groups it is indeed still "politically incorrect" to bring up issues of rethinking the relationship of religion and the left. This is a long-standing position of "faith" for the secular left, and in this area the left is, ironically, very traditional and very conservative. Ribuffo, for one, calls for a reconsideration of school prayer, putting forward his own view that a "local option for a moment of silence in public schools is a tolerable social compromise rather than a serious threat to freedom" (1995: 175–176). Ribuffo is one of several voices now calling for a basic rethinking of the notion of a left politics as a purely secular project—and this is offered as one path to broadening the appeal of a new left politics to the community of religious believers who are already turned off by the Robertsons and Falwells. Yet clearly it is only a small opening wedge for real change in the historic relation of secular and religious left.

Even in those organizations, such as Democratic Socialists of America (DSA), which have for some time now taken this issue seriously, the main struggle is over basic tolerance of religious left views within the organization, not an acceptance of religious belief as an equal partner with the secular left, a fundamental mainstay for a renewal of socialist politics. The DSA has had, since 1977, a religious caucus, now called the Religion and Socialism Commission, and yet the members of this commission often feel that they are marginalized by the secularist mentality of the democratic socialists. John Cort, responding to the DSA Chair Alan Charney's call ("Back to the Beginning") for a rethinking of DSA's politics, objected to Charney's listing of social movements that could be harnessed to a renewed left politics:

> He [Charney] says, 'There are four social movements that stand out: those based on people of color, gender, environment, and the unionized workplace.' conspicuously absent from this list: religion. Mike Harrington once said that the only significant left in American is the religious left. Apparently Comrade Charney hasn't noticed it (1995:32).

The DSA Religion and Socialism Commission publishes its own newsletter, *Religious Socialism*, without any support from DSA's budget. Although DSA has probably done the most on the American left in opening itself up to religious socialism, religious DSA members see their task as one of full and equal acceptance of religious experience within a broad socialist movement. Gary Dorrien (1992), in a lead article in DSA's journal "Democratic Left," introduces several reasons for this full acceptance: key among them is the Christian-Jewish socialist tradition, which is a decentralized and cooperative concept of socialism, an antithesis to the nationalization project of the old secular left. Dorrien further argues that after the secular left's predictions of the "death of religion," the now-weakened left could well use some practical experience from religious socialists in dealing with isolation and prejudice while remaining true to their vision. Finally, Dorrien argues that "democratic socialism has been defined and led through most of its history by white middle-class Eurocentric males. The task of reconceptualizing democratic socialism can gain much from contemporary religious socialism, which includes a rich variety of African American, feminist, liberationist, and environmentalist theologies" (1992:16). Dorrien devotes much of the article to introducing a wide literature of religious socialism.

It seems to me that there are good reasons now to fundamentally rethink this ongoing opposition, in favor of a much more open and supportive position, which would see progressive ideas of religion and faith as a possible mainstay of a renewed left politics, capable of challenging the trends of global and local capitalism, and capable of reaching much more of the potentially sympathetic audience for its message of social justice.

First of all, the position of the churches, both Protestant and Catholic, within Western societies has changed. They are no longer state or near-state religious institutions, and their privileged role in society has been much reduced. The historic separation of church and state has been accomplished, despite some lingering points of contention, such as religious Christmas displays in public parks in the United States or the recent controversy over crucifixes in Bavarian schoolrooms. In a fundamental sense, religion is no longer necessarily an institutional mainstay of the state system or the economic order, and in its practices it is now a social movement—a new social movement, a part of the new social fragmenting and individualization of Western society, and potentially an important component of a new left politics. In many ways, the old left has become more socially established and a more institutionalized part of the state (the democratic and bureaucratic welfare state) than organized religion. This disestablishment of the church—of organized religion and its values—is in part what fuels the right-wing Christian Coalition in the United States. The Christian Coalition is of course a new social movement, and its politics are anathema to the left, but the religious critique of modern society is in good part a critique of modern capitalism, if only the left opens its rethinking and accepts religious experience as a motivating force for social justice.

Another factor that has changed since the Holocaust is the gradual decline in the European churches of official anti-Semitism as the functional substitute for anticapitalism. Before the Holocaust, both Catholic and Protestant clergy preached and practiced anti-Semitism as a form of scapegoating, a substitute for a critique of the existing social order. Anti-Semitism as part of the church's social thought was also expressed in attacks on Jews as carriers of alien doctrines from the left, including, of course, communism. In the interwar period of economic instability and weak democracies in East Central Europe, religious anti-Semitism played a key role in the collaboration between conservatism and an ascendant fascist politics. In 1936, the Polish primate would still write, in a pastoral letter to the faithful: "There will be a Jewish problem as long as the Jews remain. . . . It is a fact that the Jews are fighting against the Catholic church, persisting in free thinking, and are the vanguard of godlessness, Bolshevism, and subversion" (quoted in Toibin, 1995: 40). The distance traveled between that interwar Catholic church and the church today, even with a conservative Polish pope at the helm, is startling, and it has to be taken seriously by the left.

So long as the church continued to use an anti-Semitic lens for its critiques of both liberalism and socialism, it was probably impossible for the organized faith to speak with a socialist voice against the amorality of capitalism. Marx had recognized this long ago in his essay "On the Jewish Question," a much misinterpreted early work in which he argues, using socioreligious allegory, that through the spread of capitalist relations and the universal power of money, the Christian has now become Judaized, and that any critique of the role of the Jew must now lead to a critique of the entire capitalist system, not just a scapegoating of one ethnic-religious minority. Marx's longer-term perspective here was telling, but only after the trauma of the Holocaust and the virtual extermination of "real existing" Jewry in much of Europe. The shame of religious collaboration with the fascist extermination project finally transformed Christian thought and practice in the West. Finally, organized religion in the West has removed anti-Semitism from its own political agenda and has therefore opened its own social thinking to the type of systematic critique from which a socialist politics may emerge. (The same cannot be said of organized religion in Eastern Europe, where the Orthodox Christian faiths still practice blatant anti-Semitism, which is now being mobilized in the traditional fashion as a substitute for an anticapitalist critique. Once again, the spread of capitalism is denounced as the work of Jews or Jewish agents in business, politics, and the media.)

If one looks, in Europe and North America, at the leading opponents of welfare state dismantling, or budget cutting at the expense of the weak and the poor, then the role of the churches, both Catholic and mainstream Protestant, stands out clearly. In Germany, many of the most progressive voices of the Social Democratic Party are Protestant pastors. The whole eastern wing of the SPD in reunified Germany has been dubbed the party of Protestant clergy, because the overwhelming proportion of its leaders has been drawn from the progressive clergy. In the United States, the most influential voice speaking out against the trashing of the social safety net has arguably been the Catholic Bishops' Conference.

In my home state, New York, where the Republican governor, George Pataki, has submitted a state budget which slashes social spending to make room for tax reductions for business and the well-off, the most prominent opposition has come from progressive religious voices within churches and temples. While agreeing with the need to reform welfare programs, the New York State Catholic Conference also urged state leaders to "offer more concrete help to families seeking to rise from poverty" (*Catholic Sun*, November 23, 1995: 9). The statement continued: "The federal government is poised to abolish the welfare program as we know it. The state will now be faced with compelling moral and legal responsibilities of caring for poor families, with substantially less dollars and far more freedom." John Kerry, executive director of the Catholic Conference, testified before the New York senate, "The bishops assert it is a moral imperative to deal with poverty in positive and constructive ways which promote the dignity of the human person, enhance self-sufficiency, protect children and families, and provide a safety net for the poorest and most vulnerable in our state."

The Protestant New York State Council of Churches, representing 4,000 congregations and (nominally) 4 million members, has also spoken out against the attacks on welfare and social spending by the new Pataki administration. On November 27, 1995, they put out a press release to publicize their opposition to the new conservative offensive in New York state, on grounds that it was both immoral and unnecessary. This press release was based on a "Vision Statement" of the Council of Churches drawn from the inspirations of Matthew 15:32-38, and reads in part:

> As the Christian Church, we confess our sins of faithlessness in the power of God and we confess our greed and idolatry of power and affluence. For the sake of all, we call upon the people of Christ in New York State to renounce their fear of scarcity and the limitations on action and ministry that it brings.
>
> We know that a government serving narrow self interest is harmful to individuals, families and communities. It denies them respect and dignity; robs their life-giving spirit; and humiliates and isolates them. In every generation and in every desert, the prophets have called such governments unjust.
>
> Therefore: As the baptized of Christ,
>
> —Believing in the abundance of God's Creation, midst the fear of scarcity, we are compelled to work for a just distribution of society's wealth.
>
> —Believing in God's unconditional acceptance, in the face of those who use our shame to divide us, we are compelled to reach out and embrace all.
>
> —Believing in God's hospitality, we are compelled to welcome all persons into families and communities where they belong, and respected, and have enough.
>
> As the household of Christ, with other households of faith, and with all other people of heart and will, we commit ourselves to provision for the crowds of neighbors through public policy dialogue and action.
>
> THERE IS ENOUGH FOR ALL!" (Vision Statement of the New York State Council of Churches, 1995)

In elaborating on the Vision Statement, the Council of Churches said that the state budget "must provide for the most vulnerable among us and not put more money in the pockets of the wealthy and the corporations through yet another tax cut." This statement is also worth quoting at some length:

> The council Monday announced the opening of its campaign to stop further erosion in services to the poor, elderly, children, the disabled, single mothers and their families, and low-wage workers, which they see as part of the 1996–97 budget that Governor George Pataki will present sometime next month. . . .
>
> In a recent story, the New York Times pointed out that, in Manhattan, the income disparity between rich and poor is greater than that in Guatemala. That gap is growing in all cities, towns, and villages in New York and all but the wealthy will feel its effects, whether it means hunger at bed-time more nights every month, or that a youngster will not be able to attend a state college because of the sharp rise in tuition.
>
> "This is a moral issue," said Archdeacon Michael Kendall. "God's creation is plentiful and provides enough resources for everyone. Think of the parable of the loaves and fishes. Four thousand hungry people gathered on the hill-side saw only scarcity while Jesus saw abundance. When all had eaten from the five loaves and two fishes, there were baskets full to overflowing with the excess."
>
> There is enough wealth for everyone to live in dignity, the church leaders declared. There just isn't enough for the few to hold all of the abundance, leaving scarcity for the masses. "God intends abundance, not excess. Greed creates misery, and the gap is ungodly. People of faith must stand and be heard."
>
> "No one needs to be excessively wealthy while others go hungry," they said. The program of the council has a simple message, and it's in the name: JUSTICE IN THE GATE: THERE IS ENOUGH!
>
> "We have problems in our state and we acknowledge that we need to make adjustments in the way we do the people's business, but we also need to protect our most vulnerable and neediest people, as well as the air they breathe and the water they drink," Dr. Arleon Kelley, council director, said. "Many of our people voted for change, but these weren't the changes we voted for!" (Press release of the New York State Council of Churches, November 27, 1995)

The Council of Churches called upon all citizens, of all faiths, to join in a campaign which would turn back the attack on the weak and the poor. The council will advocate an alternative budget which, though it does not want to be called socialist, clearly has socialist aims of solidarity and economic justice:

> We will challenge every Christian, indeed, every person of faith, to live out of their hopes, not their fears in order to transform this Scrooge-like climate of meanness that seems to pervade the public arenas of our life into generosity. We will again remember that God's economy is not capitalism or socialism.

God's economy is about justice—that each may share in the abundance of creation—that each may have enough, because there is enough!

. . . In the precincts and communities of New York we will join with others to ensure every potential voter is registered—and knows how to participate in the public debate out of hope, not cynical self interest.

—In Albany we will advocate budget policies that are a 'Whole' society solution.

—These policies must be rooted in an equitable revenue plan—not one that continues to shift the responsibility from the corporations to the individual or one that shifts responsibility from the wealthier to the middle class and the poor, all under the guise of tax cuts to create jobs. They won't. Today all capital is global.

—These policies must demonstrate we are a caring community that provides for the common good first so every person and family has the opportunity to reach their full potential. All should have access to quality health care, education and shelter. Children, women and families matter! And if one should stumble or be unable to compete and need our help for a time, we should not begrudge it.

—At the same time, our public policies must be effective, they must be efficient. Efficiency is borne out of creativity—new understandings of our interdependence however, not continuation of past bureaucratic assumptions that measured success in terms of more money and more specialized staff. More is not the solution to every need." (Arleon Kelley, Executive Director, New York State Council of Churches, November 27, 1995)

One of the more visible opposition forces to Pataki's budget cuts in social spending in my region is the Central New York Labor-Religion Coalition, combining local AFL-CIO leaders and religious leaders such as Auxiliary Bishop Thomas Costello and Rabbi Daniel Jezer. This is by far the most effective voice for the plight of workingpeople who face downsizing in corporate employment and defunding of education, health care, and welfare spending at the state level (Costello and Jezer, "Addressing the Labor Question," *Syracuse Post-Standard*, April 13, 1996).

On the national level as well, the religious opposition to Republican attacks on welfare and social programs has been clear and often more visible than opposition from secular groups. In the fall of 1995 during the budget struggle between President Clinton and the Republican Congress, the National Conference of Catholic Bishops met in Washington to appeal for social programs and welfare spending as moral obligations of a decent society. Cardinal Keeler called for political leaders to defend "the unborn, the poor, the weak and the immigrant" (*Catholic Sun*, November 30, 1995: 4). The bishops reaffirmed their support for social solidarity on the tenth anniversary of the bishops' pastoral "Economic Justice for All." Bishop John Ricard of Baltimore, chairman of the domestic policy committee, said that the pastoral "has shaped our public advocacy and our church's support for children, families, especially the poor children and families. This reflection not only calls for the pursuit of the common good, but insists that concern for the poor and the destitute is at the core of the common good"(ibid). The bishops used the meeting also to mark the twenty-fifth anniversary of the Campaign for Human Development (CHD), which has distributed over $250 million to 3,000 self-help projects. Bishop James Garland of CHD released a statement entitled "The Cries of the Poor Are Still with Us: 25 Years of Working to Empower the Poor," in which the church describes poverty in America as "a social and moral scandal that continues to wound our nation deeply" (*Catholic Sun*, November 30, 1995: 5).

This religious campaign far overshadows, at this point, any opposition coming from the Democratic Party, the trade unions, the civil rights leadership, or any other secular group. I am aware that these groups have also made their views known, and their opposition has sometimes been ignored by the media, which seem to have joined in a consensus of silence that will be pierced only by longer-term organized and publicly visible protest. Yet many of the secular groups are concerned with protesting against only a part of the conservative budget offensive—namely the part that has an impact on their clientele, their special interest audience. This is a politics doomed to failure, and it will be rightly seen as self-serving and hypocritical as well. On the other hand, the protest from the churches speaks on behalf of a broad coalition of people and seeks to mobilize opposition on the basis of a moral imperative that incorporates many things secular socialists likewise support. Here is a broad fertile ground for common cause, if only the left on its part will make efforts to connect with this progressive force. Instead of focusing on issues—especially abortion and separation of church and state—that are indeed points of contention between the secular left and some (but by no means all) church organizations, there could well be a historic rapprochement between the secular and religious lefts, a searching out of common ground and quite frankly a "benevolent neglect" of some issues, not unimportant but not the most important either, that have divided them. At the end of the twentieth century, there is no longer any reason that the basic antagonism between the secular and religious left cannot be overcome; if the right can put together a coalition that includes both Pat

Robertson's Christian Coalition and Milton Friedman's libertarian free marketeers, the left can also, if it chooses to abandon sterile sectarian feuds, embrace a coalition of progressive forces, and make room for disagreement under the "big tent." In many areas, the religious left has done a much better job in reaching the broader masses, hungry for change and willing to commit to it; this is nowhere more apparent than in the developing nations, where the Catholic church, in spite of the antipathy of Pope John Paul II, has been gradually changing sides in the struggle of the poor for a decent and just society.

The emergence of a progressive left within the Christian church has been gradual, accelerating with the antiwar role of the Clergy and Laity Concerned in the 1960s and 1970s, and affected in good measure by the development of an orientation toward liberation theology—the "option for the poor"—within the Catholic church in the developing nations, especially in Latin America and the Philippines. In Central New York, where I have lived and worked for the last twenty eight years, the Maryknoll Order of Brothers and Sisters has been especially affected by liberation theology, becoming a strong advocate of Christian socialism in its missions and activities throughout the third world. I have been especially impressed with the dedication of these religious workers to a cause that we share. With the collapse of communism, the crisis of the Cuban regime, and the decline of socialist revolutionary prospects in Latin America lately, liberation theology supporters have done some rethinking of their own, and have admitted past mistakes in forming too close an involvement with a particular party or regime; yet it seems likely that the legacy of the "option for the poor" will continue as long as social injustice is so blatant throughout Latin America; indeed, some (Szulc, 1995) have argued that this is the great hope for the future of the Catholic church, despite the misgivings of the current pope. Liberation theology is itself the continuation of a trend towards progressive social activism which already was taking shape with Catholic Action in the 1930s. This experience did not fail to have an impact on the church in Europe and North America; the passing away of an older generation of Irish-American conservative cardinals in the United States has made room for a gradual shift in the social policies of the Church. Recent polls of Catholics in the United States show a trend toward greater demands for democratization within the church, especially from Catholic women and younger believers (Niebuhr, 1996). In 1987, for example 57 percent of the Catholics surveyed thought that the local parish, and not just the bishop, should have a say in selecting its parish priest, and this had risen to 74 percent by 1993. In the same poll of 1993, a majority of Catholics expressed support for lay participation in deciding institutional church decisions: 63 percent felt that laypeople should help decide on the ordination of women, despite Pope John Paul II's flat refusal to open this matter for discussion. These surveys showed that while Catholic women were more religious than Catholic men, they were also more supportive of democratization in the church.

Especially in the United States—which has, in comparison with Western Europe, a stronger religious sentiment and religious practice and a much weaker tradition of labor unionism and explicitly social democratic parties—the counterbalancing role of a progressive religious left relative to the forces of capital and business should be correspondingly more important (Steinfels, 1996). A recent study by Verba, Scholzman, and Brady (1995) confirms that organized religious groups offer a useful forum for political socialization into progressive social work and advocacy on a wider scale than any other institution in American society. This religious community offers the most widespread contacts with ordinary workers and the less affluent for potential political mobilization, whereas professional and business groups reach predominantly upper-income and highly educated strata. Although one might hope that a renewed left politics could be a broad-based and rejuvenated union movement, the fact is that religious institutions remain, in the United States even more than in other Western democracies, one of the most readily available avenues for a politics which opposes the dominance of capital, and which counterposes values based on human and social needs. Father John A. Coleman, a Jesuit priest, argues that over the past two decades religious community-based organizing has been far more successful in addressing social goals than is commonly realized: "Nor does the Christian right represent the only faith-based political movement that is growing and having an impact. . . . No institution in America generates as much social capital as the churches" (quoted in Steinfels, 1996). Coleman notes the difficulties facing progressive religious organizations, which are often reluctant to bring openly religious views into what is often perceived as purely secular politics; he also notes, "Exclusive liberal philosophies that force the religiously devout to submit to gag rules before they will be allowed to act as legitimate citizens seem neither democratic nor liberal." Yet there is a growing sentiment for an involvement of progressive religion in political life, and this is a much-needed social force for a renewed left politics. The secular left would do well to accept and welcome this contribution, and not assume that religious political activism must be socially conservative or that it would necesarily contaminate a progressive political agenda.

In Austria and Germany as well, attempts by the pope and his close collaborator Joseph Cardinal Ratzinger to impose reactionary bishops or cardinals has led to grassroots mobilization of the faithful—most recently among the generally conservative Austrian Catholic community against the aggressively authoritarian Archbishop Krenn—demanding a voice in such appointments and in local practices. In Germany, also known as a stronghold of the conservative church hierarchy, 1.4 million Catholics signed a parishioners' church initiative "We Are the Church," supporting the participation and deliberations of the faithful in the workings of the church, including church appointments and issues of celibacy, women in the church, and questions of sexuality. Most of the signers were between ages forty and sixty (Köpke, 1995: 21), people who were long committed to their faith and unwilling to abandon it but also committed to changing the relationship between the hierarchy and the faithful. This democratization movement inside the Catholic church itself is further testimony to the changed and still changing nature of the church, and it suggests new possibilities for a progressive alliance of secular and religious left groups.

I have just finished reading an article by Mathias Greffrath in *die Zeit,* which reviews the weighty growth in Germany of a new literature marketing "values" and "virtues," much in the fashion of Bill Bennett's *Book of Virtues* in the United States. In fact, one of the leading new works by Ulrich Wickert in this genre is entitled "*Buch der Tugenden,*" which in English would be the "book of virtues." Greffrath notes with suitable disdain the sudden heavy marketing of such entrepreneurial efforts to install or reinstall conservative values and virtues in German society. The rebirth of morals will not, in his view, come out of such right-wing entrepreneurial salesmanship. He notes the juxtaposition, under the corporate roof of the media giant Bertelsmann, of television channels which every evening show the numbers (with appropriate video enticements) for telephone sex and channels that are concerned with the moral crisis of modern society and are commercially assigned a spiritual orientation (1995: 16). On the other side, however, Greffrath also comes down hard against resignation and a knowing cynicism, the option chosen by many disappointed or disillusioned idealists of an earlier time. His hope is that a new global sense of moral responsibility and ethical behavior will emerge from the bottom up, from small deeds of individuals and small groups, taking on themselves ethical responsibility for the problems which now affect others. Greffrath argues that no grand, well-financed project can produce this new global morality (*Weltethos*), but that it will grow, if at all, out of the birth of a world society beyond the already existing world economy. The alternative is a new world division, requiring a new wall, such as the famous *Limes* constructed by the Romans through the middle of Germany to separate the civilized Roman world from the barbarism of the wild Germanic tribes:

> Conscience is created in the definition of borders, and how we here in the North draw the borders between us and the others, how broadly we define the moral community which we belong to—that will determine, if a global conscience will emerge or if a new Limes will divide the world of the favelas from our world. If we allow the blank spots to spread across the globe, then our conscience will have to be numbed, to define great parts of the world as not belonging, to exclude them, to separate from them. One can do that, and the result would be a precarious security and global loss, sadness and a not decreased feeling of threat"(16; my translation from the German).

Against this new division of the world into "rich civilized" and "poor barbarians," there is only a moral answer, which comes not from any traditional past or from present institutions, but from the conscience of each of us. Greffrath bases the hope for this new global conscience on the growing realization of our interconnectedness that the global economic order is creating—has already created—with all of its destructive effects:

> We don't need any Kantian "must" anymore; we need only awaken to the consciousness of that which is conveyed, seen, enjoyed, suffered every day: the world society. It isn't going well for it, and the question is whether there are enough good-hearted men and women (Paul Kennedy), who will assert themselves against the destructive forces of the global economy. It is an equation with 6 billion unknowns and a power about which no one knows, if it is enough: the feeling of connectedness, belonging, and obligation. Brecht called it kindness (16).

Whether one takes this vision of a global morality for social justice and a kinder treatment of others without borders in a formally religious or a more secular fashion, it is a factor that a new left politics should build upon in its widest and most inclusive sense.

In 1997, the center-right government coalition under Chancellor Kohl began a far-reaching debate on an extensive program of finance and tax reform to overhaul and in some respects to rein in the generous social programs of the much-admired Sozialstaat, in the name of economic competitiveness (*Standort Deutschland*) and under the budgetary necessity of fulfilling the requirements for the European Monetary Union (EMU). This project, spearheaded by proponents of an economic liberalism that would transform Germany's social market economy into a more orthodox neoliberal economy, is controversial within Helmut Kohl's Christian Democratic Union, and it is resisted (as one would expect) by the opposition Social Democrats, Greens, and Democratic Socialists. Germany in the 1980s had no equivalent of Thatcherite or Reaganite politics, but it is now faced with a new political offensive that would, perhaps in milder form, follow these models.

But it is significant to note that, in this moment of truth for the German welfare state, the Protestant and Catholic churches have spoken up most clearly against the neoliberal course, and in favor of a maintained and reformed *Sozialstaat* based on social solidarity and social justice. A joint eighty-seven-page statement, "For a Future of Solidarity and Justice," issued in February 1997 by the Council of the Evangelical Church and the German Bishops Conference, demanded the rescue through reform of the German *Sozialstaat*, rather than its creeping dismantling (*schleichendes Abbau*). This important intervention from seventy-eight Catholic and nineteen Protestant church leaders is perhaps the most ambitious religious political initiative in Germany since the Protestant church supported the Ostpolitik and the formal recognition of the Oder-Neisse border with Poland in the 1960s (Piper, 1997: 11). Although the statement lacks precision in its call for a "social, ecological and globally responsible market economy," it nonetheless, as Nikolaus Piper of *die Zeit* concludes in his semicritical analysis, has given voice to the concerns and existential worries of many people over the future course of German society. It has also placed the two largest churches in opposition to any butcher-knife attacks on the German social market economy, and it has expressed this opposition in terms of religious moral commitment to social justice and solidarity. Here is a new opening for a secular-religious coalition to counter the new neoliberal offensive in Germany, and to work out an alternative that would renew through reform the commitments to social justice which made the German model so impressive in the postwar era.

Despite the fact the I am a nonbeliever, and come from a secular political background, I have felt for some time not only that the left is missing a good opportunity to broaden its base, but that the political left, generally, in opening itself to religious progressives in a renewal of its politics, can gain tremendously from the practical experience of the religious workers—who in many cases are much closer than the secular left to the real world of workers, families, and communities. A renewed left political agenda needs these perspectives if it is to reestablish an organic link to those most negatively affected by the current globalization of the capitalist economy.

C. Socialism and Markets, Property, Competition, Efficiency: For a Dynamic Socialism

Over the first half of this century, socialists have struggled with the opposition of economic planning and market efficiency. The Leninists, once in power, were inclined to take as much control of the economy as was possible into their own hands—the party and the state—but even the early Bolsheviks were divided over the issues of what was possible. In the 1920s, therefore, the Trotsky-Preobrazhensky model of central state planning for a completely nationalized economy was advanced, based on Trotsky's understanding of and admiration for the German mobilization for "total war" in 1917–1918. Trotsky argued for a similar forced-draft mobilization of the backward Russian economy to prepare its industry for the next war. But there was also a considerable faction behind Bukharin which wanted to retain a "mixed" economy with significant roles for private property and free markets in retail, small-scale industry, and agriculture, with the "commanding heights" of the industrial sector in the hands of the state. The experience of the NEP period of rapid reconstruction after the civil war had already impressed on a part of the Leninist party the need to rethink its earlier "war communist" views of how to run the economy. Bukharin sought that elusive "third way" between plan and market which has occupied so much of innovative socialist thinking on the modern economy. In the end, the Stalinist decision to adopt, in hyperbolic form, the centralized planning or command economy model was a political decision based on maintaining the political monopoly of the party and the future military security of the regime. The Leninist party logic could not, in the end, stand for the rising political challenge of the kulak class in the countryside. The regime also opted for a forced industrialization model that guaranteed a military mobilization of economic resources in anticipation of a new war with the West, perhaps specifically with Germany. The grounds for this decision were thus peculiarly Leninist, relating again to the drive for conquering and holding state power. It was assumed, of course, that the Leninist control of state power would eventually direct policy toward meeting social needs, but for the lifetime of the communist regime in the Soviet Union, it was extraordinarily difficult to break away from the original model of heavy industry related to military capacity, and the decision not to open economic debate beyond the boundaries of the party. The Soviet planned economy, through its sixty or so years of evolution, remained a variation of a wartime mobilization economy, in both its explicitly military and its civilian sectors. The deformations of the Soviet model have been spelled out for a long time now, but the collapse of communism also laid bare the extent of some problems—such as massive environmental pollution and crude lack of attention to safety standards—which still endanger the lives of Russian workers and which cannot possibly be connected to any type of "socialist economics." Earlier analyses of these aspects (Enloe, 1975; Kelley et al. 1976; Ophuls, 1977), as useful as they were in pointing out additional systemic problems of Soviet-style planning, could not begin to expose the full range of these problems. The exposure of the industrial working class to daily hazards of Soviet industry is a final telling comment on the betrayal of the working class by the Soviet planning model.

In the West, social democrats, in an evolutionary fashion, opted for acceptance of a market economy, but with a series of reservations, which led then to a search for mechanisms to regulate, macromanage, and socially steer the results or outcomes of a still capitalist market system. The Swedish socialists had already given up on nationalization in the 1920s; the German social democrats formally accepted the wisdom of the marketplace in their Godesberg Conference in 1959; and the British Labour Party waited until 1995 to dump its historic "clause 4" commitment to nationalization—yet practice in almost all cases outran theory in Western socialism, and in fact the great majority of social democrats, socialists, laborites had decided that the capitalist market economic could not be eliminated, but could be socially reformed. For socialism in the West, therefore, the question was one of democratically establishing structures and agencies for regulating and modifying the free market, of moderating its volatility through government action far short of comprehensive planning, and of leaving the general direction of economic development to private decisions of capital interests. This politics of democratic social regulation assumed that national governments could effectively control the behavior of capital within the borders of the nation-state, and for perhaps forty years after World War II, this assumption was probably accurate. It was based on a wide public consensus that national government intervention in economic affairs could redress perceived failings of the marketplace, and was necessary to provide social security, labor peace, and political stability for both labor and business.

This consensus has now broken down; the ability of capital to escape effective regulation and social control within the nation-state, and the fiscal crisis of the Keynesian welfare state resulting from the globalization of capitalist dynamics as well as from other causes, has now brought the statist regulatory project into doubt.

What are socialists to do? At the moment, the wisdom of the deregulated free market dominates, and the direction of change is toward accommodating demands of capital; governments are scrambling to attract capital to their territory and are willing to bid down regulations, taxation, and social benefits to pull in new investments. The Republican concept of decentralization of policy down to state or local level is aimed at accelerating this already dominant current, to multiply the number of units needing to reduce their social demands on capital investments in order to compete with each other. The levelingdown is just one more sign of the political ascendancy of capital freed from the fetters of nation-state social democracy. It is proof, if there needed to be proof, of the silly notion of a humane modern capitalism, or of the "corporation with a soul" or of capitalism with a human face, all propounded to convince people that modern capitalism had changed basically in character. Modern capital, indeed the most modern sector of capital, has chosen to escape social restraints in search of higher profitability, maximizing (at least short-term) profitability regardless of social costs to particular localities, regions, or nations.

It is clear that the conditions which made possible a viable, even dominant social democratic politics in which the nation-state would steer the economy and regulate national capital to social ends—in short social state Keynesianism—have fundamentally changed, requiring a no less fundamental rethinking for a viable left politics in this as in so many other areas. And, as in so many other areas, it would be advisable to look at the critique of Keynesianism from its opponents, to see if there are useful ideas that can be incorporated into a specifically socialist rethinking of the politics of markets, private property, and economic efficiency.

In his search for a workable socialist economics, Alec Nove provided, over the years of the cold war, a useful critique of the failures of Soviet-type central planning. His credentials as a critic of communist "command economics" are strong and reach back a long way. He has also considered some features of the Yugoslav and the Hungarian "market socialist" experience, and the lessons from Western European nationalization policies, in his search for a new synthesis between plan and market that would be practical and still socialist. His work on a model of "feasible socialism," first presented in 1983, energized the debate among Western socialists on a renewed socialist economic project. His recent work on *The Economics of Feasible Socialism Revisited* (1991), included such features as the following:

(a) The predominance of state, social and co-operative property, and the absence of large-scale private ownership of the means of production.

(b) Conscious planning by an authority responsible to an elected assembly of major investments of structural significance.

(c) Central management of current microeconomic affairs confined to sectors (and to type of decision) where informational, technological and organisational economies of scale, and the presence of major externalities, render this indispensable.

(d) A preference for small scale, as a means of maximising participation and a sense of "belonging." Outside centralized or monopolised sectors, and the limited area of private enterprise, management should be responsible to the workforce.

(e) Current output and distribution of goods and services would whenever possible be determined by negotiations between the parties concerned. There should be explicit recognition that this implies and requires competition, a pre-condition for choice.

(f) Workers should be free to choose the nature of their employment. . . . in cooperatives, or on their own account . . . or in private enterprise.

(g) As an unlimited market mechanism would in due course destroy itself, and create intolerable social inequalities, the state would have vital functions in determining income policies, levying taxes (and differential rents), intervening to restrain monopoly power, and generally setting the ground-rules and limits of a competitive market. Some sectors (education, health, etc.) would naturally be exempt from market-type criteria.

(h) It is recognised that a degree of material inequality is a pre-condition for avoiding administrative direction of labour, but moral incentives would be encouraged and inequalities consciously limited. Unemployment is an evil to be minimised.

(i) The distinction between governors and governed, managers and managed, cannot realistically be eliminated, but great care must be taken to devise barriers to abuse of power and the maximum possible democratic consultation" (245–246).

Nove's rethinking of a socialist economics provides for a huge role for the state "as owner, as planner, as enforcer of social and economic priorities" (247). Nove counted on the presence of a small and closely watched private sector to provide some measure of competition and an outlet for individual enterprise, yet with strict limitations on the possibility of large income from ownership of property, the basis for a capitalist class (220). Nove would allow free enterprise to build up a business, but at some point this larger enterprise would have to be converted into a cooperative or socialized firm, with appropriate compensation for the owner. His vision of a feasible socialism is still very much state-centered, though with much expanded roles for cooperatives and for workers. A multiparty democracy with strong protection of individual rights would allow for steady response by citizens to the workings of the system, as well as the possibility of a popularly chosen return to capitalism in case of widespread dissatisfaction. Yet there is in Nove's blueprint for a feasible socialism still much of the style of thinking that defined revolutionary socialism—the elimination of the capitalist class. For Nove there might be room for individual entrepreneurs and entrepreneurship, but not for a capitalist class to represent a competing social order. In that sense, although democracy would still allow for a capitalist revival, this could not be promoted by a capitalist class with significant capital resources. The politics of this feasible socialism would still require, in its implementation, overcoming the existing capitalist class, and building a powerful socialist state capable of enforcing the new groundrules of the economy. Although Nove's plan would allow for competition in the nonprivate sector, and would permit some private sector competition as well, this is undertaken largely for the sake of efficiency within the boundaries of democratic state planning and socially conscientious public authority. Certain industries would be forever in the state sector, and some large areas (health care and education) would be forever outside the market sector.

But how would this permanent structuring guard against the growth of bureaucracy and abuse of monopoly power? How would this provide for dynamic change over time, which has, under capitalism, made some key industries of the past (steel, mining) shrink to modest proportions and others (computers, telecommunications) grow to tremendous influence? Would a feasible socialism have any such dynamics, or would it be ever afraid of technological innovation and new, unanticipated, developments? In much of Nove's analysis of past mistakes and future prospects, it sounds as though an old issue is being treated in an old way: through still another attempt at creating a democratic socialist state that would keep some very basic market tendencies from going beyond small-scale effects. But if this is the case, it would also not allow for larger-scale changes or innovative dynamics to fully develop, unless a much higher level of certainty, or security, could be given to the larger community that it would not disturb the economic order. My suspicion is that this feasible socialism would be risk-averse to a much greater extent than Nove perhaps would admit, and that it might well become a fairly unimaginative and frankly boring social order. This of course is one of the charges made against communism—that when it was not terrorizing its opponents, it was a boring and very undynamic social and economic order.

Nove freely admits that there would be mistakes and that not all social ills would disappear under his feasible socialism, yet the main danger he sees is not the threat of "a vote to 'restore capitalism' " but that in so "'political' an economy, especially in income and price policy and in investment, . . . the resultant stresses and strains will lead to economic crisis, which could disrupt both the economic and the political balance" (247). My concern is that Nove underestimated the degree to which the enlarged state has itself become problematic, and to which its power over citizens is resented, so that another state-centered socialist politics would engender much more citizen opposition, and demands for less planning and social controls. A strong liberal politics would be required to redress the heavy statism of Nove's feasible socialism; perhaps this would be accommodated through the democratic process, but if it were to weaken the state planning function, it would again open the door, democratically, for the reemergence of a capitalist class and the dynamics of class conflict. In short, Nove's innovations are directed to problems of the democratic nature of state planning, to problems of efficiency, and to building up forms of cooperative competition for a feasible socialist economics. But he

pays little attention to the problems inherent in heavily statist strategies, and his preferred model is one that weighs, I fear, heavily against
economic dynamism and flexibility. Of course this seems to be one of
the classic trade-offs of socialist politics: more security for the individual and community might well be seen as requiring less change, or
only an evolution slow enough not to unduly disturb previous expectations. But is this of necessity a permanent feature of any socialist
politics?

In economic policy, as in many other questions of a renewed socialism, Michael Harrington was an intellectual pioneer, and his ideas on
policies for a new socialism are worthy of special consideration. He
posits a new socialist commitment to more local, personalized, systems for delivering social services, and for social ownership on a decentralized basis:

> Questions of efficiency—sometimes posed as profound choices relating to life
> and death—are important even in the nonmarket sector, even when they are
> answered in cooperative and decentralized ways. That point relates to the
> broader concept of the commitment of the new socialism to *decentralized*
> forms of social ownership. It is not merely in the delivery of social services
> that such an approach opens up new spaces for personal freedom and cre-
> ativity. It also provides for the possibility of bottom-up control of the economy
> on a human scale (1989: 242).

Harrington goes on to elaborate an approach that would recognize
individual entrepreneurship in production as a desired goal of a renewed socialist politics. In speaking about enterprise-level democracy
in a future socialist political agenda, Harrington seeks to enlarge the
socialist vision of human creativity to include managerial and business
initiative:

> . . . if there is to be genuine grass-roots autonomy, then there must be a
> market space—modified by planning priorities, of course—in which the demo-
> cratic enterprises are free to exercise their communal imagination and inter-
> act without supervision from above. If, however, all decisions are made by
> central planners, even if they are working under the instructions of the people,
> one would lose that new source of productivity. For the latter requires that
> the enterprise—private or public, large or small—has the possibility of coming
> up with new ideas and products. That leads to what must seem to be a very
> heretical thought for a socialist: there must be sources of individual and col-
> lective gain in the process (243).

What Harrington is describing for a new socialism is an expanded
respect for decentralized business initiative, which may come from a

community or from an individual. And the motivation for initiative will be material incentives, "so long as there is scarcity and discretionary income, so long as there must be a social concern with economizing inputs and therefore linking performance and success, there will be a need for material incentives" (243). At the same time Harrington wants his new socialism to retain democratic economic planning, so that "within the context of a plan, markets could, *for the first time*, be an instrument for truly maximizing the freedom of choice of individuals and communities" (247). Harrington rejects the sharp choice made by Alec Nove between plan and market, and says, "What is critical is the *use* of markets to implement democratically planned goals in the most effective way. That, it must be said, involves a danger: that the means will turn into the ends" (247).

This rethought economic politics is an attempt to create a "third way," a synthesis between comprehensive nationalization (plan) and privatization (market). In accepting market incentives for individuals and collectives, Harrington is fully aware that the force of self-interest—now, it is hoped, a means to an end for a socially just economic order—could well become the end itself, and it would entail bringing contradictory elements into his new socialism. This is what happened, many socialists would argue, in the evolutionary course of European social democracy: arriving at a technocratic politics of more efficient management and better growth rates as the top priorities, and forgetting the original aims of a socialist economics. But he argues that there is no other way: "At the same time, to repeat an earlier warning, there is no socialist market utopia. Making self-interest—including collective self-interest—the instrument of community purpose will be a contradictory, and even dangerous, idea for the foreseeable future. It is also necessary" (244). In this respect Harrington goes much farther than Nove in accepting a new and higher level of risk-taking to gain the benefits of economic entrepreneurship.

The question that arises is: just what remains of planning in Harrington's new socialism? And what socialist purposes does it really serve? On these points Harrington is rather silent, perhaps because this will remain to be fleshed out in practice and cannot be foreseen now, but perhaps there is less to "democratic planning" than there seems to be at first glance. For example, "democratic planning" could not, in order to make use of market efficiency mechanisms, undertake comprehensive planning of economic production, employment, wages and salaries, or research and development. It could not, if it is to avoid the errors of bureaucratic statism, involve a large centralized oversight of the economy. And if it focuses on making use of market efficiencies, it has to consider "marketization" of even such sectors as health care—though Harrington cites health care as a success of the Keynesian welfare state model precisely because it was withdrawn from the market sector. (239) This is really an open political question about a popularly perceived need to intervene in market-type economic processes with social political capital (i.e., socialist politics) to trade off some capitalist market efficiency for greater social efficiency. And as Harrington notes, this trade-off may well, as in the health care sector, lead to rising costs, in part due to the loosening of market-type constraints on individual consumption of health services. Is there a way to maintain the commitment to universal access to health care over the long run simply through the expenditure of social political capital, or will this type of intervention give rise to attacks on the inefficiencies and fiscal crises of socialist policies? The answer, it seems to me, is that no durable socialist policy of intervention in the market-type economy could work forever without challenge, because such intervention is loaded with contradictions, which over time will bring unintended but unavoidable negative effects (as well as worthwhile social benefits); but I don't see this as such a terrible dilemma for a new and revived socialism, if we can accept that socialist politics (like conservative and liberal politics) contains some severe contradictions and shortcomings, which will need criticism (always) and revision (steadily) and defeat (at longer intervals).

What appears from left reform proposals on socialism and the market is once again an attempt to fashion a stable position for a left political agenda, that could maintain itself over the longer term, escaping both the pitfalls of Soviet-type central planning and any abject submission to capitalist market dictates. Harrington does recognize a need for some risk-taking, and he sees some of the inherent contradictions involved in attempting to use market mechanisms for socialist purposes. Rather than trying to achieve some "socialist market utopia," Harrington argues for the necessity of risk-taking for the sake of reaching a new socialist politics; he does so reluctantly, but why? In part because he is still tied to the achievements of the Keynesian welfare state, as much as he criticizes it for its bureaucratic failings. In part because he is aware of the powerful pull of material incentives, especially at the individual level, even for the so-called postmaterialist generation (244). Perhaps it is simply not possible to achieve any stable

socialist position, but rather possible to achieve only successive socialist challenges and counterbalances in a dynamic market economy, just
as it is not possible for capitalism to achieve any stable synthesis by
which it could escape political condemnation and renewed challenge
for its social and ethical failures.

Robert Heilbroner has been one of the most prominent intellectual
critics of modern capitalism, Western socialism, and Soviet communism as competing economic alternatives. In 1990, with the collapse
of European communism and the capitalist transformation of Chinese
communism (cf. especially Chen, 1995, for the undermining of socialist economic ideology in China), and the erosion of Western social
democracy well under way, Heilbroner offered his reflections on the
end of an era in which socialism seemed not only possible but "within
easy grasp. Mainly it would require the nationalization of the Fortune
list of five hundred leading industrial corporations, which would there-
after be administered by a Central Planning Board" (1990: 91). Now,
in his epitaph for the end of economic planning, Robert Heilbroner
noted that as early as the 1930s, not only conservative economists
like Ludwig von Mises but also socialists like Oskar Lange had pointed
out the dangers of a centralized planning system. Lange, citing some
ways around some of the difficult problems of pricing in a planned
economy, added; "The real danger of socialism is that of a bureaucratization of economic life" (1990: 92). And yet Lange also noted that
the same danger also was present in monopoly capitalism, perhaps in
even greater measure. But although Lange was right about the trend
toward bureaucratization of the largest corporations in the era of large-
scale industrialization, the capitalist system did have its own dynamics
for countering this bureaucratization of the firm—the ability of more
enterprising capitalists to compete effectively with the large corporate
bureaucracies, and eventually to force them to "downsize" and break
up into their component units in the search for more flexibility (This
meant, of course, the capability of firing large numbers of employees)
and to increase the risk of employment at all levels (naturally much
more at the bottom, but reaching high into management as well). By
the 1980s downsizing and corporate flexibility were of high priority in
Western capitalism, in keeping with the general trend toward more
decentralized production and more individualized products.

Heilbroner's analysis pays homage to the dynamism of the private
sector, "where individuals and corporations do all the things they are
unable to do in a centrally planned system: innovate, expand, con-

tract, and otherwise seek to enlarge, rescue, or change their markets. This activity is what gives capitalism its simultaneous inner growth and inner decline; and it is apparent enough, weighing both sides in the balance of history, that successes have outmatched failures, and growth has outpaced decline" (97). There is also, says Heilbroner, a specifically capitalist need for public sector intervention of some sort, in effect, to save market capitalism from itself, from its own negative social effects:

> Capitalism is thus as intimately entangled with planning as it is with the market. Its entanglement is called not planning but economic policy, and I need hardly add that economic policy is very different from central planning. . . . Planning is therefore the manner in which a capitalist society attempts to control its destiny (98).

Heilbroner applies this concept of capitalist planning to the emergence of postcommunist economies in Eastern Europe, which will lead them from a situation of "not socialism" to some sort of capitalism (and not some elusive "third way"). What Heilbroner is getting at is that the only working model of economic development now in play is capitalism, of one variety or another. This hegemony of ideas will be likely to inhibit even the thought of an alternative order:

> It seems unlikely in part because one residual effect of the collapse of Communism is apt to be an inhibition of the social imagination. In larger part, however, my skepticism stems from an absence of plausible social blueprints whose realization seems worth the risk of venturing beyond the terrain of capitalism (99).

Heilbroner leaves only some prospect that within the foreseeable future environmental challenges stemming from economic growth will force some type of socially organized and legitimized constraints on capitalist dynamics. Whether this could be called capitalism or socialism is doubtful, says Heilbroner, at least as we have become familiar with these terms. It would be much more constraining to the dynamics of capitalist growth, and therefore "it would be difficult to call the final social order capitalism." Yet "socialism as a social order designed to ward off ecological disaster will of necessity be a less agreeable undertaking than socialism as a design for the benefit of our grandchildren in the absence of such an overriding challenge"(100). In Heilbroner's view, the last remaining rationale for constraining capitalist economy is the impending threat of environmental catastrophe, and whether such mechanisms as might evolve can already be ideologically labeled is doubtful.

Heilbroner's pessimism does not encourage rethinking any type of economic planning, but then again, he is giving his farewell address on an old issue of state-centric socialism with its solutions of economic planning; he is remarkably silent on any socialist futures that rejects statism as a goal, and is fully aware of the negative consequences of bureaucratic forms of problem-solving. But why is this? Certainly, given Heilbroner's long experience, he is aware that socialism was a vibrant movement before the advent of economic planning, whether Soviet or Western Keynesian. Why would socialists have an alternative economic policy already developed, since it is only in recent times that the older socialist strategies of either comprehensive central planning or democratic macroeconomic steering have become clearly moribund? Only now are the barriers to rethinking of socialist economics falling, and only now is the severe critique of past strategy being accepted widely within the left itself. With a few years of postcommunism now past, the collapse of the Soviet system seems more like an emancipation from old deadends (Nagle, 1992) than a residual barrier to the social imagination of left political thought. Heilbroner himself at one point says that "collapse of the planned economies has forced us to rethink the meaning of socialism" (98), but then he decides that the only conclusion is that all notions of economic planning are dead. This is a possible interpretation, of course, but not by any means the only one. With all of the social polarization of income, wealth, and opportunities that the new gobalizing capitalism is bringing—along with the dismantling of all types of social security programs—a socialist politics has a broad potential audience for new ideas, which will come from the bottom up and will be likely to steer clear of statist solutions. In fact, within a few years Heilbroner was contradicting his earlier pessimism and canceling his funeral rites for socialist economics. In a foreword to a collection of articles on market socialism, he remarks:

> I do not think the outlook betokens despair. Capitalism continues to be, as it always has been, the agency of its own undoing. The task of socialists is therefore not to wring their hands, but to dust off their clothes and go to work. They will not lack for an agenda. What I think they should also bear in mind is that the testing of socialist ideas with small initial letters is not only valuable in itself, but helps clear our minds about what really constitutes the Socialism of the future (1994: xvi). Perhaps nothing revives the spirits of

socialism as much as the sight of the terrible contradictions inherent in the newly unleashed globalizing capitalism.

Part of the problem of these left debates over the tension between democratic socialist planning versus market efficiency is that it misses the real dynamics of capitalist growth—not just efficiency but individual entrepreneurship tied to the emergence of new technologies. Joseph Schumpeter, in his classic *Capitalism, Socialism, and Democracy* (1942), had already argued this position, but Schumpeter had himself doubted the capacity of a capitalist entrepreneurial culture to reproduce itself. Daniel Bell (1996), one of the most telling critics of capitalist culture, nevertheless argues that it is this combination of entrepreneurship and technological change, both uncharted and not amenable to planning, that fuels economic growth. Bell may be mistaken in thinking that technological change cannot be planned to some degree (perhaps in some negative sense, as in the avoidance of some paths of technological development), but his point is telling. The dynamism of entrepreneurship and technological change provides capitalist flexibility and adaptation, but also destroys the cultural foundations of existing capitalist society. The traditional socialist debate about planning versus market leaves this most dynamic aspect of capitalism pretty much out of the picture and focuses instead on efficiencies of the market with a given productive technology. Bell, like Schumpeter before him, saw this as a flaw of Keynesianism, which rested too much on assumptions of a constant technology. Bell's conclusion in this regard is that planning cannot address this aspect of a market economy, and if socialists want to retain longer-term market dynamics, they must reduce the role of planning to accept this. Bell's suggestion is that socialists focus on the question of social values to give a normative direction to the economy. Therefore, socialists might use planning as a normative economic tool involving not the actual planning of the economy but a kind of counterfactual theoretical model against which actual economic performance could be measured in the distributional realm, just as "perfect competition" and "general equilibrium" are used as heuristic tools regarding efficiency.

Of course this leaves unanswered the question of what practical use such normative economic tools would have in shifting economic outcomes to meet distributional goals, unless Bell is convinced that the power of social norms (the value system) is by itself sufficient to change the investment patterns of capital. But this is precisely Marx's wager—Marx believed that private capital was inherently amoral and antisocial and therefore always looking for private gain (accumulation) and seeking to escape the social question. Marx saw, along with the efficiency drive of the capitalist through division of labor, the larger dynamics of capitalism, and he welcomed its power to overturn and destroy the old order; but he saw a socialist revolution as needed to humanize modern technological progress. For Marx the solution was not to freeze technology, but to have it respond to broad human needs rather than to the owners of capital. Marx never could spell out how a socialist society could retain these dynamics of technological innovation, which he welcomed as the dawning of a new era in which the abolition of poverty, for the first time, was feasible, not utopian. Yet in the twentieth century, this part of the problem for a socialist economics has been, to a great extent, neglected, and most energy has been directed to issues of efficiency within a given production technology.

The Bolshevik "industrialization debate" of the 1920s occurred in the aftermath of a German economic mobilization for "total war" that impressed many observers, both inside and outside Germany; the notion of a state apparatus mobilizing the full economic resources of a nation and directing them to state goals did not seem unrealistic. The incrementalist evolution of the Western social democratic regulatory regime was more of an inductive search for greater social security, moderation of the volatility of business cycles, and modest redistributional steering. All this was based on a vibrant popular base of support for challenges to capitalist power. At the outset of the rise of socialist parties to governmental power, there was no clear plan about planning. Only gradually did the state come to be seen as a potential ally of labor politics, and state agencies as effective mechanisms for redressing concerns of a broad majority of the population. Now that era has ended, the Keynesian state and the Soviet planning models are no longer viable possibilities, and socialists must rethink what approaches they should take towards a changed economic reality. One direction for such rethinking might be to abandon the search for an institutional framework that would solve the issue of plan versus market in any lasting fashion, and rather accept the need for an ongoing political struggle between socialist economy and market economy. The message might be formulated as another abandonment of "endism" in the economic realm, which leads to a very different kind of socialist politics, one less tied to the state, or to control of the state, and more dependent on rebuilding a broad-based socialist movement as the prerequisite for any challenge to the newly dominant post-Fordist capitalism.

There is something of this new attitude in some recent work by Frank Roosevelt and David Belkin, who edited *Why Market Socialism?* (1994), a thoughtful collection of voices from *Dissent* from the mid-1980s to the present. Roosevelt comes to grips with the opposition of Marx and market by rejecting Marx's endist perspective:

> Although the market socialist critique of Marx must be taken seriously—I, for one, have come to reject his abolitionist position—it is still necessary to pay careful attention to Marx's argument. He exposed many of the defects of capitalist markets that will not just disappear with the establishment of market socialism (123–124).

After a careful consideration of Marx's views on the sources of human alienation, commodification, and commodity fetishism, Roosevelt comes to the conclusion, which he supports, that market socialism will not be able to reconcile the goals of efficiency and the Marxist goal of overcoming commodification: "Simultaneous and commensurate progress toward all of these goals is impossible because some of the goals conflict with each other. For example, democratic decision making at the grassroots level—say, within enterprises or local communities—may conflict with asserting control over the general direction of society . . ." (135). Roosevelt's vision of market socialism is still that of a containment strategy, to "attenuate" (134) the instability and fluctuations of market-type growth, to "contain the market," and "to fashion and preserve a social ethic, strengthen community life, and achieve a better balance between competition and cooperation" (135). What is relatively new here is the acceptance of a never-ending struggle, a recognition of the contradictions between market economics and social goals, which can be dealt with in an ongoing political contest but not resolved. If socialists want to retain the positive aspects of the market, they must develop a longer-term perspective of continuing political struggle and therefore a flexible, dynamic, socialist politics.

David Belkin, reviewing Brus and Laski's critique of market socialism in Hungary (the NEM) and Yugoslavia, arrives at a perspective on a market socialism that includes "indicative planning" but without state ownership, a vigorous role for certain economic projects but not a large enough role to "destroy the rules of the game" (163), and extended participation for workers within enterprises. Belkin sees this market socialism as one which "doesn't need to be realized as a 'bounded system,' but which can abide as a perpetual restless 'movement toward' rather than as a consummated end, with its aspirations for solidarity and participation and justice existing in ongoing, fruitful tension with the elements of competitive self-interest that also drive society" (ibid). Belkin's idea of market socialism rests on the thesis that human capital (skills, education, social experience), as opposed to material assets (such as machinery, tools, and supplies), is the key to the new era of capitalist development, and that a new socialism should try to empower this much-needed human capital. His model of "stakeholder socialism" (1995) advocates priority for stakeholders' rights within the firm on an equal footing with traditional investor rights. This notion is, of course, aimed at supporting the right of participation by productive labor in relation to its human capital investment in the production process, rewarding skilled labor much more than unskilled. It is a stakeholder model that takes up the case of the productive worker, the valuable employee; it says less about support for the jobless, for the marginalized, for those with little human capital. Belkin's model would fight to open up opportunities for these groups, but it would put much greater responsibility on individuals to take advantage of a more equitable opportunity society—to build their human capital and therefore increase their own fulfillment within the productive process.

For many on the left, even the moderate democratic left, the trend toward "market socialism" leads back to capitalism. Within the DSA's (Democratic Socialists of America) reformulation of its own political statement, there has been a running debate between Belkin and David Keil. For Keil, the notion of market socialism should not displace the eventual goal of a predominantly nationalized and collectivized economy, even if this cannot be realized in the foreseeable future. Part of Keil's defense rests on blatant traditionalism:

> The overwhelming tradition among people who have considered themselves socialists has always been that in a socialist society, the *preponderance* of production—the 'commanding heights' of the economy—*will* be collectivized, separated from the profit motive and the dictates of the market, and planned according to the needs of society. Belkin's articles noted this, calling openly for a break with the traditional definition (Keil, 1995: 28).

To say the least, it sounds odd for a socialist, who argues that society can be radically remade, to argue for the retention of some idea on the basis of "tradition," a distinctively conservative valuation. Keil, however, argues that if profit motives and private property are allowed to operate within a market socialism, these elements will drive the system back towards capitalism:

Now we learn that perhaps a collection of *private* firms will solve these problems *without* escaping the dictates of the market, *without* displacing the profit motive (on the contrary *making use* of the profit motive!), and without instituting a plan under control of the society as a whole. Let's be clear—some people may call this socialism, but it is a description of a marvelously reformed *capitalism* in which the actual economic and social laws that have determined capitalist development, underdevelopment, and collapse so far will have been somehow overturned! Socialism, by this new apparent definition, is a kind of capitalism (29).

Keil then attempts a partial defense of Leninism and the usual denunciation of the perversions of Leninism by Stalin. Keil's views call for a retention of the goal of a fully collectivized economy that would suppress the profit motive, private property, and the "dictates of the market," democratically, of course. This vision is forthrightly a traditional Marxist proletarian scenario, keyed to nationalization (socialization), societywide economic planning, and a labor party based on trade unions as the bulwark of socialist politics. Despite the general trend in discussion toward market socialist alternatives, there is clearly still strong opposition to this path of renewal, an opposition that sees it as another stage of Keynesian reformism, accommodating itself to the dominance of capitalism.

Once again, aside from all other areas of disagreement, Keil's vision of socialism is an "endist" scenario, in which individual greed, the profit motive, and private property are abolished once and for all. These "endist" schools of thought will always see accommodation or utilization of ideas borrowed from conservatism or liberalism as sellouts or fatal flaws, which will doom any socialist politics based on them. But if, as I have argued above, the endist concept is itself flawed, then a reworked socialist politics may well have to utilize worthwhile insights from its ideological competitors and produce a new synthesis which doesn't aim at some final, permanent triumph of one value system, but which accepts the ongoing nature of political struggle among a plurality of partially valid value systems.

It is possible, therefore, to take a different attitude toward reformulation of socialist politics on economic matters, if one drops the expectation of ever achieving a final solution to this puzzle. Continuing economic change is necessary for lifting broader segments of humanity above poverty, and it is also the potentially desirable result of liberating human creativity. Socialist politics in the modern era adapted itself to the rise of industrial capitalism, which Marx saw as working positive as well as negative wonders in destroying traditional agrarian society. With capitalism now entering a new period of expansion and transformation, a new socialist concept is clearly necessary, but it might also learn from the experience of the industrial era that economic transformation is to be expected and accepted as an opportunity to improve upon the past. Since capitalist economic change brings new contradictions and new conflicts (with class conflict being strategically important), a socialist politics must aim at challenging the power of capitalism, but it must expect that this struggle will be ongoing and steadily changing.

Indeed, one of the failings of nationalization and state planning (whether comprehensive or dirigiste) was a tendency to view socialist regulation and steering mechanisms as once-and-for-all solutions to specific problems of the current capitalist production order. Yet—and this may be one of the few useful points from the regulation theory school (Aglietta, 1987)—the capitalist order, while going through a period of one dominant type of regulation, is open to basic changes and is capable of moving from one type of capitalist strategy of accumulation to a new and more elaborate form. There is reason, therefore, if one does not expect a final triumph (or at least not within the foreseeable future), for a socialist economics to view itself as necessarily provisional and subject to changes in environment that will reduce the effectiveness of its current political agenda. A new socialist politics might well want to modify its own selfunderstanding in this regard, which would imply the need for a more active socialist community or a more participatory socialist culture. One of the weaknesses of Western socialist statism was the tendency of the popular base, at the highpoint of Keynesianism (or even at the high point of Soviet communism), to take a more passive attitude, leaving social responsibility to the "official" regulatory and welfare agencies.

The above review shows that there has been some movement in this long-running debate on the left, with proponents of market socialism more willing to accept market, and even private market, mechanisms as a useful part of a future socialist economics. Some of the proposals still show a predisposition toward statist measures as a counterbalancing force, and that is understandable, given the long history of Western Keynesianism, but at the same time it is less and less convincing in a globalizing capitalist era. More of the counterbalancing to capitalist market dynamics will need to come from below the level of the nation-state, as well as from above (see the sections below on "The New Meaning of Internationalism" and "Socialism and Democracy"). The heavy reliance on an even stronger state "containment" effort will be faced with the new international mobility of capital, which, as Marx would have expected, opted to escape social responsibility at the nation-state level in favor of no social responsibility at the global level. Even if this were not the case, the new models of market socialism do not seem to have appreciated the negative aspects of statism per se, the pubic disaffection with big and bureaucratic methods of problem-solving. To be sure, there is a renewed emphasis on workers' participation and community participation in enterprise decision making, but in almost all of these proposals there is still reliance on the state to do the heavy lifting, and this, even in a democratic system, has developed a heavy bureaucratism that alienates citizens—the very opposite of what a democratic socialism aims to achieve.

A few of the proposals show movement toward a less statist approach, and toward acceptance of a never-ending struggle of socialist values with market outcomes. At least Roosevelt and Belkin are ready to end the old socialist idea of a final solution, a once-and-for-all framework for containment. And yet we can go further still. Socialist economics has, I would argue, always been a response to the social failures of the dominant type of economy, in every era. Thus it is primarily reactive and takes much of the given economic order as a "working hypothesis." In the era of urban industrial capitalism, the modern socialist response proposed a political challenge from the new urban working class, and its political agenda in the West helped to fashion a set of state regulatory and distributive mechanisms to achieve some of its values (much more, looking back to the Great Depression era, than is perhaps realized in the current era of disillusionment on the left). This socialist response was specific to the shape of the capitalist economy of that era, more centrally fixed in investment, more congruent with the nationstate. Capitalist interests, once willing to compromise within the Keynesian democratic welfare state, have utilized (did they actively promote?) new technologies which permitted effective investment, communication, research, production, and management in a much more scattered pattern (cf. Knox and Agnew, 1994: esp. chap. 7), less bound by local community mores or national consensus. The new globalizing capitalism is made possible by new technological breakthroughs, which, on the whole, are able to give a new geographic, and therefore political, flexibility to capitalist interests. More and more, this spatially decentralized capitalism can choose from various geo-

graphic bidders what obligations, if any, they are willing to abide for
its investment; this neo-Fordist stage of capitalist development thus
can take advantage of economies of scope (Knox and Agnew, 1994:
229) as well as economies of scale, regaining a dominance that it had
lost after the Great Depression.

Since the shape of capitalist economy has changed and is still changing, Keynesian nation-statist mechanisms are increasingly weaker and
less effective and bring more distortions of their own; production, the
workforce, the family, and social expectations have changed remarkably over the past thirty (or sixty) years. It seems likely that a rethought socialist response to the new circumstances must also be much
more flexible, more decentralized, much more able to work across
geographic spaces in order to organize an effective political counterweight.

D. Socialism and Popular Culture: Crime, Family, Nation

One of the many failings of the political left in recent times has been
its social distance from the commonsense notions of ordinary people,
including mainstream working-class people. It has often been painful
to listen to the left's logic on social issues which people are concerned
about, such as the breakdown of family life, the rise of violent crime,
or the loss of valued cultural traditions. Far too often, the left has put
itself on the side of small minorities whose interests, while important,
frankly turned most people off to the larger messages of socialist politics. The only reason the conservative attack on left "political correctness" has had any success is that it does rest on a wider perception
that the left is woefully out of tune with mainstream culture and wants
to impose its own alien language and literature. Although this is for
the most part a disinformation campaign, it is based on just enough
real role models of a totally alienated and alienating left to be plausible
for a large part of the public (cf. Conant, 1995).

In focusing on goals of peace and disarmament through the antiwar
and peace movements, the left has seemed to set itself against the
nation; in its defense of women's and children's rights, the left has
been all too easily pictured as antifamily; in its defense of artistic freedom and critical expression, the left has opened itself to attack as
both elitist and immoral; and in its concern for the rights of accused
and convicted criminals, contemporary left politics has been seen as
condoning crime and neglecting the rights of victims. In all of these

areas, and many others, postwar left politics on social issues has gradually developed a talent for painting itself into a corner, cutting itself off from the daily concerns of ordinary workers and employees, and allowing the political right to capture a wide range of social issues without a contest. What follows is a harsh and blunt attack on the myopia of this type of left social values politics, and a plea for a sensible alternative much more faithful to the ideals of socialism. In this section, I want to argue that a renewed left politics does not have to alienate the larger potential audience, and that it can defend the rights of minorities more effectively by building new bridges to mainstream working-class and middle-class citizens.

Many on the left fully realize how small a minority they are, but they do not necessarily feel any need to rethink their politics in order to speak to a larger public. In fact, some on the left wear their minority status as a badge of courage. Barbara Ehrenreich, Honorary Chair of DSA, has put forward the following argument:

> This is as good a time as nay to abandon all traces of deluded populism, or perhaps the word I want is "majoritarianism." As long as there has been an American left to be part of (since the 1960s, that is) it has presumed to speak for "the people," the "working people," or at least some vague grouping of "progressive forces." With Gingrich characterizing even the conservative-Democratic Clintons as "enemies of normal people," it should be clear that we on the left are far from "normal." We represent a teensy-tiny minority at best. In fact, the number of Americans who consider themselves "on the left" is probably smaller than the number who have had contact with extraterrestrial beings.
>
> In the past, this kind of deluded majoritarianism led to all sorts of problems—or what an old-fashioned doctrinaire leftist would have called "errors." Leftists tended to crumble when they realized that "the people" were rejecting them yet again or persisting in "false consciousness." Or they tended to drift ever rightward in order to make their (decreasingly principled) views more palatable. They tossed what they saw at the moment as the more controversial issues (abortion at times or gay rights, or welfare rights) in order to advance what seemed to be a natural winner, like our clear, departed notion of universal health insurance.
>
> But what's wrong with being a minority? The condition of being an embattled minority is an inevitable part of the life-cycle of any political movement—any movement with principles. . . . So rant. Be the lone voice in the wilderness, the different drummer, etc. You are different—and whatever you say, you're lucky to get a hearing at all (Ehrenreich, 1995: 84).

Ehrenreich is correct in the sense that the there is no shame in being the voice of a small, even tiny, minority; and certainly that fact alone has not deterred socialists from sticking to their political views. Her argument is well known to American leftists, who have always been in the minority. But this minority has not in recent memory seemed so isolated from the mainstream culture, and that might well tell us something. Also, there is certainly no special glory in just holding a minority view per se; that would indeed be an elitist position, which disdains popular culture and commonsense understanding. The current situation is different from that of the 1950s and 1960s, and it points to the need for serious rethinking, not of core principles but certainly of the politics that attempt to realize these principles. In my opinion, the dichotomy that Ehrenreich draws between holding on to one's principles and compromising them to curry favor with the masses is classic but also classically false. It is perfectly possible that the left can rethink its politics—part of the normal political life-cycle—in order to strengthen its principles as a feasible alternative to the existing social order. Why does such rethinking and renewal have to represent some kind of sellout of principle? Do we never need to rethink the politics of the left? Does the left forever stick with a losing political formula, which becomes a quaint political antique, beautiful in form but useless in daily life? One could argue that maintaining some brand of principled purity in politics, self-isolating for the left, is an even more insidious betrayal of those principles, since it alienates potential allies and makes their realization less likely. In fact, this is the core of my argument: that left politics in defense of selected social issues has become self-isolating and has unnecessarily built even more barriers to the achievement of socialist goals. I believe there is a better left politics now being gradually born, which will be true to our principles and more challenging to the capitalist system.

When any conservative political or social leader denounces the left (socialists in Europe, "liberals" in the United States) for its defending criminal's rights or for bringing charges of police brutality, what is the standard response from the left? The knee-jerk reaction (yes, it is knee-jerk) is to blame the economic system, the inequities of the social order, for producing conditions that lead so many to criminal behavior, and to denounce racism and bias in the police and the court for singling out blacks (in the United States), or immigrants (in Europe) for prosecution, while big-time corporate (white-collar) crime is either ignored or treated with kid gloves. In general, not a word will be said about justice for the victims of crime. There will be no call for more effective punishment of crime, but rather a call for understanding the extenuating social circumstances of the accused criminal, and a call for better and more costly rehabilitation of criminals (offer free education, treat their drug addiction, build their self-esteem, or whatever). The left directs much of its rhetoric and political efforts towards improving the treatment of the accused and imprisoned. The left follows a politics of tolerance and rehabilitation with respect to crime and criminal behavior (except of course when the criminals are white cops, as in the Rodney King case, or rich pirates like Leona Helmsley). That type of left politics appeals only to a small group of minority activists and the most alienated opponents of the political system, for whom virtually every aspect of society is by definition unjust and every form of resistance is justified. This is a simple-minded, dogmatic conclusion drawn from the correct perception that there are many inequities in the current system, especially for racial, ethnic, or immigrant minorities; that there is prejudice in the administration of justice, and that there are indeed broader socioeconomic causes for the decline of whole communities and the rise of social pathologies such as broken families, drug addiction, and crime.

The left has not been wrong in pinpointing the inequities suffered by minorities under the dominant capitalist order, especially in the period of decline of the Keynesian welfare state. This emphasis is based on objective realities, and is not, as the political right has charged, based on just prejudice against the system or an ideological myopia (although that does exist, to exert its influence on how these realities are interpreted and politically expressed). Much evidence, for example, supports the perception of broad injustice within the current legal system; it is estimated that the cost to American society of white-collar or business crime is twenty times the cost of blue-collar or street crime (Yeager and Clinard, 1980: 8–9); Hans See (1990: 190–191) has estimated the costs of business crime (*Wirtschaftskriminalität*) in Germany at between $20 billion and $50 billion annually. Yet most law enforcement is directed against street crime, and very little against corporate or elite criminality. The infamous looting of the saving and loan industry during the Reagan years cost American citizens over $200 billion (cf. Nagle, 1992; Pizzo, Fricker, and Muolo, 1991); very little of the stolen loot was ever recovered, and very few of the key perpetrators ever went to jail (or even had to stand trial). The top law and accounting firms that profited from the looting of the S&Ls through fat fees for fraudulent auditing and certification of rigged property sales to inflate paper assets were able, without exception, to reach out-of-court settlements by which they paid back a small fraction of ill-gotten gains while ensuring that the records would be sealed forever and no law or accounting partner would face personal criminal liability (Nagle, 1993); the law firm Kaye, Scholer, Fierman, Hayes, and Handler paid back $41 million; Jones, Day, Reavis and Pogue paid $24 million in damages; the giant accounting firm Ernst and Young had to cough up $400 million; Deloitte and Touche repaid $312 million; KPMG Peat Marwick repaid $186 million; and Arthur Andersen and Company paid $82 million. The Resolution Trust Corporation, which was set up by the Congress to sell off assets of failed S&Ls and to recover stolen moneys, reported that only about $2 billion had been recovered, or less than 1 percent of the total losses. Most repayments from law and accounting firms would be covered by their insurance, not by the partners personally, and so these costs would simply be passed on (socialized) to later customers through higher insurance rates. Jon Madonna, CEO of KFMG Peat Marwick, announced, "Settlement at this time represents, over all, an intelligent business decision" (*New York Times*, August 10, 1994: D1). This colossal ripoff of S&L assets in the 1980s went virtually unpunished, except for a few financial pirates like Charles Keating of Lincoln Saving and Loan or Texas renegade banker Ed McBirney, who were not part of the established financial elite but expendable nouveau riche interlopers. The pilfered assets were not recovered, and the losses had to be covered by ordinary taxpayers. The class bias of American justice could not have been more clearly exposed, and yet this was an issue not taken up by either of the major parties in the 1988 election campaign, because both Republican and Democratic political elites were implicated. (George Bush was personally linked to it through the nitwit machinations of his son Neil at Silverado Savings and Loan.)

This is all quite accurate as a left critique of existing capitalist society, and it should remain a part of a renewed left politics. But in order to recover credibility on a whole range of social issues, a new left politics needs to regain the connection it once had with the legitimate concerns of Main Street workers and their families. One way to push the necessary debate on the left over the so-called social agenda is to recognize the pitiful failure of standard left responses currently, and to reformulate positions that are in fact much more consistent with socialist values. Crime as a social issue is a key example. The recognition of flaws and biases in the current justice system, and the bias in favor of upper-class (read moneyed) interests, does not in itself address the real fears of citizens about high levels of crime, especially violent crime. It was believed by progressives, both liberal and socialist, that crime was a product of poverty and of the effects of poverty on families, neighborhoods, and individuals. If poverty could be eliminated or drastically reduced, crime rates would also decline. It was also believed that brutal treatment of prisoners was both inhumane and ineffective, but that more positive rehabilitation was possible through practical education and humane treatment to build self-esteem. This progressive policy alternative was gradually introduced into the American penal system after World War II. And for a while, from the late 1940s to the early 1960s, more progressive prison policies, combined with low unemployment rates and the widening of economic opportunities, did seem to reduce crime in the United States. The experiences of the Western European democracies were broadly similar. But then, just when economic prosperity was reaching new peaks in the 1960s, and when prison reform had achieved new breakthroughs, crime rates in the United States, and to a lesser degree in the European democracies as well, began to rise again, accelerating in the 1970s, to reach new, much higher, plateaus in the 1980s, where they have generally remained since (cf. Gurr, Grabowsky and Hula, 1977). Since the 1970s at least, we know that crime and criminality are not just a product of absolute material poverty; and we—unfortunately—know that social rehabilitation of prisoners is very difficult, even with much greater expenditures and more elaborate resocialization efforts. Currently, in the United States, the recidivism rate—that is, the rate at which former convicts are rearrested and convicted of a new crime within three years of release into society—is between 60 and 70 percent (cf. Nagle, 1995: 122–126). The United States now incarcerates over 1.3 million people in federal, state, and local prisons and jails, at a cost of over $20,000 per prisoner annually. The United States is an exceptionally violent society among the Western democracies, but the trend towards higher levels of crime, and even violent crime, was visible in Europe as well. Only in the most socially conservative advanced industrial country, Japan, are rates of crime and violence still very low by international comparison. Fear of crime has emptied inner cities of middle-class residents and viable businesses, decapitalized them, and reduced certain areas to zones of general lawlessness both by professional criminals and by local police. Residents live in fear of criminals, but do not cooperate with the police. The police are themselves fearful and resentful of the tasks imposed upon them, and frustrated by lack of support from the community and the courts. They are all too often likely to engage in criminal activity themselves, to become part of the basic criminal enterprise network, further eroding any hope of legal protection for law-abiding citizens. In these circumstances, local police forces cannot reasonably be expected to render honest and humane service to the community.

These circumstances are not new or special; they exist in most poor nations, where criminal gangs and corrupt police and courts make it impossible for citizens to expect justice from their "justice" system. From Mexico to Nigeria to Turkey to India, poor urban neighborhoods suffer from lawlessness and violence by both criminals and by criminal police. Rich neighborhoods protect themselves with private armed guards, iron fences, and domestic security systems; rich merchants pay for death squads to murder, sometimes in purposefully savage ways, criminals (often children) who threaten their businesses. In the rich Western democracies, these circumstances were believed to have been overcome in the postwar era, with widespread prosperity and more modern rehabilitation methods, but these circumstances have been returning, even amidst impressive wealth.

What should the left say about this? It should say, of course, what it has been saying—that without meaningful employment, whole communities will continue to suffer from endemic crime and violence. It should also say that injustices in the legal system, police brutality, and court bias need to be redressed. But a new left politics must also pull back from defending the criminal as just a product of the environment, and a rethought left should not emphasize understanding of violent actions, no matter how bad the social circumstances have been. The left might also consider that a decent police presence and adequate police protection are just what the community needs, and that always bashing the police as the enemy does nothing to achieve this goal. A renewed left politics might, for a change, try to establish decent relations with the police, by making it clear that the left also stands on the side of law and order (the provision of personal safety and physical security for all citizens), and that it advocates policies which can help police do a good job with decent means. A left politics on crime needs to distance itself from crime and criminals, who are a problem (though not the only problem of course) for poor and working-class neighborhoods, and put itself squarely behind the majority of the community and the police (Not all police are racists or corrupt, and the police should also be considered as victims of the crime-ridden inner city environment.)

A renewed left politics must speak to the needs of the larger (much larger) community of law-abiding workers and their families, who suffer most from the depredations of violent criminals. They are also a product of their environment, and they have chosen not to engage in crime and violence; they are still trying to make a living through honest labor; they are the ones who need the real protection of the law and the police. They are the victims who deserve first priority right now in a socialist agenda to fight crime while trying to gain support to reshape the economy through a longer-term economic agenda. Socialists recognize that economic change for the better will take time, and that many of the violent criminals can never be retrieved, at least not through any coherent rehabilitation program; the aging process may do more than any professional therapy to turn former criminals away from crime.

The current legal system must be supported in a new effort to regain control of poor neighborhoods and to reduce the fear of crime, even while a socialist politics tries over the longer term to reform the judicial system; a new left politics on crime should be a law-and-order politics for the benefit of the great majority of law-abiding working people, aimed at an equitably applied law and a socially just order. A socialist vision of a better society must include a well-developed role for enforcement of law. Any conceivable socialist order will need a police force, and will require good community relations between residents and police. Socialists need to rethink their attitudes about law enforcement and criminality; criminals are not social rebels fighting capitalism (although some radical criminologists like Richard Quinney once propounded this view), nor are they socially progressive allies of the left. The police are not everywhere and forever the enemy, and genuine appreciation for honest and humane policing should be an evident (i.e., explicit and visible) element of a new left politics on crime. Violent criminals are, for the most part, believers in the absolute priority of self-interest; of private profit at any price; of a free market capitalism, devoid of any social rules of conduct often espoused by radical right libertarians. The drug dealers and pimps and organized gangs are on the side of capitalism; they are capitalists, of the most crude and exploitive type; they may make a few donations to buy protection and curry favor with local residents, but their overriding goal is maximizing private capital with no concern for the social costs to their communities or families, to say nothing of the larger society. The left needs to abandon any illusions about this subject and needs to put itself squarely on the side of law and order for the sake of the community. The left stands for social security, and one of the most basic aspects of security is physical security, the freedom from violence and pervasive fear of violence. The clear commitment to support law and order in every community is an elementary part of a socialist politics of security for all, not only the well-off who can afford to live in private secure communities and fortress estates. A rethought socialist politics would emphasize this commitment first and foremost, rather than abandoning it to the conservative right, which has no interest in security for the poor or the working-class but who can and will mobilize working-class and middle-class fears for a purely punitive politics—in the absence of any feasible alternative from the left. Only with established anticrime credibility can the left hope to get support for its proposals to reshape the economy and reinvest in inner-city and working-class neighborhoods. No one can expect productive investment to return to many of these local communities and stay there unless the social issues of crime and violence are also addressed at the same time. A rethought left potentially has a lot to offer, not only to the poorest communities most ravaged by crime, but to the larger society, which has reasonable fears and would dearly like to find an effective way out. The left knows already that community organization, with a network of "community watches" or patrols, combined with good relations with local law enforcement, is the most effective method for preventing crime. There is a lot of good experience from the Cuban Committees for the Defense of the Revolution, or the Soviet druzhini, which, despite the undemocratic nature of these regimes, still holds some valid lessons for crime-fighting through social organization within the local community.

Fortunately, there is growing support for "community policing," involving more police officers on neighborhood street patrols, and an extensive linkage of formal police forces with community groups and with responsible citizens in each neighborhood setting. The recent experience of New Haven, which introduced "community policing" under the leadership of Police Chief Nicholas Pastore, has shown that there is a progressive left alternative to current right-wing demands for even more punitive sentencing and still higher levels of incarceration. This approach involves the police much more intensively in the local community, and requires a reciprocal commitment to cooperation and responsible involvement from the community.

In a recent review of left politics regarding crime in America, Bruce Shapiro summarizes the issue, and the new opportunities it presents:

"Can the left—given our affinity with the dispossessed, our commitment to civil liberties—effectively engage the right on that ground? I think so; but only if we are willing to risk making a radical connection between street crime and social issues that incorporates people's basic desire for safety" (1996: 20). Shapiro believes that ignoring this basic reality—the fear of criminal violence—has made left politics voiceless on the issues of street crime, neighborhood violence, and imprisonment. Only by building on people's desire for personal security, and supporting measures that make sense in terms of fulfilling that desire, can the left rethink these issues and revive its relevance:

> If the left is to have a revived politics of crime it must begin with those sorts of connections; to make of community safety a call not for "law and order" and vigilantism but for grass-roots activism; for constructing democratic institutions in neighborhoods and cities that can keep young people from crime and make a genuine difference to those who may be crime's victims (Shapiro, 1996: 21).

Massive incarceration has been tried, and more massive incarceration will not solve the basic problem; rehabilitation of seasoned criminals is unlikely. A renewed left politics can get a hearing for its solution—justice with jobs—only if it clearly commits itself to fighting crime and supporting neighborhood security as prerequisites. But if the first words from the left are yet another plea for prisoners' rights or another attack on the police, most citizens will simply tune out the rest of the message. Does the left forever want to achieve nothing in the area of fighting crime, or would it prefer to link up with the legitimate concerns of citizens who would like to see a society in which their personal safety could be more secure?

What has been said about crime as a social issue is nothing compared with the myopia of the left on family issues. How is it possible that a socialist politics, which once was easily able to present itself as the defender of working-class families, has lost that important terrain to a bunch of pseudo-Christian preachers of an outdated family caricature? But this is precisely what has happened, as the left moved from a politics of meeting basic needs—material, educational and physical needs to a politics of liberation from the paternalistic authoritarian family, which was happening anyway, more under pressure from a changing economy than from any sexual revolution or counterculture. In this change of course, the left confused antiauthoritarian politics on the family with an antifamily politics generally. This required a lot of muddled thinking, sometimes under the influence of a radical bourgeois feminism which was indeed antifamily but also antisocialist, sometimes under the influence of a 1960s cultural radicalism of the universities (which was antiestablishment but also ultimately more about new middle class lifestyles for a still upwardly mobile educated class).

When one asks what the left stands for as regards the family, the most common response is the right of women to choose abortion. Other responses include the right of gays to marry, or the protection of children from parental abuse. These are not unimportant issues, but they are perceived—all of them—as antifamily, because they are not embedded in a more positive commitment of a left politics to support families as a cultural institution valued by the broad majority of citizens, even though they may disagree on just what constitutes a "family." The issues that the left has chosen to defend are not the central concern of most families, and they do not address the broad range of issues threatening the quality of family life. If the left chooses to develop its own positive politics for the family, it will be able to get a hearing for its own notions on what constitutes a good family life and what are the real threats to that goal.

Much of the left's problem in this area can be rectified by bringing the family back as a focus of socialist politics. The left does not need to accept the patriarchal authoritarian family of Christian right imagery in order to put family values back into its politics. It does need to recognize the values of a healthy and happy family life, with a diverse and pluralistic range of family forms and traditions, as a main part of what most people desire ("the pursuit of happiness"). Socialist politics aims at securing that pursuit of happiness for all kinds of families, across all classes and all divides.

Michael Lerner, editor of *Tikkun* and one of the leading thinkers for a left renewal, has called for a progressive "Contract with American Families" as an alternative to the right's "Contract with America":

> and in the fall of 1996, before the elections, we propose a national Family Day that would be convened by the progressive forces, and which would draw national attention to the fact that the main enemy of families and loving relationships is the very values that the Right's competitive market produces. Finally, and at a moment likely to shape many people's perceptions, someone will be challenging the Right on its own turf (Lerner, 1995: 627).

This is part of what Lerner calls a new "politics of meaning," which goes beyond the left's traditional call for economic justice or equal rights for minorities, to embrace an ethical and religious response to the right's support of an even more materialist and egoistic order. Lerner is equally critical of the left's failure to respond to the right's agenda:

> Ironically, the Right is also the very force that supports the ethos of material-ism and selfishness in the world of work. It insists that economic life should be free of moral control, and that each corporation pursuing its own narrow interests without accountability to the community is the best way to produce prosperity. So it champions in the economic sphere the very values which, when brought home into personal life, as they inevitably are, undermine lov-ing relationships. How do they get away with this? Because the liberals, the Democrats, and the social change progressives have no understanding what-soever of these dynamics. They are fine at articulating the need for economic justice and individual rights but they have no understanding of the ethical and spiritual dimension of human reality—what we call the "meaning" needs. So when they hear people talking about ethical and spiritual needs, or the break-down of family and values, they assume these are merely code words for racism, sexism, homophobia or xenophobia (626).

The myopia of the left has been to assume, in recent years, that family and cultural values were universally and forever the territory of conservative politics. Lerner would take a renewed left politics back into this territory, offering an alternative that combines family values and progressive economics. It is apparent, however, that Lerner will have a tough time selling his proposal. For one, it does rely on reli-gious and moral grounds as a basis for a progressive politics of "mean-ing," a respect for the spiritual that the left has long had problems accepting. Moreover, the question arises as to what to do with the leftist critique of traditional patriarchy in the family and in society. Is this now just to be abandoned, or does the left want to exclude the older traditional patriarchal family from its range of "politically cor-rect" family types? Part of the answer lies in the much greater toler-ance of a renewed left for social values still strongly felt and embedded in people's experiences, even though they contradict some universal principles of individual freedom or social equity. In other words, a renewed left should fight for family values that provide happiness and healthy development across a wide range of family types, including those that still embody traditions of patriarchy, while at the same time supporting the ongoing struggle against patriarchy. There is certainly a contradiction here, but the left has dealt with and lived with such contradictions before. The union movement—the most progressive el-ement in the expansion of working class participation in modern soci-ety and in the building of the Keynesian welfare state—faced such contradictions earlier in this century in organizing some parts of the workforce while neglecting others (especially women and racial minorities). Later, the union movement did try to redress these failures, but in its earliest breakthroughs in order to build and maintain its broad base of support, it set priorities which did not challenge certain social prejudices. This example shows that a left politics cannot pursue all of its principles equally at all times in all locations; it must confront contradictions and choose to deal in partial success (and partial failure) if it wants to maintain political relevance. The left (like the right) cannot remake society all at once, and cannot remake society only in its own image, and its own values will come into conflict with each other on specific issues and at specific junctures. This means appealing to diverse groups with some common interests but with some conflicting values or priorities as well, and still being willing to work with people and groups whose views embody a variety of cultural values. This does not mean that the left cannot draw some clear lines, such as fighting against racism and sexism within its own coalition, but it seems to me more effective to first signal to the broad majority that there is room for them within a progressive politics, and to expect that a larger, looser left alliance will lead to valuable learning on a variety of social and human rights issues. This seems preferable to much (not all) of the current left practice of demarcation from the politically incorrect, combined with sectarian preaching to a tiny minority (which Barbara Ehrenreich cites) that holds its own views to be beyond criticism.

Education for a new left politics leads through humility and the recognition that any politics is only partially capable of addressing the needs of an ever more complex and diverse society. It means learning from one's opponents, in this case the neoconservative right. The right has developed its stranglehold on the politics of social values in large part because it claims to respect traditional culture, culture as received through the generations. Conservatism generally builds support from the wisdom that tradition provides meaning to people, and that without tradition, they feel detached and alienated from others and from their own lives. Tradition, secular and religious, gives meaning for individuals, families, nations. What conservatives fail to understand is the impossibility of freezing culture as dogma—the necessity for traditions to gradually change, and the need to experiment with new formulations in order to preserve what is worth preserving. Actually, classic conservatives like Edmund Burke did recognize this aspect of living conservatism, the ability of the current generation to add its own contribution to the accumulated culture and traditions of a nation. It was the post-revolutionary interpretations of conservatism in Europe, coming out of the reactionary views of Gustav le Bon and Joseph deMaistre, that turned political conservatism against change generally, and therefore sought to preserve the status quo, the restored monarchical order, in its entirety.

In order to reconnect a left politics with a much broader segment of the population, the left needs to rethink its own understanding of cultural traditions, and what attitude it should take toward traditional values. Michael Walzer has done some of the most innovative if controversial rethinking on the left regarding the relationship between socialist justice and the culture of a particular society. Starting with his *Spheres of Justice* in 1983, he has elaborated an image of social justice connected to the context of specific cultures, rather than to universal principles. For Walzer, the illusion of a single universalizing principle to be applied at all times for all societies, must give way to the notion of "complex equality" which is connected to the context of people's real experience. The whole thrust of Walzer's argument is advocacy of a differentiated and culturally reconnected left politics of social justice. In a more recent collection of pieces relating to Walzer's thesis, Michael Rustin summarizes:

> Spheres is a book remarkable for its commitment to understand, describe, and value the variety of ways in which human lives are actually lived, and the meanings and norms which shape them. It takes as its premise the idea that if a socialist view of the world is to be in the least bit plausible, it must be grounded in good aspects of the lives that people have now. Walzer's method is to argue not from abstract principles, like most of his fellow contributors to the debate about social justice, but from meanings grounded in everyday social experience (1995: 17–18).

This is, in part, a building of a new socialist politics by induction from actual practice, as opposed to deduction from theoretical principle (cf. also the section on "Lessons from History" in Chapter III). It represents an attempt to reformulate complex notions of social equality which keep pace with the changes under way in, especially, Western postindustrial, post-Fordist societies:

> The idea of "simple equality"—equated with sameness and uniformity, imposed or chosen—has become untenable or at least insufficient because the social experience of the majority in "developed" societies has changed so

radically. For reasons of prosperity, enhanced individual mobility, and a greater diversity of lifestyles, the resonance of the ideal of equality as a shared condition of life is not what it was (Rustin, 1995: 19).

Contained in this reformulation is an upgrading of the value of tradition, of learned culture, which necessarily implies an acceptance—based on cultural grounds (rather than principle)—of variations in what counts as justice, or morality. Is this not, however, an acceptance of conservative valuation of tradition and all of its inequities (paternalism, religious dogma, class or racial hierarchy)? Might not an acceptance of cultural tradition lead to acceptance of "complex inequality" rather than a struggle for "complex equality"? (Rustin, 1995: 27) Joseph Carens, in describing Walzer's project, calls him a "left-wing Burkean" (1995: 47): He would rather rest his moral claims and criticisms on the history, traditions, and practices of a particular community than on abstract general principles, on the rights of Englishmen rather than the rights of man (though Walzer, I suspect, would construe the rights of Englishmen much more expansively than Burke with respect to class and gender) (47–48).

Indeed, in the many rejoinders to Walzer's *Spheres of Justice*, there are repeated suspicions that Walzer has brought in an essentially conservative view of an organic community, tied to past inequalities that have become part of the cultural heritage of that society. How, then, can a socialist notion of justice pay respect to such cultural truths, especially in view of their legitimation of inequities? Yet David Miller, a sympathetic interpreter of Walzer, argues that this vision is anything but conservative, since Walzer's requirements would include the following:

A decentralized democratic socialism; a strong welfare state run, at least in part, by local and amateur officials; a constrained market; an open and demystified civil service; independent public schools; the sharing of hard work and free time; the protection of religious and familial life; a system of public honoring and dishonoring free from considerations of rank or class; workers' control of companies and factories; a politics of parties, movements, meetings and public debate (*Spheres*, 318 quoted in Miller and Walzer, 1995: 9).

Still, a good point is made by Walzer's critics—that he has gone quite far down the road to accepting community norms and cultural traditions as taking primacy over external principles of justice; Walzer specifically says as much:

> Every substantive account of distributive justice is a local account. . . . One characteristic above all is central to my argument. We are (all of us) culture-producing creatures; we make and inhabit meaningful worlds. Since there is no way to rank and order these worlds with regard to their understanding of social goods, we do justice to actual men and women by respecting their particular creations . . . Justice is rooted in the distinct understandings of places, honours, jobs, things of all sorts, that constitute a shared way of life. To override those understandings is (always) to act unjustly (Spheres, 314, cited in Carens, 1995: 49).

Walzer's anthropological acceptance of cultural relativism would seem to leave no opening for criticizing any social setting except one's own immediate one (and how immediate?); perceived injustices in other cultures should not be overridden, because that would be unjust. And what of international solidarity across cultures? What of the growing interpenetration of cultures, which makes any closed sense of community unrealistic? As Carens notes, Walzer himself chooses to criticize the German cultural concept of citizenship based on *ius sanguinis* (law of the blood) in denying citizenship to Turkish guest workers who have lived and worked in Germany for decades, or for their children born and raised on German soil. Yet Carens (1995: 50–52) also suggests a possible way out, in that it is for Germans, the German political community, to wrestle with this issue, since it involves not only their cultural tradition of defining who is a German, but also their cultural tradition of liberal democracy. That is to say, the decision rests with the community of Germans to decide; only within that culture can there be a democratic decision, at a time that is appropriate for that community, to revise its concepts of citizenship and to abandon parts of is traditional understanding in favor of strengthening or maintaining others. This is a cultural relativism that leaves the question of justice up to the current understanding of the community members, with the hope that progressive democratic politics will continue to develop a new understanding of what is fair, what is just, what is morally responsible.

In one sense, Walzer seeks to escape a strictly American, or Western, concept of social justice, to avoid the imposition of current Western understanding on nonwestern circumstances. Yet any move in this direction leaves open the question as to what role an international socialist politics can have in an era of globalizing capitalism, what effects are produced simply by the existence of different standards of justice (role models, vanguards, success formulas, cultural borrowing) among societies or communities which are ever less isolated and less self-contained (cf. Barry, 1995). Some sense of the wider world of standards of social justice is missing from Walzer's concept, and in the face of the post-Fordist world economic order, there must be some role for comparisons across borders.

Some of Walzer's critics reply that there must still be some universal minimum principles of justice, against which any local understanding can and should be measured. Amy Gutmann argues for a fixed set of moral considerations to be embedded firmly in a theory of complex equality:

> Fairness, individual responsibility, equal citizenship, and the dignity of persons do not constitute the social meaning of specific goods. They are not adequately conceived as contingent cultural facts, which we just happen to hold and can readily change at our collective will. They are not master principles, which claim to dominate all sphere-specific distributions. . . . They are moral considerations that make sense across a wide range of societies, and inform our self-understanding as well as our social understandings. They do not threaten tyranny nor do they point in the direction of simple equality. They render many spheres less autonomous than they otherwise would be, but they do not obliterate their boundaries. Quite the contrary, they point to a conception of social justice that is complex but not sphere- specific. Such as conception would serve us well both here and now, and into the future (1995: 119).

Gutmann's argument for limited cultural autonomy in the formation of standards of social justice, while holding on to some overarching moral principles, offers one possibility, but what is the dynamic connection between the two contending approaches?

Let me, in this regard, try to integrate some (though only some) of the insights here of Michael Lind. Lind, former wunderkind of the neoconservative right, former protégé of William F. Buckley, and former editor of the *National Interest*, a mainstay intellectual journal of the political right, suddenly broke with the Republican right in the early 1990s, denounced its politics of inequality, and became the first notable intellectual defector from the right in an era of conservative triumph. Lind is no friend of the new left of the 1960s, and in this regard he could be seen as returning to the earlier postwar class liberalism of the Keynesian welfare state project, with its concentration on class politics as its driving force. Lind's argument is that the left, in the 1970s and 1980s, has lost its connection with mainstream class politics embedded in American national culture, and that to fight the Republican politics of class warfare against the working class, the left must itself regain that connection. A left politics cannot do that if it constantly puts down mainstream working-class culture, with all its suspicions about multiculturalism and its retention of more traditional views of family and religion. Lind is clear that parts of this American national culture are "politically incorrect" on issues of women's rights, black consciousness, and new libertarian lifestyles; but he argues that the left has made these issues into group entitlements, whereas the older class approach, which aimed at mainstream integration of all citizens regardless of color or gender, was and still is the correct and winning way for the left to put together a competent challenge to the conservative offensive.

In his recent work, *The Next American Nation*, Lind (1995) calls for a renewed "liberal nationalism" which returns to class confrontation instead of cultural critiques of mainstream American lifestyles. Lind is critical of the left abandonment of class priorities after the 1960s for "marginal" issues like abortion, and of its concentration on the plight of specific minorities, like blacks and gays. He advocates instead an embrace of American national culture and nationalism, by a class-conscious left politics. He wants a renewed left politics of restricted immigration to protect Americans' jobs, an end to group entitlements, and a return to the American "melting pot" ideology. Instead of favoring black consciousness or black nationalism, or Indian rights, or bilingual education in an attempt to retain distinct racial or ethnic cultures, the left should support integration and assimilation into the larger American national culture. Lind sees the left's support of group rights and entitlements as not only a failure, but collusion with a white overclass strategy of division and diversion from the core class inequities of modern American society. In a recent debate in *Dissent* on affirmative action, Lind mounted a no-holds-barred attack on the multicultural left as "racist, snobbish, and antidemocratic, authoritarian, and profoundly insincere (1995: 470). While Lind was the most blunt and even vicious of the left critics of group identity politics of the multicultural left, he was not the only critic. One of the most interesting points of the *Dissent* debate was its openness and frankness; even those defenders of affirmative action like Joanne Barkan argued that the left should "drop the defensiveness about scrutinizing individual programs. Affirmative action begs for democratic management—for careful design and monitoring by the people who live with it. When a fair evaluation shows a program to be ineffective, fraud-ridden, wasteful, or unjust, the left should endorse revamping or drop-ping it" (1995: 463). Barkan, however, is not very convincing that affirmative action can regain a wider base of popular support, nor does she really have any alternative to offer (as Lind does). On the whole, the remaining left defenders of affirmative action were clearly on the defensive, and within the left the tide is turning against con-tinuation of group identity politics, and toward some return to class-based politics.

In a recent review of *The Next American Nation*, Richard Rorty praises Lind's ability to focus on the emergence of a new economic "overclass," the oligarchic winners in the class warfare being waged against working-class America. While disagreeing with Lind's total trash-ing of new left and identity politics, Rorty summarizes the main thrust of Lind's argument in a way that I think is persuasive and which points the way to rethinking a left politics with a strong connection to work-ing class thinking and culture:

> Lind may well be right, however, that there is no hope of social and economic equality unless the blue-collar "Reagan Democrats" can be convinced that the enemies of the oligarchy are their friends. He may also be right that the abandonment of racial preferences is the price that liberal politicians will have to pay to regain the allegiance of those blue-collar voters. Most of that price will, as usual, be paid by poor black people rather than politicians or intellectuals. But it may have to be paid nonetheless. It will take a lot of class consciousness to defeat the oligarchy, and Lind makes a good case for saying that we will not get sufficient class consciousness if we continue to insist on racial consciousness. He is certainly right in suggesting that the "politics of identity" has made it a lot more difficult for all of us to get economic inequal-ity in focus (1996:110).

In a interesting non-American review of American race politics, Christoph Scherrer and Lars Maischak, two young scholars from the German left, cite as dead ends both Jesse Jackson's "rainbow coali-tion," and the halfway sticking point on the path to racial integration (1995). They also point out the growing tendency toward a black na-tionalism and especially the Nation of Islam—as racial separatist poli-tics within the black community, and judge that also to be a dead end. The alternative of the moderate Democratic party elite, with which Clinton and his advisors are most connected, is a strategy of "deracialization," a downplaying of race as the cutting edge of anti-poverty and welfare politics in favor of a return to a politics which looks at economic and social need regardless of race (Scherrer and

Maischak, 1995: 1455–1456). They blame the failure of Clinton's politics of deracialization, especially his failure to pass a universal health care program, as a sign of the danger of losing both the white working class and the black community as popular bases for a moderate Democratic majority coalition. Their most interesting conclusion is that, in the last analysis, the solution to America's racial divisions and its racial conflicts, and the responsibility for a solution, rests with the majority white culture: "The key to a just participation of blacks in the social life of the USA rests with the actors of the dominant culture. It is therefore the task of those who thanks to their birth [were born] into this dominant Euroamerican dominance culture, to work against racism in their 'own' ranks." (1459) They connect this conclusion to a frankly idealistic call for white leaders to take clear positions against racism and to challenge their own culture to rethink the meaning of "race." But one could just as well ask: what real grounds do you have for expecting that moral appeals will carry the day, without some "commonsense" grounding in the existing culture of the white working middle-class? For this is precisely the point that most needs to be addressed. If one believes that the past left politics on race, which included major moralistic and moralizing appeals against racism, was and is still effective, then that is clearly the way to go. I doubt, however, that this is the case.

Appeals for racial justice now face a new economic reality, which has instilled fears, both real and unreal, into the dominant white culture about greater job and educational opportunities for black citizens. When the American economy was growing at a healthy pace in the 1950s and 1960s, enough good jobs were being created to satisfy most (never all) of the expectations of the white working class, with enough left over to accommodate the rising expectations of urban black workers. In that situation, the calls for greater economic and social access to mainstream opportunities for black citizens could just barely maintain a majority politics within the Democratic party. (Even so, the Republicans immediately saw their opportunity, and launched their Southern strategy, now reaching its peak payoff, to profit from Democrats' risk-taking on this integrationist path.) This strategy paid off for the Democratic party in this era—amazingly so—but it also became seen as a group identity politics that spoke to the interests of specific disadvantaged groups, not to the interests of the working class as a whole. Over the last two decades, however, the American economy has evolved in technology, in inequality of new work roles, and in decentralization both domestically and globally, so that aggregate growth does not produce as many good and long-lasting jobs, but rather produces much greater economic insecurity in the working class, both white and black. Moral calls, or a left politics aiming for greater economic justice for black citizens, now must face an entirely new environment in the job market, with little prospect for short-term improvement.

Scherrer and Maischak have accurately identified the key to greater racial justice—namely the politics of the dominant white culture. The ability of the minority culture to shape majority politics has always been limited, and therefore any progress toward a more just society for minorities requires support within the majority culture. This recognition must lead to a corollary consideration: what rationale would, in the current situation, attract a broad base of support within that dominant white culture for a progressive politics? I would argue that without a commonsense rationale for white workers to unite with black workers in a politics aimed at healthy job creation and greater job security for all workers, the race-specific call for more access for black workers will continue to fail, and will only help the antiworker agenda of the right. Here again, as in so many other areas relating to popular culture, the appeal of a left politics to justice for specific identity groups today, unlike the situation in the 1960s and 1970s, is a losing strategy, which needs to be rethought. This does not mean giving up on principles of social and economic justice, but it does require abandoning practices that are now barriers to the realization of those goals, and developing new coalitions based on common goals that cut across race (and other identity) characteristics.

There is, therefore, in Lind's critique of the left's turning away from the mainstream integrationist ethic after the 1960s much that strikes me as correct, and my own argument has been that the left has migrated away from the priority of class politics in search of new causes which were meant to defend specific minorities or attack specific issues rather than mount a more general defense of working-class interests against the demands of capital. And yet there are some really severe limitations to Lind's own response to this situation.

Ellen Willis, in a review of Lind's recent work, argues that Lind seems to be a younger "warmed-over" Daniel Bell: "liberal in politics, socialist (sort of) in economics, authoritarian in culture. What's new?" (1995: 212). Willis does "share Lind's dislike for the idea of racial 'authenticity,' and agree that racial preferences are a form of tokenism, the great virtue of which—from the point of view of established power—is that it doesn't challenge the class system." But for the most part Willis does not agree that multiculturalism (or at least "mainstream" multiculturalism) is some new sort of orthodoxy, but rather a more pluralist model of integration which goes beyond the earlier WASP-dominated models. Willis correctly warns of the authoritarian notion of a dominant American culture whose norms are privileged over minority cultural norms and practices. She criticizes Lind's notion of a "civic familism," which Lind describes as "Something like the 'companionate' or 'bourgeois' nuclear family, with a mild division of labor between the sexes" (quoted by Willis, 1995: 213) Clearly, Lind advocates a turning back of the cultural clock to the pre-1968 era, not in all areas, but enough so that a left politics can once again lay claim to speak on behalf of American values. Willis argues that the left must challenge the right-wing offensive on both cultural and class grounds, without giving up the goals of the new social movements, or the defense of women, blacks, gays, and immigrants. She argues that "the left can counter this powerful perception only by challenging the right's cultural as well as economic propaganda. Until people feel entitled to govern their personal lives they can't fight consistently for their economic and political interests. Democracy is a way of life" (213). Well put, and very much to the point; there is no going back to the restrictive cultural norms of yesteryear, even if that might make some people (white male workers) more comfortable again. Yet Willis herself has no answer except more of the same, and this has only deepened the alienation of so much of the working class from any left politics and has opened the door to right-populist demagoguery like that of Pat Buchanan, which has real class content but also panders to an outdated and irretrievable national culture from the past, which was so flawed that it engendered not only the civil rights movement but all of the subsequent new social movements. Willis is correct again to point out that Lind's "liberal nationalism" does not address the globalization of the economic order, the new freedom of capital to escape national Keynesian constraints, which is a major cause of distress and insecurity among the working class. "It's not nationalism we need; it's an international labor movement." (213) This too is a good point, but if the left cannot communicate with the working class in terms that are understandable and make sense, then no national solidarity, and certainly no international labor solidarity, will emerge. Once again, if the left takes seriously its loss of voice as the voice of labor, it must renew its bonds with working-class culture, with American national culture, with American working-class values. It achieved this in the past, without abandoning all efforts to reform those national cultural values; in fact, looking back, a lot of progress has been made. Lind's prescription does not take into account the fact that the working class is itself very different from what is was only thirty years ago, in particular with much greater representation of women—more highly educated, much more diversified, and much more dispersed in service sector jobs. Any retrieval of the left's voice for the working class and for a class politics will inevitably be a different voice and must reflect the changing social composition and understandings of employees. But a new left politics must speak for workers and employees generally, not for black workers, or women workers, or gay workers as separate groups, and certainly not in general and systematic opposition to the interests of white male workers. The evolution of a new working class "common sense" must have "common" as the key, if it wants to build coalitions that can achieve majorities.

Michael Tomasky (1996) bluntly argues that affirmative action's political support as a "reparations policy" is gone, and that the continuation of affirmative action as a "diversity policy" is both self-defeating and unfair. He notes that in a recent national survey, 75 percent of respondents said they opposed preferences on the basis of past discrimination; even among African-Americans, 46 percent opposed such preferences. Tomasky's conclusion is that the left must argue instead for a primarily class-based agenda to address the needs of the working-class poor, even though this would mean less direct attention to the needs of the African-American poor. Only a class-based post-affirmative action policy is capable of majority support, and especially from the white working class, whose support is vital and whose objections to earlier left rationales are compelling. Can such a new beginning succeed? Can the working class be won over to a new common ground that looks not at race (or gender or ethnicity) as the basis for redress of grievances, but rather at economic class? This is not hopeless, because the new economic trends that hurt some workers now—and some workers worse than others—also undermine the opportunities for other workers later, and will cut deeper later, if there is no common challenge to the capitalist agenda now. And it now seems as though the left political debate on this and other "cultural" issues is heading in the right direction.

A lot of white middle-class men of my generation (in their mid-fifties) can well look back on their own attitudes toward blacks, women, and especially gays, and be astounded at the abandonment of prejudices and stereotyping practices that in the 1940s and 1950s were part and parcel of the American national culture. How did this come about, if the dominant culture was so flawed? Clearly, the culture contained and still contains the mechanisms for change. That culture did change, and the left in most cases led the way. Conservatives, on the other hand, fought against virtually every change regarding treatment of these groups, but they lost in every case; they cannot turn back the clock. Many of the outspoken conservative demagogues have in their own personal lives no real interest in traditional family or moral values; Newt Gingrich and Rush Limbaugh are not serious about religious values, and their marital behavior is anything but a model of traditional American norms. How is it, then, that these guys can speak with forked tongue and get a hearing, while the left, which should stand for decent jobs and social security needed to support a healthy and happy family life, gets portrayed and perceived as antifamily and anti-American? Of course the right has tremendous financial resources and institutional backing; but this was always the case, even when the left had a much greater access to the popular national culture. The left, I would argue, was most effective when it was an organic part of the mainstream class-based movement for change, and was ineffective and increasingly self-defeating when it lost its larger vision, which was and still should be connected to class politics. Not everything is simply class conflict, but without class struggle as a central theme of a left politics, the left ends up in a politics of division, which only helps the ruling elites perpetuate their control with greater ease.

None of this is intended to make the white ethnic working class into some sort of dominant category for a new class-based politics. The demographic decline of the old white working class alone would prohibit any straightforward return to the old New Deal or Great Society coalition that Rorty and Lind, in my opinion, are prone to glorify in any case. Younger union and political thinkers who speak from the white working class perspective are aware of their diminished numbers and declining political clout; there is rethinking required on both sides for a reconciliation. A new class-based left politics, however, must still find some cultural reconciliation with the still-important white ethnic working class.

Is there not some creative synthesis here, between the recognition that a left politics must work within the framework of what people are culturally ready, or close to ready, to accept, and adherence to the principles of an open and democratic society, tolerant of many lifestyles and minorities? In her critique of Lind, Willis at various points says that the left indeed has supported some ideas which give credence to the right's cultural propaganda war against the left agenda as un-American or anti-American, alien to the society. Why then don't left political thinkers, those more amenable to Lind's critique if not to his political alternative, spend more time and effort clearly and bluntly separating themselves from the sectarian cultural left, from the special pleading left, from the separatist and group entitlement left? Why don't left spokesmen and spokeswomen in fact denounce the doctrinaire left sectarians and begin to engage the mainstream culture on its own terrain, taking its culture seriously (though not uncritically) and understanding that if there are many ways toward a more integrated society, the older goal of mainstream integration is still one of them, as long as it is open to all citizens on equitable terms. If Willis and others agree that post-1960s left sectarianism has produced some wrongheaded and obnoxious notions, why not come out frankly and strongly against these notions? One way for the left to find its way back to a dialogue with American national culture rather than a harangue against its failings and vices is first to criticize, as Lind does, those separatist, doctrinaire, anti-Americanist elements that still find some silent acceptance as part of the left political agenda. Recent debates on the left have been much more open and honest, using straightforward arguments and dropping the use of code words or euphemisms; this itself is a sign that the debate is causing a shift of thinking on the left. If Lind is correct on so many points, though wrong in his alternative project, then we can still borrow from his critique while searching for another alternative.

In fact, what Walzer, Miller, Rustin, Gutmann and Lind are working toward is a way of recognizing the validity of cultural standards and traditions, as a precondition for rethinking a politics of social justice that connects with those cultural understandings. The big message in this discourse is that the disconnection between traditional left politics of economic justice as a universal principle and the social concerns of citizens and families can be overcome only by coming to terms with real existing cultural norms, which can change, and do change, but which cannot simply be trashed if the left wants to get a hearing for its notions of social justice. This is a very significant break-through for a reformulated left politics on the widest range of social issues, for it signals, far in advance of any real solutions, a willingness to borrow from the treasure chest of conservative values, and to learn from conservative critics the importance of cultural norms and existing meanings for gaining entry to the broadest-based audience on issues where the left has most recently been absent.

The most basic insight is that there already exist, in various forms, cultural notions of social justice which can be mobilized for the left, if the left is willing to work within these contexts rather than preaching universal principles from the margins or from a position largely alien to broader cultural traditions. In the history of the Communist Party in the United States, this would have been called Browderism, the Americanization of communism, but this effort was always undercut by the party's loyalty to Moscow and its ideological dependence on Moscow. It is common wisdom on the left that socialist movements in other countries (China, Vietnam, Cuba) made their revolutions by adapting socialist revolutionary politics to the local situation, by adapting the universal to the local. Likewise, for better or worse, the gains of Western democratic socialists were in large part made possible by their acceptance as part of their national community. Social Democracy in Germany was notable for its desire to become a fully accepted political partner, and it was a partner from the beginning—to Marx's dismay—willing to demonstrate its commitment to working within mainstream German culture and traditions. The working-class politics of democratic socialism was organically rooted in the local community and its culture, its traditions, even those, like patriarchy in family life or certain religious beliefs, which stood in conflict with universal socialist principles. This tension in practical politics between commitment to principle and acceptance of existing culture is not new; the negotiation between principled but isolated dissent (which might be necessary in some situations) and a locally pragmatic, culturally acceptable politics is an ever-present problem, not only for socialists but for liberals and conservatives as well. I am arguing for a course correction in the direction of greater cultural pragmatism in the area of social value politics, *in the face of strong evidence that the left has become too socially isolated to provide an effective alternative.* This is the key proposition advanced here: that the evidence of the left's social self-alienation from the popular culture is overwhelming. From this it follows, I believe, that such a marginalized left cannot

share of reborn conservatives (like Podhoretz in the United States) is I think testimony to its essential nuttiness. Yet it is worth recalling that in the initial encounter between Old Left and New Left in the 1960s, these Leninist sects were able to compete for a part of the young generation which was interested in a reformulated left politics in the West; and the notions of a Western revolutionary left, fed by the French general strike of 1968 and the student revolts throughout the West, did not seem so impossible. It is truly fortunate that the Greens in Germany were able to attract most of the activist youth of this period to its own banner, saving it from real political isolation and strengthening German democracy in the process (Nagle, 1989); this rescue was achieved in the face of resistance from the established parties which had lost touch to their own youth. These Leninist sects have now disappeared, and their absence (the extinction of Leninism) does make some difference for the current period of left rethinking. This may seem a minor change, since these groups did not have very much practical effect, but they did for a time (in the 1960s and 1970s) attract some parts of leftist youth, and they did provide a significant ideological division, which at that time could not be ignored. The demise in the early 1990s of the weekly radical *Guardian*—an independent Leninist voice with some credibility in the United States during the cold war era, and a leader in the 1970s effort to build a revolutionary party in the United States—is symptomatic of this change on the left.

It should not be forgotten that the mainstream democratic left in the cold war era succeeded in a two-front struggle, against both bourgeois (conservative-liberal) and Leninist opponents. There is in historical perspective really nothing like the basic changes in the treatment of labor, and the redistribution of benefits of growth to labor, which matches the Western Old Left experience. The achievements of this strategy in the twentieth century have been enormous (cf. Harrington, 1989: chap. 1; Piven, 1992; Heidenheimer, Heclo, and Adams, 1990), and this success formula cannot simply be abandoned and its gains thrown overboard, to be replaced by the tender mercies of the free market, as current conservative attacks intend, either gradually or through "shock therapies."

Frances Fox Piven's edited volume (based on a 1988 conference) on the future of labor parties in postindustrial society offers various thoughtful analyses, all sympathetic to labor party politics and its achievements, of the reasons for the decline in labor's fortunes; there are some differences in degree and specifics, yet all the authors, covering the advanced capitalist democracies of Europe and North America, agree on the general nature of the current trend, and almost all agree that the Old Left approach has no chance of reversing the trend without basic reworking of progressive left politics (Piven, 1992: 18–19). Even if labor parties may still win some elections, and temporarily replace conservative parties in the national government, "the specific economic and social arrangements which nourished the labor politics of the past have changed too much to expect the revival of class politics in familiar forms" (19). Piven and others who have been close to Western labor and social democratic politics during the cold war era now admit that this type of left politics is in irreversible decline, that its historic time of achievement and new ideas lies in the past. Yet Piven, in her concluding passage, foresees that labor politics will still be the centerpiece of a renewed left, through a co-opting other new progressive elements:

> Perhaps in countries where labor politics remains strong, these new political currents will be absorbed into older labor formations, as environmentalists and feminists are being absorbed into some European labor parties. In the United States, however, the Democratic Party remains a bulwark of entrenched interests that is unlikely to yield or adapt unless assaulted by protest movements in the future (264).

This seems to me a minimalist vision of accommodation between the Old and New Lefts. If the Old Left were indeed able to absorb the new social movements, it would probably be on terms much closer to the Old Left politics, which would mean less rather than more innovation, less rather than more rethinking of the political agenda.

Among New Left thinkers, there is also a gradual breaking away from the "politics of identity" and a self-criticism of the their role in promoting a politics of division. Todd Gitlin, one of the leading lights of the New Left in the 1960s and 1970s, now has strongly and openly repudiated left sectarianism, which had championed specific groups (African-Americans, women, Hispanics, gays, Native Americans) and in the process has lost contact with the rest of American society, including the white ethnic working class. According to Gitlin, the reaction to the New Left among this white ethnic working class has given political opportunities to people like Buchanan and Perot, while abandoning the left's most valuable asset, the claim to speak for the common good—as Giltin puts it, the "common dream" of Americans. Gitlin tells his own personal tale of rethinking, which is all too familiar to white male intellectuals who have been dismayed that we, now in our fifties, are viewed with increasing suspicion because our time has passed; we are now part of an older generation of white male intellectuals whose careers and lives have, despite youthful rebellion, been surprisingly comfortable.

I take issue with Gitlin's indictment of the New Left because of his relative neglect of the historical context of the 1960s—this is surprising for a writer who has made his career analyzing the 1960s and its politics. For myself, the New Left's rejection of established party politics—and particularly of the Democratic Party's unionized working class and party machine—was a useful and progressive break. That undemocratic machine politics would be resented more and more over time, and needed the challenge of open competition on all issues, outside of formal party channels of power, by spontaneously formed social movements. Remember that the major parties in the 1960s had refused to provide a choice, or even a meaningful debate, on the Vietnam War; both mainstream Democratic and Republican leaderships had squelched open debate in their own parties, until the antiwar movement took to the streets and turned to alternative candidates who broke party ranks. Quite naturally, the New Left critique of normal party politics was extrapolated from the Vietnam War issue to virtually all issues, and confronted power through issue-oriented movement politics.

For those of us who remember being roughed up in antiwar demonstrations in the 1960s, for those of us who worked for McCarthy only to find that the Democratic Party machine was not about to allow a free and fair debate over the war issue, for those of us who experienced, in our political youth, the joy of rejecting closed-door elitist politics, the New Left was a healthy reaction by citizens who wanted to participate in political life, who had a just cause, and who took some risks to open up the system to wider debate and participation. For this the New Left has no apologies to make. The New Left rejection of George Meany's union boss politics, of Mayor Daley's Chicago machine politics, of Lyndon Johnson's and Hubert Humphrey's war politics, was a giant step in the right direction. Of course it also alienated lots of white working-class patriots; witness the rise of George Wallace, the forerunner and still the most dangerous model for antileft populist politics. I don't see how the New Left could have avoided this break and still made its opposition to the war clear. The "Get Clean for Gene" strategy of McCarthy's primary campaign of 1968 was an attempt to avoid offending working- and middle-class feelings about cultural or lifestyle differences, and get a decent hearing on the war issue; it made little difference at the time. The break over what a progressive politics should look like was not just about hair length, or dress codes; it was a fundamental challenge to the limitations that an oligarchic elitist politics placed on the emerging new civic culture, a culture which was better educated, more confident of its own voice, and less submissive to traditional authority. While some of the cultural backlash against the New Left might have been reduced, in general it was pre-programmed; it was a political cost that had to be paid. The positive achievements of the social movement politics of the 1970s and 1980s still stand, with all their blemishes and excesses.

As Gitlin rightly says, over time the politics of the New Left, cut off from common dialogue with the mainstream working class, or the working middle class, was left to concentrate its political efforts through groups that were more politically marginalized, also outside the realm of mainstream society and political life, the so-called new social movements. In the course of this evolution, group-specific "politics of difference" became hardened into fractionalized identity group politics, lacking a common vision for the larger society (unless one accepts a tolerant pluralism of divided identity groups as a sufficient and positive vision, which at its best was represented by Jesse Jackson's rainbow coalition). Gitlin's break with this evolved version of New Left politics is symptomatic of the search for a reconnection to mainstream American history, culture, and politics for a renewed left: "What is a Left without a commons, even a hypothetical one? If there is no people, but only peoples, there is no Left" (quoted in Stimson, 1995: 791). Catharine Stimson argues that Gitlin exaggerates the sectarianism of feminism and underestimates its achievements; she notes, tellingly, that Gitlin pays no attention to the use of identity politics on the right, especially the religious right of Pat Robertson, which dwarfs any politics of division among the New Left camp in its own mobilization of (threatened?) religious identity in order to dominate the political agenda on special issues of family, education, the media, and the arts. Yet in the final analysis Stimson agrees with Gitlin and sees his conversion as a sign of a growing consensus on the left, the now mature New Left, that a renewed left politics must regain a common vision of a better society, rather than separate and separatist visions of better treatment for specific groups: "Gitlin will prove persuasive to many.

He also belongs to still another, growing population. It consists of people who seek social justice, the reciprocal recognition of diverse groups and the cultivation of a cosmopolitan, if contested, national unity" (Stimson, 1995: 792). At the same time, Stimson hopes that new "common ground" for a revitalized progressive politics will have more room for women and minorities as well as white ethnics.

Here the achievements of the New Left, of the new social movements, make possible a new concept of progressive polices for mainstream America because the mainstream itself has been transformed over the past thirty years. The opening up of job opportunities to blacks, to women, to Hispanics—the breaking down of barriers (obviously not all barriers) to millions of individuals—has worked its way through the economic and social system. The problems of mainstream America now include the problems of millions of full-time women employees throughout the occupational spectrum, of millions of African-American blue- and white-collar workers, of Asian-Americans and Hispanics in numbers that defy any narrow definition of an ethnic white working class. There is no reason to expect that a revitalized left vision of "common ground" will omit the interests of women, or blacks, or other minority. There is, however, every reason to expect that the common ground of working America will be the new focus of this politics; and this represents an important lesson learned in the rethinking process. The problem now is how to develop a new synthesis between the Old and New Lefts, which can build on common ground.

There has been much talk in the Old Left about accommodating the new social movements, about making room for environmentalists, the women's movement, and third world solidarity movements within the left coalition. The nascent coalition between environmental "green" politics and the social democratic or "Keynesian" left in Europe and America is one example of this discussion. If we look at Germany, building a coalition ("a majority to the left of the Christian Democrats") between the two has been very difficult, and the terms of the dialogue have shifted considerably. Andrei Markovits and Philip Gorski (1993) chronicle the emergence of the German Greens as the most innovative and authentic political creation coming from the Left in the history of the postwar Federal Republic. This movement-party, which split from the old SPD Left, embodied a specifically postwar left democratic critique of the existing system:

> The Greens' liberalism has led them to disdain and mistrust the state in all its forms. Moreover, liberalism has taught the Greens to extol the individual's autonomy vis- á-vis all political power. The Greens' libertarian anarchism,

derived from the New Left, rendered them the enemies of all mega-bureau-cracies and technocratic strategies of problem-solving. Lastly, the Greens' anchored socialism of the old Left made them bitter opponents of capitalism (1993: 276).

Despite all of the internal factionalism and feuding, the German Greens represented the most thorough, and most important challenge to the Old Left politics from the left itself. In Germany especially, with its history of Marxist influence in the SPD, and the SPD's special history as the most disciplined and best organized vehicle for the politics of social democracy on the continent, this achievement was indeed an important breakthrough. From the 1970s onward, the Green movement-party became the most important political innovator on the left, exerting a "greening" influence on the Old Left and becoming a driving force in the realignment of progressive politics in the Federal Republic. The Greens also succeeded in rescuing the great majority of the generation of rebellious students and youth of the 1960s ("die 68ers") from the fatal temptations of other antisystem politics (for example, the terrorist Baader-Meinhof Red Army Faction, the anarchist Spontis, or the various Maoist sects (K-Gruppen)). In this respect, the Greens' attraction of leftist dissident young people in the 1970s and 1980s into democratic participatory politics performed a great service to German democracy (Nagle, 1989), which the established parties (SPD, FDP, and CDU/CSU) were unable to achieve. The great good deed of the German Greens was to take the political risk of joining the electoral struggle, risking defeat and abandonment, in the effort to save a generation of German youth from permanent political alienation, and they succeeded. In the course of this struggle for the hearts and minds of the "68ers" generation, they became the vehicle for political innovation on the left and began the process of challenging German Social Democracy to change itself (Nagle, 1989: 153–154).

Markovits and Gorski argue that the Wende (turning point) of 1989 has created a new environment for the Greens and their politics. First, it has brought them face to face with new issues arising from unification, which the Greens opposed in 1989–1990 (with no sense of that political imagination and innovation for which they had become popular well beyond their immediate following). Second, the collapse of East Germany gave the Greens (and the SPD) a chance to abandon the "anti-anticommunism" of the cold war era, which, together with the politics of reconciliation (Ostpolitik) of Brandt and Schmidt (and continued by Kohl) had become an excuse for not criticizing the communist systems of Eastern Europe. (A part of the Greens, led by Petra Kelly, does not fit this description, and Kelly put herself at odds with much of the Green movement with her steady and vigorous support for dissidents in communist systems.) As I have argued elsewhere (Nagle, 1992), the collapse of communism was in this sense a "liberation" of the Left from the no-win politics of anti-anticommunism. For better or worse, the Greens now have to confront their past failures in this area, but they also have an opportunity to become innovative again and to continue to broaden their politics beyond the environmentalist-feminist-antiwar core. The failure of the peace movement or the Greens to provide any leadership in the Bosnian war issue—especially in view of the catastrophic effects of the Kohl-Genscher push for quick recognition of Croatian independence in 1991—shows that this process of rethinking will take still more time. Joschka Fischer, however, has shown his continuing capacity for political rethinking of Green politics on issues of war and peacemaking, and the debate within the Greens is, at least as of this writing, the most open and vigorous of all the parties. Certainly the Greens stand head and shoulders above the defensive rearguard accommodation of the Scharping leadership of the Social Democrats.

Indeed, after the 1994 elections, in which the Social Democrats polled 36 percent of the vote (a modest 3-percent gain), the SPD leadership has failed miserably to put forward a clear and convincing alternative to the policies of the ruling conservative-liberal coalition, which despite its own failures has had an easy time governing with a very thin majority. It now appears that the Social Democrats are really uncertain in their ideas and dissatisfied with their own leadership, as the splits and resignations in the summer of 1995 have shown. To most observers, the SPD has not used its time in the opposition to renew its own agenda; the fragile beginnings made by Oskar Lafontaine with respect to environmentalism and by Bjorn Engholm with respect to rethinking the party organization and the social welfare state were lost with the 1990 election defeat of Lafontaine and the resignation of Engholm, and have not been continued by Scharping. In the mid-1990s, the Social Democrats as a party had no new ideas to offer, and were reaching new levels of crises within the party organization. It may well be that the Greens will become still stronger partners in the debate/dialogue between Old and New Left, while the SPD will either break free of its intellectual lethargy or lose still more credibility. The gradual decline of the traditional social democratic politics accelerated in 1995, with defeat of the SPD candidate by a Christian

Democrat in the city of Frankfurt, a longtime bastion of the SPD, and a disastrous showing of only 26 percent of the vote in the autumn elections in Berlin (where the SPD had once received over 60 percent of the vote). Even at this late date, old-time SPD leaders like Anne-Marie Renger, from the right wing of German Social Democracy, still call for loyalty and unity, which only make sense if there is some viable program to defend and a capable leadership to present it. To those who want to reopen issues of leadership and overall direction of the party, Renger says: "Discussion is good, loyalty is more important" (1995: 1). The short-term outlook for German social democracy, long considered the most coherent and most durable presence in European politics, is miserable, and it changes all previously held assumptions. Those in the United States who have regarded German Social Democracy as a much stronger and more solid base for reworking a left politics must now regard it as deeply troubled, with major splits at the top and massive voter defections at the base. Certainly the image of a strong social democratic party and a strong labor movement in Germany which many on the American left have looked to with envy (see, for example, the outdated perceptions of Jo-Ann Mort on the strength and vitality of German labor politics, 1995) has now been shattered.

In short, the Old Left in Germany has never looked weaker in the postwar period, while the New Left Greens are at least potentially capable of leading a reform-oriented politics to challenge the Christian Democratic dominance. The relative shifting on the German Left from the Social Democrats to the Greens may give more weight to the New Left antistatism and social movement perspectives, and finally destroy the Social Democrats' illusions about being able to simply coopt the environmentalist and feminist causes through some rejiggering of SPD policy. Perhaps this most recent series of defeats was finally necessary to convince reformers in the SPD to take bold initiatives, and bluntly challenge the "normal " politics of the current leadership. Rudolph Scharping was ousted as the Social Democrats' leader in 1996, and the Kohl government's performance has declined in recent years, giving rise to new hopes for a change in government. There may now be some new opening up of party debate, led perhaps by the ambitious maverick Gerhard Schröder, who is at least willing to explore new ideas and break with old positions; a clear reform of German Social Democracy, however, is not yet in sight.

In Europe generally, the political landscape, which had been gradually shifting since the 1970s—with the growing challenges to the old left success formula from the free market right and from the new social movement left—has now become unhinged; in the short term the right has the clear advantage, since it has predominated in the undoing of the Keynesian welfare state and has offered a return to unfettered, unregulated capitalism as a cure for the social ills of the last thirty years. The idea of a renewed democratic socialism which could coopt the new social movements while retaining its previous commitments to social welfare has been dashed; the rethinking of the relationship between Old and New Left will be much more complex and difficult, and will involve much greater transformation than was foreseen earlier, or even in some current analyses (such as Piven's volume offers).

In the United States, the debates over NAFTA and the Clinton health care plan have spurred a rethinking of relationship between the Old and New Left. The election of Bill Clinton in 1992, despite his record as a centrist New Democrat, gave many on the left the hope (or illusion) that a new Democratic administration could still push through some important social legislation and could stop the hemorrhaging of the Keynesian welfare state.

An old and typical debate of the postwar, cold war era, is whether the left should have worked within the Democratic Party, as the Democratic Socialists of America (DSA) have done for many years, or whether it should have worked exclusively on building a party to the left of anything the Democrats could support, as the various left groupings and sects attempted in the 1970s and 1980s. Even in the elections of 1992, some part of the left looked to a new Clinton presidency as an opportunity to finally accomplish old business of the left agenda in the area of national health care, and to forestall new initiatives of the Reagan-Bush right in the form of the North American Free Trade Association (NAFTA)—designed to further undercut labor's position in the postwar Keynesian economic consensus.

This era has now come to an end, and the experience of the first two years of the Clinton administration, culminating in the disastrous election defeat of the Democrats in the 1994 Congressional elections, has put an end to this typical form of left debate, and has opened a new phase in the difficult development of a post-cold war politics of the American left. The debate over NAFTA, the fate of national health care, and the 1994 elections marked, in a short time frame, a climax of more gradual developments in American politics, especially painful for those on the left. It is perhaps instructive to look at this time frame and some of the key events that have ended an era of American left politics.

The fashioning and the fate of Clinton's plan for national health care—so much touted in 1993 as a progressive plank in his otherwise centrist platform—came to represent the bankruptcy of not only Clinton himself but of the Democratic Party as a political force through which to finally accomplish the long-standing goal of health care as a basic right for all citizens. By the end of 1994, the midterm Congressional elections brought a resounding end to any hope of even moderately progressive initiatives from either Clinton or the Democratic Party.

The accelerating support given to NAFTA in 1993 by President Clinton, and his (for once) resolute opposition to organized labor in seeking and getting bipartisan support for NAFTA, made clear that labor had lost its clout in the Democratic coalition. This was reconfirmed by Clinton's push for a final GATT agreement, and its passage in 1994, again with a bipartisan coalition in Congress and exclusively business support. The American left, having viewed these developments with growing dismay, has no choice but to thoroughly rethink its politics and to offer a progressive alternative to the new political consensus, which has now taken a giant stride to the right. In some ways, the most recent period is a final defeat for the postwar Keynesian consensus on the welfare state and its promise of some compromise with labor and other working-class interests and at the same time, it is a signal for a new direction for left policies and strategy. What lessons have been learned from these events, and how have these lessons influenced the language of the left in the search for a new political agenda in an era of conservative dominance?

The Democratic Socialists of America (DSA), which was formed from the merger of the Democratic Socialist Organizing Committee (DSOC) and the New American Movement, is the leading socialist group that during the cold war years worked both inside and outside the Democratic Party to promote, step by step, a progressive political agenda on the basis of democratic socialist values. Led for many years by Michael Harrington (until his death in 1989), it continued the tradition of Norman Thomas as the idea center for the progressive left and the promoter of specific programs for eventual cooptation by the progressive wing of the Democratic Party. DSA is a member of the Socialist International and follows a path of European-style social democracy; in the absence of a significant American party descended from a socialist tradition, the DSA has represented this tradition within and outside of the Democratic party. For the postwar period, the agenda of DSOC and DSA was the completion, through broadening and deepening, of the welfare state programming begun during the New Deal. As long as the Democratic Party was the majority party (it had a majority in Congress for all but a few brief interludes over the past sixty years) , and as long as the Democrats were still committed to the fundamental outlook of the New Deal—that government should and could play a positive role in regulating the economy and legally mandated and publicly funded social security and welfare—DSA argued that this was the only practical opening for the left to make an impact. DSA includes has some members of Congress (Ronald Dellums, Democrat of California), officials in the AFL-CIO (Tony Mazzochi of the Oil and Chemical Workers, George Kourpias of the Machinists, Susan Cowell of the Garment Workers, John Sweeney of the Service Employees), and highly visible left intellectuals (Cornel West, Manning Marable, Barbara Ehrenreich, and Theda Skocpol).

In 1992, the DSA supported Bill Clinton once he had become the presidential nominee of the Democratic Party, despite Clinton's long-time association with the more centrist or conservative Democratic Leadership Council, which Clinton once headed, and which included such other centrist figures as Senator Charles Robb of Virginia and Senator Al Gore of Tennessee. In the last preelection issue of its bi-monthly publication, *Democratic Left*, DSA noted hopefully that "if ever a year had all the preconditions for progressive politics, 1992 is that year." (September–October 1992; 2) DSA argued :

> the American people want government to play a role again in promoting the life opportunities of its citizens. . . . belatedly, in its characteristically mixed fashion, the Democratic Party has begun to respond to this sea-change in the political climate. The party is shifting from more narrowly targeted to more universal programs, family leave, national health care, affordable housing" (ibid).

While recognizing that the Democrats and Clinton were also committed to "free trade," military intervention on behalf of national interests, and were not committed to a more comprehensive single-payer Canadian-type health care program, DSA argued that Bush had to be defeated in order to open up "political space for a revived progressive politics in America" (38). The role of DSA during a Clinton administration would be to push him from the left within the broad Democratic coalition, to have a voice within a governing party with at least some progressive leanings. DSA further opposed third-party candidacies at the national level, although advocating local grassroots challenges.

Perhaps the most prominent programmatic item in DSA's support for Clinton was health care reform, which Clinton had adopted as his own, following the success of Harris Wofford in his race for an open Senate seat in Pennsylvaniain 1991 on a platform focused on this issue. After Clinton's victory, *DL* editorialized that now that the Reagan-Bush era had ended, DSA's role would be to push Clinton from the left through popular organizing, to guard against his moving to the "responsible" center, and to criticize the new Administration when it showed too much "caution" (Clark, 1992: 2). Maurice Isserman, a DSA leader in Boston, compared Clinton to Kennedy, arguing that like Kennedy, Clinton was a moderate Democrat, "a cautious politician, not a crusader with a bold agenda for social change" (1992: 22). Isserman felt that if anything, Clinton had more progressive potential than Kennedy, since Clinton was a product of the antiwar and civil rights movements of the 1960s, had engaged in some forms of political protest, and had paid a political price in his later career: "At the start of the Clinton presidency, there is the potential, if no guarantee, that the Left can again play a significant role in American politics" (23). In a critique of Clinton's adminstration after its first five months in office, Joanne Barkan of DSA took note of Clinton's lack of direction, and lack of conviction, as well as his political weakness among the American public generally, but still gave him credit for modest legislative gains including voter registration, family leave, the bio-diversity treaty, college loan programs, abortion rights, and his commitment to health care (1993: 2) In other words, despite many misgivings and many signs that Clinton lacked any solid commitment to a progressive political agenda, the DSA strategy remained one of critical support, as the best opportunity for realizing left political goals within the givens of the existing power structure.

Perhaps the best example of DSA's strategy of critical support for Clinton came during the formulation of the his health plan in 1993, and the attempt to get this plan through the Democratic-controlled Congress in 1994. The DSA organized a special Health Care Task Force and attempted to raise funds for lobbying the administration and Congress in favor of a single-payer national health care system similar to the Canadian system. It mobilized its members to write letters, make personal contacts with representatives, and engage in publicity aimed at pushing elements of a single-payer plan into Clinton's plan. Throughout 1993, as Clinton's plan was taking shape in his Health Care Task Force, DSA debated whether to push its own preference (the single-payer system) against the Clinton (managed competition) alternative, or to critically support the Clinton plan, emphasizing its features of universality, comprehesiveness, and fairness in financing (Cowell, 1993). Already in the 1993 run-up to the Congressional consideration of the Clinton plan, eighty-eight members of the House and five senators endorsed the single-payer option. Theda Skocpol argued that this was a historic window of opportunity to finally accomplish national health care in the United States, after a long history of past defeats (1994; 6–7). In some ways, public awareness of the problem, political movement in government circles, and proposed solutions had a chance to come together in the 1990s, a chance that had been lacking for decades. Skocpol advocated a popular education campaign to counter right-wing charges that single-payer plans were illegitimate socialist politics, which meant more government control and coercion. In the course of the debate in 1994, over 100 members of Congress, led by Representatives Jim McDermott and John Conyers in the House, and Paul Wellstone in the Senate, supported the single-payer plan. When it was explained to the public, the single-payer plan scored well in opinion surveys. But as it became clear that Clinton's health care task force was virtually ignoring the single-payer option in favor of "managed competition," which would preserve the profitable role of private insurance industry, the DSA was faced with the classic choice: oppose Clinton's plan, or offer support for it as the best that could be achieved under the present circumstances.

DSA took a special poll of its members regarding what strategy to follow; 670 members responded to a mail-in survey in early 1994, and the results give an impression of DSA's political orientation at that time. With regard to Clinton's "managed competition" (as originally presented), 46 percent of DSA respondents chose the "oppose it" option, while 36 percent wanted to support it, and 52 percent wanted to support it critically (multiple options could be chosen); (DL, March–April 1994: 9). Asked whether support for the single-payer option would force Clinton to water down his own plan further to get Republican and conservative Democratic support in Congress, 45 percent of DSAers agreed, while 51 percent disagreed. Sixty-six percent agreed with the goal of preventing division between supporters of the single-payer movement and critical supporters of the Clinton plan. Finally, regarding the best strategy to get a single-payer plan through Congress, 47 percent wanted to continue opposition to the president's plan, and 48 percent wanted to support it critically, while attempting to get some single-payer principles into the legislation. Thus the DSA membership was considerably split over Clinton's health care plan, which ignored the more left-progressive single-payer approach but nonetheless offered an opportunity for some movement toward universal, secure health care coverage. Additionally, the DSA worked hard in 1994 in support of state-level single-payer health plans, which were on the ballot in California and Massachusetts. (The California plan, which would have represented a major breakthrough towards a state-level Canadian-type system, was defeated in November.)

The dilemma of DSA regarding health care was clarified somewhat by the outcome of the Congressional debates, and by an extensive media campaign funded by the insurance industry against the Clinton plan throughout the spring and summer of 1994; the Clinton plan was also attacked as "socialistic" on right-wing radio talk shows. In response, Clinton backtracked on virtually every element of his original plan, until finally none of it remained. The mobilization for health care reform had ended in failure, and the DSA strategy had revealed the weakness of the Clinton administration as a stalkinghorse for progressive health care reform.

As regards using Clinton's presidency as a barrier to the NAFTA proposal drafted by Bush, the democratic left soon found itself in a position of trying to mobilize an anti-NAFTA coalition against both Clinton and a bipartisan Republican-Democratic majority in Congress. The preelection hope that Clinton would somehow stand up to transnational corporate interests proved to be illusory; at best Clinton would tack on two commissions, with little authority in any of the three NAFTA countries, to hear appeals on enforcement of labor and environmental codes. The probusiness vision of free trade would remain the living core of NAFTA, a furthering of freedom for capital to escape national regulations in search of the most favorable conditions for investment. In an important test case, American labor unions put their diminished weight into a coalition which included some organizations of the "new social movements": environmentalists and Naderite consumer advocates. Missing conspicuously from this progressive anti-NAFTA effort were the women's groups. Yet the anti-NAFTA effort was a ground-breaking attempt to pull together elements of Old and New Lefts in the US, in opposition to both major parties. Its failure to persuade the major women's groups to join the effort was also symptomatic of the lack of any natural or easy coalition of progressive forces; in some conversations, (Naderite) Public Citizen activists admitted that women's groups were still hopeful that even a centrist Clinton presidency was a useful barrier against right-wing attacks on abortion rights, and that Clinton's policies and appointments were still favorable to the women's movement. The American women's movement, which is heavily middle class in orientation and leadership, simply did not see NAFTA as a priority issue, and in particular did not see NAFTA adversely affecting working women in both the United States and Mexico. This lack of support from the women's movement was a severe loss for any project of building a progressive coalition independent of the Democratic party.

Additionally, the progressive anti-NAFTA coalition was matched with a populist anti-NAFTA coalition led by Ross Perot and Pat Buchanan, who mobilized opposition to free trade and ties with Mexico on the basis of protectionist, antiforeigner, and isolationist sentiments. Thus the new beginning of reconciliation and practical coalition-building between Old and New Left in the United States not only faces opposition from the dominant probusiness free trade consensus of establishment Democrat and Republican elites, it also must compete with an emergent right-wing populism which in the short term has easier access to popular resentments and commonsense understandings of what is at stake and who is to blame. Both Perot and Buchanan have a much easier time speaking to the working middle class of mainstream America, and their populist rhetoric combines both class-based anger and scapegoating. Eric Alterman has remarked on Pat Buchanan as a candidate for the 1996 Republican Presidential nomination:

> Nearly a century and a half after the publication of the Communist Manifesto, America has its first Marxist presidential candidate. He focuses workers' anger on corporate greed and larceny. He even invokes the great man's writings to attack free trade, the sacred cow of the global elites' post-cold war ideology. Unfortunately, he's also a reactionary Republican who scapegoats gays, immigrants, blacks and, until recently, Jews (1995: 654).

It is a testimony to the current weakness of the left's links to the mainstream working class that a nationalist populism gets a better response than any left-progressive coalition, even one including the trade unions. The struggle to build a new coalition of both Old and New Lefts will involve, as William Greider (1993) has noted, a change in common sense thinking so that neither anti-foreigner isolationism and America Firstism nor an individualistic competition on a new global scale are the standard alternatives. The first attempt to build a new commonsense which links domestic and international concerns—which sees cooperation across borders as necessary for the interests of labor as well as environmentalists, consumer groups, and supporters of human rights—did not fare very well in the anti-NAFTA campaign. It revealed all the weaknesses of both Old and New Left groups, but at the same time it did begin the process of overcoming old antagonisms and rethinking old positions.

Even before the 1994 elections, which confirmed the shift to the right among the mobilized electorate (that is, those who actually voted), the DSA had been forced to rethink its strategy of critical support. In a first postelection analysis, Alan Charney, the national director of DSA, blamed Clinton for choosing to back a conservative Republican agenda on GATT, crime, and welfare reform; in this situation, he argued, "the net effect of Clinton's various political choices was to aid and abet the formation of a Republican majority in Congress" (1994: 13). Clinton's strategy of riding the health care issue in search of new support from the political center failed, in Charney's view, because "support for health care reform is not simply a question of need and self-interest. It also requires a positive attitude toward government— an attitude sorely lacking among the new center. (And the administration didn't help matters by proposing such a cumbersome and complicated initial health care plan)" (13–14). On too many issues, Clinton had chosen to take the Republican side instead of building a broader progressive coalition.

But this was exactly what most people expected from Clinton in the first place; he was not expected to take "left" or "progressive" positions on a wide array of issues, so it is hardly surprising that, except for some selected areas, his agenda was close to long-standing Republican and conservative positions. What lessons could the DSA draw from the fate of both the single-payer and Clinton health care proposals, the last best chance to enact comprehensive health care, a major item missing from the social welfare agenda since the Great Depression? Would this grand failure now change the DSA strategy from critical support to principled opposition of Clinton's adminstration, and concentration on popular organizing in opposition to Clinton's agenda? This was Charney's general conclusion, since he now sees no possibility of working with Clinton unless Clinton moves to the left on a host of issues, most notably NAFTA and GATT:

> As we in DSA help to lay the groundwork for a trinational campaign calling for a social charter for NAFTA, we are not only helping to build a crucial movement for the future of the left in Mexico, Canada, and the U.S.—we also happen to be preparing an effective bridge issue for the post-Clinton era (14).

On the other hand, Charney held out the option for future support if "Clinton reverses his commitment to the right-wing version of global economic integration" (14).

On further reflection, the DSA leadership concluded that the electoral realignment evident in the 1994 elections meant that the remaining loyal Democratic party base, of "White social liberals, African Americans, a diminished trade union movement, and scattered activists from a diverse array of social movements" was only a small part of the electorate, but "for the first time clearly progressive." (Charney, 1995: 31) In this sense, the longtime strategy of DSA, propounded by Michael Harrington—to social democratize the Democratic Party—had been realized. But this potentially progressive base was ideologically on the defensive, unable to maintain the partial gains of the past, and still lacking "a strategy and a program for the next left" (ibid). Sadly, this represents today the same state of affairs that Harrington himself described in his work *The Next Left* (1986). In the last ten years, as the elements of the old progressive coalition continued to erode, no new "next left" has emerged, and the failure of health care reform has led to the realization that "inventing such a coherent 'next left'—a left that squarely recognizes the implications of the globalized economy—is the central task awaiting us" (ibid). Charney raises the task of creating this new vision of a left politics above the level of electoral calculations, since in his view only a coherent new vision can put a left agenda in a position to win, both inside and outside the electoral arena.

DSA's longtime pattern of critical support and popular organizing on behalf of progressive elements in the Democratic Party and its programmatic commitments, followed by major disillusionment but often gradual gains in the expansion of the postwar welfare state, may now have been exhausted. The failure of health care reform may be symptomatic of this turning point, at which a familiar debate within the democratic left may no longer be relevant to the current politics. With the abandonment by a sitting Democratic president of the more progressive aspects of his original platform, and the loss of congressional control by the Democrats, the political assumptions of this strategy must be rethought, and new strategies appropriate to the new constellation of political forces must be developed.

The leaders of DSA have at this point reached a curious impasse, whether they recognize it or not. On the one hand, the erosion of the traditional base of the Democratic Party through the final defection of the Southern white vote is taken as some sort of fulfillment of a requirement for making the Democrats a more progressive vehicle for socialist ideas and proposals. At the same time, DSA leaders seem to admit that the long-standing role of American democratic socialists, which was to provide an inspiration for the liberal left of the Democratic Party, is at the moment impossible to continue, since the democratic left has no inspiring vision of a more just future society to offer. Even if one accepts the first proposition, which is tenuous, the admission of a failure of political imagination on the left means that DSA cannot sustain its long-standing strategy within the Democratic Party. The failure of the Clinton health care proposal, Clinton's determined support for an antilabor and antienvironmentalist GATT, and the culminating debacle in the 1994 election, have laid bare the futility of continuing the "insider electoralist" strategy in the absence of a rethinking and renewal of a coherent and broadly attractive vision of an alternative society.

The new weakness of labor and of labor-based politics alone makes it necessary for the Old Left to be more innovative and more accommodating to those New Left forces that were once anathema to labor unions and labor parties. The new social movements themselves have in the meanwhile become much more established as a normal part of the political landscape, and have lost much of their earlier momentum and political volatility. There is now serious rethinking of the "politics of identity" born from the New Left, and a call by some of the former leaders of the 1968 generation for a return to a politics of common ground (Gitlin, 1995). The Old and New Left are unable to achieve their political goals without each other, and both now face a dominant conservative politics that threatens to roll back earlier partial gains. The end of the cold war has also eliminated the antidemocratic Leninist voices from an earlier Old Left split, clarifying the debate somewhat. In this era of shifting political and party landscapes, we should expect a series of coalition-building projects to produce a more lasting synthesis of the Old and New Lefts. Some of these will fail miserably, as with the first SPD-Green coalitions at the state and local levels, and some will usefully reveal the need for much more work, as with the anti-NAFTA coalition of 1993, but these projects have already become a legitimate arena for overcoming the critical weakness of the left, whereas in the 1970s both Old and New Lefts viewed cooperation with each other as either a political sellout or political suicide.

The split between the Old and New Lefts in the 1960s was not a mistake or a betrayal of left politics in general by either side; it was a first sign of the inherent and serious limitations of the Old Left politics of the Keynesian welfare state. The Old Left was indeed too comfortable with cold war anticommunism, which demonized progressive third world regimes and sent millions of young (mostly working class) men to fight and die for horrible regimes. The Vietnam War was the right place to take a stand on this for the New Left, whereas the Old Left politics had bought into anticommunism and was now paying the price. The Old Left had become indeed too comfortable with continued exclusion, marginalization, and demeaning of many groups in the industrial Keynesian structure of opportunity, including blacks, women, gays, and other minorities. The Old Left, especially in the trade unions, was still a part of the problem in the 1960s, not a part of the solution. And importantly, the Old Left had bought into an economic growth model that was destructive to the environment, and paid virtually no attention to water pollution, air pollution, or toxic wastes.

In all these areas, the New Left launched a forward-looking politics of protest movements: the antiwar and third world solidarity movements, the black power movement, the gay rights and women's liberation movements, and the environmentalist Green movement. These movement politics have had their own successes over the last thirty years, even against both Old Left and the conservative opposition. In the course of this movement politics of the New Left, the demographics of the workforce and of the left (Old and New) have changed considerably. And, after thirty years, the New Left also is faced with unmistakable signs of the limitations of its own politics, including its excesses, its intolerance and its self-isolating features.

Now is the time, and the time had to arrive, since no one could seriously believe that the New Left had found the final answer to a progressive politics valid for all eternity, for a reconciliation of Old and New Lefts, a gradual formulation of a new synthesis, capable of combating both the national-populism of the right, and the sectarian identity politics of the left. This is not so amazing, and in fact the cornerstone of this rebuilding has already been laid; the logic of the emerging synthesis is to build a broad coalition that will encompass a new working class made up of people from much more diverse backgrounds and lifestyles, united around a commonsense politics of opposing the conservative capitalist offensive that threatens all of them—some earlier and more seriously, but sooner or later all of them.

F. Socialism and the State: An Antibureaucratic Dawning

The left has always done a fine job of critiquing the capitalist structures of power that systematically deny to the poor and working classes access to the tools of a decent life. In this, socialist theory provides a wonderful corrective to the overweening ideologists of the market; the project of a "social science," which Marx considered to be his lifework, has continued to produce ever more sophisticated and telling analyses of the ways in which power structures of capitalism evolve to meet new challenges, without ever giving up the core privileges of ownership of the means of production. Yet when it comes to a socialist critique of the structures of power in the progressive left of the political landscape, the motivation has been much less—understandably, since once again there is no need to do the work of conservatives and liberals in attacking those organizations that call into question the power of money or the domination of capital.

Yet on some occasions the power structures on the left have become key issues of debate. The Leninist "party of a new type" was criticized from the beginning by socialists both within Russia and in the West as an organizational formula that could lead to abuse of power by a new "socialist" elite. From Luxemburg and Martov through Trotsky and Fromm to Khrushchev and finally to Gorbachev and (yes) even Yeltsin, the organization of the Leninist party was a constant subject for critique by those outside and intermittently inside the Communist Party.

Why was the issue of Leninism able to break through the barriers that so often smother self-criticism of power structures within the left? Perhaps first and foremost, Leninism was a direct challenge to the emerging Western socialist view of expanding democratic participation by working-class parties in a long-term reform socialist project. Lenin's revolutionary vanguardism was a competitor against which democratic socialism had to fight from the very beginning, since any acceptance of Leninist views would make democratic left politics in the West impossible. The attempts to create some sort of synthesis between Leninism and democratic socialism (for example the USPD in Germany, the Independent Labor Party in Britain) could be attractive for a moment, but were shortlived because of the immediate contradiction between the two strategies. (This is another area where Marx and Engels are of little use. They still were tied to the possibility of "dual" development within an organizationally intact left politics, as in Marx's "Address to the Communist League" after the failures of 1848, and Engels's later "Two Tactics of Social Democracy." Both Marx and Engels saw the evolution of the two paths after 1848, greeted both as possibilities, but refused to deal with the growing contradiction which would split the socialist movement in Europe and, after World War I, would lead to generations of mutual denunciation and intraleft warfare.) The split between the social democratic left in the West and the Leninist vanguard revolutionaries in the East was one of the areas that demanded some critique of organizational abuse of power by the left itself. However, a general critique of organizational logic leading to abuse of power was left to a few faithful adherents of spontaneous worker revolution such as Luxemburg, and some advocates of workers' syndicalism such as the young Robert Michels. Both Luxemburg's and Michels's critiques of organized power relations within the left tended to be marginalized, or used mainly by antisocialist observers in their overall attack on socialism. As democratic socialism gained ground in the Western liberal democratic framework, these critiques were written off as the work of "idealists" whose continued support of spontaneous self-mobilization and self-organization by the working class was simply unrealistic. Their commentary about the rise of a bureaucratic mentality within the labor movement and within social democratic parties was ignored, and they became outcasts from the politics of social democracy. Symbolically, Luxemburg was killed by one of the death squads (from the extremist Freikorps) whose antirevolutionary terror was utilized and tolerated by the first SPD government of the flawed Weimar democracy. Robert Michels like many socialists after the disillusionment with socialist parties after World War I, underwent a political conversion to the right—in his case to the cause of Italian fascism; Michels migrated to Italy and ended his life as a devoted follower of Mussolini.

In the Soviet Union, and then in other communist regimes, the criticism of bureaucratic power within the party-state apparatus surfaced intermittently, most clearly with Trotsky in the 1920s, with Khrushchev in the destalinization campaigns of the 1950s, and finally with Gorbachev's glasnost, perestroika, and demokratisatsia reforms. In the Czechoslovak communist system, the short-lived breakthrough of the "Prague spring" in 1968 presented the beginnings of a democratic humanist critique of bureaucratic state power, but democratic reform was considered so hostile to Soviet power that its suppression was necessary. In the early politics of the Solidarity union movement in Poland (1980-1981), bureaucratic state and party power were challenged by the vision of a self-managed society, a revival in good measure of Luxemburg's critique and of her remedy: spontaneous grassroots action and selforganization. The suppression of both the "Prague spring" and Solidarity did much to alienate those critical of state socialism (communism) from socialism generally, and to send them (for example, Adam Michnik) over to the liberal or conservative camps.

In China, Mao's periodic rectification campaigns (cf. Gong, 1994) were part of his ongoing battle with party and state bureaucratism and what he perceived as bourgeois elitism. His complex views about the continuation of the class struggle even after the revolutionary seizure of power in 1949 were, in retrospect, one of the most thorough examinations of the tendencies towards bureaucratic abuse of power in a communist state, yet Mao insisted that this was due to remnants of the bourgeois and Confucian mentalities of the past, which only the "great proletarian cultural revolution" (1966–1975) could eliminate. Mao's disastrous remedies to combat the ills of bureaucratism and the rise of new privileged elites discredited his analysis, which was in good measure sound. But Mao refused to consider the possibility of bureaucratism and elitism as phenomena of the new order itself, apart from any traditional cultural influences or any atavism of the overthrown business class.

The rise of democratic socialist parties in the West to the status of government power, and the hard-won acceptance of organized labor by business and government, accelerated the professionalization and bureaucratization of the organized left, so that the democratic left also became part of the structures of power and were in no way immune to the abuses which arise from longer-term organizational imperatives (as Michels had predicted with his "iron law of oligarchy"). After World War II especially, with the rise of the welfare state and the huge expansion of government regulation and social services, new civil service bureaucracies emerged, to be populated, in good conscience and simultaneously in their own self-interest, in large measure by supporters of the democratic left and its Keynesian social welfare state politics. In Britain this new bureaucratic class (the "salariat") has grown to be one of the mainstays of Labour's political base, in Germany the civil service unions and teachers' unions are the mainstays of the SPD; and in the United States the civil service unions and the teachers' unions are the most dependable mass base for the liberal agenda of the Democratic Party. With the sharp decline in membership in the industrial unions (steel, mines, autos, chemicals), the public sector of organized labor becomes ever more prominent in the popular base of Western social democracy. In a period of growing insecurity for much of the working and middle class, the security of government employment and job tenure for teachers makes these sectors easy right-wing targets for arousing popular resentment and hostility. Although no one in teaching and civil service is making big money, these positions are seen as privileged and guaranteed through the bureaucratic power of the social democratic (in American parlance "liberal") welfare state.

The trade unions, pretty much across the board in the postwar West, achieved a remarkable new status; they were in their heyday—the 1950s and 1960s—important partners in the rise of the Keynesian welfare state. In Europe they were generally more powerful than in the United States; in Scandinavia they were major players, and even where the union movement was quite divided, as in France and Italy, they were now, for the first time in their history, part of the political establishment. Trade union leaders changed their own image as well, leaving behind the earthy working-class language of a George Meany for the moderated middle-class bureaucratese of a Lane Kirkland. (Of course there were still some throwbacks like Arthur Scargill of the Miners Union in Britain, but these colorful characters are remarkable precisely because they are now so exceptional.) But the deindustrialization of the Western economies, the decentralization and globalization and downsizing of production units, and the technological revolution in production requirements for human labor, have all weakened the trade unions, with no end in sight. Now that they are in decline, labor unions appear more and more relics of an earlier age, fighting a purely defensive battle for privileges for an aging portion of the workforce. In some labor unions—for example the Longshoremen's union on the East Coast—the average age of members is over fifty, and their average yearly income is more than $40,000. In the case of the Longshoreman's Union, this was part of a thirty-year agreement that ended class warfare on the docks in the 1960s, guaranteeing labor peace, an end to resistance to technological change (containerization), in return for a gradual downsizing through natural attrition of the workforce with high salaries for the veterans of the earlier struggle. In Germany, the once mighty Miners' Union (IG Bergbau) has shrunk to less than half its membership of forty years ago (even with the addition of 90,000 new miners from the former East Germany), and almost half of these members are retirees. IG Bergbau's leaders decided in 1995 to merge with the Chemical Workers and the Leather Workers (*Deutschland Nachrichten*, October 6, 1995: 4). The recent announcement of proposed merger of automobile workers', chemical workers', and steel workers' unions in the United States is a similar sign of the times. This trend toward merger and consolidation of long-independent unions is a sign of their weakness as separate bargaining collectives, but not yet a sign of any conceptual renewal of labor unionism as a social movement.

Unions had by the 1990s achieved a new and unenviable status: they were now weakened and on the defensive across the board, and declining in numbers of members; but at the same time they were seen by large sections of the population as too powerful and abusive of their power. For many people, the union movement is no longer a movement but an entrenched bureaucracy led by undemocratic bosses interested mainly in their own salaries and fat retirement packages. The Donovan Commission surveys among American workers found that a majority of the unorganized wanted some form of collective representation, but not the kind offered by the image of American unions. Unionism has become, in the minds of perhaps most workers themselves, a negative feature of the social and political landscape, an established bastion of authoritarianism (bossism) that is hardly attractive as a defender of their interests. For young workers and employees, with a few exceptions for some minority workers' groups, union organization is not even on their conceptual radar screen.

A survey of attitudes conducted for the AFL-CIO by a prolabor consulting firm found general support for the idea of unions combined with heavily negative attitudes toward union leaders and the AFL-CIO. The findings, taken from broad opinion surveys and eleven focus groups across the United States, showed that "mostly, unions are discussed as something no longer relevant, as symbolized in the frequently used short-hand, 'they're dinosaurs'"(Kelber, 1994). Of the four-fifths of Americans who were in nonunion households, only 29 percent had positive attitudes towards unions, with 39 percent negative and 32 percent neutral. Only 22 percent of respondents felt positively disposed toward the AFL-CIO, versus 33 percent who felt negative. However, most Americans felt that unions have a positive impact on their members' benefits and incomes, and that unions give workers more say in the workplace. Still, only 25 percent felt that unions were concerned about all workingpeople, versus 65 percent who felt that unions were concerned only about their own members. There was strong criticism of union leaders and their behavior. One criticism coming from the focus groups was that "many people—especially low-income working people—believe unions are not responsive to their members. They see unions as largely undemocratic bureaucracies that impose decisions on their members from the top down" (ibid). Forty one percent of the respondents felt that union leaders were out of touch with their members, whereas 42 percent felt that they were responsive to members. The report stated: "We believe that this sense that unions are not fully democratic institutions and are not truly accountable to

their members is one of the greatest problems faced by the labor movement today" (ibid). This report, which was published in March of 1994,
was not mentioned in the *AFL-CIO News* nor in any other AFL-CIO
publication, nor did any member of the AFL-CIO Executive Council
comment on its findings while Lane Kirkland and his associates still
headed the labor federation. The Lane Kirkland years were a disaster
for labor—years of an entrenched conservative union bureaucracy. Even
with the ouster of Kirkland and some of his closest associates, it will
take a major effort for the labor movement to live down this legacy:
"Until unions are once again seen as advancing a broad agenda on
behalf of all working Americans, they will face very serious upper
limits on the possible support they can receive from the general public" (quoted in Kelber, 1994).

To be sure, in Germany and elsewhere in Europe the union movement is still much stronger than in the United States, but even there
the trend is the same, and the unions' image is declining among the
public and in the working class itself. In Germany, a series of scandals
rocked the German Federation of Unions (DGB) over the past decade,
including financial scandals that bankrupted its Heimat finance corporation for low-cost housing. Recently, the head of the prestigious and
powerful Metalworkers (IG Metall) was forced to resign after being
caught in an insider trading deal. Insider trading was not illegal in
Germany but it was considered unethical. Although the DGB is certainly still a powerful player in German politics, it is viewed as part of
an establishment which is itself increasingly alienated from the concerns of workers. Unionism is widely viewed as part of the past; it
perhaps had its justification in an earlier era, but it has now ossified
into a "special interest" for smaller, still privileged segments of workers and is out of touch with current realities for the great majority.

These are sweeping generalizations, I know, but are they incorrect?
Are there masses of workers who really want to join unions, who view
unions as their own, who would become active on behalf of union
organizing? Do unions present ideas that make sense to blue- and
white-collar workers, and especially to the younger generation entering the work force? I think not.

In the renewal of a left politics, one area for thorough criticism
should be the bureaucratic, antidemocratic, bossism of the unions.
The renewal of the Labour party in Britain was spurred on by a series
of humiliating defeats at the hands of right-wing ideologist Margaret
Thatcher, who built her popular base of support on union-bashing.
With the unions weakened and politically immobile, reforms within

the Labour leadership under Neil Kinnoch, John Smith, and now Tony Blair have begun to remove unions from their positions of privilege within the party. Blair, as the most recent Wunderkind of this renewal, has even enjoyed engaging in a kind of union-bashing himself, and has risen in the opinion polls as a result (Krönig, 1995). Without putting too fine a point on it, the old-style union leadership needs to be opposed if it cannot contribute to the renewal of a left politics, and the renewing left leadership can now do this and still not alienate working class popular support. It appears that the left must and can repair its relationship to the unions without breaking its ties to a labor constituency, which itself agrees in large measure with the antiunion critique of power and privilege. Blair's New Labour (in some ways like Clinton's New Democrat) is a first and partial recognition of the need and the opportunity to take labour politics in a new reformist direction, one which both borrows from the antiunion sentiments used so effectively by the Conservative right, but which rejects the injustices and inequalities of Thatcherism, the quick accumulation of wealth by new insider speculators, and the insecurities of "shock capitalism." Only some combination of the two will be credible; the revived left must distance itself, clearly and bluntly, from old unworkable political formulas (above all from the traditional orthodoxy of Labour's Clause 4 nationalization of industry), while just as clearly and bluntly attacking the multiple massive failures of the newly unbound capitalism.

Blair's reform path for Labour may not be the whole answer, and a good part of it rests with the attractive personality of a young (42 at the time of this writing) Tony Blair, both authoritative (or authoritarian?) and full of conviction, which could evaporate. Blair is media-savvy, and propagates a message of breaking social privilege, improving education, and getting Britain's economy on a competitive footing internationally. His message is an attempt to blend a modern and classfree meritocracy with the labourite sense of communitarianism (*Economist*, 1994), and this synthesis will face tough testing. But the Blair experience of speaking bluntly to the unions, as a vital part of reforming social democratic politics in Britain, is itself solid evidence of the basic feasibility of this project. The solid parliamentary election victory by New Labour in May of 1997 elevated Blair to Prime Minister, and has given him a new chance to develop his reform course for labour.

The Blairites are of course hated by the old-line labor intellectuals for their perceived abandonment of the welfare state. Peter Townsend (1995), writing in *New Left Review* (which despite the title is pretty much Old Left), offers a withering attack on the Labour Party's own *Borrie Report on Social Justice*, which under John Smith's Labour leadership was searching for a way to modify Labour's adherence to its old and losing political formula, while developing a new approach to achieving a socially just order. Townsend is correct in viewing the Borrie report as the opening wedge in prying New Labour away from its old welfare statist approach, and building instead a policy of more equitable social "investing" in human capital for employment. For Townsend, this borrows from Thatcherite notions of individual enterprise and competitiveness and gives up unnecessarily on the historical achievements of the welfare state. Blair's path may try to appeal to a broader middle class, but it will not, in Townsend's view, redress the growing inequality and poverty in Britain. Townsend sees another path for Labour—a much more active and militant defense of the welfare state, combined with a transnational effort to build a European welfare state within the confines of the European Union.

The problem with Townsend's critique is that it flies in the face of 15 years of electoral defeat for Labour in Britain; Townsend seems to think that if Labour leaders were just more resolute in their defense of the old welfare state system, their popularity would soar and they would be returned to office. He neglects to offer any critique of the failings of nationalization of industry and bureaucratic statism or union feudalism, which fueled Thatcher's rise to power. Blair may not have the final synthesis yet, but his challenge to the old guard was a first step to serious rethinking for Labour; and Blair is a committed Europeanist, who would have Britain sign on to the European Social Charter, which, flawed as it is, is still the beginning of a European network of rules and regulations to protect labor and provide for transnational legal redress of grievances for the largest working class aggregate in the industrial democracies. Here Townsend and perhaps other defenders of the traditional welfare state would agree with Blair, and this is a significant turnaround in the thinking of the old guard of the Labour Party, who for a long time had been very anti-European, convinced that Britain's insularity could help protect labor without international commitments. Townsend himself now says that a labor government:

> must act internationally in the first instance to protect economic and social health. This will mean working with European allies to argue for the introduction of forms of regulations over multinational corporations; closing loopholes in cross-national taxation; protecting nationally-based companies and individual employees by means of more democratic company laws; using the

European Union Social Charter to improve labour law; promoting international links between trade unions; facilitating the internationalization of democratic pressure groups; encouraging cross-national links between city authorities; and, in particular, taking new initiatives to foster relationships between
First and Third Worlds (148).

This would of course require a real change in attitude of the main
British trade unions, but it is at least a first sign that even the most
traditionalist defenders of the national-level welfare system are now
supporting a campaign of democratic labor internationalism (cf. also
the later section on "The New Meaning of Internationalism"). Blair's
New Labour agenda is in fact advocating just this approach, but with
a much more critical view of union bureaucratism and the need for
democratization within the unions and the Labour Party.

Townsend offers some good challenges for Blair and New Labour
thinking, and his own transnationalism is itself a good change from
the past insularity of Labour thinking of the past, but Townsend's
account has no explanation for the success of Thatcherism and the
decline of Labour in the 1980s, and therefore does not come to grips
with the need to reformulate a labor politics that goes beyond statist
approaches and more calls for government bureaucracies. Townsend
still calls for a future Labour government of enlarged size and scope:

Events in the public sector will be crucial, for public-sector employment is the
critical direct and indirect factor. . . . A future Labour government cannot
afford to neglect the unanswerable case for greatly enlarged public-sector employment. The case must also be made to the multinationals that the benefits
of such a policy would be in their long-term interests and are even a condition
of their continued stable operation. Without positive promotion of the public
sector, Labour's attempt to appeal to the private sector is bound to take on
the features of appeasement (146).

One of the really notable developments of socialist politics in the
twentieth century has been its state-centeredness. Leninism was first
and foremost a politics to conquer state power, which then evolved
into the consolidation of state power and its expansion into every
sphere of human behavior. More than anything, Leninism was a politics about the control and exercise of state authority. With the huge
tasks which Leninist regimes posed for themselves—of warding off
hostile external threats (yes, there were such threats; it was not all
paranoia), bringing backward economies into the industrial age, and
of creating a new socialist order, while at the same time suppressing
internal dissent—the size of the party-state apparatus grew enormously,

and this state apparatus (the *nomenklatura* class) quickly developed its own self-interests. Stalin, at the peak of his tyrannical power over the entire system, was able to use blood purges as a mechanism to rejuvenate and revitalize the ruling elites (Nagle, 1977: chaps. 9–10), but after his death and the taming of the apparatus of terror (in the first wave of destalinization under Khrushchev), bureaucratization, with its attendant ossification of thought and action, became the hallmark of the mature Soviet system.

The Brezhnev years (and the Andropov and Chernenko years) were a triumph of Soviet bureaucratic collectivism. The aging of this "managerial modernizer" generation into decrepitude was a physical symbol for the Leninist model at the end of its life span. This bureaucratic order had some advantages (it was not so scary as "high Stalinism," and it did, in its own bureaucratic way, pay greater attention to public needs), but it represented no vision of socialist emancipation, and its professional managers did not believe in socialist ideology or dream of building a future socialist society. In its final years, the reformers around Gorbachev public acknowledged that the Leninist project had failed— had led to stagnation and decay, and that something new had to be tried. As the Soviet reform of the latter 1980s project evolved, it became apparent that Gorbachev had no clear vision or path to a revived socialist politics, but rather was only committed to opening the door to free discussion and ultimately democratic choice among contending alternatives, including rejection of socialism. Gorbachev's real radicalism in the Soviet context was precisely his unwillingness to reimpose order in the name of order itself, which had become the standard reflex of the bureaucratic state.

Western social democratic politics was not nearly so statist as Leninism, because it maintained a firm commitment to democracy. The democratic commitment of Western socialism guaranteed a vital antistate and antibureaucratic opposition, with which the state system would have to contend. The Keynesian welfare state was not imposed by force or by trickery on an unwilling public; it evolved in stages from the broad public reaction to the failures of laissez-faire capitalism and the minimalist state. At each step of the way, vigorous dissent by powerful and well-funded interests against the expansion of state regulation and broadening of bureaucratic oversight of economic and social affairs simply lost out in free and fair electoral competition. The right-wing attacks on the specter of "creeping socialism" had their chance in the political arena and lost. The right-wing notion that "the people" never wanted big government is just plain nonsense. Conservative forces had every opportunity to turn back the trend towards big government, and they failed for more than sixty years—an amazing record of failure that can be explained only by general popular support for the (social democratic) politics of a state-centered commitment to social welfare, modest redistribution, and security.

But this democratic mechanism for criticism of the social demo-cratic statism of the past sixty years has now produced a sea change in public perceptions. Now the public believes that the state and its regulation regime are part of the problem; now the public believes that paying higher taxes in an attempt to get better results will not work; now the government is seen as too intrusive and too distant from citizens' concerns. This change is much further advanced in the United States than in Europe, but even in Germany, with its long tradition of an honest and efficient civil service, the expansive statism of the postwar era has produced now a trend toward public skepticism about government regulation and intervention. At the beginning of the century, the state system received tax revenues of less than 10 percent of gross domestic product; by the 1980s, this figure had reached the range of 30 to 50 percent (Heidenheimer, Heclo, and Adams, 1990: 187; Nagle, 1995: 51). Conservatives and liberals had warned about the breakdown of the ability to govern at every step of the way, had prophesied catastrophe and economic collapse, had tried every scare tactic to stop this progression. Now it seems clear that a basic change in public attitudes has set in, and the left must reckon with this new fact. Just as conservatives and free market liberals have been reluctant to face the truth about their decades-long failure to turn the tide through the democratic process, so Western socialists have been reluctant to recognize and accept new public antistatist and anti-bureaucratic attitudes.

Does this mean that the public, including large segments of the blue-collar working class and white-collar employee class, wants to dismantle government programs and simply turn everything over to the free market mechanism? Not at all. The dominant public mood is a desire for social security without government bureaucratic intrusion and onerous taxation. A good illustration of this can perhaps be gleaned from the health care policy area in the United States. In 1993, Clinton's plan for a national health care system was launched on a wave of public support for universal health care coverage that could not be taken away. Yet the plan went down to humiliating defeat after a well-

orchestrated campaign directed against the image of a new governmental health care bureaucracy. The opponents of the Clinton plan,
whatever the merits or accuracy of their attacks, had an easy time
turning public opinion around and making it possible for a Democratic-controlled Congress to be scared into total inaction. The presumption of government bureaucratism, even in advance of its occur-
rence, is now dominant, and can be readily mobilized; twenty or thirty
or forty years ago, despite the best efforts of the right, the reverse
was true. On the other hand, in 1995, with the new and very conservative Republican majorities in Congress, the Republican plan for cutting Medicare and Medicaid spending and sending responsibility for
health care to the states has also run into heavy skepticism from the
elderly and the poor. While Newt Gingrich has done a masterful job of
presenting the reforms as the salvation of Medicare and Medicaid,
much of the public is rightly suspicious about the real intentions and
aims of a conservative politics which never supported public health
care in any shape or form. Conservatives, it should be noted, have a
lot of negative baggage to carry when they say they only want to save
and improve these programs. Nor can they simply say that they want
to dismantle Medicare, or even Medicaid, because they know that the
public wants some basic government commitment to health care. Conservatives have a long track record of opposition to government public health care, so that they are not trusted on this or on other issues
of social welfare and security.

The issues of left statism and support for nationalized bureaucratic
approaches to social problems still permeate the rethinking of a left
politics. In the fall of 1995, Democratic Socialists of America (DSA),
one of the most open and diverse socialist groups in the United States,
was undergoing a reformulation of the its political platform, and one
of the chief lines of cleavage involves those who still see the democratic state as an ally (at least potentially) of the left, the only ally with
enough clout to counterbalance capitalist interests. DSA's draft platform, written by a select national steering committee, has been sub-
jected to thorough criticism in *Socialist Forum*, the bulletin of open
discussion about the course and activities of DSA. At least one faction
of DSA has taken a strongly antistatist and antibureaucratic line. Joanne
Barkan, a longtime DSA activist, argues against any program of state
control of industry in the platform :

> The paragraph announces that the state might own industries such as steel,
> auto, and petrochemicals. This sounds loony in 1995. Why would the state

do a good job of managing entire industries that have become highly diverse, decentralized, and competitive? To save jobs? No—because—as the document states in the same paragraph—state-owned industries would have to compete and might go bankrupt. Protection against the cruelties and capital mobility and deindustrialization lies in industrial policy; stable currency exchange rates, brakes on international capital flows, labor unions, public education, and training programs. State ownership is not the answer (Barkan, 1995: 10).

Although the draft platform did move toward some kind of "market socialism" in its recognition of the utility of market mechanisms for efficiency and productivity, Barkan still sees much in the draft that represents old and worn-out proposals:

> The document in profoundly defensive. Confronting long term and dispiriting difficulties for the left, the authors dig in their heels, raise old familiar flags, and proclaim that conditions are ripe for "the movement." Not only does wishful thinking displace sober analysis; the wishes are mostly obsolete. The social movements theme might as well have been written in 1983; the urban economic democracy theme sounds like 1973; and the state-control-of-the-commanding- heights theme qualifies as an antique (11).

On the other hand, some—like Ron Baiman of the Chicago DSA—fear that there has already been too much endorsement of the market, of private enterprise, of market efficiency. Baiman and others fear that "market socialism," moving away even partly from the goal of a socially planned economy, eventually leads to the "capitalist road" or capitalist rebirth: "The notion that one can sanction market based outcomes and then regulate or otherwise redistribute them to address some of the problems . . . is extremely probematic. . . . Market socialist systems create extreme incentives to revert to straight capitalism because of elite self interest as is occurring in China" (Baiman, 1995: 8). Although there is no direct defense of a state-owned and state-planned economy in this argument as the immediate goal for any new socialist politics, there is a rear-guard defense of that as a long-term goal, and a different lesson is said to be learned from the collapse of Soviet-style central planning and bureaucratic statism. For Baiman, "the collapse of the Soviet regimes can be attributed to a power (read private property) grab by its bureaucratic elite as much as a failure of central planning and public ownership." In other words, it was a betrayal of socialist principles by the Soviet *nomenklatura*, and their desire to become a "normal" bourgeois elite with real ownership of property rather than just a "new class" with only collective benefits from running the party-state apparatus (as Djilas once described). There is certainly a power grab for private property underway in the ex-Soviet Union and the other formerly communist countries, but Baiman himself points the finger of blame at the bureaucratic elites which developed in the hyperstatist Soviet system. Still how can one avoid bureaucratic statism from developing its own interests and its own self-protective politics, which—as Michels warned long ago—increasingly diverge from the original intent of the movement?

The left has long believed that the achievement of state power, whether democratic (evolutionary pluralist) or Leninist dictatorial (revolutionary conquest), opened the way to either eliminate capitalism and private property or at least moderate and shape its outcomes toward social justice. Even in the aftermath of the collapse of Leninism, and the accelerating erosion of Keynesianism, it is hard for many on the left to believe that without state power there can be any effective challenge to capitalism. But at the same time, there is an opening for rethinking why national state power for the left has not succeeded in creating socialism through the Leninist path or has reached the end of its possibilities in the postwar Keynesian welfare state democracies. Socialists must produce a thorough critique of bureaucratic statism in order to rethink their politics on the state, and on nonstatist strategies for a new left.

In 1996, the DSA continued its debate over socialist politics and big government under the title "The Left and Limited Government," with David Belkin taking the lead in questioning the left's traditional support for growing government regulation and social control over wider stretches of the economy. Belkin, in more direct terms than would have been possible within the left only a few years ago, argues that the public critique of big government, bureaucratic authoritarianism, and government inefficiency is not just "false consciousness" or the result of a well-funded conservative offensive. He takes seriously the notion of the government's becoming too intrusive and too large a factor in our lives, and he argues for a kind of left Madisonian doctrine of balance between too minimal and too dominating a state; the key, of course, is the substance of government policy and intervention: on whose behalf, from whose decisions, and from what motives. In Belkin's words:

> The left must become more engaged in the debates about government efficiency, tax burdens, welfare incentive effects, and so on. These issues matter to millions of Americans. If we don't like the right's proposed policy reforms (privatization, flat tax, workfare, etc.), then we must propose our own. What

we must not do is endorse the status quo, which is what the left ends up doing when it ignores popular anger at government. . . . the American left must seek relatively non-statist solutions to the major problems facing American society today (1996: 6).

Belkin once again advances the concept of "stakeholder democracy" as a decentralized and nonstatist approach to building social accountability into enterprise behavior; while this idea is not yet fully formed, its main thrust is to give greater credit to market mechanisms for their efficiency and nonbureaucratic flexibility, while trying to provide measures of popular accountability into market economy. Belkin's ideas still encounter dogmatic resistance from traditionalists such as Ron Baiman and Chris Lowe, but the progress of this debate within DSA, which does act as a forum for much of the intellectual left in the United States, is itself indicative of how far the left has already come in breaking intellectual taboos, questioning long-standing positions, and offering new alternatives.

A renewed left politics needs to think carefully about the antistatist and antibureaucratic spirit of our time. The backlash against the welfare state is not the creation of conservative ideologists, right-wing talk shows, or ambitious young Republican leaders. These actors have only taken full advantage of new attitudes toward the welfare state and its visible agency, the government bureaucracy. A renewed left politics will, in my opinion, not be credible unless it too comprehends the popular anger at the social-psychological distance that has grown up between government and citizen. But this is very different from giving up on the function of public power in providing social security to those same citizens. The renewed left politics will stand on firmer ground in continuing to defend a public commitment to welfare, social security, and distributive justice, especially now in the new era of insecurity and risk (Beck, 1995).

From my own perspective, it should be possible to join a critique of bureaucratic statism, which never was an end of socialist politics, to a reaffirmed and reworked commitment to a basic social security net. The reliance of the Old Left on the state, and political control of the state, needs to be questioned. This will in any case be required over the short run, since the state now is siding more and more with the demands of a newly unchained globalizing capitalism. The nation-state and its institutions, even if democratic, cannot by themselves re-create the regulative boundaries of Keynesianism; the state institutionalist approach of Western social democracy can have only a declining role in a renewed left politics; more effort needs to be directed toward rebuilding the left as a social movement, that is, as a popular movement with its own strong roots and daily contact to the lives of the people, rather than as official state welfare programs and civil servants. The relative decline of the nation-state as the locus of potential countervailing social power over capital must give way to left organizing both below and above the national level. International networking of left movements will need to confront the power of capital across national borders, and localism will need to mobilize communities and regions to challenge capital and to direct resources so that they can meet social needs without the aid of the state.

Some of this rethinking will be advanced by the impending downsizing of the regulative social state, which will ipso facto require nonstate defenders for social and community needs. The effective control of the state will more than likely be in the hands of new antisocial free market advocates. The left will not be able to count on the established welfare state as a political given; the model of citizen mobilization pioneered by the New Left and the new social movements will gain further weight in a renewed left.

The democratic left in the West became too dependent on the state and its social and regulatory agencies. One of the most disheartening signs of the times has been the virtual absence of organized popular opposition to the dismantling of welfare, health care, and social security in the existing system. As Michael Walzer said, in looking beyond the welfare state, "Even if the welfare state were to be perfected under the best possible conditions and under socialist auspices, the dangers of bureaucratic omnicompetance and popular passivity would not be avoided" (1982: 148). The growth of bureaucratic welfare statism, because it did take care of some problems, and because it removed itself from the local community, encouraged a kind of passive attitude which now hampers political mobilization against the conservative assault on social welfare.

Perhaps this current passivity is also related to the ambivalence of many citizens about the welfare state; on the one hand, people are generally supportive of its goals and commitments, but on the other hand they are increasingly hostile to its size and its methods. They also believe that it has failed to motivate too many individuals with its welfare and social benefits, but rather has created new syndrome of dependency on the state. Such claims by a Charles Murray are often linked to racist or antiforeigner prejudices, but there is enough evidence of this welfarist dependency to be taken seriously, by those on the left who want the left to succeed. Many of the traditional responses of the left in this debate are still appropriate: without decent education, without decent jobs in sufficient numbers, without health care, without child care support for the "working poor," the conservative solution is no solution at all to poverty and social need, but only a vehicle for a tax reduction for those who want to separate themselves from such problems. The left also responds that welfare for the poor is a small portion of the federal budget (about 1 percent in the United States), while "corporate welfare"—tax loopholes for corporations, subsidies for industry, government gifts of property or property use to industry and agrocorporations—is much larger. But although this is correct, it is politically lame if it does not come to terms with the issue of welfare dependency that bothers most working-class people—the image and reality of some who live off the labor of others when they could be working.

If the left wants to get back into this debate, it must itself recognize that welfare dependency has not been the solution; socialist values aim at emancipating individuals from need and from fatalistic acceptance of degrading conditions. Producing dependency, in whatever form and from whatever motives, is not part of a socialist agenda. Michael Harrington, one of the foremost rethinkers of socialist politics, whose death was a tremendous loss for the renewal process, saw the new dependency in part as "a generational shift in which the benefits of the welfare state become one more fact of life for those who did not have to struggle for them, something to be exploited for convenience" (1989: 135). Harrington defends the achievements of the welfare state, even in its impersonal and bureaucratic format, but, citing the work of Fred Siegel, he concludes:

> the new entitlements coincided with, and even reinforced, a certain fragmentation and depersonalization of all of social life, a decline in solidarity, and a rise in possessiveness and what Siegel calls 'dependent individualism.' A welfare state that sought collective solutions to the problems of working people was put to uses for which it was never intended." (136)

This is perhaps inevitable over the long-term, as programs become institutionalized and people figure out how to manipulate the system. I have heard much the same commentary made by my socialist colleagues in Germany, who defend the much more generous welfare system there while at the same time recognizing how, especially among the younger generations, people have learned how to milk the system not out of pressing social need but for personal convenience.

The line between helping people and fostering dependency is often blurred, and no one can pretend to know exactly where the border runs. No one expects that the record of social welfare, of public benefits for those in need, can be perfect. But on the other hand, socialists themselves should be the first, not the last, to recognize the failings of the current welfare system, and want to change it. The earlier worry (which I also shared) that left criticisms of welfare state practices would only play into the hands of conservative antiwelfarist politics is now outweighed by the recognition that antiwelfarist attitudes are now so prevalent that further stonewalling on this issue will only deepen the credibility gap between a left political agenda and the average citizen.

David Belkin (1995), in an impressive critique of commonly held left beliefs on the extent and causes of the new inequalities in the United States, finds that the decline of the middle class has been overstated, and the reasons for it have been mistaken. He finds that much more of the "new poverty" has to do with household composition, and that much of the new inequality is mitigated in a life-cycle perspective on lifetime earnings (rather than a one-year snapshot of distribution of income). In fact, his analysis points to technological change and immigration as more potent threats to low-end wage earners than either globalization or free trade. Belkin sees the Keynesian state as modestly succeeding in its redistributive functions, and therefore he views the growth of taxation in the Keynesian state as representing a real (not imagined) threat to the middle-class family's interests. What Belkin is getting at is that middle-class anger at the welfare state is not just a fantasy of right-populist demagogues, that the Keynesian welfare state has reached or exceeded some sort of upper limit and has come to be viewed as "unjust" by millions of middle-class citizens:

> One positive result of this is that . . . the after-tax and benefit degree of household economic income inequality is much lower than the pre-tax household money income degree of inequality. But at the same time, the net distribution of income away from the middle class—away from most working Americans—emerges as an "objectively" legitimate concern, comparable in magnitude to the distributional impact of changing labor compensation shares, and much better established than the latter as a long-term phenomenon.
>
> Considering this, one can begin to entertain the subversive idea that making governments rather than transnational corporations the targets of popu-

list anger is not purely a matter of "false consciousness." This is not to deny the ugly subtexts of some of this anger—racism, homophobia, and so forth. It is simply to say that "the politics of scapegoating" isn't the whole story. The American welfare state, as cramped and pinched as it is by Western European standards, really does impose heavy enough costs to invite the skeptical scrutiny of those who mainly pay for it—the middle class (Belkin, 1995: 19).

This is indeed a subversive idea for the left, but it is one reason why the left needs to take seriously the loss of support for the welfare state among a broad element that once supported it. Along with all of the other negative by-products of welfare statist approaches, this loss of mainstream support must be included as one of the most harmful, since it has added to the self-isolation of the left (cf. also the earlier section on "Socialism and Popular Culture"). The antistatism and antibureaucratism which fueled the new social movements in their beginnings in the 1960s and 1970s, need to reach a new stage of evolution in rethinking left politics. Belkin warns that:

> The familiar (if somewhat toned down) socialist reflex—to trace all societal problems back to private markets and to counterpoise more or less directly state-centered public solutions—is not compelling today, and it would still not be compelling even if the changes in contemporary capitalism were as calamitous as the left makes out (20).

Belkin's own preference is for a new socialist politics to focus individual workers' desire to control more of their own economic assets—their human capital. According to Belkin, the new era of capitalism is characterized by a remarkable increase in the weight of human capital (education, skills, and social knowledge) in the overall composition of capital assets, from 60 to 80 percent of total wealth in most Western democracies, according to estimates by the World Bank (ibid). Belkin argues for a socialist politics of empowerment of human capital, the demand for participation by the owners of human capital (workers and employees) comparable to participation by investor capital. This "stakeholder socialism" would build not on state ownership or schemes of workers' control, but on extension of participation to human capital "investors" in firms:

> "Stakeholder governance is closer to what is found in Japanese "coalitional" firms, or under German co-determination, or in the participatory ESOP—and even in some "ordinary" profit-sharing American firms. Considerable job security is restored, but conditional on greater managerial flexibility within the firm; tying a chunk of employee compensation to the bottom line is allowed,

but conditional on greater employee empowerment within the firm. This is
what prevents long term disinvestment in human capital—and also what makes
the stakeholder model such a hot potato for the (accredited) owners and managers of conventional capitalist corporations. (It can also be a hot potato for
labor unions adapted to adversarial combat with conventional owners and
managers, but that's another story (1995: 21).

In this critique lies the basis for a much more individualized socialist
politics toward "transformation of relations of production." It is a politics that puts more responsibility on the individual worker or employee
as a stakeholder, an owner of human capital, at the same time that it
pushes for democratic empowerment of stakeholders in the economy.
Belkin's views may be criticized for borrowing from the logic of capitalist investment, which legitimizes the oversight and monitoring of
capital as a right of individual private property. On the other hand,
much of Belkin's argument is more in tune with Marx's goals of individual empowerment in production as the path toward overcoming
alienation in the capitalist production system, advancing labor's rights
to match those of the capitalist investor. (But the capitalists were also
alienated in Marx's view, even though their power was affirmed through
their alienated relationship to production.)

The focus of Belkin's model is on productive workers and employees, not on welfare dependents or the jobless poor. The socialist goal
is empowerment of those with human capital assets, rather than support for those who have few, none, or negative assets. This is a major
revision of priorities, since it requires the left to reconnect with those
who have jobs, even good jobs, and to address their middle-class desires and needs for fulfilling work and respect in the production system. It is part and parcel of the perceived need by some on the left to
reorient its politics towards the mainstream, to respect the real concerns of the working middle class, and to offer an alternative vision to
address those concerns. It means opposing continued statist dependency and promoting measures that grant participation rights but with
more individual responsibility for finding fulfillment within the production system. Does this mean that the left should turn away from
defending the poor and excluded? Does it mean abandoning state-
funded programs of support for their needs? In some sense, the honest answer must be yes. A new left politics that opposes dependency
must aim at phasing out bureaucratic statist approaches (which are
not solutions anyway) in favor of policies which open new opportunities but rely on individual initiative and motivation. This would include

real enforcement of antidiscrimination laws, reorienting education towards building individual human capital, and giving even low-wage earners some legal rights of participation in responsibilities in their firm. It would aim to free individuals from prejudice and traditional barriers by enforcing proworker laws but would not promote government bureaucracy or government ownership as a part of the "solution."

Although it remains to be worked out in detail, the stakeholder model offers a way to approach the question of individual participation and individual responsibility in many social settings, including schools, religious organizations, and perhaps even the military. Wherever bureaucratic statism hinders individual learning and the chances for individual responsibility, a stakeholder approach may offer a nonstatist and also noncapitalist alternative, one that emphasizes the need for widespread support for social institutions through responsible participation by those with a social (not just capital) stake in their functioning.

The left can, if it chooses, offer a nonracist, class-conscious critique of welfarism and its abuses, while presenting an alternative that promotes work for all in a full-employment economy, family values, and community self-help to prevent social pathologies from reproducing a dependency syndrome. Some will immediately say that this is just a pale version of the long-standing conservative or neoliberal agenda for decentralizing responsibility while cutting programs and budgets, and in the end the public will choose the real thing over the imitation. There is considerable risk that, especially in the short run, that will be the case. The credibility of a revived left politics in this area cannot be restored in quick order. My contention is, however, that the left must restore its credibility in this area in any case, and only a left that speaks blunt truths (truths, not fiction) about public welfare programs will be trusted to offer an alternative that retains the commitment to help those in need through a reform and restructuring of public policy.

Meeting social needs without resorting to state bureaucratic tools will not be easy, and it may not be possible right away and in all policy areas. It will require a process of devolution of democratic controls from official state institutions to a wide variety of local and non-local social organizations, a process that upholds minimal standards and yet allows real room for local, nonbureaucratic controls. The trend toward elitist, self-serving rule within bureaucratic organizations of all types was formulated by Robert Michels at the beginning of the century as an "iron law of oligarchy," and this law is one of the few sociological findings that has held its own over time. Yet Michels overlooked the possibility of popular revolt against unresponsive and elitist statism, which was visible even during his lifetime and which has since become more common with the growth of state intervention in all areas of social and economic activity. A mass public is now ready for a program of antibureaucratic political reform but is also looking for ways to preserve certain essential social and economic protections against the volatility and anxieties of an unregulated market. The problems of bureaucratism cannot be solved simply by relocating government power to local or state authorities below the national level; that will over time reproduce bureaucratism and self-serving behavior at those levels. Only by a process of democratic competition over values and policies by a broader informed and interested public can we wage a constant, never-ending battle against the tendency toward bureaucratic government. And this in turn requires some real sense of ownership, some type of stakeholding, to promote both learning and participation by affected citizens. All this means abandoning the statist model of social welfare, while maintaining the priority of social needs themselves. It requires self-criticism and reform of trade unions and labor parties as well as corporations and religious bodies. Of course this will not be welcomed by many on the left, whose own commitment has been to build up the social democratic state as the mainstay of popular commitment to social solidarity and some measure of justice within a market-type economy. Yet the victories of the past cannot be defended in their entirety, and a strictly defensive strategy has no chance of winning in the longer run; it can at best only drag the process out, reinforcing the idea that a left politics has no future.

This is all perfectly natural and unavoidable in the cycle of political renewal, since renewal comes onto the agenda only when previous political models have obviously run their course and have encountered massive failure. In this area, as in so many others, abandonment of the old formula is now possible, and a new political space for rethinking the relationship of socialist politics to the state is now appearing.

G. The New Meaning of Internationalism: Democratization beyond Borders

Modern socialism has a historic commitment to internationalism; indeed international solidarity was conceived as one way to strengthen the weak position of nationally-based workers' movements in the nineteenth century. Marx's early theory of the rise of an international labor movement in Europe to politically challenge capitalism was in large measure borne out in the fifty years after it was first presented in the *Communist Manifesto*. Giovanni Arrighi argues, "The close fit of the trends and events of 1848–1896 with the predictions of the Manifesto goes a long way toward explaining the success of Marx and his followers in establishing their hegemony over the nascent European labor movement" (1990: 61). Marx's theories on the rise of a class-conscious labor movement to confront capitalism within the heart of capitalism proved superior to the views of the Owenites, the Fourierists, or the followers of Proudhon and Bakunin. Arrighi describes the making and remaking of the world labor movement as a central feature of the evolution of capitalism and the leading response to capitalism on the broadest and most general scale. Central to the Marxist project was the success or failure of this world labor movement, for unlike other challengers (ethnic, national, racial, gender) to specific abuses of capitalism, the global proletariat had to confront the logic of capitalism generally and develop a systematic alternative to that logic.

In the era of imperial capitalist expansion in the late nineteenth century, German Social Democracy supported the effort to establish uniform labor standards through international agreements. The SPD's Erfurt Program of 1891 developed a theme which was quite forward-looking, and which is now at the heart of the contemporary crisis of the left:

> With the expansion of world transport and production for the world market, the state of the workers in any one country becomes constantly more dependent upon the state of workers in other countries. The emancipation of the working class is thus a task in which the workers of all civilized countries are concerned in like degree (quoted in Murphy, 1994: 75).

As Craig Murphy notes, German Social Democracy, the best organized on the continent, called for both "national and international legislation for minimal labor standards, including the eight-hour day, an end to factory work for children, and the two-day weekend without work" (ibid). These demands are still relevant today, since they have not been achieved for most of workers around the world. Bebel and other leading German Social Democrats were then in the forefront of the effort to build a network of international organizations, most of them public international unions (nongovernmental organizations), to

establish a coherent framework for managing the emerging world order dominated by the great European industrial powers. The establishment of the International Labor Office (ILO) in Geneva in 1901
was the result of this effort, which was one practical achievement of
the labor movement's internationalist commitment.

Yet the twentieth century has seen the erosion of socialist internationalism, marked by the split between mainstream socialists who supported their nations' war efforts in 1914–1918, and their antiwar
opponents led by Lenin and Luxemburg. After World War I, socialism
was organizationally and conceptually split for most of the century
into warring democratic socialists and revolutionary Leninists. In that
time, on both sides of the divide, socialist politics became more oriented to the politics of national solidarity, far less to the politics of
international solidarity. The Soviet concept of "socialism in one country" was indicative of the thinking of an era. Above all, the practical
work of socialist parties was directed toward achieving state power,
the power of the national government. There were, to be sure, cases
of extraordinary international socialist solidarity, mostly in Europe and
particularly during the Spanish Civil War of 1936–1939. Yet even the
Spanish Civil War demonstrated the international splits and fragmen-
tation of the socialist movement.

Why did modern socialism, committed to internationalism among
all peoples as a core principle of its humanitarian mission, forsake this
ideal? There is no doubt that the evolution of socialism of this century
has been indeed a nationalization of socialism, as Belgian socialist
Paul Henri Spaak once noted (cited in Harrington, 1989: 145). The
main reason, aside from all the particular failures and misunderstand-
ings, was that a national-level socialist politics was feasible, whereas
the conditions were not ripe for a truly international socialist politics.
At the international level, it was, as the experience of World War I
indicated, too easy to split labor loyalties by the simplest, crudest application of appeals to nationalism. Within a given country, it was also
possible to divide labor by utilizing ethnic, racial, religious, gender,
status, and generational cleavages, but there the sense of a common
interest among workers from different backgrounds could be moderately sustained. Protestant and Catholic workers had some social contacts with each other; Polish miners in Germany had some solidarity
with their German coworkers; women and young workers were family
to the larger working class milieu. At the national level, socialist parties in the West were able to win enough votes to influence govern-

ment, and then to join a government, and finally to lead a government; this was predicated of course on the ability of socialist leaders to appeal for support in the interests of the national working class, and to argue that they would be the beneficiaries of an elected socialist regime. The commitment of Western socialists to liberal democracy for their nation as the path to socialism was at the same time a commitment to the nationalization of socialist politics. The boundary of liberal democratic politics became the boundary for democratic socialist politics. This formula had its measure of success (and its failures) and became part of the Keynesian postwar compromise: a welfare state democracy of the nation.

The Leninist regime in revolutionary Russia was initially very internationalist in its politics; Lenin did predicate his concept of revolution in backward Russia on its spread across Europe, especially to industrial Germany. But once the revolutionary uprisings of 1918–1919 in Germany, Hungary, Finland, and elsewhere in Europe had been brutally crushed, the Soviet regime turned its attention more towards maintaining itself in a context of hostile capitalist encirclement. In the 1920s, with the victory of the Stalinists as Lenin's successors (cf. Daniels, 1960, for a good account of this struggle for the conscience of the party), Soviet internationalism became an extension of Soviet foreign policy, as a forward line of defense of the Soviet Union and the power of the Soviet regime.

The record of the next decades of Soviet power is one of constant betrayal of communist parties and communist activists abroad in the name of protecting that power, which became synonymous with the interests of world revolution. From the Spanish Civil War to the sellout of German communists in the Molotov-Ribbentrop pact to the betrayal of the Chinese communists in their long battle with the Kuomingtang, foreign communist parties were manipulated mercilessly, with the loss of countless lives among the most dedicated cadre. In Stalin's paranoiac "great purge" era of the 1930s, and then again in the anti-Titoist purges of 1948–1952, foreign communists of unshakable loyalty to the ideals of communism were imprisoned, tortured, and murdered, all because of the dictates of the Moscow power center and the submissiveness of most foreign communist organizations to the leadership of Moscow. It is not surprising that such "internationalism," in the course of sixty years of Soviet dictates, earned itself a horrible reputation. Both socialists and antisocialists in the rest of the world marveled at the misguided and misused idealism of foreign communists and at the hold of an uncaring Soviet dictatorship over the international communist movement. Arthur Koestler's famous *Darkness at Noon* recounts the psychological conditions of such a mentality, from his own experience; anticommunists pilloried local communists as disloyal to their own nation, and were over and over supplied with evidence of their submission to Moscow's directives. Democratic socialists also had to fight hard to avoid being smeared as stooges for Soviet interests, "dupes of the communists," meaning dupes of Moscow.

This stench of Soviet internationalism was evidence that this was a perversion of socialist internationalism, a strategy that caused great harm to a legitimate ideal. It must, of course, be added that Western socialists, in good part, had abandoned the terrain of socialist internationalism to the mercies of the Soviet regime. Had Western democratic socialism maintained a more positive alternative to Soviet internationalism, the credibility of a left internationalism might have survived, but this was not the case. Abandonment by the West in favor of a national Keynesian politics and Soviet manipulation for its own national interests combined to undermine the cause of a working-class international movement through most of the century.

Capitalist modernization in the age of industrial revolution created a new economic interdependence of peoples, under the domination of capitalist interests. This newly created environment, in the European context, made the older guild socialism and peasant socialism obsolete. It was no longer possible to confront the power of capital at just the local level; despite some internationalization of capitalism, however, it was possible to build a counterbalance to capitalist interests at a national level, since the technological preconditions (in finance, communications, and transport) for today's globalizing capitalism had not yet appeared). On the other hand, the interests of the working class of the capitalist core nations were often at odds with the interests of workers and peasants in the nonindustrial and nonwestern colonies. While there was a humanitarian sense of solidarity between the socialist parties of Europe and the socialist-nationalist liberation movements of the colonies, there was no overriding economic interdependence of interests. Although socialist parties were committed in theory to granting independence to colonial peoples, they were not quick to do so in practice; Western socialist parties never developed any project to offer full citizenship to colonial peoples on an equal footing with the citizens of the colonizng nation. Such proposals would have met with great opposition from many of their working-class followers, who would have considered—as they still do—the third world worker as a wage competitor. Then, as now, the predominant view of labor across the divide between rich nations and poor nations was one of protectionist isolation from the competition of low wages and benefits. This strategy worked as long as capital investment in the major production lines was still located in the core industrial nations and had not yet been sufficiently depreciated to require replacement, and communication, transportation, and financial connections in poorer third world nations were too costly, inefficient or unreliable. Increasingly, this strategy has eroded as the preconditions for new industrial investment in low wage, low benefit nations have been met. Although, as Knox and Agnew (1994: chap. 7) point out, the preponderance of industrial capital investment is still in the high-wage, high-benefit, rich democracies, the new opportunities for runaway capital have already remarkably shifted bargaining power to the side of capitalist interests, and have left both labor and the Keynesian welfare state in a long-term defensive, losing position. How will labor and social democracy respond to this new internationalism of capital, which has already ended one political era?

Many of the thinkers most closely associated with labor party politics in the postwar era have recognized the basic problem but have been unable to come to grips with the absolute need for fresh thinking and breaking with the now-losing defensive politics of national-level Keynesian statism. Frances Fox Piven's volume (1992) on labor parties in the postindustrial era, which includes some of the most prominent authors sympathetic to democratic socialism, has virtually nothing to say about the need for a new internationalism of labor politics, although there is some recognition of a new international division of labor that undermines the continuation, even in reformed fashion, of a purely national-level labor politics. Most attention is devoted to the significant differences among varieties of Keynesian welfare statism—for example among Sweden, Germany and the United States—or to strategies for managing or adapting to the decline in labor's political clout. The bigger issue of developing a left politics to confront the new international division of labor and to begin to fashion a new counterbalance against globalizing capitalism is virtually ignored. In this respect Piven's volume represents no new thinking on this issue, and tries to seek ways of minimally adjusting social democratic politics to what is a qualitatively changed situation.

But even among some pretty traditional defenders of the national Keynesian welfare state, there has been some change of heart on the necessity for a new left internationalism. Here the new thinking sees a need for an internationalist effort to preserve the welfare state at the national level. Peter Townsend has been one of the staunchest defenders of the old welfare state, and a constant critic of the revisionist New Labour leaders, especially Tony Blair. Yet Townsend himself, after a trenchant critique of New Labour rethinking on the welfare state, comes out in favor of a new internationalist approach, focused both on the European Union and on the global context, as a new line of defense of the national welfare state. Townsend and perhaps other traditionalist defenders of the welfare state would agree with Blair, and this is a significant turnaround in the thinking of the old guard of the Labour Party, who for a long time had been very anti-European, convinced that Britain's insularity could help protect labor without international commitments. Townsend says that a new labor government:

> must act internationally in the first instance to protect economic and social health. This will mean working with European allies to argue for the introduction of forms of regulations over multinational corporations; closing loopholes in cross-national taxation; protecting nationally-based companies and individual employees by means of more democratic company laws; using the European Union Social Chapter to improve labor law; promoting international links between trade unions; facilitating the internationalization of democratic pressure groups; encouraging cross-national links between city authorities; and, in particular, taking new initiatives to foster relationships between First and Third Worlds. To such a strategy must be added measures to monitor the development of multinational companies and to democratize the IMF and the World Bank in ways which will raise the representation of Third World populations and also the social interests of poorer groups in the rich countries. The problem with existing institutions of the international finance community is not just their exclusion of Third World countries, but also their exclusion of the poorest fifth or two-fifths of the populations of the rich countries. The treatment of refugees seeking asylum and of temporary workers in Europe are prime examples of this lacuna (1995:148–149).

This advocacy of a combined national-international strategy for labor has some new elements, but its means look very similar to the old labor politics at the national level: a national job-creation program for the public sector, income redistribution measures, anti-discrimination protection for women, children, and minorities. Townsend's view of the European Union itself is that—for example on pension guarantees—"it is far from being in any position to establish an acceptable federal scheme" (148). At least there is movement toward recognizing the need for a more solid regional and international politics, even if the main focus is still on the national welfare state. The inadequacy of a purely national strategy for the left is now accepted more widely, though not universally.

Some new thinking that has emerged on the left has bypassed the debate on a new internationalism, preferring to develop a new social-ist politics which still takes the nation-state as its practical boundary. The Austriallian laborite activist and theorist John Mathews, recogniz-ing the emergence of post-Fordism, elaborates a model of associative democracy as the unifying principle of a new socialist agenda. Mathews still sees the national government as the regulator of international capital, the only effective weapon against misbehavior by multinational corporations (MNCs):

> In a democratic economy, MNCs will, in my view, be allowed to continue operations, but subject to a "good citizen" code of behaviour. The difficulty of enforcing such a code is acknowledged, but there is no alternative if the for-eign policy of the democratic government is not to be dictated by MNCs. . . . a code needs to be backed by adequate sanctions for misbehaviour (defined, for example, as excessive repatriation of profits and tax avoidance; plant closure without adequate consultation or warning; inadequate local process-ing or research and development; restrictions on export activity by subsidiar-ies, and so on)—and the most effective sanction of all is outright nationaliza-tion (1989: 151).

Mathews argues against putting too much faith in internationalism, although at the same time he is aware of the power of international capital to escape national-level social and democratic controls:

> I do not know whether globally-operating MNCs will remain in perpetuity. I am skeptical as to whether they will ever come under adequate regulation by some supranational authority. . . . And so the only feasible path forward seems to be to bring their operations in each country under control within that country, with all the inevitable difficulties this will entail. The liberal and social democratic governments which have allowed the MNCs to grow to their present size, have left the democratic world with a terrible burden and ob-stacle to overcome, given the global reach and power of these organizations, and their capacity to play off one government against another. However, they are not insuperable, and are likely to be tamed by a combination of national enforcement of "good behaviour," combined with some international initia-tives (151–152).

Mathews suggests that nations may group together (as in OPEC-type cartels) to enhance the market for their own similar products. Or the United Nations may be able to set up international public enter-

prises, such as the proposed (but then abandoned) International Sea-
bed Authority of the 1970s. In this area Mathews seems to have an
outdated vision of the problem; it is not just the existence of MNCs,
nor their considerable political weight in the economies of less developed nations, that is now at issue. It is the whole new complex of
research and development, investment and finance, communications,
transport, decentralized manufacturing, and worldwide marketing that
now has outrun the capacity of even the largest nation (such as the
United States) to regulate or enforce any code of behavior. And nationalization now hardly seems a credible threat; the French experience of 1981–1982 was a last attempt by a Western socialist government to use nationalization as a mechanism for control and for steering
overall economic performance, and it failed miserably . Harrington, a
sympathetic commentator on Mitterrand's agenda, concludes:

> National Keynesianism, we have seen, no longer works in a transnational
> economy. The experience of the French socialists in the early eighties was a
> dramatic confirmation of that fact as the stimulus decreed in Paris helped to
> create markets—and jobs—for the West Germans and Japanese at the ex-
> pense of the French (1989: 207).

The capability, in a short period, of French investors to decapitalize
the French economy disciplined the Mitterrand regime and forced it to
completely reverse its economic policies. The power of capital to discipline even a majority socialist government in a relatively strong nation such as France indicated already in the 1980s which power was
ascendant, and which power in decline.

Mathews's mention of regional or product cartels also misses the
point; OPEC aimed at disciplining the Western oil multinationals on
behalf of larger national capital interests, mostly antidemocratic. And
they still left the oil multinationals as strong players in the industry,
once they had paid OPEC's price at the point of production. If this
example shows anything, it shows the tremendous difficulty of disciplining national capital in an era of globalizing opportunity structures
for capital.

Some in the labor movement have recognized the need for a strategy to match the globalization of capital, but their attitude toward the
new technologies that underpin the capacities for a globalized production are mixed. Dave Broad, writing in *Monthly Review*, which
has not been known for much new thinking on the left, argues that
globalization now is a continuation of early waves of globalization in

the expansion of capitalism. Broad describes the advancing signs of the "degradation of labor, feminization of labor, housewifization of labor, informalization of labor, casualization of labor, and peripherization of labor" in the new wave of capitalist globalization (1995: 24). All of these trends, he argues, are presented in the media as technologically driven aspects of the new requirements for "flexible production" of the new post-Fordist era, but are really only aspects of capital's new dominance over labor, its power to treat labor as a commodity without any regard for individual human needs or wider social needs. Praising the achievements of the national-level social movements which carved out the democratic welfare state, he calls for their revival, but he also recognizes that in the current period, "now more than ever we must accelerate the work of uniting these movements into a global coalition" (30). Broad looks to support for regional social charters "along the lines of that included in the negotiations for the European Union, but better" (30). At the same time, however, he advocates a left political challenge to technological developments which borders on antitechnological dogmatism: "Technologies and their applications are the product of human choices. Some can improve our lives. Others should be done away with if they serve to further exploit people and destroy the environment. This may involve transforming First World lifestyles by, for example, replacing personal transport with improved and expanded public transportation systems" (29).

The premise that technologies are products of human choices and human resources is fine, and certainly a left politics can and should seek to affect the path of technological development and application, but to simply state that some technologies should be "done away with" smacks of a politics of suppression, and a supposition that progressive forces can know which technologies should be done away with, presumably forever. This attitude toward technology would seem to put the left in the position of seeking to resist technological change through selective abolition, rather than continuing social and democratic management. The globalization of capital certainly makes destructive applications of new technology possible, but I would not want a renewed left politics to put itself in the (antiprogressive and ultimately losing) position of preaching technological suppression, even in the name of social or environmental goals. I can just imagine the response to Broad's suggestion that personal passenger cars should be "replaced." What kinds of new state bureaucracies and police mechanisms would have to be set up to accomplish the suppression of the private automobile? Broad's recognition of the problem does not need to lead to his proposed solution, which can easily be seen as a new technological police state, presumably on a global scale. Social regulation and democratic controls, at both national and international levels, are not the same as absolute suppression, which presumes a lot more knowledge and certainty about the uses and abuses of technology than anyone possesses. In opposing the extreme capitalist position of technological change with no social control, Broad has ventured into the dead-end opposite extreme of technological selection and suppression as determined by the left. Once again, the left needs to get over notions of "endism," here in its approaches to technological change. The notion that things can be settled once and for all is a mirage; it leads to bad means which will lead only to bad results, and which will lose support because they don't make sense to ordinary people. Any notion of a renewed left attempting to stifle technological change as a response to the technological innovations that have given global capital its current (and temporary) advantage should be rejected as backward-looking. The left needs to devise its own positive approach to using technological innovation for promoting social justice and better lives, and this involves much more flexible response mechanisms that leave questions of technological application open for ongoing discussion and democratic review.

More realistic is the treatment of the international order issue by Craig Murphy (1994) in his historical account of the development of international organizations in the modern era as a concomitant to the emergence of a world economy. Here labor played a minor role in earlier waves of international organizational development. But one future internationalist project that a renewed left politics could support is that of a global and ecological Keynesianism. Some visions of global Keynesianism as a solution to certain problems of developing nations began to be advanced in the 1970s and 1980s. Some of the early dependency theorists of the 1960s shifted their ground to advance a new strategy for development which would involve a reform of priorities for Third World governments and international development agencies like the World Bank.

> Rather than spending the bulk of development funding to serve the politically important interests of the local bourgeoisie and of relatively privileged workers in urban areas, Third World governments would have to focus on increasing the incomes of the vast majority, the rural poor. Policies would have to begin by focusing on basic needs, go on to focus on improving human capital,

and finish by abolishing the economic inequities sapping initiative and preventing the kind of agricultural revolution that seems to have preceded the 'takeoff' of all societies presently enjoying mass production and mass consumption (1994: 249).

The global Keynesian model would require the North to accept much of the South's proposed New International Economic Order (NIEO) but would also require new coalitions between Northern and Southern regimes. In the view of Hartmut Elsenhans, a German global Keynesian theorist, the rich Northern regimes would have to support "those segments of the (Third World) State-classes which are in a position to enforce structural change. Often, these reformist segments subscribe to the Marxian critique of capitalism. This is only to be expected as long as the industrial countries of the West use the principles of the market economy as a pretext to reject welfare measures in Third World countries, and the redistribution of income on a global scale" (quoted in Murphy, 1994: 249). As Murphy notes, in the midst of the cold war, these proposals did not receive a very favorable hearing, but they did begin a strand of thinking about an alternative international economic order that combined socialist, liberal, and increasingly environmentalist priorities. The first Brandt Commission Report of 1980, even though it appeared just as the Soviet invasion of Afghanistan was smashing the first East-West détente and reaffirming the logic of the cold war, did get some attention in Europe. But it was the Reagan-Thatcher project of the 1980s that gained power and ideological credibility, while the alternative project of global and ecological Keynesianism had little chance of political acceptance. As a result, the current era is defined by growing inequality both within and between nations, with no short-term prospect that labor can mount a counterbalancing force to globalizing capital interests.

The existence of great inequalities within the context of an ever more flexible capitalist production system, and the ideological support from free market fundamentalism for acceptance of whatever degree of inequality the market dictates, has now realized the worst fears of well-paid Western workers—real wage competition with low-wage, low-benefit job-seekers from the poorer nations. Elsenhans estimates that by the end of the century, globalizing capitalism will create a third world industrial workforce equal to that of the rich Western nations. The "danger of downward equalisation" for the Western worker is being realized, and rather quickly (quoted in Murphy, 1994: 252). The end of Fordism now means the end of mass consumption by a wide section of the working class, creating even greater inequalities in the rich nations and raising the specter of underconsumption of pre-Depression times. Murphy cites the reemergence of a new series of debt crises in the 1980s, which also characterized the Great Depression, and which undermined efforts to stimulate new growth. In short, there is good reason to believe that a new type of Keynesian alternative may soon be called for, when the increasingly volatile and unregulated global capitalist order creates its next catastrophe:

> In the short run this outcome may have seemed to be a boon to northern investors, just as the antilabor policies of the 1980s must have seemed to be a boon to many OECD employers. But this was only a temporary respite, what Gramsci would call a reassertion of "domination," not the reestablishment of a long-lasting hegemony. In the 1980s, capitalists might be able to dominate workers as they had in the interwar years, and the U.S. might be able to dominate its Free World allies (North and South) the way European members of the Entente dominated Weimar Germany, but in both eras the world order crisis remained (253).

Murphy sees the crisis of the new globalizing capitalism already appearing, since "new forms of international labor resistance have been growing in many of the more populous newly industrializing countries where liberal fundamentalists hold out the greatest hope for finding relatively inexpensive and relatively skilled labor to staff the new 'global' factories: places like Brazil, Mexico, Poland, and South Africa" (266). Moreover, these new labor resistance movements are international in scope, with "alliances with global ecological, human rights, peace, and women's movements that have arisen in the political space created by the waning world order. Examples include the consumer boycotts organized by Greenpeace and the Interfaith Center on Corporate Responsibility of the World Council of Churches" (266). We might well add that many of the new labor movements have strong religious backing, especially in Latin America and the Philippines, from the liberation theology wing of the Catholic church (cf. also the earlier section on "Socialism and Religion") But also in Korea and South Africa, the religious support for labor has been an important factor that should be included in the rethinking of a left politics of internationalism. Despite the recent triumphalism of the world order of Reagan and Bush, Murphy argues that there are just as many signs of the emergence of a new global ecological Keynesian world order, which seems at this point to be *the* major alternative.

Increasingly, labor unions see the necessity of forging international labor alliances that can engage in effective bargaining with internationally dispersed corporations; new forms of solidarity campaigns, a focus on women's rights, and consumer boycotts are emerging as new or reborn tactics of international labor (Stand, 1993). International campaigns focused on one corporation (Schantz, 1992) and cross-border organizing (Coughlin, 1995) are increasingly apparent as tools of a renewed labor internationalism, although the longer-term effect of individual campaigns is not clear. Coughlin argues that to succeed, labor must effectively organize millions of new members of the new international workforce. This requires basic democratic rights in each country, and an end to anti-labor terrorism with impunity by employers and the state. In the debate over NAFTA, the issue of one-party authoritarianism and state suppression of independent unionism in Mexico was not effectively used to oppose its entry into a free trade zone. In the European Union, at least certain standards of political and civil rights for labor, a basic part of a democratic system, are required for new member countries.

On the other hand, after the end of the cold war, it should be more difficult for American foreign policy to justify support for regimes that brutalize labor movements with soldiers and death squads. North American and European labor organizations can mobilize their members against support of antidemocratic regimes in the developing world, increasingly freed from the Cold War logic, and aware that their own fate is connected with the success or failure of the global labor movement. In this coming struggle, the war of ideas may already have tipped in favor of a global democratic opening for a new wave of labor politics. In the nineteenth century, in the gradually democratizing West, it was impossible to keep labor from joining in democratic politics, although in practice the struggle for union recognition was very difficult and often violent. And it was inconceivable that Western democracy could continue to maintain itself without permitting a free labor movement from organizing to represent workers' interests, just as it is now inconceivable that democracy can survive in durable fashion outside the West without some similar opening to labor.

The passage of NAFTA in its antilabor and antienvironmentalist form was a wake-up call for North American labor organizations. The anti-NAFTA coalition forged some important new links with Mexican independent labor, environmental and political organizations, which failed, however, to mount an effective campaign against NAFTA from the left. Arguably more effective was the anti-NAFTA right-wing populist campaign led by Ross Perot and Pat Buchanan, which fed on current protectionist, antiforeigner, and antiimmigrant sentiments in the United

States. As noted earlier, missing from the left-liberal coalition (mostly labor, environmentalists, and consumer advocates) were the women's groups, which did not see NAFTA as an important enough issue for women workers, either in the United States or in Mexico. A post-NAFTA analysis by José LaLuz of DSA recognizes the need of the left to make clear what is at stake for working-men and -women, and their families, in the integration of the North American economies, but also to put forward a positive alternative, including a "social charter" for raising labor standards, for enforcing labor laws, and for democratizing the Mexican political system:

> I think that we needed to have our own vision of what kind of trade for North America would have been good for all, and that's where we failed. It was a lot more of, "We are against this thing," as opposed to, "Here's the kind of agreement that we have to offer that will benefit the many as opposed to benefiting the few." But we have got to make sure now that we build on what is there, and in order to do that, we're going to have to put what exists to the test. For instance, if environmental rights and regulations are being downgraded in any of the three countries in order for one of the countries to become 'more competitive' at the expense of people, then somehow we're going to have to denounce that, to expose it. But we must also offer our own alternative vision of what it would mean to protect the environment in the three nations (LaLuz, 1994: 3–4).

At the same time, LaLuz is concerned: "I'm afraid that sometimes we lack imagination in terms of how to do something like this" (4).

No doubt the re-education of the labor movement will be a massive undertaking, of international solidarity with progressive forces, overcoming generations of past neglect -mainly in the service of cold war ideology. The AFL-CIO's American Institute for Free Labor Development (AIFLD), long headed by William Doherty, was an instrument of American cold war policy, hostile to progressive (socialist, populist, radical, or communist) unionism in any nation. AIFLD, supposedly an institution for promoting "free" trade unionism, regularly funded right-wing, pro-American unions tolerated by right-wing dictatorships, while ignoring or justifying the terrorization of progressive unionists. David Bacon, for twenty years a union organizer, recounts the legacy of cold war unionism of the AFL-CIO, now that American unions needed to build ties to Mexican workers to oppose NAFTA:

> After NAFTA, U.S. workers felt the full impact of the international department's disastrous betrayal. Forty-five years of cold war politics in Mexico had built no

relationships based on solidarity. It they wanted a common front with Mexican workers, or those in other countries, they would have to build it from scratch (1995: 573).

Especially in Latin America, therefore, building connections to progressive labor, to authentic democratic parties and to social organizations which support structural change will involve a lot of rethinking, and some serious truth-telling about past mistakes and betrayals of international labor solidarity. The Germans would call this "overcoming the past" (*Vergangenheitsbewältigung*, which was applied in Germany to face up to the legacy of the Nazi era and to move beyond it); and this would help clear the way, and clear out remaining old cold warriors, for a new beginning. A first important step in this direction was taken by AFL-CIO's new president, John Sweeney in dumping William Doherty after thirty years at the head of AIFLD; Doherty's forced resignation in January of 1996 may be an important turning point for building international labor solidarity and rejecting the AFL-CIO's cold war policy of support for repression of independent unionism in the developing nations. Maybe American labor is entering a process of rethinking its strategy for labor, although this is only a modest beginning, which would have to be followed by substantial positive outreach to authentic labor leaders in other countries, and which would therefore have to challenge the United States' established policy of extreme hostility to organized labor anywhere that its business interests are at stake. This would have to be integrated into a longer-term vision of a global Keynesian economic and environmental project to challenge capitalist interests, and it would require an international labor and environmentalist solidarity capable of resisting nationalist and isolationist sentiments.

Of course the difficulties of implementing a new global and environmental Keynesian project would be enormous. It would require commitments by newer industrializing nations not to repeat the environmental disasters of the older European powers. It would require the most developed economies to adopt new policies that promote both leisure and welfare in a new and more equitable division of socially necessary labor time. Now, on a global scale, "finance would again have to be made a servant of the welfare state in order to prevent cascading monetarism and guard against capital flight as different states or regions arrive at different social pacts" (Murphy, 1994: 267). Yet there would be benefits for business and international trade as well, since one of the causes of the current economic stagnation and mass joblessness in both the industrial core nations and the developing third world nations is a lack of purchasing power for the great majority of families, shrinking the size of the effective (money-demand) market for products. The new hyperliberal economic globalism, in escaping from the national Keynesian compromise, has undermined the success formula of the old Fordism; the new international Keynesian alternative offers the prospect of widening of markets through greater employment and international pay equity, a leveling up of the poor, and social security for the displaced in the transition to a more integrated global economy.

H. Socialism and Democracy: A Unifying Universal?

There are those who saw Marx's original project as a theory of universal democracy. Shlomo Avineri, in his interpretation of Marx's lifework as a continuation of the universal humanism of the young Marx, describes Marx's vision as a universalizing democratization project, one which has its roots in a liberal humanism but which takes the class-limited liberal project and projects it onto a future classless society. For Marx, "true democracy" was communism, that self-governing society of the future, in which the state would have both withered away and been transcended (Avineri, 1968: chap. 8) In this regard, although Marx and Engels had a complex and dual-track attitude toward real existing parliamentary democracy in the nineteenth century (cf. esp. Hunt, 1974), their project for a modern socialism was also bound up with their vision of a free society. For Marx and Engels, liberal democracy or parliamentarianism meant democracy for the bourgeoisie—bourgeois democracy in literal terms—and continued alienation for the proletariat. From the early writings of Marx, there is a definition of the future communist society in which all are free, all are empowered (as we might say today), and all are materially able to develop their capacities to their fullest.

Marx's image of the all-around or full development of the individual in a future communism is a possible working definition of a democratic society, going beyond liberalism but holding on to a profoundly democratic vision for the future. "In place of the old bourgeois society, with its classes and class antagonisms, we shall have an association, in which the free development of each is the condition for the free development of all." This was the grand vision of Marx and Engels in their 1848 Manifesto (quoted in Nagle, 1991: 38). Thirty years later, Engels reiterated this:

> In making itself the masters of all the means of production to use them in
> accordance with a social plan, society puts an end to the former subjection of
> men to the own means of production. It goes without saying that society
> cannot free itself unless every individual is freed. The old mode of production
> must therefore be revolutionized from top to bottom, and in particular the
> former division of labor must disappear. Its place must be taken by a organi-
> zation of production in which, on the one hand, no individual can throw on
> the shoulders of others his share in productive labour, this natural condition
> of human existence; and in which, on the other hand, productive labour,
> instead of being a means of subjugating men, will become a means of their
> emancipation, by offering each individual the opportunity to develop all his
> faculties, physical and mental, in all directions and to exercise them to the
> full—in which, therefore, productive labour will become a pleasure instead of
> being a burden (Engels, *Anti-Dühring*, quoted in Nagle, 1991: 39).

Marx and Engels used the terms emancipation, liberation, and freedom to describe the entry into a socialist stage of human development. Marx particularly used universal suffrage to describe the goal of
a self-governing society. They did not use the vocabulary of parliamentary democracy, and what they had to say about the parliaments
of their time was mostly negative, except insofar as the advance of
parliamentary government mirrored the decline in the power of the
monarchy and aristocracy. Marx and Engels frankly distrusted the institutions of parliament, seeing in them another, more subtle mechanism for class control. They paid little attention to the details of the
evolution of liberal democracy going on in their century. And they
made few statements about what a socialist governance, in the transition to communism, would look like. Marx's eulogy to the defeated
Paris Commune in 1872, including his remarks on directly elected
representatives to the Communal government, and his statement about
the possibility of peaceful transition to socialism in the most democratic nations (Holland, Britain, the United States) were pretty thin on
specifics, and they demonstrate that Marx had given little thought to
this problem and preferred to concentrate more on the problems of
revolutionary struggle. In this respect Marx and Engels missed one of
the major political developments of their own time, and they therefore
left little to indicate what the relationship between socialism and democracy should be.

On the other hand, Marx in particular held firm to his antistatism,
insisting that the dialectical process leading to "true democracy" must
mean the withering away and the transcendence of the formal state as
a separate entity above society. Avineri, in his critique of both Leninist
and social democratic statism as deviations from the original Marxist
perspective, argues that for Marx, the winning of universal suffrage

for the proletariat was, in good Hegelian fashion, dialectically both means and end toward communism. He cites Marx and Engels's formula in the *Manifesto*, "The first step in the revolution of the working class is to raise the proletariat to the position of ruling class, to win the battle of democracy" (quoted in Avineri, 1968: 204). The popularization of the writings of the young Marx in the 1960s, with their emphasis on antistatism, was of major importance for the thinking of the New Left in the West, which would challenge both Leninism and Western social democracy precisely in these terms. Now, in the 1990s, perhaps the moment has come for a healthy antistatism to regain its place in a reworked relationship between socialism and democracy.

In practice, of course, Western socialists did support democracy, the representative or liberal democracy that was presumably the historic project of European liberalism. The early leaders of German Social Democracy—and especially Eduard Bernstein, the great reformer of Marxist thought—steered their socialist politics into the mainstream of liberal democracy, and accepted, first in practice, much later in theory, the politics of liberal democracy as the road to socialism. Indeed, Bernstein and not a few others considered that, in the wake of the abject failure of German liberalism in the latter part of the nineteenth century, social democrats would have to take up the cause of liberal democracy themselves, as a requisite for pursuing their evolutionary path to socialism. In those fateful moments of 1918-1919, when spontaneous uprisings by armed workers were spreading across Germany, the newly installed Social Democratic government even chose to use the forces of reaction (the Kaiser's military command and the Freikorps death squads) to protect the fledgling Weimar Republic against the Spartacists; a bargain with the devil, as the later history of Weimar demonstrated, but also a testimonial, signed in blood, to the commitment of German Social Democracy to a democratic parliamentary politics. During the Weimar years, no party was more loyal to the democratic principles of the system than the Social Democrats; even in the last months of the Republic, German social democracy could not conceive of armed resistance to the rising conservative-fascist coalition, could not bring itself to plan for effective armed struggle after the Nazis came to power. The history of Western socialism has no guilty conscience about its adherence to democracy, even to liberal democracy, in the course of this century. Compared with the politics of conservatism, which collaborated with fascism and reaction through the first half of the century, and with the politics of economic liberalism, which opted to protect property over individual freedom in much of Europe during the interwar period, Western social democracy can look back at its own constant support for democracy and the restoration and expansion of democracy.

Yet, in the current crisis of the left, there is also a need for rethinking about the relationship between socialism and democracy. Much of this is connected to the need to rethink the relationship between the left and the state, and to rebuild a left politics as a social movement rather than as a set of bureaucratic state institutions. The original acceptance by Western socialism of liberal democracy as the vehicle for its project carried an acceptance of all the features of the Western liberal state, which for several generations served the democratic left well. The once oppositional and socially radical ideas of the democratic left have become the state establishment over the course of this century, and at the end of the cold war have become a set of hindrances to the further development of a left politics. Liberal democracy, like any organized politics, is subject to ossification, stagnation, bureaucratization, and loss of innovative energy; and so the great welfare states of the West—still democracies of course—have been subject to these trends. A new socialist politics therefore must take a fresh look at the role of democracy in its future agenda; the commitment to democracy needs to be renewed through a revised image of what constitutes democratic experience from the perspective of the left.

Norberto Bobbio, the Italian critic of Marxist theory from a liberal socialist position, has long argued that Marxism has no political science, no detailed theory of the state, and certainly no elaborated theory of a specifically democratic socialist state (Bobbio, 1987: chap. 1). Bobbio's insight was presented first in the 1970s when participation in the Italian government by the large Italian Communist party seemed possible:

> When I say that a genuine alternative model of a socialist state does not exist—that is a model thought through in as much detail as the model of the representative state, elaborated and refined by the great tradition of liberal thought—I am referring to the fact that the efforts of socialist political thought, especially its Marxist wing, have been concentrated almost exclusively on the critique of representative democracy, and have neglected the need for a blueprint of the state that is to replace it. But even this critique has remained so superficial as to seem self-evident or sterile (77).

Bobbio is highly critical of the socialist politics of the past for their relative neglect of this area, which has allowed liberals and conservatives to claim that socialism and democracy are incompatible, whereas for Bobbio they should be inseparable. Bobbio's own brand of "liberal socialism" has long argued that the "democracy trend" should be recognized as a potential ally of the left, if the left will embrace it, and will push for democratization as its own guiding principle. For Bobbio, the socialist presumption of a widening of political democracy to economic democracy is crucial, yet he:

> would simply point out that a permanent feature, one just as common to capitalist as to socialist states, is the removal of economic power from the province of democratic control, i.e. from below. It is a basic fact—one of those facts which all utopian reformers of society have come up against and been powerless to resolve—that the major political decisions in economics (on which depend the minor ones as well) in socialist countries just as much as capitalist ones, are taken autocratically. . . . Yet it is precisely in this field, the field of democratic control of economic power, that the battle for socialist democracy will be won or lost (101).

Bobbio is himself a skeptic regarding the prospects for such a democracy, yet his main point is that the left needs to "reflect and meditate on the events of history, to renounce slogans, ready-made formulas, catechisms, the bombast of the initiated, to give up showing off doctrinal purity with a high and mighty air, or the use of the obscurantist jargon of factions and sects, and instead get down to the serious business of studying the mechanisms of power. . . .(101–102). There are no shortcuts in this work, and at the same time the left must be ready to start anew, "even preferring to be taken for someone who has everything to learn rather than someone who knows it all already (ibid). Bobbio's critique is not new, but it reads today, in the post-cold war era, much more convincing than when it was first presented, and its insights are more critical.

John Keane has said of Bobbio's argument for a "liberal socialism":

> He concludes that the Left needs democracy in order to live up to its old promises of greater equality and solidarity with liberty; and that, in view of the systematic failure of the Left to keep these promises, its full acceptance of the democratic method would radically alter the methods, policies and public image of the Left. It would become a synonym for the democratic fight for greater democracy." (Keane, in Bobbio, 1989: xxvii)

In fact, Bobbio argues that the "democracy trend" from strictly political affairs to the larger social sphere is one of the main features of modern political progress:

Today, if you want an indication of the development of democracy in a country, you must consider not just the number of people with the right to vote,
but also the number of different places in which the right to vote is exercised.
In other words, to pass a judgement today on the development of democracy
in a given country the question must be asked, not "Who votes?" but "On
what issues can one vote?" (1989:157).

Bobbio's vision is that a renewed left politics should adopt a radical
democratization—indeed, the goal of universal suffrage—as its leading
principle. He intends that the political project of liberalism, that is the
political institution of representative democracy, be extended within
civil society. Religious bodies and unions, as well as business enterprises and organizational bureaucracies, are possible candidates for
this democracy trend. There is more than a little irony in Bobbio's
injunction that the left needs to completely and unequivocally embrace democracy and democratization as the method for its own renewal and fulfillment. This sounds very much like Marx's goal of universal suffrage, the extension of human freedom and real choice into
every sphere of life. Bobbio, however, has been a lifelong critic of
Marx, yet how does his call for a "democracy trend" as the leading
principle of a new left politics diverge from that of Marx?

For Bobbio, the search for "universal suffrage" carries a clear and
steady affirmation of representative democracy over direct democracy,
which has often been the left's, and especially the New Left's, vision
of true democracy. Bobbio argues, to the contrary:

If one democratic trend is to be seen nowadays it is not, as is often mistakenly
maintained, the substitution of direct democracy for representative democracy (which is, in any case, impossible in large organizations), but the transfer
of democracy from the political sphere (where the individual is regarded as a
citizen) to the social sphere (where the individual is regarded as many-fac-
eted); for example, as father and son; as spouse; as entrepreneur and worker;
as teacher and student and student's parent; as officer and soldier; as admin-
istrator and client; as producer and consumer; as manager of public utilities,
and so on. . . . Consequently, current forms of democratic development
cannot be interpreted as the affirmation of a new type of democracy. Rather,
they should be understood as the occupation of new spaces, which up to now
have been dominated by bureaucratic and hierarchical organizations, by some
of the traditional forms of democracy (1989:155–156).

As is typical of Bobbio's writings, he is skeptical about the ultimate
possibilities of this principle of democracy for a renewed left. He is
especially pessimistic about the technocratic tendency in modern society which reduces the chances for citizens' participation in deci-

sions. He is worried about the tendency toward hierarchical bureaucracy to emerge even in liberal, representative, democratic institutions. And he is especially concerned about the undemocratic and manipulative power of the mass media. "All of these are also modern trends, which contradict the democratic assumption of free and full development of the faculties of individual citizens" (Keane, in Bobbio, 1989: xxi). As Keane rightly notes, Bobbio's writings leave us with more riddles than answers, and yet he has been steady in his support for a left "democratic trend," since long before the current crisis of left politics was widely recognized. Bobbio's position, despite his distaste for the New Left and for Marx, in fact incorporates much of their own radical antistatist and antihierarchical politics, while rejecting the New Left "illusion" of direct democracy and Marx's primacy of the economic over the social, cultural, and political.

Some lessons for this rethinking may come from the postwar experience in Germany, where a very generous and efficient but very bureaucratic and statist welfare democracy led to a split on the left between a prostatist Reds and the antistatist Greens. Here Andrei Markovits and Philip Gorski recommend that the left adopt a universalizing democratization as the core principle of a revitalized left politics. Their concern is that, with the collapse of Leninism in the East and the slow erosion of social democracy in its familiar form in the West, in the absence of some unifying principle, the left will fragment:

> Yet there clearly exists a universalizing principle around which social democracy and the Left could rally and redefine themselves. It is *democracy* pure and simple, without any qualifying adjectives such as "liberal," "constitutional," "parliamentary," "popular," and yes, even "social." Democracy in this case would denote the constant struggle for the weak and poor and disadvantaged wherever they might be, regardless of system and "ism." It would be a position of true antinomy and critique against any entrenched power anywhere (1993: 285).

Whether intended or not, this formulation is quite close to that of the young Marx, but it extends the concern of a new socialist politics to all areas, without privileging the economic or class issue. Marx saw the economic organization of society as the key to all other issues, which were of lesser consequence and could best be addressed through radical change in the economic system. Markovits and Gorski, like many others on the left, now seek to redress what is seen as Marx's neglect of issues of culture, nation, gender, race, or environment. In their view:

this democratically-defined left would criticize American racism in the United States as vociferously as it would oppose Cuba's anti-gay policies, Serbian oppression of Albanians in Kosovo, as well as Croatian discrimination against Serbs. This universalizing democracy would plead for more workers' control, more individual rights, more empowerment for regular citizens, more community responsibility, more egalitarianism, regardless of the "system " (285).

Is there no need here for any priorities, or for any ordering of importance? Can a new left agenda take on all these issues equally, with only the principle of democracy as a guide? Or, perhaps more pointedly, are there no contradictions inherent in a "universalizing democracy" that seeks simultaneously to uphold any underdog, oppose any entrenched power? What about, for example, an entrenched democratic state which seeks to put down extreme right-wing violence or threats of violence? What about the use of state power to maintain separation of church and state, or to enforce certain codes of conduct that contradict a long-held tradition of a religious minority? It should be noted that Markovits and Gorski do not give an example of defending a religious minority in their listing of tasks for a democracy-defined left. Is it always so clear which interest is dominant and which is underdog? Nevertheless, the focus on democracy as the universal principle for a new left politics is attractive; in this regard, the Greens' contribution in the German context might be not only beneficial for that case, but a pathblazing example for other contexts as well.

In yet another sense, democracy can become the unifying principle for a new left politics, as the equalizer of uncertainty in uncertain times (of great transitions). Helmut Dubiel (1994) argues that the current stage of economic development in the West is marked by a dramatic reduction in the socially necessary work time needed for production. This was already foreseen as a crisis of Western "dominance of surplus" by Herbert Marcuse, the intellectual forerunner of much New Left thinking. The paradox of this condition is that at the same time that production is increasing to produce greater surpluses, more and more people are driven out of work, especially women, young people, and older workers. Dubiel sees in this situation a chance for a left democratization of risk:

A left treatment for this "domination of surplus" is just now being outlined. It would have its unity in the principle of a democratic distribution of uncertainty. First of all it would involve a reduction of individual work time and making its application flexible. The democratic distribution of this reduced work time would have to be surrounded with a basic security guarantee, unconditional, a citizen entitlement. Whoever speaks of "uncertainty," seems to suggest that it concerns only a transitional phase. From the beginning of written history we can see epochs of collective existential uncertainty, in which old patterns of meaning collapsed and new certainties were not yet established. The special feature of our posttotalitarian epoch is that we can no longer expect new certainties. The totalitarianisms of the twentieth century were hopefully the last great efforts to base politics on supposed certainties. In the posttotalitarian era the uncertainty over the course of history itself has become the orientational center of politics. Democracy is the institutional form to treat this publicly recognized uncertainty. While earlier societies justified themselves through a horizon of questions to which the answers were already fixed, democratic societies are based in an institutionalized questioning of themselves (1994: 5; my translation).

Dubiel sees a left politics centered on democratization of risk as a flexible and therefore once again plausible response to the current situation. Once again, a New Left vision rests on an overcoming of "endism" in all its forms, reconciling a left politics to the openness of historical developments, and promoting a left politics that is relevant to the possibilities of a new era. A political project of democratizing social risk on a flexible and open-ended basis seems, for Dubiel, a possible path for a renewed left.

The Western left has, in practice, steadily supported liberal democracy, and many of the gains of Western democratic liberalism, as opposed to economic liberalism, have come from the major contributions of the left, often well in advance of mainstream liberal politics. Yet the idea of liberal democracy, of a parliamentary representative institution, was not the idea of socialists. This has meant, as John Mathews has noted, that:

> Social Democratic and Labour parties have always had an uneasy relationship with democracy. It was not "their" system, but one which they inherited, and have adapted to their own ends . . . yet the truth is that virtually all the gains won by the SD/L movement this century have been achieved under the protection of democracy. The creation of a public sector, the establishment of universal social security and health, education and welfare services systems, the upholding of economic activity and employment through Keynesian fiscal and monetary policies—all this has been achieved by SD/L parties wielding influence through a democratic state (1989: 1).

So what is new about the current situation, and what areas are ripe for a rethinking of the relationship of socialism and democracy? First and foremost is the critique of those organizations which have been mainstays of the democratic left politics, and which were once seen as authentic representatives of working-class and community interests, but which have suffered from the bureaucratization of power and have come to be seen as part of the problem, not part of the solution. The question of democracy is not related just to formal government institutions, but covers those civic organizations that claim to represent the interests of noncapital-owning interests. In the late period of the Keynesian welfare state, these organizations are seen as distant from the problems and perceptions of their members and potential members, in part because they are not democratic in their organizational culture and are not seen as belonging to their rank-and-file membership.

In the era of post-Fordist capitalism, the question of socialism's relation to democracy becomes once again problematic and at the same time central, according to John Mathews, the longtime Australian labor activist who has developed a vision of associative democracy as a new response for the left. In his *Age of Democracy: The Politics of Post-Fordism* (1989), he outlines a new social democratic and labor strategy that aims, first and foremost, at launching a new democratization trend as both means and end for a new left politics. In the search for a new strategy for social democratic and labor parties, Mathews analyzes the current deadend of Keynesian (Fordist) politics and argues that the answer lies in:

> democratization of economic and social life. Without democratization, any notion that ordinary people can influence the debate on our social future as much as IBM or Exxon, is ludicrous. We need to implant a *culture of democracy*. My conclusion is that democratization must now be seen as the prime strategic goal of the labour and social movements. It is the precondition for social advance. Moreover, it seems to me to be the only viable response to the industrial challenge of effecting a rupture with Fordism, and the immediate challenge posed by the New Right (1989: 220).

This criticism must be directed above all against the unions, whose leadership has become a professionalized oligarchy (just as Michels foresaw long ago), able to utilize a central autocratic power to maintain its positions and avoid grassroots intrusions into decision-making. What was (perhaps) necessary in an earlier era for effective organization of poorly educated or semiliterate factory workers, and what undeniably did achieve some leverage for organized labor in the Keynesian welfare state, is simply unattractive for the new generations of employees. And the lack of attention within traditional organized labor to issues of women's employment, or to the representation of young workers, or to the organization of part-time or decentralized service-sector workers, has meant that unionism has become less and less relevant for the emerging conflicts of post-Fordist capitalism. Aside from all the problems which face organized labor in the new globalizing economy, and which call for a real and sustained internationalization of labor organizing, the unions long ago ceased to be a movement, and many unions became privileged and entrenched interest groups in an era of growing inequality of income and wealth. Not only the middle class are outraged by unionized school janitors in New York or New Jersey who do little work and get paid $45,000 and up. I know, this isn't typical of all unions, and so what if a few lucky workers are able to beat the system? But where is the recognition within organized labor of the terrible corrosion that this causes? Where is the recognition on the left that abuses of power, even in small fiefdoms, ruin the chances for labor to attract public support for its organizing, bargaining, and strike actions? The democratization within the left needs to be forthrightly and bluntly addressed. Typical of the left today is the call for economic democracy, without any mention of democratization of those organizations most vital to a left politics, starting with the trade unions.

Alan Charney, national director of Democratic Socialists of America, in a recent editorial, says that "economic democracy is the only hope for saving political democracy." Further, there is only one class-based institution, the trade unions, which "has the capacity to take the lead in putting forth a new strategy and program for the next left" (43). Charney then lists five "fundamental changes that need to take place in the union movement—many of which have already begun."(ibid) Each of the changes is worthwhile, including transnational organizing, speaking for working people as a whole, alliances with social movements, recognition of the new role of immigrant workers for unionism, and a programmatic commitment to economic democracy. Yet Charney nowhere even mentions democratization within the union structures and the union movement itself, as if this were not even an issue. Fortunately, Charney's view, which maintains some traditional taboos of the democratic left when speaking of trade unions, is not the only view within DSA. Charney's views on the potential of trade unionism are still trapped in that tradition, whereas a renewed trade unionism is impossible without serious criticism of its own bureaucratism and its lack of democratic credentials.

Harold Meyerson, also a DSA leader, authored a pair of articles on the crisis of organized labor in the United States, in which he recounted the findings of AFL-CIO focus group studies that showed that the word *dinosaurs* was the most common connection to unions. Recent polls in the United States show that workers not only are skeptical about the effectiveness of unions in representing their interests, but are also doubtful about unions as democratic institutions (Meyerson, 1995a). There are some positive signs that a round of self-criticism is taking hold in the AFL-CIO, and that for a first time in decades, change is now on the agenda. Meyerson cites the change in leadership at the top, the resignation of Lane Kirkland, that epitome of union bureaucratic thinking, and the defeat of his chosen successor, Tom Donovan, by the somewhat more progressive and activist John Sweeney -as the opening round in a labor "perestroika" for a new era of unionism. He cites the new wave of union mergers—foremost among them the auto workers, machinists, and steelworkers—as an emerging trend. Within this trend toward merger is the new support by UAW's president Steve Yokich for a NAFTA-wide union of metalworkers in Canada, the United States, and Mexico, to bargain more effectively with transnational corporations. There is also a chance for a generational breakthrough of more activist unionists, who include far more women and minority leaders than the older union bosses. Meyerson notes the new leadership's commitment to devoting union resources to organizing on a level not seen in generations. And finally, the campaign of the reform unionist coalition "has legitimated (well partially) the idea of public dissent and self-criticism" (1995b:5). Meyerson is cautious about how much democratization will actually be realized by the new leadership, yet he places this change in leadership in the context of other changes that might well push a democracy trend within the unions:

> It's particularly auspicious that the merger movement coincides with the legitimation of dissent and internal democracy that the challenge to Kirkland and the Sweeney candidacy have offered. As the AFL-CIO's own polling shows, Americans are far more enamored of workers' rights than they are of unions, and the larger the union, the less enamored they become. A more accountable and diverse leadership will be indispensable to a union movement seeking to grow. At its best (and the UAW in the 1930s and 40s is a prime example), a union achieves a kind of oxymoron status; it's a democratic army (9).

Since the election of Sweeney as AFL-CIO chief, there have been some modest signs of renewed union activism, and Sweeney has publicly committed himself to a new and more activist, more militant unionism. Speaking to a group of labor, business, and government leaders in New York City on December 6, 1995, the new AFL-CIO head summarized his new approach:

> The carrot and the stick. The "stick" is this: On behalf of workers and their families, the leadership of the new AFL-CIO is going to challenge our unions to get busy doing what we are supposed to do. It's not just happenstance that our nation's 20-year wage decline has coincided with a 20-year decline in the power and effectiveness of the labor movement. I firmly believe, and I know some of you agree, that strong unions are vital to a thriving, high-wage economy. But, quite frankly, we haven't been holding up our end of the stick. . . . We're going to renew and rebuild our labor movement by pouring vast resources into organizing from the Sunbelt to the Rustbelt and from software writers to sweatshop workers. Our message to American workers is simple but powerful: Whether you wear a blue collar, a white collar, a new collar, or no collar, we can help you make your job better (Davis, 1995).

The question is whether this new labor activism will be based on a more democratic unionism, with regular chances for membership participation, open discussions of union actions, and responsibility of union officers to members. Sweeney himself comes from an older generation of unionists, but his election—and even more the examples of Kirkland's ouster and the defeat of Donovan as his named successor—may have set in motion a trend that does not depend just on the top leaders to maintain and build on.

Yet even within Sweeney's SEIU (Service Employees International Union), the battle for the democratization of the American union movement has just begun, and the older generation of union bosses will not be overcome quickly or easily. In Los Angeles, the SEIU was successful in organizing janitors from the Latino community into a militant workers' protest ("janitors for justice"), able to confront the largest employers in the area. The percent of janitors represented by unions went from 10 percent in 1987 to over 90 percent today. But in 1995, rank-and-file dissidents of the union felt it necessary to use the tactics of militancy within the union itself, criticizing the union leadership for being "unresponsive, undemocratic, even racist" (Nazario, 1995). They ran an opposition slate called the Multiracial Alliance in Local 399's executive board elections, and won a majority of seats. But the longtime incumbent president, Jim Zellers, has attempted to thwart the new board majority, prompting a running intra-union struggle over hiring, policies, and procedures governing Local 399. The conflict pits an insurgent, largely Hispanic rank and file against a non-Hispanic older union leadership and union leadership style. The

American union movement has avoided this type of struggle for a long time, and it now appears that it will become one of the painful hallmarks of the rebirth of the union movement, as unions broaden their base and become a stronger and more representative voice for the working class in a new era. At times this struggle within the union movement will appear to weaken it, and the conflict may indeed provide opportunities for discrediting the new unionism or splitting its membership into disunited factions; but in the longer run this conflict is, I believe, one more sign of the revitalization of this crucial sector for the new left politics. The birth of democratic insurgency within the unions is a further connection to the universalism of democracy as a centerpiece for a new left politics.

This type of analysis from within democratic left circles is not so new, but it is getting a lot more attention these days. It seems now that the movement within labor has emancipated thinking about what labor needs to do to become again a social movement, and it is in this sense that the call for democratization is essential. The democracy trend already had one earlier success (again partial) with the election of Ron Carey as head of the Teamsters Union, and the legitimation of the Teamsters for a Democratic Union (TDU) within the union. While the old corrupt, crime-linked Teamster bosses have not yet lost their hold in some regional fiefdoms, the growing competition—more or less democratic, more or less open—in this largest and for a long time most corrupted union was also a positive sign. But the question of retaining a democratic culture within the unions, and preventing a new bureaucratization and bossism from reemerging (the "iron law of oligarchy"), still remains to be bluntly addressed. Even a new, more socially diverse, and younger leadership is no guarantee at all against the re-establishment, after a while, of a new bureaucratic oligarchy. The sad experience of the Farm Workers' Union under the originally charismatic leadership of Cesar Chavez is a case in point, in the not so distant past.

Here the experience of the New Left, the Greens, and the new social movements generally may be useful. Rules that limit terms of officeholding, limit the powers of leadership, and raise the requirements for open debate and member approval, are part of a systematic attempt to develop and maintain a bottom-up democratic culture within an organizational framework. (I am well aware that the German Greens, over time, have gradually become more professionalized and have dropped some of their earlier restrictions on leaders, and yet there is good evidence that, while the trend toward professionalization and bureaucratization are strong, the democratization trend is also strong and its effects are long-lasting though obviously not uncontested.) In Germany, the example of the Greens' internal culture of open debate and dissent has affected all the major parties, which have been shamed into introducing some elements of a "democracy trend" into their own organization (cf. Nagle, 1989; Markovits and Gorski, 1993). Although there is no final solution to this dilemma—no "endism" here either— there are ways of opening up the organizational culture of the trade unions, or of developing other workers' associations with more democratic practices. The ideas and experiences for democratizing the internal life of a social organization from the new social movements provide at least some connection between the goal of democratic socialist culture and the need to rethink and reshape the union movement.

The idea of democratization is increasingly being counterposed to the ideas of antidemocratic challengers in the post-cold war era. Benjamin Barber notes in "Jihad against McWorld" (1994) that both international market laissez-faire and religious fundamentalism are "waging war against the nation-state and therefore undermining its democratic institutions." For Barber, the laissez-faire free market has not lost its basic impulse to escape any social control, including and perhaps especially democratic control. The libertarian economic dogma of laissez-faire capitalism, which has occupied much of American, and more and more of European politics in recent decades, now sees the liberal democratic state as its enemy, a hindrance to market forces and an alien force to be beaten down.

Jack Kemp may still talk about "democratic capitalism" as the shining ideal for the future, but in fact Kemp has nothing to say about the reality that global capitalism increasingly seeks out undemocratic environments (China, Mexico, Indonesia, the Philippines, Pakistan), where authoritarian regimes deny labor rights, where workers can vote only for conservative or very conservative right-wing parties, and where labor, environmental, and human rights activists are kidnapped, tortured, and murdered on behalf of the economic elites with no protection under the law. Kemp and other ideologues of the Chicago school may still preach a connection between democracy and market capitalism, but this has nothing to do with economic realities of our times. Multinationals are pushing to find sites for labor and production where they can escape democracy, where they can set up shop with the least interference from a democratically elected government, and where they can in fact rely on an undemocratic state to enforce tough labor "discipline" and submission to capital. Rhetoric aside, the entire globalization process is fueled by capital's conscious vision of escaping from even the modest social democratic confines of national Keynesianism. Fortunately, this is also fueling a growing recognition within the trade unions that their future interest is tied to real democratization wherever multinational firms set up their operations; the future course for labor is now both internationalist and democratic as the best hope for creating a counterbalance to the power surge of globalized capitalism (Borosage, 1996). A renewed socialist politics is now clearly on the side of democratization on a global scale as central to its own vision, while capitalism is veering more toward an anti-democratic orientation as central to its globalization project.

Viewing the liberal democratic state as the enemy, the ascendant economic orthodoxy of the Chicago school has tipped over into a suspicion of democracy itself; one should not be surprised that those on the right increasingly seek to limit the scope of democracy as part of their basic program of reducing state power. Not just the state and statist bureaucracy, but democratic politics generally, are now targets for the dominant right political thinkers, since it is democratic politics that legitimizes social regulation on capital and markets. "Democracies want markets, but markets don't want democracy," is Barber's conclusion. Barber's perspective is mainly left-liberal, but his insight is most helpful for the renewal of a left politics. Political liberalism is hopelessly split between its Jekyll and Hyde faces, its commitment to private property and its commitment to individual liberty; political liberalism on the whole, and especially today, is too much in love with McWorld to give priority to democratization. Conservatism is also split between its own illicit love affair with Jihad (not the Islamic Jihad of course, but the Christian right Jihad), and its kinder, more democratic, impulses of preserving and consoling. At this moment, after the collapse of socialism's "Leninist evil twin," the democratic left has an historic opportunity to renew itself through a unique, leading role as the agent of democratization, the new socialist middle against the extremes. The antidemocratic extremes of free market and religious fundamentalism are the two forces which must be challenged if democracy is to survive and thrive. Precisely for this reason, the new socialist politics should occupy the space for a democratization project now opening up in the post-cold war era.

I. Marx, Marxism, and Socialism

The relationship between Marxism and socialism has been a subject of intense debate within the left almost from the first official status given to Marx's ideas as the theoretical base of the German Social Democratic Party in the 1870s. As many have argued (Rosselli and Bobbio among the best from the Italian left), this began a process of institutionalization of Marx's ideas that reached absurd levels under the Soviet regime. This official Marxism then—in my own view as well as that of so many other critics on the left—became stultified and incapable of providing the penetrating social critique of existing society, whether Western social democracy or Soviet communism. Above all, Marx and Marxism became associated with the abuses of power and the crimes of the Stalin and post-Stalin regimes in the East, and with socialist notions of nationalization, bureaucratic statism, and welfarism in the West. As I have described elsewhere, the discovery (or rediscovery) in the West in the latter 1950s and 1960s of the writings of the young Marx revived the relevance of Marx for another generation of critical left analyses, and in my own experience this was the launching pad for a course on Marxism which I developed and taught for more than twenty years at Syracuse University.

The concept of a humanist Marx, or Marxist humanism, reached a significant young intellectual audience in both Western Europe and Eastern Europe in the 1960s; but this current of thought was unable to overcome the official Marxism-Leninism of the communist regimes of Eastern Europe, so long as the Soviet Union remained to ensure that no democratic socialist experiment would be allowed to emerge. With the military intervention against the "Prague spring" if 1968, the best chance for a humanist and democratic socialism in East-Central Europe was snuffed out. (The Polish communist regime's military suppression of the populist-socialist Solidarity union movement in 1981 reinforced the point that only the collapse of communist imperialist control from Moscow would provide an important precondition for evolution of a postcommunist socialism in that region; cf. Mahr and Nagle, 1995) . The discussions of humanist interpretations in the West (cf. Avineri, 1968; Mclellan, 1970) based on the young Marx evolved into a more comprehensive debate over the coherence of Marxism itself, including whether Marx needed to be periodized into pre-Marxist and mature Marxist years. Louis Althusser (1979) took this line to its idiotic extreme, and this debate eventually got very tiresome, which was then a de facto victory for official Marxism. Nonetheless, Western Marxism at least had the freedom, after the McCarthy-era taboos and sanctions were broken in the latter 1960s, to engage in a critical debate about Marx's ideas and their consequences for a socialist politics. Here too I must admit that citation-mongering from Marx got very tiresome at times. Even without a strong party or state to institutionalize Marxism and bureaucratize the administration of Marxist analysis, there was still some tendency for many to appeal to Marx as a final authority, or to avoid putting themselves directly at odds with Marx's ideas. This tendency, often noted by antileft critics of Marxism, needs to be brought into the debate over a more useful relationship of Marx's ideas to a new and revived socialist politics.

My course in Marxist theory was by far my most satisfying teaching experience for many years, and it offered me the opportunity to constantly review and revise my own ideas about Marx, Marxism, and the relevance of Marx's ideas to a contemporary politics of socialism. I am not a scholar of Marx, and I do not pretend to have any great insight into many of the intricacies of Marx's thought. I have learned over the years from fairly extensive reading that there is a wide spectrum of possible interpretations of Marxist theory, with a tremendous range of implications for a politics of socialism. How else could the writings and ideas of this nineteenth-century middle-class German Jewish intellectual have been adapted to reformist and revolutionary practices, in various cultures around the world, so far from Marx's own experience and time? It must in retrospect appear astounding that the socialist ideas of most of this century have been dominated and overshadowed by the ideas and contending interpretations of this single man, Karl Marx.

Is it now time to break with Marx, to consign his ideas—and even more his methods of analysis to the "dustbin of history"? More important, what remains of Marx's ideas after more than a century of historical experience and interpretation; and what are the prospects for future use of his thought? Several basic points can be made on the first aspect of this issue. First, as many Marxists have themselves pointed out, the timetable that Marx expected for the achievement of socialist revolution, and the relatively short transition to communism, were much too optimistic. Marx, as well as liberal ideologists of the nineteenth century, had a poor appreciation for the staying power of tradition, or social habit, and of resistance to change, whether driven by capitalist or socialist revolutions. Most clearly, it seems to me, Marx and other ideologists who welcome radical change (and this would include today Heidi and Alvin Toffler, promoters of the "third wave" and the conservative ideologists of laissez-faire) mistook the trend toward systematic change for a continuing and irreversible victory over social culture and traditions built up over centuries and maintained through successive waves of "radical" transformation. In this sense, Marx suffered the same limitations of thought as all "endist" philosophers, who believe that there will be some inevitable (or necessary) triumph of one value system over all contenders, once and for all.

It is time now to put Marxist "endism" in the category of failed perspectives on a much more complex and ongoing contradictory human condition, which does not allow for such a final solution. Socialists have certainly been helped by the belief that history was on their side, that socialism would one day succeed despite all current setbacks. Generations of young idealists, militant workers, and suppressed peoples around the globe have taken heart and overcome fatalism with the aid of such future-oriented visions.

More than a century after Marx's death, however, it now appears that this "escalator effect" of standing on the side of inevitable historical progress needs to be abandoned. For one thing, socialists of the previous mold have made so many predictions about the imminent crisis of capitalism (here especially I need to mention Sweezy and Magdoff of *Monthly Review*) that they have made socialist analysis unconvincing and even laughable. Clearly capitalism has had and still does have immense adaptive power; it goes through periods of "crisis," which lead to newer, more efficient, and still socially destructive forms of capitalist economy, but which never threaten its basic continuation. Socialists need to think in terms of a longer struggle without any clear victory, once and for all. All this may sound like Bernstein's "the movement is everything"—and it is related to Bernstein's notion of an evolutionary socialism, pieced together over a long period of smaller struggles for emancipation and participation of the working class in bourgeois society and political democracy. But my notion here is that socialist politics can never assume that past gains are secure, and that the smaller struggles accumulate to form an evolutionary road to a socialist society. The experiences of European fascism in the 1920s and 1930s proved that political democracy, which was the necessary precondition for Bernstein's evolutionary socialist strategy, could itself be abandoned by liberal political forces. More recently, the erosion of the social democratic welfare state in the West is further evidence of the tenuous or reversible nature of partial gains of a socialist politics. In short, a new socialist politics may need to mobilize support without either an evolutionary or a revolutionary certainty of final victory.

Would this vision of a left politics of continuous struggle—in which victories are never secure, and setbacks are also certain—be enough to energize a committed base of popular support? The answer lies in the ultimate value of a decent society with social solidarity, a strong commitment to community welfare, and a socially just order. These are values that, I believe, have found historically broad support and continuing attraction for most citizens. Socialist values, despite the best efforts of capitalist media systems to discredit them, despite the worst abuses of power in their name by communist regimes, have not only survived but are deeply engrained in the life experiences of most people. In an era of increasing inequality between classes, regions, nations, and generations, in a post-cold war world of global capitalist power unchecked by forces of social equity or democratic accountability, socialist values (and conservative values as well) will find an ample social basis for their political agendas. The question is, rather, on what basis these values can be spelled out in a practical political agenda that neither abandons the ideals of equity, justice, and community welfare, nor promises more than can be reasonably achieved in the current situation. It is the question of connecting, or reconnecting, a left politics with a "commonsense" understanding of those people most oriented toward the basic values of socialism.

Can Marx still be useful in the formulation of a new socialist agenda? My years of teaching Marx indicated the continuing power, for myself and my students, of his trenchant critique of capitalism's dynamics. Marx's own times were tied to the rise of a pre-Fordist, Taylorite capitalism; this was to be superseded in the twentieth century by the Fordist model, which went beyond what Marx had experienced but for which Marx's ideas were still relevant. There is good reason to think that, in the transition from nation-state Fordism to a newly volatile, wild global capitalism, Marx's theories will be immensely useful as a method of analysis, while his own prescriptions for possible political action will be less relevant. This is entirely in keeping with his own—and even with more Engels's own—life experience, since by the 1880s Marx had accepted the notion of plural paths to socialism, and Engels had in his last years even given up on "barricades uprisings" for socialist revolution in the European context.

Ironically, the *Wall Street Journal* paid homage to Marx in a lengthy feature just at the time of the disintegration of the Soviet Union. In a series of interviews with leading scholars, mostly non-Marxists, Henry Myers concludes that Marx, along with Freud and Einstein, has done most to shape our century, and will continue to have great and lasting influence: "But even as the newly liberated peoples of Eastern Europe and the Soviet Union celebrate Marx's apparent eclipse, others are finding fresh insights in his work. For Marx's revolutionary analysis concentrated exclusively on capitalism, not socialism, and even now, severe abuses can spring from unbridled capitalism" (Myers, 1991:A1). After duly noting the limitations of Marx's insights, and his inability to see some of the possibilities for moderating capitalism without over-throwing it, Myers concludes:

> In a general way, however, Marx's views still carry enormous weight and almost surely will do so well into the next century. His concern for ordinary workers and his belief that the government should look after them will con-tinue to echo through economic and political discourse. Few people want a return to unbridled capitalism; even ardent free marketers say some govern-ment intervention into economic affairs is necessary. The debate now is over what kind and how much (1991: A4).

Despite Myers vulgarization of Marx's views on government taking care of workers, which forgets that Marx wanted workers to take gov-ernment into their own hands, thereby taking care of themselves, this judgment does have some validity. Marx's work has done much to shape the continuing critique of capitalism, and as long as capitalism remains strong, so will Marx's insights into its working.

There is really nothing either sad or regrettable in this judgment. Marx will continue to be one of the great thinkers in the socialist tradition; at the same time, a socialist renewal will be in some good measure a post-Marxist socialism, and that is also good. The domi-nance of Marx's ideas in socialist thinking should give way to a more pluralist debate and contention of ideas, more conducive to building democratic tolerance in the socialist movement, and less vulnerable to misuse of theory through institutionalization or official recognition as dogma. Socialists might even try especially to avoid raising any ver-sion of the socialist vision to an "official" status, and encourage an ongoing pluralism of contending ideas within the broader socialist community. This pluralism of ideas was part of the nineteenth century socialist movement; Marx borrowed often from Owen, earlier from

Proudhon and Saint-Simon. What was missing then was a more conscious attempt to value a democratic pluralism of socialist ideas for its own sake. With another century of experience, perhaps that consideration could now be given greater priority.

References

A

Birnbaum, Norman (1993). "Identity Crisis on the Left" *Nation* (August 23–30) 211–212.

Conant, Oliver (1995). "Saving Democracy in the English Department," *Dissent* (Spring) 273–275.

Harrington, Michael (1986). *The Next Left*. New York: Holt.

Kennedy, Paul (1993). *Preparing for the Twenty-First Century*. New York: Vintage.

Knox, Paul, and John Agnew (1993). *Geography of the World Economy*. New York: Edward Arnold.

Leicht, Robert (1993) "Wenn die alten Lehren wanken," *die Zeit* 42 (October 22) 3.

Markovits, Andrei, and Philip Gorski (1993). *The German Left: Red, Green and Beyond*. New York: Oxford University Press.

Nagle, John (1992). "Befreiung vom Kommunismus: Denkanstöße aus dem Amerikanischen Sozialismus," *Sozialismus* (October).

Sigal, Clancy (1992). "The Karma Ran Over My Dogma" *Nation* (May 18) 651–666.

Tarzynski, Steve, and Christine Riddiough (1995). "Rethinking DSA," *Socialist Forum* 24 (October) 42–46.

Wiener, Jon (1995). "Looking for the Left's Limbaugh," *Dissent* (Spring) 160–164.

B

Cort, John (1995). "Back to the Real Beginning," *Socialist Forum* 23 (Summer) 30–32.

Cox, Harvey (1996). "The Transcendent Dimension," *Nation* 262:1 (January 1) 20–23

Dorrien, Gary (1992). "Discovering the Spiritual," *Democratic Left* 20:1 (January–February) 15–17.

Greffrath, Mathias (1995). "Vom Gewissensbiß zur Politik—Wider Tugendphrasen und wohlfeilen Zynismus," *die Zeit* 45 (November 10) 16.

Hampshire, Stuart (1974). "Epilogue," in Leszek Kolokowski and Stuart Hampshire, eds., *The Socialist Idea* New York: Basic.

Howe, Irving (1994). "Thinking about Socialism," in Frank Roosevelt and David Belkin, eds., *Why Market Socialism?* Armonk, New York: Sharpe.

John Paul II (1991). "Centesimus Annus," reprinted in *Origins* 2:1 (May 16, 1991).

Köpke, Wilfried (1995). "Ein Votum für den Aufbruch," *die Zeit* 48 (December 1) 21.

Meidner, Rudolf (1993). "Why did the Swedish Model Fail?" in R. Miliband and L. Panitch, eds. *Socialist Register* 1993. London: Merlin Press. 211–228.

Niebuhr, Gustav (1996). "Getting Below Surface of U.S. Catholics' Beliefs," *New York Times* (April 13) 11.

Piper, Nikolaus (1997). "Gott und das Geld," *die Zeit* (March 7) 11.

Ribuffo, Leo (1995). "Religion, Politics, and the Latest Christian Right," *Dissent* 42:2 (Spring) 174–176.

Steinfels, Peter (1996). "The active churches and synogogues of America have let people work for social and political goals," *New York Times* (May 4) 10.

Szulc, Tad (1995). *Pope John Paul II—The Biography.* New York: Scribners.

Toibin, Colm (1995). "The Paradoxical Pope," *New Yorker* 71:31 (October 9) 36–41.

Verba, Sidney, Kay Schlozman, and Henry Brady (1995). *Voice and Equality.* Cambridge, MA: Harvard University Press.

C

Aglietta, Michel (1987). *A Theory of Capitalist Regulation: the US Experience.* London: Verso.

Belkin, David (1994). "The Turning Point," in Frank Roosevelt and David Belkin, eds. *Why Market Socialism?* Armonk, NY: Sharpe.

———— (1995). "Our Back Pages," *Socialist Forum* 24 (October) 12–23.

Bell, Daniel (1996). *The Cultural Contradictions of Capitalism.* Twentieth Anniversary Edition. New York: Basic Books.

Chen, Feng (1995). *Economic Transition and Political Legitimacy in Post-Mao China.* Albany, NY: State University of New York Press.

Enloe, Cynthia (1975). *The Politics of Pollution in Comparative Perspective.* New York: McKay.

Harrington, Michael (1989). *Socialism: Past and Future.* New York: Arcade

Heilbroner, Robert (1990). "Reflections: After Communism," *New Yorker* (September 10) 91–100.

———— (1994) "Foreward," in Frank Roosevelt and David Belkin, eds. *Why Market Socialism?* Armonk,NY: Sharpe.

Keil, David (1995). "For an Alternative Draft," *Socialist Forum* 24 (October) 28–31.

Kelley, Donald and Kenneth Stunkel and Richard Wescott (1976). *The Economic Superpowers and the Environment*: the United States, the Soviet Union, and Japan. San Francisco: Freeman.

Knox, Paul and John Agnew (1994). *The Geography of the World Economy*. Second Edition. London: Edward Arnold..

Nagle, John (1992). "Befreiung vom Kommunismus: Denkanstöße aus dem Amerikanischen Sozialismus" *Sozialismus* 18:10 (October)

Nove, Alec (1991). *The Economics of Feasible Socialism Revisited*. London: HarperCollins.

Ophuls, William (1977). *Ecology and the Politics of Scarcity*. San Francisco: Freeman.

Roosevelt, Frank (1994). "Marx and Market Socialism," in Frank Roosevelt and David Belkin, eds. *Why Market Socialism?* Armonk,NY: Sharpe.

Schumpeter, Joseph (1942). *Capitalism, Socialism, and Democracy*. New York: Harper.

D

Barkan, Joanne (1995). "Affirmative Action" *Dissent* (Fall) 461–463.

Barry, Brian (1995). "Spherical Justice and Global Injustice" in David Miller and Michael Walzer, eds., *Pluralism, Justice, and Equality*. Oxford: Oxford University Press.

Carens, Joseph (1995). "Complex Justice, Cultural Difference, and Political Community" in David Miller and Michael Walzer, eds., *Pluralism, Justice, and Equality*. Oxford: Oxford University Press.

Conant, Oliver (1995). "Saving Democracy in the English Department," *Dissent* (Spring) 273–275.

Ehrenreich, Barbara (1995). "Thoughts on Being in the Minority," *Socialist Forum* 24 (October) 84–85.

Gurr, Ted, and Peter Grabosky and Richard Hula (1977). *The Politics of Crime and Conflict*. Beverly Hills, CA: Sage.

Gutmann, Amy (1995). "Justice across the Spheres" in David Miller and Michael Walzer, eds., *Pluralism, Justice, and Equality*. Oxford: Oxford University Press.

Lerner, Michael (1995). "Stop Liberals and the Left from Blowing It Again in 1996," *Nation* 261:17 (November 20).

Lind, Michael (1995a). "Affirmative Action" *Dissent* (Fall) 470-472.

——— (1995b). *The Next American Nation*. New York: Free Press.

Miller, David and Michael Walzer, eds. (1995). *Pluralism, Justice, and Equality*. Oxford: Oxford University Press.

Nagle, John (1992). "In Banks We Trust" in Hans See and Dieter Schenck, eds. *Wirtschaftverbrechen: Der innere Feind der freien Marktwirtschaft*. Cologne: Kiepenneuer & Witsch.

——— (1993). "Ein justizkritischer Nachtrag zum US-Bankenskandal der Savings & Loan," *BCC-Info* 2: 2 (1993).

——— (1995). *Introduction to Comparative Politics: Challenges of Conflict and Change in a New Era*. fourth edition. Chicago: Nelson-Hall.

Pizzo, Stephen, Mary Fricker, and Paul Muolo (1991). *Inside Job: The Looting of America's Savings and Loans*. New York: HarperCollins.

Rorty, Richard (1996). "Sins of the Overclass," *Dissent* 43:2 (Spring) 109–112.

Rustin, Michael (1995). "Equality in Post-Modern Times," in David Miller and Michael Walzer, eds., *Pluralism, Justice, and Equality*. Oxford: Oxford University Press.

Scherrer, Christoph, and Lars Maischak (1995). "Abschied von der 'farbenblinden' Gesellschaft," *Blätter für deutsche und internationale Politik* 12 (December) 1451–1459.

See, Hans (1990). *Kapitalverbrechen*. Düsseldorf: Claasen.

Shapiro, Bruce (1996). "How the War on Crime Imprisons America," *Nation* 262:16 (april 22) 14–22

Tomasky, Michael (1996). "Reaffirming Our Actions," *Nation* 262:19 (May 13) 21–24.

Walzer, Michael (1983). *Spheres of Justice*. New York: Basic.

Willis, Ellen (1995) "A Neocon Goes Back to Class," *Nation* 261:6 (August 28) 211–214.

Yeager, Peter, and Marshal Clinard (1980) *Corporate Crime*. New York: Free Press.

E

Alterman, Eric (1995). "Loose Buchanan," *Nation* 261:18 (November 27) 654–655.

Barkan, Joann (1993). "Clinton at Five Months," *Democratic Left* (July–August) 2.

Charney, Alan (1992). "Elect Bill Clinton," *Democratic Left* (September–October) 2.

——— (1994). "The Meaning of 1994," *Democratic Left* (November-December) 13.

——— (1995). "Present Progressive," *Democratic Left* (January-February) 31.

Clark, Jack, (1992). "Clinton and Us," *Democratic Left* (November–December) 2.

Cowell, Susan, (1993), "National Health Care: The Next Steps," *Democratic Left* (September–October)

Gitlin, Todd (1995). *The Twilight of Common Dreams: Why America is Wracked by Culture Wars.* NY: Metropolitan Books.

Greider, William (1993). *Who Will Tell the People?* New York: Simon and Shuster.

Harrington, Michael (1985). The Next Left. New York: Holt.

——— (1989) *Socialism: Past and Future.* New York: Arcade.

Heidenheimer, Arnold, and High Heclo and Carolyn Teich Adams (1990). *Comparative Public Policy : The Politics of Social Choice in America, Europe, and Japan.* New York: St. Martin's.

Isserman, Maurice (1992). "The Times, They are A-Changin' Again?" *Democratic Left* (November–December) 22.

Markovits, Andrei, and Philip Gorski (1993). *The German Left—Red, Green and Beyond.* New York: Oxford.

Mort, Jo-Ann (1995). "Labor's Troubles," *Dissent* (Spring) 179–182.

Nagle, John (1989). "The West German Greens: An Evolving Response to Political Conflict," in L.Kriesberg, T. Northrup, and S. Thorson, eds., *Intractable Conflicts and Their Transformations.* Syracuse, NY: Syracuse University Press.

——— (1992) "Befreiung vom Kommunismus: Denkanstöße aus dem Amerikanischen Sozialismus," *Sozialismus* 18:10 (October) 65–70.

Piven, Frances Fox, ed. (1992). *Labor Parties in Postindustrial Societies.* New York: Oxford University Press.

Renger, Annemarie (1995). "SPD Honors Its Past, " *The Week in Germany* (October 13).

Skocpol, Theda (1994). "Has the Time Finally Arrived?" *Democratic Left* (March–April) 6–7.

Stimson, Catharine (1995). "Acting Up and Opting Out," *Nation* 261:21 (December 18) 791–792.

Wilpert, Gregory (1993). "Revolutionary Cadre Politics and Terrorism," in Andrei Markovits and Philip Gorski, *The German Left—Red, Green and Beyond.* New York: Oxford University Press.

F

Baiman, Ron (1995). "Reponse to: 'A New DSA Political Perspectives Statement,'" *Socialist Forum* 24 (October) 7–9.

Barkan, Joanne (1995). "Wishful Thinking," *Socialist Forum* 24 (October) 10–11.

Beck, Ulrich (1995). *Ecological Enlightenment: essays on the politics of the risk society* (translated from *Politik in der Risikogesellschaft*) Atlantic Highlands, NJ: Humanities Press.

Belkin, David (1995). "Our Back Pages," *Socialist Forum* 24 (October) 12–23.

———— (1996). "The Left and Limited Government," *Socialist Forum* 26 (Summer–Winter) 4–6.

Economist (1994). "Labour's Ladder of Opportunity" *Economist* (October 8)

Gong, Ting (1994). *Politics of Corruption in Contemporary China* Westport, CT: Praeger.

Harrington, Michael (1989). *Socialism: Past and Future.* New York: Arcade.

Heidenheimer, Arnold, Hugh Heclo and Carolyn Teich Adams (1990). *Comparative Public Policy: the Politics of Social Choice in America, Europe, and Japan.* New York: St. Martin's.

Kelber, Harry (1994) "LaborTalk: AFL-CIO Shocked by Survey It Commissioned," *Leftnews email* (December 18).

Krönig, Jürgen (1995). "Der große Reformator," *die Zeit* 40 (October 6) 4.

Nagle, John (1977). *System and Succession: The Social Bases of Political Elite Recruitment.* Austin, TX: University of Texas Press.

———— (1995). *Introduction to Comparative Politics: Challenges of Conflict and Change in a New Era.* fourth edition Chicago: Nelson-Hall.

Townsend, Peter (1995). "Persuasion and Conformity: An Assessment of the Borrie Report on Social Justice," *New Left Review* 213 (September/October) 137–150.

Walzer, Michael (1982). "Politics in the Welfare State," in Irving Howe, ed. *Beyond the Welfare State.* New York: Schocken Books.

G

Arrighi, Giovanni (1990). "Marxist Century—American Century: The Making and Remaking of the World Labor Movement," in S. Amin, G. Arrighi, A. G. Frank, and I. Wallerstein, eds., *Transforming the Revolution.* New York: Monthly Review Press.

Bacon, David (1995). "Laboring to Cross the NAFTA Divide," *Nation* 261:16 (November 13) 572–574.

Broad, Dave (1995). "Globalization versus Labor," *Monthly Review* 47:7 (December) 20–31.

Coughlin, Ginny (1995). "Power Across Borders: From global solidarity to global organizing," *Democratic Left* 24:5 (September-October) 14–18.

Daniels, Robert (1960). *Conscience of the Revolution: Communist Opposition in Soviet Russia.* Cambridge: Harvard University Press.

Harrington, Michael (1989). *Socialism: Past and Future.* New York: Arcade.

Knox, Paul, and John Agnew (1994). *The Geography of the World Economy.* second edition. London: Edward Arnold.

Koestler Arthur (1941). *Darkness at Noon.* New York: Macmillan.

LaLuz, José (1994). "Social Justice in the Americas," *Democratic Left* 22:3 (May-June) 3–5.

Mathews, John (1989). *Age of Democracy: The Politics of Post-Fordism.* Melbourne, Australia: Oxford University Press.

Murphy, Craig (1994). *International Organization and Industrial Change.* New York: Oxford University Press.

Piven, Frances Fox, ed. (1992) *Labor Parties in Postindustrial Societies.* New York: Oxford University Press.

Schantz, Penny (1992). "There is Power in a Union: International Labor Solidarity in West Virginia," *Democratic Left* 20:5 (September-October) 16–18.

Stand, Kurt (1993). "Global Thinking, Global Action: The New Labor Internationalism," *Democratic Left* 21:5 (September-October) 29–30.

Townsend, Peter (1995). "Persuasion and Conformity: An Assessment of the Borrie Report on Social Justice," *New Left Review* 213 (September-October) 137–150.

H

Avineri, Shlomo (1968). *The Social and Political Thought of Karl Marx.* Cambridge: Cambridge University Press.

Barber, Benjamin (1994). "Zwischen Dschihad und McWorld," *die Zeit*, 42 (October 21) 16.

Bobbio, Norberto (1987). *Which Socialism? Marxism, Socialism and Democracy.* Minneapolis: University of Minnesota Press.

——— (1989). *Democracy and Dictatorship.* With an Introduction by John Keane. Minneapolis: University of Minnesota Press.

Borosage, Robert (1996) "Global Reach: Workers Fight the Multinationals," *Nation* (March 18) 21–24.

Charney, Alan (1995). "Present Progressive" *Democratic Left* 23:3 (September–October) 43.

Davis, Warren (1995). "Sweeney's Speech to NY Bosses," *labornews email* (December 10).

Dubiel, Helmut (1994) "Was, bitte, ist heute noch links?" *die Zeit* 12 (March 25) 5.

Hunt, Richard (1974). *The Political Ideas of Marx and Engels.* Pittsburgh, PA: University of Pittsburgh Press.

Markovits, Andrei and Philip Gorski (1993). *The German Left: Red, Green, and Beyond.* New York: Oxford University Press.

Mathews, John (1989). *Age of Democracy: The Politics of Post-Fordism.* Melbourne, Australia: Oxford University Press.

Meyerson, Harold (1995a). "Labor Pains," *New Yorker* (October 30)

——— (1995b). "Perestroika on Sixteenth Street," *Democratic Left* 23:5 (September–October).

Nagle, John (1989). "The West German Greens: An Evolving Response to Political Conflict," in L. Kriesberg, S. Thorson, and T. Northrup, eds., *Intractable Conflicts and Their Transformation.* Syracuse, NY: Syracuse University Press.

——— (1991). *Looking at Marx: A Student Manual.* Syracuse, NY: Center for Instructional Development.

Nazario, Sonia (1995). "Hunger Strike Marks Union's Split," *leftnews email* (August 11), from *Los Angeles Times* August 8, 1995, Home.

I

Althusser, Louis (1979). *For Marx.* London: Verso.

Avineri, Shlomo (1968). *The Social and Political Thought of Karl Marx.* Cambridge: Cambridge University Press.

Mahr, Alison and John Nagle (1995). "Resurrection of the Successor Parties and Democratization in East-Central Europe," *Communist and Post-Communist Studies* 28:4 (December).

Mclellan, David (1970). *Marx before Marxism*. New York: Harper and Row.

Myers, Henry (1991). "His Statues Topple, His Shadow Persists: Marx Can't Be Ignored," *Wall Street Journal* (November 25) A1.

Chapter V

Three White Guys Named Mike: Their Progress Report

In the summer of 1996 I happened to be browsing in my local Barnes and Noble superstore, a pleasant pastime for my tastes, and noticed three new entries, almost side by side, on the nonfiction display at the entranceway. There in front of me lay Michael Lind's *Up From Conservatism*, Michael Tomasky's *Left for Dead*, and Michael Lerner's *Politics of Meaning*. From the names and titles alone I guessed that this trio of new works could provide me with some new inputs for my own rethinking of a left politics, and perhaps with some luck could offer some broader perspective on just how far this rethinking had progressed, at least on the American scene. These were the works of three white American males (three white guys named Mike), and were not necessarily representative of much new thinking from feminist or African-American corners of the overall left spectrum; but after a few weeks of reading and evaluating these three works, I decided that they did, as a group, represent for me a good overview of where the process of rethinking and renewing a left politics stands, what has been achieved, and what remains (lots) to still be accomplished. Moreover, I believe that the symbolic appearance in the same political season of three innovative essays by this trio of white male Americans is a telling sign of where the left discourse on renewal stands, in all its glory and agony. I am much impressed by the symbolism of this chance trio, and have taken this as a clear sign of a breakthrough in the difficult struggle to rebuild a viable left politics. In some ways, my optimism about the process of left political renewal was affirmed by this partially coincidental event. Coincidence in the world of political discourse is often not chance happenings at all, but early, telltale signals of what is to come on a much larger scale and with much greater political impact—down the line. What follows is a review of major points of rethinking and renewal from these recent works, and of what I view in them as signs of progress in the left renewal project.

A. Michael Lind in Search of a Progressive Political Debate

I start here, as I started with my reading, with a recent work by Michael Lind, accurately and provocatively titled *Up from Conservatism*. I, like many others on the left, have been dismayed over the years by the defection of valuable intellectual talent from the left, often accompanied by parting shots: accusation and proclamations of emancipation from false ideas and dogmatic practices within the left intellectual community. This emptying out of left intellectual talent went hand in hand with the salaried promotion of a cadre of right-wing conservative thinkers and promoters of new (or refurbished) conservative ideas. Clearly the tide of talent, whatever one might think of the specific ideas represented, went from left to right—a historic reversal of the preponderance of intellectual thought in the West since the Great Depression. Although one might continue to disagree with this exodus, arguing instead that dissident voices on the left should stay with the "cause" and try to influence the course of left politics within the broad left spectrum of ideas and groups, it could not have been more apparent that for many talented and insightful people, this was either no longer intellectually attractive or so personally conflictual that exit to another political standpoint was preferable.

Notable intellectual defection had of course marked the left intellectual movement in the West at earlier points as well; in the period after World War I some former left syndicalists defected to fascism especially; and in the aftermath of the show trials and the 1939 Molotov-Ribbentrop Pact, many in the West and in the United States broke not only with the pro-Soviet left but with all leftist politics. Yet in these earlier periods there remained a strong current of fresh left thinking, new critiques of Western capitalist societies and a hopeful and future-oriented politics based on an alternative vision of a more just, more humane society. Even in the 1960s, the discovery or popularization of the writings of the young Marx, the humanist Marx, the Marx with insights on human alienation in modern capitalist society, found resonance with young intellectuals who were then actively opposing the Vietnam War and Western imperialism abroad, and domestic racism and self-centered consumerism in their prosperous, liberal democratic societies. But by the latter 1970s, the decline of a coherent left vision for younger intellectuals had set in, and middle-aged political thinkers—who had once populated the pages of progressive journals and had produced early works of some promise for continuing the evolution of a viable left politics based on a compelling vision of a better society—were moving on or moving out. By the time of the collapse of the Soviet empire and the Soviet Union itself, the young Francis Fukuyama could even cobble together a semi-Hegelian analysis of the end of ideological struggle and proclaim an end to viable left political thinking about the future of human society. More and more, the new ideas for change and reform being actively promoted and disseminated through Western society were from the right, from conservative thinktanks and conservative journals. So when, in late 1992, Michael Lind, one of the new generation of carefully groomed and generously supported intellectual talents of the American conservative movement, defected and went over to the left (the center-left to be sure, but for any careful reader clearly the left), this was at least an anomaly of recent times, and perhaps an important harbinger of something important yet to come. And it was.

Michael Lind has provided in his recent work convincing evidence of the exhaustion, after thirty years (from 1955, the founding year of Buckley's *National Review*, to the mid-1980s), of vital and challenging intellectual debate on the conservative right, and the calcifying institutionalization, and power-seeking corruption of the intellectual core of the conservative movement. That this has been charged all along by the left was both unconvincing and until recently, wrong; the Buckley conservatives and the post-1968 neoconservatives had provided a valuable critique of the Keynesian welfare state, and had worked to revive a conservative politics, which had been intellectually exhausted after the Great Depression and the failure of Western conservatives to clearly and firmly denounce European fascism.

Lind's work is remarkable for its clear and telling presentation of the intricacies of postwar conservatism. It is a valuable contribution to the history of an ideological revival, one that Lind believes has gone wrong, but a rethinking and a revival nonetheless. Lind would have remained a conservative if the neocons of the 1970s had been motivated and capable of fashioning what he terms a "one-nation conservatism" along the lines of German Christian Democracy or French Gaullism (1996: 47–48). For Lind, a one-nation conservatism included elements of Catholic social thought, the concept of a social market economy, and a solidarity across classes that commits the upper class to support welfare state measures for the entire society. In the early postwar years, Peter Viereck, Reinhold Niebuhr, and Arthur Schlesinger Jr. represented the core of a moderate centrist conservatism along these lines. Lind's story is one of growing dismay at the failure to build a one-nation conservatism in America, and disgust at the conservative elite's embrace of a "two-nation" formula of supply-side economics and populism based on white resentment: "The capitulation of the neoconservatives in the 1990s, following the defeat of the new conservatives in the 1950s, has doomed the enterprise of an intelligent, moderate, centrist conservatism in the United States. This was a project to which I was committed for a decade. The story of the failure of one-nation conservatism is, in a small way, my own story" (46). Lind's purpose here is to expose this failure in the most glaring way: "It is too late to rescue American conservatism from the radical right. But it is not too late to rescue America from conservatism" (269).

Most interesting is Lind's analysis of the Southernization of American conservatism, the gradual defeat of the Eastern moderate wing of the Republican Party and the rise of the "Southern strategy," which in Lind's evaluation becomes the leading strategy for American conservative politics nationwide. This conservatism, which claims to be radical—even revolutionary—is in fact counterrevolutionary, built on a program of eliminating the past sixty years of American political tradition and taking American society back to the pre-Depression era of class warfare, probusiness government, and raw manipulation by moneyed elites of religion, ethnicity, and race in order to divide and rule. Lind details the "money connection" from right-wing foundations led by radical ideologues of unfettered capitalism to the journals and thinktanks, which churn out policy manifestos and groom would-be policy wonks (such as Lind in his decade among them), to the populist organizations that provide the mass base for the movement. Lind is at the top of his game when quoting from Michael Joyce, head of the right-wing Bradley Foundation, at a *National Review*-sponsored conference in Washington. After quoting extensively from Joyce's address, Lind concludes:

> If further proof is needed for my contention that much of today's conservative political theory is merely Marxism which the substitution of "bourgeois" for "proletariat" and "culture" for "class," it can be found in Joyce's call for enlisting art and literature in the service of Republican conservatism, a program

that is indistinguishable, except in its content, from the aesthetic orthodoxy of American communists during the 1920s and 1930s (92).

The issue that for Lind represented the breaking point was the refusal of conservative intellectuals to confront Pat Robertson on his crackpot theories of how the world works, theories involving Illuminati, Masons, and European (read Jewish) bankers. Under the general heading of "no enemies on the right," conservative strategists have continued to accept Robertson's conspiracy theories as respectable and useful elements of their movement, since the Christian Coalition provides a mass base of support for the right's otherwise all too elitist economic agenda. Lind and a few others had tried to prod conservative movement thinkers to repudiate Robertson's ideas, or at least to repudiate the anti-Semitism that they incorporated, but without effect. When Norman Podhoretz, a founding father of the neo-con right, argues that despite some flaws, Robertson's ideas were quite okay with him, Lind comments: "For Podhoretz, it seems practically any lunacy can be forgiven the conspiracy-mongering leader of a mass movement, as long as he supports Israel" (112). The inability of the leading intellectual forces on the right to break with Robertson and to denounce his weird and harmful ideas was for Lind a final proof that the right had lost its capacity for reasonable self-criticism, in favor of the pursuit of power through whatever religious fundamentalist ideas, however distant from reality, would provide the critical votes and workers for the conservative cause.

As an insider to this internal feud, Lind can report the depth of cynicism of many thinkers on the right, including one (unnamed) editor of whom Lind reports: "He wanted to know why I was so critical of the religious right. I told him that its leader was a crackpot who claimed that Jews and Freemasons were running the world. What more reason did anybody need? The conservative editor replied: "Of course they're mad, but we need their votes" (117). This is not peculiar only to the right's treatment of Robertson; it also characterized the right's refusal to denounce far-right cults and armed militias, and its accusatory stance against federal government and federal law enforcement role. Several of the new "Gingrich revolutionaries" elected to Congress in 1994, including Helen Chenoweth of Idaho, have themselves pushed various conspiracy theories. (Chenoweth believes that black helicopters are conducting surveillance flights to monitor patriotic groups, and that there are plans to round up patriots and put them in concentration camps). By failing to separate conservatism from crackpot demagogy, the right has opted for a seamless strand of connections, which help legitimize far-right ideas and their representatives.

The right's defense of Robertson was part of a larger project—adapting the Southern strategy as the national strategy for the Republican Party:

> The new southern-style conservatism is much more radical than Taft's midwestern conservatism or Buckley's Manhattan conservatism or the Beltway conservatism of the neocons in the 1980s. Neo-southern conservatism unites intense hostility to the national government with ruthless, cutthroat capitalism. The politics of neo-southern conservatism is based on the 'culture war'— a euphemism for the old-fashioned southern demagogy that distracted poor white voters from the realities of their exploitation by the rich and the corporations by means of theatrical denunciations of blacks, Catholics, Jews, atheists, homosexuals, modern artists, Darwinian biologists, and various other supposed enemies of the people." (119–120)

Of course, there were reasons why the right was able to mobilize millions of middle Americans around crackpot themes and social populist resentments, and Lind traces these, as he has done in earlier works (Lind, 1995), to the 1960s New Left. For the new Lind, the old New Deal was the height of progressive practical politics in America. Lind extols both the New Deal and the Great Society, and asserts:

> Had history turned out differently, had the FDR-Truman-Johnson-Humphrey wing survived as the dominant force in the Democratic party into the 1970s and 1980s, the continuing vitality of New Deal liberalism might have given credibility to the moderate Eisenhower-Rockefeller wing of the GOP. In such an America, it seems doubtful that Ronald Reagan would have been elected in 1980 or that a Republican Congress would have come to power in 1994. If the Democrats during the past generation had been identified, like Lyndon Johnson and Hubert Humphrey, with race-neutral civil rights reform, generous entitlements for wage-earning Americans, and a foreign policy that avoided the extremes of pacifism and paranoia, then a second, integrationist phase of the New Deal might have succeeded the segregated first phase. Racial quotas and supply-side economics might have been equally unknown. Had color-blind New Deal liberalism survived, it is unlikely that the United States, on the verge of the twenty-first century, would be in the control of a Washington cabal of reactionary white politicians from the South and West and their corporate sponsors (23).

Lind blames the defeat of New Deal liberalism as much on the wrong-headed 1968ers as on any attractive ideas from the New Right of the 1970s and 1980s. For Lind, there were no good reasons for the New

Left—only an unrepresentative, favored generation who wanted to reject the authority of their parents, and who found an outlet in the Vietnam War. For Lind, this rebellion in fact "resulted from conformity to the tradition of the tiny subculture from which the New Left emerged" (26–27). Lind, who was born in 1962 and therefore did not experience the 1960s generational rebellion from either the perspective of a young adult or that of the parents of that time, simply finds it impossible to justify the New Left politics on any grounds, and he cannot find any redeeming value in the 1960s. Lind's own idea of a new progressive politics centers on what he calls "national liberalism," a color- and gender-blind, integrationist, welfare-oriented revival of the New Deal and the Great Society for the post-cold war era. This is a center-left liberalism, which seeks to build a broad middle majority to continue that grand tradition.

For example, on the economy, Lind argues:

> The national liberals rejected both socialism and laissez-faire for what used to be called "the mixed economy" and what is now called "the social market'—a system of private property and free enterprise characterized by government entitlements protecting citizens from the vicissitudes of the market and a substantial degree of regulation in the public interest. The model of capitalism that prevailed in the economic competition with communist countries is social-market capitalism, not laissez-faire capitalism. Once again, the national liberals have been vindicated by history, and their leftist and conservative adversaries have been discredited." (261)

Likewise, on the cold war foreign policy of containment, and on racial integration, it was national liberals who were correct, holding a middle position between left and right. Lind had previously outlined , in his *The Next American Nation*, his vision for a future viable center-left politics, which would "combine features of the conventional 'left' and the conventional 'right'" (266). It would end affirmative action and racial quotas in favor of stronger antidiscrimination laws and stricter enforcement; defend and reform (not destroy) the welfare system; restrict immigration; and, in foreign policy, defend the interests of the United States as a great power through a strong but not overblown military. On the question of free trade, Lind argues for protection of national security interests; his nationalism contains a good dose of caution on the ideology of free trade, and on the role of a strong national government in determining national security priorities with respect to the international economy. Comparing his vision with that of the Clinton neoliberals who share many goals of the New Deal and the Great Society—such as full employment, universal health care, a good public education system, and racial integration—but now seek to downsize and decentralize government, Lind argues, "In most cases, the neoliberals are mistaken—the goals of big-government liberalism can be achieved only by big-government means" (268).

I have lots of reservations about Lind's "national liberalism," not least its blind eye to the globalization of capital, a new factor that has enabled capital to undertake its new offensive against the Keynesian welfare state, against the "social market economy," against every class compromise that was constructed to enable the West to prevail in the cold war against the appeal of a communist alternative. Lind has virtually nothing to say about this. There is in his nationalist vision virtually no place for international labor politics or labor organizing. Lind is likewise silent on many of the failings of big government welfare statism; for the most part, he holds that the conservative attacks on tax burdens, the failings of public education, and illegitimacy are "hoaxes," based on little empirical evidence, a perverse use of statistics, and well-marketed folk tales of the horrors of big bureaucracy. Lind does not seem to take seriously the acceptance of these attacks by large parts of his white ethnic middle America, from some personal experience of their own. His views on the success of the new conservative offensive give too much credit to corporate funding and conservative idea-marketers and political spin-masters, and not enough to the common sense of citizens. Although Lind does a great service in defending the successes and even historic triumphs of New Deal and Great Society policies, he is too quiet on the self-limiting boundaries of those policies, which account for the emergence of the New Left and the challenge of identity politics, and the rise of a Southern strategy of conservatism on the right. Lind pays no attention to the growth of a new suburbanized and more conservative middle class as a result of the successes of the postwar Keynesian formula, a new middle class of white ethnics migrating from the big cities into a new status, and unsurprisingly, into a new political outlook. The fact that these new middle-class arrivals, and the many wannabes still aspiring and working to gain this status, had little interest in advancing the mobility of other, culturally more distant groups such as blacks, Hispanics, new waves of non-European immigrants, and to some extent women (although here the picture is far more complex), is also basic to understanding the outer limits of the old New Deal coalition, and the new opportunities offered to Republican conservatives for reviving their own electoral base. Without some recognition of this enormous shift in class interests among the older European ethnic groups that made up the original New Deal coalition, Lind's call for a revival of this old formula seems less than convincing; and it also helps to explain why Lind cannot come to terms with the new politics or later the New Left challenges to that old formula.

A revitalized progressive coalition must include great parts of the New Left constituencies among blacks, Hispanics, women, and environmentalists, but it also must, as Lind argues, recenter the political debate by speaking effectively—in terms of class—to his "vital center" New Deal audiences. The working class of the 1990s is very different from that of the 1930s or the early 1960s, and there are legacies from the New Left which are worthwhile retaining (for example the emphasis on democratic participation, applied—for example—to unions). The left-liberal call for democratization within the Democratic party, as I remember it from my own political work in 1967–1968, was a reaction to nondemocratic, corrupt practices such as those employed against the McCarthy campaign (Eugene McCarthy was clearly from the old New Deal tradition, and did not represent any kind of "identity" politics), following the disgraceful treatment of the integrated Mississippi Freedom Democratic party challenge delegation at the Democratic convention in 1964. Lind does not understand that the erosion of the Roosevelt-Johnson-Humphrey tradition did not arise out of some adolescent "acting out" pranks, but from a series of serious challenges against the limitations placed on many citizens in their jobs, lifestyles, and politics under the hegemony of the postwar Keynesian warfare-welfare state. The challenge to the postwar Keynesian consensus from the New Left was in fact an early, perhaps premature, effort at rethinking a left politics in reaction to its glaring flaws and shortcomings. It was not a temper tantrum of an irrational younger generation (although one can certainly find examples of such), nor just a mistaken whimsy—now to be simply dismissed and thrown away.

Nonetheless, Lind's vision of a revived progressive politics does show the way toward a new synthesis, or new alternative syntheses. He utilizes the best of conservative criticisms (although he does not utilize the best of earlier New Left thinking), and his project is aimed at regaining the broad center ground of American politics; he offers a vision with wide appeal, even though I believe its international aspects need to be extended and revised considerably. Lind's work of-

fers hope that vital new thinkers are in fact abandoning the right because of its rigidified thinking and its refusal to deal with its own dark
side, the demagogy of the Robertsons and the Buchanans. I believe
that, although new, young intellectual talent still being groomed in the
right's power nexus, the best and brightest will seek out and will be
drawn to the more interesting and more open intellectual debate on
the left.

B. Michael Tomasky on a Commonsense Left Politics

The second Mike is Michael Tomasky, whose work *Left for Dead—
The Life, Death, and Possible Resurrection of Progressive Politics
in America* sounds many of the same themes as does Michael Lind,
but with an important difference. Tomasky comes to his analysis of
the left with a sympathy and understanding for the New Left politics
which came out of the 1960s. Unlike Lind, who believes that 1968
was an unnecessary and unmitigated disaster for a viable center-left
politics, Tomasky, a former reporter for the *Village Voice*, one of the
leading lights of the generational politics of 1968, shared, at one time,
many of the rationales for the break with the Old Left labor-centered
politics. For him, the New Left was a necessary recognition of some
severe failings of the Old Left, with its exclusion of women and minorities, its hostile attitude toward gays, its support for imperial American wars overseas and for the national security state generally. Yet,
thirty years later, Tomasky, like many others of that generation who
were also antiwar, profeminist, and proenvironment, now sees "just
how wrong things have gone—how notions that were useful and exciting and new in 1968 have stiffened and have, in the hands of lesser
intellects than Foucault and his contemporaries, turned into tepid paro-
dies of themselves" (1996: 23).

A major theme throughout Tomasky's work, and perhaps the underlying message tying together many diverse strands and stands, is
the need for a sense of a practical progressive politics. In so many
ways, Tomasky finds that once useful ideas have been taken to impractical or nonsensical extremes. Of course, one can argue that sticking
to principle is required, that compromise or partial measures only
water down a left agenda and end by making significant or radical
transformations impossible. This is, of course, the age-old question,
fought out by all change-oriented movements, of all persuasions: the
weighing of principle versus pragmatism. Tomasky clearly has decided

that what remains of the left, and especially of identity politics, has become entirely impractical, has lost touch with the commonsense of most Americans ("self-marginalization"), and has thus turned into an impediment to the very causes it supports:

> An excellent example of this is the hate speech debate. Here we find in convergence emery lamentable tendency the left falls prey to: the emphasis on group identity and the outright denial of either individual or universal identity (and also of universal values, such as freedom of speech); the forging ahead through the legal byways without attempting to establish anything approaching popular consensus; and the reliance on finely wrought legalistic arguments that will do nothing at all in practical terms to change the world—except, possibly, to harden and strengthen the opposition. The end result is that the First Amendment is placed at risk, with little hope that the types of speech these proposed codes seek to punish will actually ebb and the ironic prospect that such laws, if enacted, will be used against the very "oppressed groups" they're intended to protect (44).

For Tomasky, the supreme irony is that historically it was the left which fought hardest for freedom of speech and its protection under the law, as a fundamental requisite both for individual political liberty and for political organizing on behalf of progressive causes. Here Tomasky bluntly attacks what many on the left have believed but have silently tolerated for years: the political correctness doctrines of a small and self-marginalized sect, which lead nowhere and change nothing:

> Finally, the equating of speech and action, an idea that the critical legal theorists lifted from antipornography warrior Catherine MacKinnon, blurs the line between the rhetoric of empowerment and the real conditions of people's lives. The idea that speech and action are the same thing is absurd, as is the idea that placing a cordon of disapprobation around a certain type of speech can have any impact whatsoever on the world's material conditions (49).

This accusatory language is remarkable because it comes from someone who has, despite all the craziness and ill-conceived projects of left identity politics, decided to remain on the left and fight openly and vigorously for a different left agenda. This is another sign of the sea change among intellectuals and political thinkers, who are deciding not to defect to an intellectually stultifying and ideologically perverse right-wing. (The neocon migration is a past tense happening—it is now history, not prophecy.) Those who were committed to some progressive left ideals and who deplore the nonsense of—and the perversion of left politics by—small self-marginalizing sects, are becoming more hopeful that a new, rethought progressive politics is possible, and that the alienated sectarianism of the left can be overcome. Even if there are major questions about how long this will take, and what form a new politics will assume, there is a feeling that the intellectual struggle worth fighting is on the left.

Tomasky provides valuable insights into how the American left got into its current predicament, and how many of its ideas had antecedents in earlier periods. For example, identity politics was clearly present in the New Deal coalition and in the union movement, when Irish, Jewish, Italian, Polish, and other ethnic groups formed factions of that coalition, and an "ethnic balance" was required for city politics in Chicago and New York and for union organizing committees. Tomasky also gives credit to the more recent causes related to identity—which, however, have gone wrong in their rejection of assimilation into the larger society as accepted first-class citizens, no more and no less:

> Within today's left, identity is, if not everything, then at least the dock from which all investigations are launched.
>
> This is by no means all bad, and in fact many developments that are rooted in identity politics have had a salutary effect on the broader culture. The women's movement has given American women many opportunities, and gay men and lesbians see much more tolerance than they once did. The writing of history has changed dramatically for the better, and we're more aware of the cultural biases in our history and national mythology (79–80).

Yet while there have been gains for each identity group in opportunities in the larger culture, in political terms this focus has been a disaster. Tomasky argues that this disaster has led in many cases to a pessimistic "postmodernist" view, derived from a poor interpretation of Michel Foucault's writings, that downplays the political struggle with the state and stresses instead the struggle of the most marginalized out-groups. This was part of the turn by the more radical identity warriors against mainstream working-class politics, a turn away from concepts of class struggle and visions of challenge to the economic order:

> There are signs that identity's stranglehold of leftist politics is abating. Perhaps the battering the left has taken in the culture wars, combined with the right's undeniable triumph at the polls, has finally caused the left to rethink these questions. Kennedy, West (his role in the march aside), Henry Louis Gates, Jr., and K. Anthony Appiah among the African American thinkers who have tried in their writings to find a place where the particular and the

universal can meet. . . . People will always organize themselves around group interests. But when the group interest pushes everything else to the side and makes demands on others that are intolerant, unreasonable, and against the spirit of critical inquiry—which the left, in better days, held dear—then something has gone terribly wrong. And until it's fixed, nothing will change (94–95).

In a series of essays, Tomasky argues for a soul-searching rethinking of traditional left approaches to welfare, immigration, affirmative action, and health care. In each area, he gives some history of how the left arrived at its positions during the postwar era, and why in each case the left's preferences have created, alongside some clear gains, new sets of problems and negative consequences that need to be addressed. In each case he recognizes as legitimate many of the grievances by middle America that conservatives have used to advance their larger agenda. And he show how the left can only offer viable alternatives by taking those grievances seriously. In the debate over immigration control and treatment of immigrants in the United States, for example, Tomasky argues:

> The left is not going to win this debate by accusing people who express legitimate concern of prejudice and leaving it at that. Screaming *j'accuse* is not a program. Nor is it a vision of what the American nation should be (138).

Instead, some leading conservatives, including William Bennett and Jack Kemp, have criticized the anti-immigrant Proposition 187 in California but at the same time have laid out an alternative policy—including stepped up border patrols, better policing of fraudulent documents, speeded up deportation of illegals convicted of crimes—that addresses people's concerns without pandering to racism. Robert Scheer and Joel Kotkin, from left-liberal perspectives, have reframed the issue as one of enforciing existing laws, which already outlaw, for example, the exploitation of illegal immigrant labor.

On another issue, health care, Tomasky sees merit in the left's push for some sort of single-payer system and hopes that the debate will focus less on adopting the Canadian model than working out an American model. Such a model would be:

> adapted to meet certain American needs and expectations, and [this would] make it less pervious to the standard criticisms. Specialty care and technological innovation, for example, which America does seem to do better than Canada, are real concerns. Finally, people who can afford it and want it must

be able to buy supplemental insurance, and that should be a clear part of the plan. Some single-payer advocates oppose this, but it seems to me obvious that a $110,000-a-year family of four will never be sold on a plan that limits them to the same treatment that a $35,000-a-year family of four gets. This does not mean creating class divisions; just the opposite. If the $110,000 household and the $35,000 household both support the plan, cross-class solidarity has been created, with the middle class and the poor (or nearly poor) united. Ralph Nader, GM's Jack Smith, and representatives of the College of Surgeons, up on a stage together with a supportive president, would have far more impact on the public than Ralph Nader and four lesser goo-goos (185)

The figures that Tomasky uses in this example are indicative of his concern that a new left politics (but not the New Left of the 1960s) should center its attention on a broad middle majority, because without such support there is no hope of aiding the poorest minorities. Tomasky makes regular use of the practical wisdom of offering aid to meet the needs of members of the middle class in order to build cross-class coalitions and attract support from segments of the body politic who already have some political resources and clout.

The key to building or rebuilding a practical left politics is a renewed ability—and therefore a renewed will—to make coalitions across group boundaries; this means a "big tent" strategy in which many members of the new movement will disagree on specific issues, and will continue to disagree, without, however, breaking off cooperation in the larger project:

We find smarter ways to spend our energies than finding bigots under every bed; there are no litmus tests for black authenticity,. . .; a straight white male is not immediately suspect if, say, he opposes affirmative action; we can talk about the problem of welfare not only as a function of race- and gender-based oppression, but as a problem that has behavioral attributes that must be addressed; we can discuss illegal immigration similarly; the white working class is not some totemic object of derision and contempt, but comprises actual human beings who can be appealed to as a possible source of cooperation and power; we can even revive the notion of a working-class culture that leaps over ethnic and racial boundaries . . .; enemies and allies of progressive thought can be identified and named as they really stand. . .; finally, people can express legitimate disagreement with a group line without being automatically accused of some kind of -ism." (194)

For Tomasky, the basic rule of political survival of species is adapt or die; he credits the conservative movement with having done just that, and having shaped its new ideas to address real problems and conditions of middle American, even though they added "emotional appeals to people's worst instincts, . . . lies and false promises about things like tax cuts and supply-side economics. . . . They adapted" (212).

I have some problems with Tomasky's proposed vision of a resurrected left agenda, however; it seems largely geared to the European social-democratic model, which is now itself in crisis. Tomasky recognizes this in part, but argues that even in an era of downsizing in both public and private sectors, European countries have handled this much more through shorter work-weeks (199). He argues that American workers should have more vacation time (since most workers in Europe have three or four weeks of paid vacation). Yet I'm not sure that Tomasky recognizes just how badly strained the social democratic model in Europe has become, and how much new thinking needs to address the painful transitions that model is now undergoing. To American progressives, Western Europe has been for a long time a more generous and more humane social welfare state, but it is now necessary to rethink this basic orientation, since that model cannot continue as it is. Tomasky is on stronger ground when he argues, with regard to the single-payer health care plan, that a specifically American adaptation must be proposed, rather than trying to adopt the Canadian system. Probably there will be some period of cross-national debate and influences from left political innovations, which may first have success in one country, and then be considered and adapted for another country. That too is part of a broad strategy of adaptation, to see what works and what doesn't; there are no current blueprints for the left to borrow, so that in each country and region there will be homegrown experimentation combined with close observation of new trends in other polities.

C. Michael Lerner and the Cultural Revolution of Meaning

The third Mike is Michael Lerner, founder and editor of *Tikkun* (which means healing and transformation), the leading Jewish intellectual journal of progressive politics. Lerner brings to the rethinking process for a progressive politics a dynamic spiritual or religious element as a central element of renewal—something that is not found in either Lind's or Tomasky's writings. Lerner's book, *The Politics of Meaning—Restoring Hope and Possibility in an Age of Cynicism* argues for nothing less than a cultural revolution: from a social ethic of selfishness and materialism to one based on love, compassion, and solidarity. Of the three works, his is clearly the most visionary and the most openly— even aggressively if one might use this term- idealistic. Lerner argues passionately that the alienation produced by American consumerist, self-centered institutions and practices is the root cause of the wide-spread feelings of cynicism and hopelessness, even in the midst of great wealth and technological sophistication. For Lerner, American society needs a fundamental cultural shift, though this might seem impossible in the face of all the resources which support, reinforce, and reproduce alienating patterns of behavior, which bothers people but also channels their responses into more of the same self-defeating searches for more goods and more selfish affirmation.

Lerner, who holds doctorates in both philosophy and psychology, is at his best when he is critiquing the social bases of widespread problems that eat away at the meaningfulness of people's lives, and distract people from identifying the real sources of their distress (Is this another version of "false consciousness"?) He is also at his best when he offers a progressive agenda that differs qualitatively from today's standard "liberal" and "conservative" political formulas. At many points Lerner's arguments remind me of parts of Kantian philosophy dealing with the possibility of overcoming alienation by acting as if the life of humankind is the end in itself, and should not be treated as mere means to (someone else's) ends. In some passages one could read much of the young Marx (whom Lerner cites occasionally) as a radical humanist critic of capitalist society, and the promoter of a vision of a nonalienating alternative society:

> Assume man to be man and his relationship to the world to be a human one: then you can exchange love only for love, trust for trust, etc. If you want to enjoy art, you must be an artistically-cultivated person; if you want to exercise influence over other people, you must be a person with a stimulating and encouraging effect on other people. Every one of your relations to man and to nature must be a specific expression, corresponding to the object of your will, of your real individual life (Marx, 1978: 105).

But above all, there is much of the philosophy of Ludwig Feuerbach and his "Essence of Christianity" in Lerner's extended essays on the failures of liberalism and conservatism, the perverse version of Christian meaning advanced by the religious right, and the alternative of achieving the essence of Christianity through actual practice—that is, personal service to the lives of others. For Lerner, as for Feuerbach, the true measure of religious spirit, and the only way to overcome an alienated image of a distant God, is through recognition of the God force in each of us, and daily practice of love, charity, and service to one's fellow beings.

Lerner's synthesis, a "politics of meaning," is most important for its reliance on specifically religious and spiritual values, which he combines with both traditional and more recent (i.e. Old Left and New Left) experience:

> Most of the ideas in this book derive from the Bible and from all that I have learned from the biblically based religious traditions, from my study and practice of psychoanalysis, and from various progressive political movements of the past centuries, particularly feminism and ecological theory (Lerner, 1996: ix).

Lerner, while coming from an explicitly Jewish religious tradition:

> seeks to translate this ancient biblical truth into a contemporary language that can be grasped by a nonreligious person. I am calling for a "politics in the image of God," an attempt to reconstruct the world in a way that really takes seriously the uniqueness and preciousness of every human being and our connection to a higher ethical and spiritual purpose that gives meaning to our lives." (ibid, 4)

The fact that Lerner is coming, in an unabashedly straightforward way, from this religious foundation into the competitive arena of re-shaping a progressive left politics for our times is one of the great services of his work. His thinking represents a growing stream of entries into this struggle for renewal from the religious and spiritual left, which, as I have argued earlier, needs to be heard and received as a vital element. For Lerner there is no question of second-class citizenship for a religiously based progressive politics; there must be a break with the long-standing secular left notion of "leaving your religion at the door," as the basis for participation of progressive believers alongside progressive nonbelievers. While one might disagree with certain aspects of Lerner's strategy for a "politics of meaning," or with some of his agnosticism about "capitalism"—which is, however, not so different from the long and honorable tradition of working within the system to change the system, and to test the limits of change—I as a nonbeliever have to admire his blend of militancy and call for radical cultural change and his synthesis of religious beliefs into a forward-looking politics that evokes the progressive side of many religious traditions and secular approaches as well.

Of the three Mikes, Lerner is the most radical, and the most vision-ary. His politics goes far beyond Lind's call for a "national liberalism" to counterbalance the power of corporate capital, and well beyond Tomasky's "evolve or die" formulation for a new, mainstream left syn-thesis. Like Lind and Tomasky, Lerner takes the conservative critique of contemporary society seriously, and he shows how the right has been able to mobilize millions of people, identifying real problems while offering, in Lerner's terms, false and self-defeating answers. Yet Lerner takes on the Christian right on its own turf and develops a progressive counterstrategy that takes profound religious belief as in-deed a prime source of social healing and a curative politics. Lind and Tomasky are still mainly interested in an economic-centered left re-newal that would address the mainstream's fears and the conservative's anxieties (they do not use the concept of "alienation" in any central way). By contrast, Lerner says:

> Many liberals write these people off, but those who wish to create a progres-sive politics of meaning understand that many conservatives share with us a profound distaste for the alienation that permeates our society. Some conser-vatives imagine that if they can get away from the public realm, they might be able to preserve a personal life that offers a more humane way of relating to other human beings. Sophisticated liberals who ridicule the conservative nos-talgia for an earlier America may be correct to note its evocations of highly romanticized visions of the past—visions that obscure the real class divisions, the racism, and the sexism of the small towns whose demise conservatives bemoan. But such liberals miss the quite legitimate desire underlying this romanticization: a desire for a less alienating world in which selfishness and materialism would not rule the day (32).

Lerner is, in fact, harder on liberalism than conservatism with re-gard to what he sees as their failures to address the real (not phony or feigned) anxieties and grievances of the broad American working and middle classes. Two sections of his book are devoted to taking the conservative diagnosis of what bothers middle America as essentially sound, and using that as a basis to offer that great constituency a competitive and progressive alternative. Lerner berates liberalism for taking seriously only the plight of the "most victimized," and neglect-ing the real complaints of the white male working and middle class. In a personal and pointed historical comparison, Lerner criticizes the European left for its inability to understand the Germans' anger and alienation, which the Nazi movement was able to address and to chan-nel for its deadly and tragic purposes. The left spoke, sometimes effectively, to the economic needs of workers suffering during the Depression, but the Nazi movement offered a more attractive and meaningful community (built on the darkest fears and hatreds present within German culture at that time):

> The communal celebrations bespoke a hunger for solidarity, mutual connection, and shared values—and for many people, it was this hunger for community that attracted them to fascism. Their hatred of others was based on the degree to which they had come to believe (usually mistakenly) that the demeaned Others had actually caused the breakdown of their communities of shared meaning and purpose (88).

Lerner intends this passage to convey both the dangers that a right-wing mobilization represents, and the need for progressives to take popular anger and fears seriously, so that an effective alternative politics can be developed. Lerner therefore treats with sympathy the uphill struggle of white men in this nasty ("lean and mean") capitalist corporate world to prove themselves to be "real men" (158), and he considers how conservatism is able to channel this need into social cynicism and conservative economic "realism." His argument is that a renewed progressive politics must develop an authentic compassion for all citizens, not just those who are the most obvious victims of the system, the ones who are already at the bottom. "Giving white men a break" is Lerner's signal for a recentering of progressive politics as a first step toward mobilizing an effort to reshape the culture on behalf of the broad majority.

Lerner spends almost no time developing new strategies for "identity" interest groups, such as blacks, women, or gays. He borrows from the lessons of social organizing and its achievements during the early civil rights movement, from the women's movement, and from the environmentalists, but his politics of meaning is not built around their special visions, nor is it in any way an attempt to meld these partial visions:

> Hate radio has mobilized legitimate anger in illegitimate ways. But to counter hate radio, we need to understand more fully what is the legitimate basis of people's anger. There is no point in dismissing it with a "politically correct" insight that, in relationship to others, many Americans are privileged. It makes far more sense to understand the ways in which this privilege does not really provide ethical and spiritual satisfaction, and then to speak to this dimension of people's experience—validating their anger and redirecting it away from the traditionally demeaned targets of hate-radio attacks, and toward the ethos

of selfishness and materialism that systematically frustrates our meaning-needs
and our desire for genuine recognition and love (176–177).

What Lerner says here, and what he does not say, represents a crucial
breakthrough in the progressive dialogue; and, even more than Lind
and Tomasky, he offers a new type of political ethic for the future.

Lerner's arguments also recenter a progressive politics within the
private and social sphere, before raising questions of winning elections and governing. Unless a revitalized social movement with a progressive politics can emerge, winning elections and governing in the
name of a progressive politics will be impossible, and I think Lerner is
saying that a decisive change in the mass political culture must have
an impact in terms of electoral politics and institutional policy-making. This comes through most clearly in Lerner's epilogue on the
Clintons and contemporary politics, since Hillary Clinton used Lerner's
"politics of meaning" in an important speech and was immediately
pounded for it by the hate-radio attack dogs (especially Rush Limbaugh,
who has also targeted Lerner many times). Lerner is sympathetic to
the Clintons, who have taken the anger and anxieties of middle America
seriously as campaign and electoral concerns, yet he is critical of their
inability to push ahead on an agenda for a new politics of meaning. In
the light of the Democratic Convention of 1996, which renominated
Clinton, it seems clear from the emphasis on family values, on community concerns about crime, and even on reforming the liberal welfare model of "statist" and bureaucratic entitlement, that the Democratic Party is still experimenting with its own "politics of meaning."
Cynics may dismiss this as only electoral maneuvering, and may well
have expected that after the elections a more normal policy-making
mindset would reemerge; yet Lerner's message is that this experimentation may also be a reliable indicator of political recognition of unful-
filled needs. Such experimentation can take a progressive shape or a
reactionary and fundamentalist shape. A progressive outcome is possible if progressives are able to build their own social movement, independent of any candidate or any party. In this too Lerner gives historical credit to those social movements which have shaped our politics
over the past fifty years and whose self-mobilization from unfavorable
beginnings could eventually not be ignored by the parties and their
leaders.

Naturally, there are some questions that need more elaboration
than can be answered in one book, or at the present time generally,
about this "politics of meaning." First and foremost, Lerner leaves

himself open to charges of extreme voluntarism because of his notions of change coming about as a result of willed transformation for
a better society, without regard for the balance of power and resources
which maintain and expand the current capitalist order. This is especially apparent when Lerner goes into the use of psychotherapy groups
to further some goals of his politics of meaning. Lerner is all too
aware that psychotherapy at the individual level has a long history of
inducing adjustment and accommodation to the existing social order,
rather than challenging or changing it. When Lerner says that "building this compassion and mutual confidence can take place as people
participate in occupational stress groups and family support networks,"
he is aware that this can easily be parodied as New Age mysticism or
navel-gazing.

Many of Lerner's formulations—with their use (perhaps overuse) of
terms like *love, compassion, caring, mutual confidence*, and especially terms like *life-energy* or *spirit of God*—are ready-made to be
lifted out of context for denigration as either New Age psychobabble
or left-liberal do-gooderism. Lerner, to his great credit, will not abandon these key terms, but he does explicitly separate his ideas from
both New Ageism and traditional psychotherapy. And, to those who
doubt the potential for cultural change, he uses the example of the
feminist movement:

> to uproot patriarchy—once seemed as grandiose and unrealistic as our goal of
> changing the bottom line of our society. Yet in a scant thirty years, the women's
> movement has made unprecedented changes in the way that men and women
> relate to one another in their personal lives, as well as in the way the women
> are treated in the economy, in the media, and in politics. Similar changes are
> possible within the next thirty years in challenging the ethos of selfishness
> and materialism, and championing a meaning-orientation in every sphere of
> life (298).

I think this is one of Lerner's strongest points, and he is absolutely
right; it is obvious that the current order organizes and markets just
such consciousness-building courses and groups that aim to rework
individual behavior in pursuit of the dominant goals of our capitalist
society. Consider the immense success of the "positive thinking" literature from inspirational motivators like Dale Carnegie, Norman
Vincent Peale, and Robert Ringer to the "Success 96" mass rallies of
Peter Lowe today (8,600 people were at the Continental Airlines arena
at the Meadowlands). Along with all this, the corporate world is constantly spending big money and applying talent to invent new ways to

motivate people for success in business (Morrow, 1996). The purposeful strengthening of goals-consciousness and motivation for pursuit of goals within the system is a social activity which the current system ardently pursues; Lerner is positing, using the feminist movement as one example, a quite reasonable potential for group-based changes in consciousness as the key to his politics of meaning.

Lerner also differentiates his own concepts from those of communitarianism, as represented by Amitai Etzioni. Communitarians, Lerner argues, have downplayed the importance of economic structures, and thus their advocacy of values such as individual responsibility do not challenge the irresponsibility of the great economic business and finance structures of our society. Communitarianism also sidesteps any religious or spiritual component; it remains a purely secular intellectual project. It does not recognize the past victories of social movements, which carved out space for individual liberty and for protection against oppressive community norms, enforced either legally or through social intimidation. Lerner argues that communitarianism is a more modest and self-limiting project, since it does not challenge the core principles of capitalism which maintain and reproduce the current self-centered, alienated individual.

On the other hand, Lerner himself is agnostic about capitalism. In his discussion of policy implications of a politics of meaning, he asserts that the question of ownership of private property, the means of production, should be left open, and therefore left aside, for the immediate future. He argues that many businesspeople themselves feel the need for a less selfish, less materialistic, and less aggressively bottom-line society; that they too, or at least some important segment of business, would be willing partners in a progressive political agenda for a more caring, more humane social and economic order. Why should a renewed left write off all the business owners and managers as part of the oppressor class? Lerner suggests that the left should stop "demonizing" people in the business world, and test the proposition that if significant numbers of businesspeople may in fact also be "willing to make that shift, and explicitly fight for it within their part of the corporate world, they become part of a progressive movement for a politics of meaning" (233). This would not be a sellout for the left, but a chance to develop the broadest possible mass basis for a transformation of consciousness. If this proposition turns out to be valid, then it may well be possible to advance a transformative politics on a broad, cross-class basis. If the proposition turns out to be false, then, according to Lerner, there is no sellout, and the limitations of trans-formation within capitalism will have been revealed through actual practice. Clearly, Lerner wants to avoid another rerun of the classic socialist-capitalist debate:

> [It] is clear that the socialist/capitalist debate is a red-herring issue today. The key is not to ask, "Who owns?" but two other questions: "To what extent does the economy really serve the common good?" and "To what extent does the economy produce spiritually, ethically, and ecologically sensitive human beings who are capable of sustaining loving and caring relationships, and who feel themselves actualized and fulfilled in the world of work?"(234)

Here Lerner's break with the left tradition on the economy is clearest, and his alternative language most disturbing for those who see the underlying dynamics of capitalism as incapable of compromise or a social pact. And his vocabulary must seem to be the most idealistic and unrealistic imaginable.

And yet, has Lerner not put his finger on one of the major prob-lems of the traditional left politics, that it has been itself economistic in the extreme and has failed to speak to potential communities of support in any terms but those of material interests (of course for workers rather than capitalists)? As I have argued in earlier sections of this work, it may well be a historic moment for a reconciliation of secular and religious left currents, impossible except episodically in the past for clear and cogent reasons, but now absolutely necessary for a revitalization of left politics. Lerner's language must be off-put-ting to many, especially those who do not care to rethink a left politics except marginally; but it may be a requisite challenge for those who are willing to rethink the left political agenda and who must therefore come to grips with Lerner's core ideas, an ethically and morally based progressive vision of a better future.

D. A New Intellectual Tenor of Our Times

We cannot say that just because three innovative and insightful works appear in one season, the debate on a renewed left politics has been settled; but this debate, I would assert, has now been joined on a new and productive level. The three Mikes each show some aspect of this new level. Lind does demonstrate the new ossification of conservative thought in the 1990s, the failure of imagination and the closing down of honest and open discourse on the right. Tomasky represents the

new call for a repudiation of left sectarianism in favor of a new coalition-building that would combine the best of New Deal and New Left
thinking, while taking conservatives' criticisms seriously and reworking their best material into a new left reform project. Lerner enters the
left discourse with the most energetic and radical vision of a new
cultural shift, based on unabashedly religious and moral principles, a
turn away from all forms of left "economism." All three are part of a
new style of left self-criticism, which no longer has any fear of being
labeled "reactionary" or "defeatist" or a "sellout." It was a pleasure to
hear, at length in each case, a direct, clear discussion of the issues of
family values, welfare, immigration, affirmative action, crime, and illegitimacy, without having to bow to any left conventions of political
correctness or to be so sensitive to language that the central issues of
the argument are obscured.

In fact, it now seems clear that the right's "political correctness," as
expressed in the slogan "no enemies on the right," is the most stultifying factor in current American intellectual debate. Lind is very insightful about this issue, and the right's enforced defense of Robertson
and his organization (legitimizing by sin of omission his "world conspiracy" demagogy) will undoubtedly lose its cause the best and brightest minds, who will be repelled by this shameful collaboration. The
real discourse over paths to a better future for America is shifting
decisively to the left, and the left is now ready to host this debate.
Thinkers on the left will make their mark by leading the critical analysis of existing society, and offering new ideas for reform and change.

The achievements of the Keynesian welfare state must be reformed
in a qualitative way if they are to survive at all; "status quo" defenses
of welfarist concepts are barriers, which neither serve their presumed
goals nor advance any future-oriented vision of a better society. The
conservative analysis of the flawed nature of Keynesian welfarism made
a lot of sense to people because it had lots of good points, some of
which (on family, crime, immigration, affirmative action, and even
welfare) can easily be worked into a new left politics, to achieve a new
left vision of a more just and caring social order. Most apparent is the
relative absence in all three works of the question of "ownership" for
the means of production. I would guess that this issue will in fact not
be a major priority of the reworked left, but will be treated more as a
long-run matter that may or may not have to be replayed. Instead, the
current priority will be reestablishing some sort of counterbalance to
the power of corporations and banks, and as Lerner suggests, this

leaves room for an "agnostic" stance on the ownership of the means of production. More clear is the acceptance of markets, and market mechanisms, as useful and necessary tools of a modern economy—which, however, need to be regulated and shaped by the larger public interest, as determined through a democratic politics.

As I have suggested throughout this work, the renewal of any ideology will be profoundly disturbing to many of its past stalwarts and leading lights. This will be the time for the marginalized voices, for new converts, for earlier dissenting currents of thought to take leading roles. This is inevitable, since the successful reworking of any major ideological tradition will come out with a new conceptual synthesis, qualitatively different from its predecessor; it will shed formerly valued positions (useful in their time but now no longer viable); it will add new positions and priorities, frankly borrowed from competing political agendas. How else could anything really new emerge? Of course, this will bring new splits and new (perhaps seemingly strange) alliances into the rethought political agenda. The rebirth of a democratic and socially responsive Christian Democracy in Europe—and especially in Germany—after World War II was in so many ways anathema to older, nationalistic, class-hierarchical, and virulently antiliberal, antileft prewar conservatives, even those who had not collaborated with the fascist regimes. How could this Christian Democracy be considered conservative, when it seemed to abandon so many of the old principles and adopted so many features of liberalism and even socialism? The reworking of a Keynesian welfare statist liberalism in the West was seen as the final sellout of liberalism by pre-war adherents of the laissez-faire capitalist model, both for its statism and for its welfarist activism. And yet, nothing could have been further from the truth in either case. Rather, these were signs of a healthy renewal process, which would in both cases make postwar conservative and liberal politics viable again—and, in fact, not just in some distant future, but rather quickly, to the great surprise of their political competitors.

Something of this sort is now occurring within the post-cold war left; Lerner, Lind, and Tomasky are part of this process, which has now reached the stage of unfettered borrowing and critical discarding in order to develop the critical new synthesis. A tipping point has been reached, and the flood of new thinking now cannot be stopped. While some on the left are dismayed at the ease with which old shibboleths can be attacked from within the left itself, and will be shocked by the blatant adoption of the best ideas and criticisms from social conservatism and economic liberalism, they will no longer be able to keep this debate from traveling with its consideration of far-ranging ideas, and all ideas are now freely contestable. Those that plausibly add to a vision of a new progressive politics that can challenge the absolutism of capital, and the abandonment of social justice to the mercy of the market, will survive this debate and become part of a quite new left agenda. The excitement of new political ideas on the left is exhilarating to more and more thinkers, at the same time that it is profoundly discouraging to others.

References

Lerner, Michael (1996). *The Politics of Meaning—Restoring Hope and Possibility in an Age of Cynicism*. Reading, MA: Addison-Wesley.

Lind, Michael (1995). *The Next American Nation*. New York: Free Press.

———— (1996). *Up From Conservatism—Why the Right is Wrong for America*. New York: Free Press.

Marx, Karl (1978). "1844 Manuscripts," in Robert Tucker, ed., *The Marx-Engels Reader*. New York: Norton.

Morrow, David (1996). "Influencing People at the Box Office—Selling Success, Blockbuster Style," *New York Times* (August 24) 35.

Tomasky, Michael (1996). *Left for Dead—The Life, Death, and Possible Resurrection of Progressive Politics in America*. New York: Free Press

Chapter VI

Moving Toward a Breakthrough?
Assessments of Progress
and Change

At the end of these considerations on the processes of rethinking and renewing, I would like to present some forward-looking propositions about the consolidation of a viable left politics for our time. These clearly more speculative expectations are based on the main points presented above, which—I hope—have placed the historic renewal movement into the larger context of competing value systems over long stretches of modern history. Any speculation on the nature and timing of a political breakthrough for a revitalized left must flow from these larger contextual points.

A. Progress in the Renewal of a Left Politics Today

First of all, the current contention and strife on the left is a normal part of the cyclical renewal of larger value systems in the dialectical process of conflict and change in human societies. In chapter 2 of this work, I develop the case for viewing socialism as one of three great value systems, itself renewed by Marx and others in the 1800s; and I argue for a recognition of the long-term viability of socialism, liberalism, and conservatism, a repudiation of the "endism" of Fukuyama and earlier socialist and conservative thinkers. In chapter 3, I describe what I take to be some historic examples of renewal for socialism, conservatism, and liberalism in the wake of massive political defeats and discrediting. In each case, older dominant variants of political practice, long assumed to rest on immutable positions for socialists, for conservatives, and for liberals, were overturned and replaced in what must have seemed to be a treasonous, a historic "sellout" of long-valued positions and articles of faith. But in each case, the re-thinking process enabled a comeback, often in a surprisingly short time, and in each case the renewed politics was clearly still identifiable as socialist, or conservative, or liberal.

The growing conflict within the left today is therefore not a sign of demise or of political marginalization, but rather a healthy sign of continued reworking and struggle; this is a necessary and absolutely unavoidable element in the continued relevance of socialism as one of the three classic (in Western terminology at least) value systems for political competition. The fact that the debate on the left has been gathering steam, that Old Left and New Left ideas are being critiqued and challenged now by those who still identify themselves as part of the left political project, that taboos are falling rapidly, that sugges-tions for revision are increasingly breaking new ground, at odds with traditional left positions—all this is a sign of renewal at work. By con-trast, the icy grip of the cold war logic and the poverty of its choices—communist or anti-anticommunist—was a sign of intellectual decay and ossification on the left. The institutionalization of left thinking, either in a communist dictatorship or in a social democracy, represented the real decline of the left's creativity, which in the last decades of the cold war led to the abandonment of left politics by a large portion of its creative thinkers. The new openness of debate on the left is a breath of fresh air by comparison, and it symbolizes the continued attraction for intellectuals of a politics of social justice in an era of growing in-equality and sharper class divisions between owners of significant capital and everyone else. As I argued in the German left journal *Sozialismus* (Nagle, 1992), the collapse of communism is an intellectual emancipa-tion from the vicelike grip of the cold war, and a precondition for a basic rethinking of a left politics.

Second, many of the main issues that a reworked left politics must include in its synthesis have been recognized and clarified to the point where new solutions, new positions, are emerging. In chapter 4 above, I argued that across a wide range of key issues—including the relation-ship of the left to religious faith, markets, new social movements, in-ternationalism and democracy—new positions are emerging out of a more open and honest clash of ideas within the community of those firmly committed to the political left. There is movement on each of these fronts, and on an intellectual level, the renewal process is quite advanced. More progress has been made on some aspects than others, of course; the relationship of the secular left to the religious left still needs more critique and confession of past error and full-bodied commitment to a new beginning. As I have argued elsewhere (Nagle, 1991; 1992), I believe that the decline in the attraction of communism as an intellectual idea, followed by the collapse of "real existing" socialism in the Soviet Union and Eastern Europe, was in fact an emancipation for new thinking within the socialist left in the West. The final failure of communism freed the intellectual left from the unavoidable bad choices of the cold war: the choice of denouncing communism as vigorously as anticommunists and therefore being in some sense "joined" to the anticommunist (and antisocialist, antileftist) crusade; or defending, with all kinds of caveats and overly sophisticated devices, the ideals of communism as a necessary and historically justified alternative to capitalism (and therefore being in some sense "joined" to the existing Soviet regime and its practices). The more gradual erosion of the Keynesian welfare state in the West has also, and also gradually, liberated the intellectual left from the quandary of either criticizing welfarist democracy as insufficient, corrupting, and diluting the goals of a just and classless society, or defending it from the conservative offensive despite its flaws. It now seems to me that, in the intellectual realm at least, there is sufficient space for left intellectuals to offer innovative critiques and ideas, without having to abandon the left entirely, or having to be marginalized as eccentrics or cranks. Rather, it is now the more traditional left thinkers who are on the defensive, and who risk becoming isolated in the debate over renewal of a left political project.

Third, I believe that some individual signs—represented here by the works of Lerner, Lind, and Tomasky—may symbolize a new level of readiness for the political comeback of a left politics. The main points involved the intellectual burnout on the conservative right, as described by Lind; the readiness to confront past failings, especially of the New Left and left identity politics, dealt with by all three; and the boldness of the new politics, exemplified by the writings of Michael Lerner. These works, and others of recent vintage, demonstrate a new maturing of the rethinking process, and a coming together on many major issues. Of course, there are still many areas of contention, and no one should expect to see (or perhaps even want to see) some sort of new consensus on a revitalized left politics. Especially in the early stages of historic political comebacks for value systems, the new synthesis has been messy, less than fully elaborated, even partially self-contradictory. How could it be otherwise, given the lack (as yet) of political success that would begin a new process, not of rethinking and revitalization, but of institutionalization, codification, and traditionalization?

B. How Societies Change: Commentary from Different Quarters

All of the above provides the backdrop for a consideration of just when and how the new breakthrough will take place, and how it will be recognized as such. What are the circumstances that will give rise to a historic event or series of events which will be widely seen as the birth of this new politics, which will consolidate into political practice the rethought direction of the left for this new era? Social scientists and social theorists cannot predict such events with any great confidence; social scientists have missed too many of the crises and breakthroughs of the cold war and its end to undertake a new round of grand prognosticating now. What social science can do, and usefully so, is to look at trends, to track the course of change, and to speculate that at some point or points, quantitative changes will be transformed into qualitative change. Following are some considerations on how political breakthroughs might occur, and what effects these might have on the emergence of a renewed left.

Daniel Chirot (1994), a Parsonian theorist of social change and no friend of socialist ideals, has offered some useful points in this regard in his most recent work on how societies change. In his argument, most societies lean heavily toward conservatism, in the sense of conserving past practices and institutions as long as they have not clearly failed. The social logic of both elites and masses is risk-averse in the absence of compelling reasons to undertake major change. Social change, he argues, can be expected only when there are severe pressures for abandoning traditional practices and embarking on some different course: "We know that human societies try on the whole to restrain change. Sometimes they do this by deliberately persecuting new ideas. They are always inherently conservative unless dramatic evidence of failure makes them change" (1994: 124). And, Chirot goes on, innovative ideas are most likely to come from "somewhat marginalized subgroups" within the larger society:

> No culture that becomes too homogeneous, too self-satisfied, or too tied to old orthodoxies will produce enough new ideas. . . . As far as societies are concerned, then, the vitality and diversity of a culture and its resistance to

uniformity now as always offer the best chances for successfully meeting future challenges (125).

Major social change, however, seems to require both new and innovative ideas, which depart radically from established wisdom; and pressures, which mainly come from clear and unambiguous signs of system failure. For Chirot, this is a trial-and-error process, open-ended, which has no guarantee of success: "We are probably no better at being able to judge ahead of time what will function than were our ancestors, though presumably we can gauge the results of any particular experiment more quickly than they did" (128).

This overall perspective matches much of the most recent debate and discussion within the left intellectual community, and within the modest but growing activism at the grass roots political level as well. In the aftermath of the supply-side utopian dreams of Thatcherism and Reaganomics, the middle class has been shaken by the realities of dismantling—even partially, in their least generous Anglo-American variants—the Keynesian welfare commitments of the postwar Western democracies, and by the cold truths of a globalizing capitalism. This has produced a new set of expectations for large portions of the population, and a new search for alternatives. The current globalization of capitalism will not be a smooth transition, and it will certainly produce sharp reactions from broad constituencies who correctly see themselves and their families and children as "losers" in the reconstruction of the political geography of work and the building of sharp class divisions in postindustrial Western societies. In this sense, we should expect that the contradictions of global capitalism will also, in the most elementary Marxist terms, produce their own antithesis. The nature of this antithesis (I would however expect choices among antitheses, as I will elaborate below) is still in the stage of coming-into-being, as the contradictions of global capitalism enforce a new consciousness among winners and losers in the process. But will this new politics of the left be a socialist politics? Does this terminology still capture the crux of a viable left politics for our times?

The British political scientist Christopher Pierson has argued that the revising of a new left politics will probably depend, as in an earlier era, on the specific challenges the capitalist process of commercialization produces, the (Schumpeterian) "creative destruction" it wreaks, and the practical opportunities available for challenging the political monopoly of capital. And in this sense, any left challenge to the capitalist hegemony in an era of global economy must still be a form of socialist politics. For Pierson, despite all the claims of postmodernism that concepts like capitalism, state, society, and most certainly socialism have become obsolete, it is still all too possible to:

> make out the rather shadowy form, if not a singular "capitalism", then certainly of relationships, institutions and practices to which the term "capitalist" may be usefully applied. So long as it makes sense to study capitalist forms and relations, and to consider alternatives to these, there is value in thinking in socialist terms. In such a context, however, it is better to think of socialist politics not as bringing us to the terminus of humanity's pre-history, but rather as a set of guiding ideas informing what is an open-ended political process (1995: 217).

In other words, no more left "endism," but certainly plenty of chances for socialist ideas to find new applications.

Pierson, who is doubtful about the market socialist project as the leading idea of a new left politics, is more confident that a renewal of socialist politics is still quite possible. The failures of global capitalism, and of the neoliberal offensive, are all too apparent. While capital is more dominant than ever, the results of its global commercialization project fall short of resounding mass approval: "At the same time, fin de siécle capitalism looks not much prettier than any of its historical predecessors. Indeed, stripped of the favourable contrast with the 'alternative' of World Communism and of the moderating influence of many social democratic institutions, it is in many ways still less attractive" (217). This is an important argument, which would predict that as we move further away from both communism and the high points of social democracy, globalized capitalism will look pretty unattractive. In much of post-communist East Europe and the former Soviet Union, and even in former East Germany, this led to a certain nostalgia (*Ostalgia* in Eastern Germany) and to a revival of left "successor" parties in second and third rounds of democratic elections. A similar social nostalgia for benefits and security now lost or threatened can be expected in the Western democracies as well. In both cases, the past cannot be rescued or reconstructed, but the socialist value culture that survives the end of communism and the slow death of national Keynesianism can provide a mass base for a rethought and revised left politics. Given the inability of global capitalism to provide for social security and social justice, a new left politics can speak to the common sense of a broad popular base about their condition, and about the need to politically confront the power of capital.

The legitimacy of the new global capitalism has already become a contentious point, recognized even by leading members of the business and finance community, such as Georg Soros. This growing recognition of a "legitimacy deficit" in the new world economic order can be harnessed to a revived left politics, and not necessarily to overthrow the whole market system, or to end capitalism once and for all, but to provide for the new era what the free market cannot provide on its own—voluntary mass acceptance. As Ulrich Beck has argued, "Let there be no illusion: a capitalism focused only on ownership and profits, which turns its back on the employed, on the social-welfare state, and on democracy, will undermine itself" (1997:53). Beck, in an article entitled "Capitalism Without Work," tracks the growth of insecure and partial employment in the West, replacing full-time secure employment with secure benefits. In Great Britain, the portion of the able-bodied workforce with traditional secure jobs is now less than one-third; in the social market economy of Germany, where no Thatcherite shock has been yet attempted, it remains higher, at 60 percent. Yet in both countries the direction of change is the same, since only twenty years ago the comparable figure was more than 80 percent (1997: 51). The emergence of growing new contradictions (though not yet the often-announced crisis of capitalism) is a sign not only that capital has escaped from the social contract of its postwar Keynesian compromise, but that this newly-empowered capitalism is also incapable by itself of providing for its own social legitimation. Yet I note that Beck, departing from traditional left visions of a final "end of capitalism," the left's version of endist utopianism, does not assert a stark choice between barbarism and socialism, but rather offers a more practical vision of a new social compromise, yet to be hammered out among contending value systems:

> The connection that exists in the West between capitalism and basic political, social, and economic rights is far more than a mere "social benefit" that can be dispensed with when things get tight. Rather, socially buffered capitalism was a response to the experience of fascism and the challenge of communism, a response developed at no small cost. This form of capitalism represents the enlightened recognition that only when people have a decent place to live and a secure job can they function as citizens who embrace democracy and make it come alive. The truth is simple: without material security, no political freedom. And no democracy—which in turn leaves people at the mercy of old and new totalitarian regimes and ideologies (53).

Beck's remedies for the growing contradiction of capitalism in the global era, from the Western point of view, point to one possible source of political breakthrough: a radical reworking of national politics as a starting point, that is, renewal within a single country. His call for refunding of public work, and investing to revive the civil society that provides the invaluable legitimation for a private market economy, is an argument built on the assumption that among the rich Western nations, the nation which first makes this political breakthrough will enjoy advantages:

> Can such a millennial reform be instituted in a single country? If the basic diagnosis offered here is correct—capitalism is becoming jobless and is creating joblessness—we are dealing with a global challenge that will sooner or later confront all highly developed societies. But the country that first finds a practicable response, that meets the risks to democracy head-on, will be ahead of the game (economically as well) (56).

Beck replays here, in some sense, the difference between Smith's English political economy of the firm and Friedrich List's continental or German concept of a coherent national economy. The first country to make the political breakthrough to a new social contract, a new form of social market economy, will also become a leader among the highly developed societies, which will then become a new pole of attraction and emulation for politics of other nations.

From these different commentaries on great social changes in general and the renewal of a left alternative for social change in our times, I have developed an image of a political community coming-into-being from a multitude of perspectives. There is no towering intellectual synthesis such as Marx offered in the nineteenth century, and there is no particular reason to expect one to emerge. Much of the politics of Western European socialism of Marx's own day was a result of local, fragmented actions, which came together only over the course of decades of struggle against the social trauma that industrial capitalism had imposed on the various societies and peoples of Europe. Even with the imposing intellectual achievement of Marx, the movement was splintered into many factions over questions of tactics, goals, and agencies of change.

By the end of the century, there was not one but two major (and several minor) paths for the socialist challenge: Leninism in the late-industrializing economies and in the most authoritarian regimes; and social democracy in the more advanced economies with democratizing regimes. Both of these very different and often viciously opposed versions of industrial-era socialism claimed a Marxist heritage. And these two challengers emerged within just the European region; today, given a globalizing capitalism that impacts more heavily on most societies around the world, one might well expect a greater pluralism of socialist new foundings. It is worth noting once again that even with the central theoretical achievement of Marx, which did indeed offer a sweeping analysis and a grand vision of the future, both Leninism and social democracy in government had to evolve from practical lessons and had to fight many intra-Leninist and intrasocialist debates over very basic issues of tactics and strategies. Marx's intellectual leadership did not and probably could not provide a left politics for his own time; rather, he offered a very elaborate theoretical model within which major questions still needed to be debated and decided. As Richard Hunt (1974) pointed out in his thoughtful study of Marx's and Engels's actual politics, the leading theorists of twentieth century socialism changed their minds or revised their commentary many times over questions of political parties, electoral competition, and parliamentary democracy, and never (in my opinion) resolved the key debate over revolutionary or evolutionary roads to socialism. What Marx could not provide for socialist politics in his day is even less probable in our times.

Since the struggle today to build an effective counterforce to the political monopoly of capital will have to be more cross-nationally interdependent and built on a greater international solidarity, we might also envision different strains of socialist politics which are more or less interconnected and which build a broad network of left politics despite very different origins and local circumstances. Samuel Huntington's (1996) vision of a clash of civilizations after the cold war may be more misanthropic than is justified, but his emphasis on unbridgeable cultural divides and the potential for cultural conflict should not be lightly dismissed by socialist rethinkers. An internationalizing socialism will have to come to terms with the need for a greater acceptance of socialist pluralism of many varieties if there is to be long-term cooperation and dependable solidarity.

My own thinking, as expressed in these pages, is a reflection of a Western experience and of Western political struggle, which is all that I can draw upon from my own life and work. Yet at least intellectually, I can see the need for a much more serious effort to engage socialist thinkers and activists in every region and every culture. This was always the ideal of socialism, as a global struggle for social justice for all peoples. Yet the nineteenth-century invention of industrial socialism was logically the product of those European thinkers who could view the workings of industrial capitalism most closely and intimately. The workings of global capitalism today are much more widespread (though not yet really covering all the globe—large segments of Africa and the Middle East, and parts of Central Asia, are just now being reached by the forces of the newly mobile and flexible capitalism), and impulses to challenge the dynamics of this capitalist era should arise from a greater plurality of cultural contexts than in the previous century, requiring a partnership among socialist tendencies based on cultural equality in order to build a truly international movement.

C. What We Can Expect, but Cannot Predict

At the end of the cold war, the social sciences came in for much criticism from the conservative political pundits, because so few had predicted the end of communism, and in general most "experts" had been surprised by the sudden and largely peaceful unraveling of the huge edifice of the Soviet state and the Soviet Union itself. There was certainly something correct in that criticism: that even major events and turning points are often impossible to forecast, even for the most talented experts in political or social analysis. And it was also fair to say that very few Western observers could, with any great precision, foretell the rapid and accelerating cascade of events which would sweep away seventy years of Leninist state power with more of a whimper than a bang.

Yet the social sciences, and comparative political science in particular, had in fact been able to track the decline of the Soviet economy, and the extreme aging of its political leadership, from the 1960s through the mid-1980s (cf., for example, Nagle, 1977). Most analysts, and especially independent left analysts, argued that the Soviet system was heading into a crisis, and that the old and increasingly feeble managerial-modernizer generation of Brezhnev, Andropov, Chernenko, Ustinov, Gromyko, Suslov, and Kosygin had no idea of what was needed to reform or rethink the Soviet system. There was a whole literature on the inability of the Soviet system to carry through reform efforts under the long-term domination of this political age cohort, which monopolized top positions on the Central Committee from the latter 1950s through the mid-1980s. Just when the realization about the need for great reform would break through, with the inevitable passing of the old generation of leadership, was not possible to predict, however. Even with Gorbachev's reform team, it was not possible to predict how far and how fast glasnost, perestroika, and demokratisatsia would move the political system.

The lesson from this experience should be that social analysis and political analysis are incapable of making good predictions about key historic events, of forecasting either the timing or the nature of watersheds in political evolution. Even a reading off of trends cannot predict that a crisis is imminent. One of Marx's greatest failings was as a judge of the events of his own time—he again and again overestimated the rise of proletarian class consciousness in both historical time and social breadth. The elder Engels was moving toward a more patient, and less vanguardist, view of this, as was especially Bernstein, for whom the whole notion of building socialism was one of practical movement, not a giant leap toward ultimate goals. In judging the progress of a renewed left toward some clear breakthrough, therefore, even the most insightful analysis should resign itself to learning from events, rather than foretelling them. Although it is always difficult for intellectuals to shy away from dramatic prognostication (after all, we might just happen to be right!), and it is always tempting to try to predict events in advance, it is probably more realistic and helpful to take a more inductive approach to understanding this formative period of a rethought and renewed left. (*Monthly Review* has made the mistake, over the years, of proclaiming an impending crisis of capitalism at virtually every sign or symptom, to the point where its annual predictions of capitalist crises have to be taken with a grain of salt.) In addition to tremendously underestimating the adaptability of capitalist economies and capitalist elites, *Monthly Review* exemplifies the left intellectual weakness for grand prognostication. I would opt rather for a more modest, even humble, capacity for broad empirical study and an associated openness in interpretation of events and trends.

None of this implies passivity on the part of the left intellectual; exactly the opposite is needed. The left intellectual is in part limited by the narrowness of his or her experience, which has always been somewhat removed from the experiences of nonacademics and nonintellectuals, but has become even more isolated since the rupture between left academe and left intellectuals after the Vietnam War and the student rebellions of the 1960s. Richard Rorty (1997) calls for a rebuilding of the linkage between the intellectual left and the labor unions in particular:

> The best thing that could happen to the American left would be for the academics to get back into the class struggle, and for the labor union members to

forgive and forget the stupid and self-defeating anti-American rhetoric that filled the universities of the late sixties.

This is not to say that those twenty-five years of inward-looking academic politics were in vain. American campuses are very much better places—*morally* better places—than they were in 1970. Thanks to all those marches on the English department, and various other departments, the situation of women, gays and lesbians, African-Americans, and Hispanics has been enormously improved. Their new role in the academy is helping improve their situation in the rest of American society.

Nevertheless, leftist academic politics has run its course. It is time to revive the kind of leftist politics that pervaded American campuses from the Great Depression through the early sixties—a politics that centers on the struggle to prevent the rich from ripping off the rest of the country. If the unions will help us revive this kind of politics, maybe the academy and the labor movement can get together again (1997: 34).

Rorty's point is well taken, although I would add that there have also been some needed and welcome changes within the labor movement and its leadership which are also transcending the "stupid and self-defeating" superpatriotic rhetoric which was coming from many labor bosses in the latter 1960s. Rorty will also be disappointed if he expects the academic left to rebuild its ties to the union movement while dropping its commitment to the new social movements of the past twenty-five years; the call for a politics of class struggle is appropriate, and that must include a new bridge to organized labor, but organized labor cannot be seen in the same "vanguard" role that it had in the era of national Keynesianism. The general recommendation to left intellectuals to get beyond academic politics and into the larger community again is fine, but it should extend well beyond the labor movement, to unorganized workers, to religious groups, to farm and rural communities, and to every group which is under the gun of global liberalism and which has the potential to become an ally of a new left-progressive coalition. The "Teach-In with the Labor Movement" at Columbia University in October 1996, which attracted 1,300 participants, was a good sign, as was the AFL-CIO "Union Summer" involving over 1,000 college students. These events, however, would have to be multiplied hundreds of times in a variety of locales before we could speak of new academic activism within the labor movement.

D. Some Inductivist Generalizations:
The Decline of Legitimacy of Global Liberalism

The left, of course, needs theory and deduction from theory in its renewal. But there needs to be a new balance between building a theory by deduction, which does presume predictive capacity, and building a theory by induction, sifting through events and then trying to generalize from them. Inductive generalizations are put forward as a theoretical proposition, a working thesis, to be tested against new information and new developments. There is less effort at the grand theorizing or paradigm-building which marked both classic Marxism and the mainstream effort to build a value-free science of comparative politics on the model of physics in the 1960s (cf. Holt and Richardson, 1970, for a good illustration of that effort, now mostly forgotten in its naiveté).

What signs can we pull together, inductively, that might tell us something about where the renewal process stands, and what we might generally expect, without attempting to predict when and under what circumstances a breakthrough might be made? I think, to begin with, there are increasing signs that those within the intellectual elite of global liberalism are becoming more aware of the declining legitimacy of that project to which they themselves are attached. It now appears to me that global capitalism has a mounting "democracy deficit" and is aware that it is losing the battle for the "hearts and minds" of citizens in various national political settings still vital for the maintenance and reproduction of the new economic order.

While the following are only a few selections from a growing literature, which now ranges from the most philosophical to the semipopularized, I believe that the ideas contained within these critiques are evidence that the political hegemony of global liberalism is threatened, and that this threat is now increasingly recognized by establishment thinkers. A major discussion of this "legitimacy crisis" was initiated by the World Economic Forum, a leading intellectual organization for the promotion of global liberalism, which holds annual high-powered conferences in Davos, Switzerland. The World Economic Forum modestly describes itself as:

> the foremost international membership organization integrating leaders from business, government and academia into a partnership committed to improving the state of the world. It is an independent, impartial and not-for-profit foundation. Since 1971 the World Economic Forum acts as a bridgebuilder between business and government. The Annual Meeting has grown into the most significant global business summit bringing together close to 2000 business and political leaders, experts academics, and members of the media, to set the global agenda for the coming year. This interface creates new opportunities for business and economic development and in defining solutions to global issues. The Forum's philosophy is reflected in its motto "Entrepreneurship in the global public interest" (WEF webpage).

In 1996, the Davos meeting focused on sustaining globalization in the face of a growing backlash and the perceived danger that the liberal globalization project could be thwarted by a populist revolt of the masses. Klaus Schwab, founder of the World Economic Forum, and Claude Smadja, its managing director, wrote an article, "Start Taking the Backlash Against Globalization Seriously," for the *International Herald Tribune* (February 1, 1996: 8), in which they broached the idea that global liberalism was in fact generating a popular consciousness of political opposition and revolt. This was written in a period of militant labor strikes in France, the antiglobalist politics of Pat Buchanan in the early Republican primaries, and the strong support among pensioners in Russia for the then-resurgent communist party. The communist leader and presidential candidate Gennadi Zyuganov was in fact a prominent guest speaker at the 1996 Forum in Davos. Schwab and Smadja admit that global liberalization is being commonly understood not as a win-win process, but rather as a process of destructive restructuring in which the destruction part is creating great anxiety and opposition to the process as a whole:

> It becomes apparent that the lead-on mega-competition that is part and parcel of globalization leads to winner-take-all situations; those who come out on top win big, and the losers lose even bigger. The gap between those able to ride the wave of globalization, especially because they are knowledge- and communications-oriented, and those left behind is getting wider at the national, corporate, and individual levels (ibid).

Schwab and Smadja recognize the growing public skepticism about whether this process will benefit them at all in the future, and they can see the pain and dislocation being inflicted right now. They also admit that "globalization tends to delink the fate of the corporation from the fate of its employees. In the past, higher profits meant more job security and better wages. The way transnational corporations have to operate to compete in the global economy means that it is now routine to have corporations announce new profit increases along with a new wave of layoffs " (ibid). In short, these two thinkers in the forefront of global liberalism admit that it is now "common sense" that in the current era, capitalist interests mirrored through the corporation are increasingly seen as opposed to working-class or employees' interests. This is an astounding admission, one that implies either a new strategy to rebuild mass support, if global liberalism is to have a "democratic" face, or the abandonment of democratic legitimation in favor of stronger measures: "All this confronts political and economic leaders with the challenge of demonstrating how the new global capitalism can function to the benefit of the majority and not only for corporate managers and investors" (ibid.). Although their own prescriptions put most emphasis on education and training—to try encourage workers to run faster to catch up with changing skill requirements—they also do put forward a social component which contradicts pure market thinking: "Meanwhile, the globalized economy must not become synonymous with 'free market on the rampage,' a brakeless train wreaking havoc. The social responsibilities of corporations (and governments) remain as important as ever. What is on the agenda is the need to redefine and recalibrate them." Furthermore, "Public opinion in the industrial democracies will no longer be satisfied with articles of faith about the virtues and future benefits of the global economy. It is pressing for action" (ibid.).

Of special interest here is the call for building a new social responsibility in a globalizing system which now has no enforcement mechanism and in which capitalist interests have spent their greatest effort on escaping from the social responsibility once imposed by democratic law at the national level. Schwab and Smadja therefore have placed on the agenda a new priority, to rethink and reconstruct this mechanism of social responsibility to counterbalance global capitalism. This would require, however, a revitalized left politics within a globalized economy, or the shattering of globalism by resurgent isolationist nationalism. What is amazing within establishment thought about this new consciousness of the collapse of global liberalism's popular base of support is that there is no accompanying recognition of the impossibility of global liberalism providing its own counterbalancing "social" value component. The dynamics of capitalism are opposed to social constraints or responsibilities; it is typical of much of this new literature, however, both to admit the crisis of globalist legitimacy and to propound a social ethic which cannot be found within the ideology of global liberalism itself.

Thomas Friedman, one of the *New York Times*'s leading pundits on international affairs, asked Schwab in a follow-up interview what motivated him to write this amazing confession of weakness with regard to legitimacy:

> In the 19th century people thought the machine was going to destroy their life as they knew it, and today many people think that globalization is going

to destroy their life as they know it. We have gotten accustomed to the idea
that globalization will inevitably succeed. But I am not so sure anymore. Those
of us who believe in globalization need to be more pro-active (1996: A19).

Friedman closes his column with the following thought:

> He's right. And the successful governments will be those able to design the
> right formula of worker training programs, tax policies that create jobs and
> preserve resources, population controls and sustainable social safety nets to
> deal with globalization. The good news is that many world leaders are begin-
> ning to understand this challenge. The bad news is that no one has found the
> formula yet (ibid.).

Friedman has it half right, and that is as far as an establishment
pundit can go on the social issue. Friedman does not even entertain
the politically incorrect idea that the reason there is no formula for
dealing humanely and ethically with globalization is that there is no
revitalized left politics which could create the necessary social counterbalance to the interests of capital. Marx had it right; capital will
never give priority to social responsibility or social safety nets on its
own, because its own dynamics, its capacity for "creative destruction," is based on sharply contrasting principles. Nevertheless, this
new consciousness voiced in 1996 at the Davos conference symbolized a new discourse, which has become a more prominent feature
within establishment thinking on prospects for global liberalism.

An interesting example comes from a feature article by journalist
Erhard Stackl in *der Standard*, the leading semi-intellectual newspa-
per in Austria. Under the title "Limits of Globalization" ("Grenzen der
Globalisierung"; 1996: 2) Stackl reviews several recent works and reports that call into question the globalization process in its current
form. He outlines how doubts about globalization are mounting, and
how dystopian images of a liberal globalized future are now being popularized and spread, at least to the informed public. Stackl reviews a
recent book of Hans-Peter Martin (an Austrian) and Harald Schumann,
two reporters for the German newsweekly *der Spiegel*, once a left-
liberal magazine but now pretty centrist. Now available in twelve lan-
guages, their book describes the new global economy as a "Globalization Trap" complete with a strategic "attack on democracy and
prosperity." Another work reviewed was by a group of experts meeting in Lisbon under the leadership of Riccardo Petrella, the former
director of forecasting on science and technology for the European
Union. Petrella's group devoted most of the volume to demonstrating

the lawlike nature of globalization, and also to unveiling its darker side; their vision is of an almost totally privatized, deregulated, and liberalized market economy in which the "driving force is survival through victory ('Sieg') over others. To be a winner is the decisive and governing principle; for the losers there is no place" (my translation from the German).

As Stackl notes, since losers may lose out as producers and consumers but remain as voters, this dark vision of the future may foster nondemocratic authoritarian rulers. The Lisbon group maintains (as does William Greider in his most recent book, *One world, Ready or Not*) that globalization is a reality which must be accepted, with all its consequences; adjustment, not denial or rebellion, is the realistic strategy, for finding the best possible place within this new system. Stackl then outlines how Martin and Schumann would reform and reregulate the globalized marketplace, including a 1 percent tax (the Tobin tax) on currency transfers to tame speculative finance, and minimum social and environmental standards in world trade. Their key point is the strengthening and democratization of the European Union as a regional organization for the maintenance of European values in the new global system. For the Lisbon group, troubling questions must be solved through global treaties; a positive example they give is the 1992 United Nations' Rio Conference on the environment, which, however has never been put into force, and exists only as recommendations and reports. For Martin and Schumann, both the Rio Conference and the new World Trade Organization (WTO) are symbols of the current process of marginalizing issues of social, labor, and environmental standards. Stackl outlines for the reader a growing conflict between a globalization process which has no priorities beyond fostering of international competition and free trade, and challenges that call into question the inevitability of the current process and demand a different path, which gives much greater attention to social and environmental issues.

Another example comes from an article by Karl Otto Hondrich, sociology professor in Frankfurt, in *die Zeit,* the left-liberal intellectual German weekly magazine. Under the title "The Fairy-Tale about the End of Work" ("Die Mär vom Ende der Arbeit"), Hondrich outlines the rationale given for the end of Keynesianism and the inexorable transformation of national economic policy to meet the desires of international finance capital in this new era of international competition. Hondrich argues that this process is not inevitable, nor can it succeed without a rebalancing in the industrial nations of the needs of productivity and the needs of social solidarity. In short, he argues that the transformations taking place now are a continuation of what Georg Simmel described a century ago, the dynamic tension between modern capitalist competition as a form of social cooperation and as a form of social conflict. Policies that are oriented only toward fostering the competitive aspect will backfire, because this capitalist competition destroys the basis for social cooperation by destroying people who fail in the competitive race. Hondrich stresses the political will in the modern industrial nations to modify the destructive side of economic competition so that individual losers remain integrated into the larger social network and do not become alienated from the entire process. The fate of the individual rests upon a massive social construction:

> Every individual performance increase in the competition rests upon immense social achievements. The most important perhaps is this: the society must say yes to performance failure—and it must integrate the performance losers. That may happen mainly through families (as in Japan) or individually (as in America) or through the social state (as in Germany). Whether the American model will succeed as the most productive, seems highly doubtful. Of course the disadvantages of the German integration model are clear, high unemployment combined with high wages and high social services. Overlooked are the productive effects of these factors: the German economy maintains a highly qualified, motivated and loyal core work force with special (dual) training; and it rests on a social capital of co-determination and balancing of interests, social partnership and international openness (1996: 3; my translation from the German).

In short, Hondrich argues that the continuation of any globalization of economic development must, in one fashion or another, return to some balance between competition that creates new opportunities for economic winners and social solidarity that buffers the situation of economic losers and keeps them integrated into the larger society. Since there is no global government, it remains for national politics to address the social issue which is now being formulated again in the most recent phase of capitalist expansion. Not only does Hondrich argue for an active national politics to innovatively take up the social issue; he argues that this is an absolute necessity, without which the nation will falter in the new global economic competition. In a nice turnabout from the usual claims that absolute economic necessity now requires only a minimal state and low taxes, Hondrich presents the absolute political necessity for an active and reformed social state.

In the recent discourse featured in *die Zeit* on the changing political economy, there is a notable emphasis on the concept of a counterbalance or counterweight to the dynamics of the liberal economy. Bernhard Wördehoff (1997), former director of German radio—on the fiftieth anniversary of the Christian Democratic Union's 1947 Ahlener Program which called for a Christian socialist "overcoming of capitalism and Marxism"—comments that the rethought conservatism of the CDU did not go so far as to adopt Christian socialism, but did promote the "social market" model, which provided for "capitalism with a human face." Now this model, with its slogan "Prosperity for all," is also history. Globalization of financial markets has transformed the message into "Prosperity for all stockholders." Wördehoff is bothered by this transformation, and cites the concern of Helmut Werner, CEO of Mercedes, that at the end of an era, the effective and necessary counterbalance has been lost. Werner argues, "Before, liberalism could develop itself further, because it had an equivalent counterweight. Now it doesn't. Therefore we must develop a new problem-solving capability in our society." Wördehoff summarizes with this thought: "How and under what conditions after this epochal watershed can we reestablish the balance between economic and social requirements, which under the pressure of communism had emerged in the form of the social market, and which so successfully withstood and defeated communism?" (1997: 6). He is not optimistic about the immediate prospects, given the lack of new ideas among establishment leaders from Kohl to Lafontaine, and the fact that there is no figure of the stature of Ludwig Erhard or Karl Schiller in sight. A similar discourse comes from Gunter Hofmann (1996), one of the leading editorialists of *die Zeit*, in the form of a plea for a new social contract, which is necessary to restore the popular support for economic policy. The call for this new social contract now has become a regular feature of *die Zeit*, which represents no radical left agenda but an establishmentarian social liberalism embracing centrist social democrats like Helmut Schmidt and socially progressive Christian Democrats like Rita Sussmuth and Heiner Geissler. Like other commentators, Hofmann is not shy about politicizing the question of capitalism:

> The Republic has changed more since the unification of 1990 than had been expected. There are lots of mutations and self-corrections underway, mostly from the bottom up—and not guided by politics. Capitalism is redefining itself daily. Therein lies one reason for confidence—and a warning for politics to reconquer lost terrain. For the political question is, whether this capitalism is moral (1996:1).

This questioning of the legitimacy of global liberalism can also be heard from the conservative right, from the English political philosopher John Gray. The most recent work by Gray, *Enlightenment's Wake*, reviewed in *Dissent* by George Scialabba (1997: 132-136). contains a strong condemnation of the ideological fixation called "market fundamentalism." Scialabba is impressed with the substantial overlap between Gray's tradition-based conservative critique of global liberalism and the left-progressive critique. While Gray supports the concept of markets as a means of promoting human welfare, he also condemns the process that destroys families, communities and traditions (ways of life) valued by people. Gray criticizes the liberal project as an assault on all these values, with little besides the ideological belief in self-interested individualism to offer as a substitute. Interestingly enough, what Gray proposes is a social market alternative, similar in overall concept to the postwar German model, in which effective counterbalances are able to reshape market outcomes to meet other values of the community:

> In all those cultures where democratic institutions are themselves elements in the common conception of legitimacy, market institutions will be stable and flourishing only in so far as their forms and workings are acceptable, ethically, culturally and economically, to the underlying population (quoted in Scialabba, 1997:133).

Gray is most harshly critical of Thatcherite incursions into British conservatism, and berates Anglo-American conservatives for having bought into "free-market extremism" of the libertarian type. Much of what Gray despises about global liberalism are precisely the elements of the left-progressive analysis; most tellingly, Gray concentrates on the shallowness of the liberal commitment to humanity and the poverty of its understanding of what most people want from life. Scialabba is clearly impressed with Gray's delegitimation of global liberalism, on the most sweeping moral grounds:

> The moral foundations of Western culture have been hollowed out. To the question "why be good?" there is now no philosophically compelling answer, even if most people don't know it yet. The name of this condition in nihilism; the eventual result may be spiritual paralysis or, worse, a war of all against all and of all against nature (1997: 134).

Scialabba plainly does not share Gray's proposed solution, which is a call for overturning the idea of endless material progress, of endless scientific mastery over nature, in favor of a kind of mystical naturalism, denoted as "releasement" (*Gelassenheit* from the German Meister Eckhart). This releasement contains an openness to nature and to the unexpected and unpredictable, an abandonment of the will to power over things and people. What is impressive about Gray's work and Scialabba's review is the commonsense understanding across political lines that global liberalism is an illegitimate and dystopian project. In this respect we can detect a new and broad-based realization that global liberalism is in trouble; its ability to command respect and voluntary compliance is shrinking, facing a mounting critique that is reaching a widening and diverse audience.

One more example comes from within the very heart of financial capitalism, from the multi-billionaire George Soros. Soros, having made his fortune, committed considerable time and resources to advancing the goals of the "open society," a concept he adopted from Karl Popper in the late 1940s. The open society, as Soros admits, was largely an underdeveloped ideal that stood out most clearly by contrast to the totalitarianism of Nazi Germany and Stalinist Russia. After the collapse of communism and the end of the cold war, Soros initially devoted his attentions to fostering the democratic transitions assumed to be under way in Eastern Europe and the former Soviet Union. His Open Society funded a variety of projects, including the new Central European University campuses in Prague, Budapest, and Warsaw, and the Open Media Research Institute (omri) headquartered in Prague, which incorporated much of the staff of the former Radio Free Europe and Radio Liberty (RFE/RL). Soros has since become disillusioned about the chances for an open society in postcommunism, but he has now turned his attention and his concerns to the West.

In the major article in *Atlantic Monthly* in February 1997, Soros outlines what he now perceives as the greatest threat: the laissez-faire ideology of the new global capitalism:

> In the Philosophy of History, Hegel discerns a disturbing historical pattern—the crack and fall of civilizations owing to a morbid intensification of their own first principles. Although I have made a fortune in the financial markets, I now fear that the untrammeled intensification of laissez-faire capitalism and the spread of market values into all areas of life is endangering our open and democratic society. The main enemy of the open society, I believe, is no longer the communist but the capitalist threat (1997: 45).

Soros's argument is familiar to those on the left, and Soros still considers his critique to be an extension of Popper's basic concept of the open society, but it is instructive to hear his case against the new monism of our times—capitalist totalitarianism:

Popper showed that fascism and communism had much in common, even though one constituted the extreme right and the other the extreme left, because both relied on the power of the state to repress the freedom of the individual. I want to extend this argument. I contend that an open society may also be threatened from the opposite direction—from excessive individualism. Too much competition and too little cooperation can cause intolerable inequities and instability.

Insofar as there is a dominant belief in our society today, it is a belief in the magic of the marketplace. The doctrine of laissez-faire capitalism holds that the common good is best served by the uninhibited pursuit of self-interest. Unless it is tempered by the recognition of a common interest that ought to take precedence over particular interests, our present system—which, however imperfect, qualifies as an open society—is liable to break down (48).

Soros argues that capitalist ideology, while valid on many points, is still imperfect, and that the current claims of perfection and historical triumph for all time are leading us to a nasty and dystopian social Darwinism. Citing the trend towards accumulation of wealth across generations, Soros states his case:

The laissez-faire argument against income redistribution invokes the doctrine of the survival of the fittest. The argument is undercut by the fact that wealth is passed on by inheritance, and the second generation is rarely as fit as the first. . . . The main point I want to make is that cooperation is as much as part of the system as competition, and the slogan "survival of the fittest" distorts this fact (53).

The open society is one that recognizes the fallibility of all doctrines, and uses (inductive) trial and error to achieve progress, mindful that advantages of open debate and free thought are indispensable. Soros specifies no particular vehicle or politics to build a counterweight to the dominant global liberalism, but he does say that "in an open society it is not enough to be a democrat; one must be a liberal democrat or a social democrat or a Christian democrat or some other kind of democrat. A shared belief in the open society is a necessary but not a sufficient condition for freedom and prosperity and all the good things that the open society is supposed to bring" (58). Indirectly, Soros is saying that open and ongoing contention among political value systems, each of which has some base of citizen support, should determine the political path. This can apply only if there is meaningful choice, if political liberalism faces an effective challenge from democratic socialism and democratic Christian conservatism (with other unnamed choices as well).

Soros's analysis is pretty tame, has no real class analysis, lacks clear understanding of the values motivating capitalism, and offers only the illusory hope that a capitalist society will somehow change its core values. Soros values political pluralism, but does not offer a strategy of principled social struggle to build effective counterbalances to the interests of capital. Yet that is not the point here. What is of interest is the growing recognition, within the economic and intellectual elites of global liberalism, that something is going terribly wrong, so off track that it is undermining the legitimacy a capitalist economy absolutely requires. The recognition that this legitimacy is in decline, and perhaps is coming to some breaking point, refutes the classic liberal notion that "society" doesn't exist, that the citizenry is an unproblematic backdrop for the free market, that the performance of the free market will naturally generate its own popular legitimacy.

None of this should be surprising, since with the end of the cold war capitalism has come out of the closet in all its glory and infamy. The left has been right to suspect all along, despite Adolf Berle's notion of the corporation with a soul, that capitalism, freed from the class compromises of the cold war, would revert to classic form. Capitalism really has no soul, no sense of moral obligation to anything deeper or more lasting than the latest market reports. The utter shallowness of capitalist dominance is now becoming rapidly apparent, far beyond the outermost boundaries of anything one could identify with the political left. In its return to open dominance, capitalism reverts to something close to the description that Marx provided long ago, still by far the most penetrating look into the lack of conscience at the heart of the free market. Most telling is that these confessions and revelations come to public attention not from left-biased media or from left-wing academics, but from establishment thinkers and anxious participants in the very belly of the beast.

E. New Challenges: Development of Far-Right Alternatives

There is now every reason to look forward to an increasingly strong series of challenges to the dominant global capitalist politics. The foregoing sections argue that the renewal of a left politics is under way, that the intellectual opening for renewal has appeared—a crucial breakthrough The main task now recognized within the left intellectual community is neither defensive retrenchment nor maintaining sacred rituals, but a thorough and far-reaching rethinking of past positions and a bold reworking of what a left politics for our time should look like. I have no doubt that the renewed left politics is on the way to becoming a real challenger to global liberalism, which I perceive, as do many others from various standpoints, as rapidly losing its mantle of legitimacy.

Another issue, however, arises from the already growing array of far-right challenges to the global capitalist agenda, from the conspiracy-obsessed religious right of Pat Robertson and the populist-isolationism of Pat Buchanan in the United States, to the new and dynamic right of Fini's postfascist National Alliance or Bossi's Northern League separatism in Italy, LePen's National Front in France, Haider's Freedom Party in Austria, and to the emergence in Germany—for the first time since 1945—of an intellectual New Right of some importance (cf. Heilbrunn, 1996).

Mark Rupert has outlined the development of two general lines of thought for challenging the hegemony of global liberalism in the United States, the left-progressive variant and the far-right variant. The two agree on many points of criticism of the neoliberal new world order, but obviously for very different reasons and with very different consequences for an alternative politics. Rupert (1995, 1997a, 1997b) analyzes the competing bases for creating a new "common sense" that could resonate with a broad majority of citizens for fundamentally reshaping the politics. In the congressional debate over NAFTA particularly—which was a defining moment of public clarification—both left and right challengers could articulate the fears and opposition of large numbers of Americans to NAFTA as a key expression of global liberalism's "common sense," and they could even share a forum for denouncing the regional free trade project.

Rupert clarifies how opposition is emerging and experimenting with new formulations; how both left-progressive and far-right voices attempt to express a new understanding of the economic and social situation that can mobilize popular support; and how these efforts are tied to a rethinking and revival of political challenge on the left and right of the political spectrum. In his view:

> In response to the harshness of post-Fordist global capitalism, neo-populist tendencies are arising which frighten some in the power bloc of global capitalism. This neo-populism is not a coherent or clearly defined political ideology, however. It represents a family of related interpretations of the American political tradition, some of which point toward possible worlds in which democratically-oriented progressives might feel at home, and others which

point down the path toward nationalist or racist conflict, and ultimately perhaps fascism (1997b).

The stakes are very high in the Gramscian struggle over what globalization of the economy means in popular common sense terms, and what that might imply for political action:

> In these ideological contests, the future shape of transnational political order may be at stake. The emerging historical structure of transnational capitalism may generate the potential for the construction of political identities and projects which transcend state-centric understandings of politics and facilitate transnational movements to contest the global dominance of capital. To the extent that the ambiguities of the new populism are resolved in ways which reconstruct political identities on the basis of economic, cultural, or racial/ethnic nationalism, this potential will be undercut. If, on the other hand, this ambiguous populism can be reconstructed in ways which broaden its core understandings of "the people" and affirm core values of popular self-determination, it could provide a necessary (but not sufficient) condition for the emergence of transnational social movements oriented towards the democratization of the world economy (1997a).

I think Rupert is right, and if this is the Gramscian battleground of popular consciousness for the next century, it may be useful to make some judgments about how the competition has progressed to date, and what the prospects are for the left progressives to win the struggle.

In the larger comparative framework, one could say that there is now in virtually every Western democracy a conceptually similar struggle, which challenges the global liberal project with a radically different and broad-based alternative. According to most estimates, the far-right alternative is ahead of the left-progressive version, and it already has some advantages over the left in terms of recognized leaders, political organization, and (as usual) resources. If one compares Robertson and Buchanan (and perhaps Perot as well) in the American case with Nader and the Green Party (or the New Party or the Labor Party) in the level of visibility, organization and funding, the judgment is clear. Robert Borosage, writing for the left-liberal *Nation*, argues that it was Buchanan's attacks on Dole within the Republican primaries of 1996 that have reached popular consciousness, that his "jeremiads on declining wages, free trade and corporate greed have exposed the depths of white male economic anxiety and transformed the national debate . . ." (1996: 18). But one could make a similar judgment about LePen's National Front in France versus some elements of the French Greens, or about Haider's Freedom Party in Austria versus the Austrian Greens (or even the socially progressive Liberal Forum), or about Fini's postfascist National Alliance and Bossi's Northern League in Italy (versus what on the left?).

Only in Germany can one still, as of this writing, say that despite the emergent intellectual New Right, the political far right (Republikaner, National Democrats, National People's Union) is still pretty weak, with no convincing leaders and only scattered organization. This does not mean that the left alternative is in great shape, however. The German Greens have evolved into at least a semicredible progressive voice for an alternative future; they have some visible and talented leaders, such as Joschka Fischer, speaking to a larger national audience, and they are at a political level of organization and even officeholding that allows them to engage other parties in rethinking German politics. A good example of this was popularized in Austria's *Standard*, in a roundtable discussion between Fischer; CDU leader Kurt Biedenkopf; and Austrian Green leader Brigitte Ederer; (*Standard*, 1996). And as Andrei Markovits and Philip Gorsky (1993) argue, in Germany the intellectual dialogue between the Greens and some Social Democrats on a new Red-Green synthesis (beyond the Old Left-New Left divide) have made some progress, although the Social Democratic Party as a whole has been lacking in vision and incapable of offering its own working-class base any attractive new ideas.

The recent large-scale defection of working-class voters to LePen in the former "Red Belt" of Paris and in a string of mayoralty elections in southern French cities, Haider's 1996 electoral breakthroughs into social democratic strongholds in "Red Vienna" are fresh evidence, if any was still needed, that the far-right alternative is making inroads into the Old Left's popular base, while the new progressive alternative cannot show any such breakthrough, but remains far behind in terms of its political evolution. After the strong showing of Haider's Freedom Party in Red Vienna in late 1996, the Socialist Party began an extensive empirical study of Haider's success formula. But these studies so far mainly reveal how immovable the Socialist Party has been, how steeped in party bureaucracy and political resistance to any real change (Zöchling, 1996: 42). There is only a beginning of taking Haider seriously, and of advancing a new politics to compete with him among the urban working class, which was for so long taken for granted as a solidly socialist electoral base. Even now, Austrian socialists have only vague formulas for renewal to present, typified by Heinz Fischer, President of the National Council, who advocates "bringing together the modernizing wings and their diverse interests under an overarching basic position," whatever that might mean (Zöchling, 44). There is still an impression that Haider is able to win votes with "quick promises," while the Socialist Party offers its own "hopefully energetic, slowness" (ibid.).

This hapless debate within the Austrian Socialist Party on competing with the new far-right challenge is symptomatic of the lag in formulating left politics even as the far-right challenge makes new breakthroughs in reaching a widening audience, and in both fostering and connecting with a new political "common sense" for out times.

There are some revealing points of comparison with the situation in Weimar Germany during the 1920s and early 1930s, a period of left and right challenges to the (weak) liberal democratic interwar regime for mass support for a radical alternative. I make no claims that the current struggle is a replay of the Weimar crisis, nor that the lessons of Weimar can be straightforwardly pushed ahead in time to the current situation. Yet I do want to suggest that the current effort to rebuild a left alternative, in a simultaneous competition with the far right, can indeed benefit from the historical lessons of the Weimar tragedy.

In the period of stabilization of the Weimar Republic (1924–1928), the coalition leadership of the prodemocratic parties (the Democrats, the Catholic Centrists, and the Social Democrats) with the overall vision of Gustav Stresemann were building a political consensus on a political economy based on bringing Germany back into the "normal" international trading system—giving its export-oriented industrial sector a chance to compete fairly on world markets, where German goods had faced boycotts and discrimination after World War I. This strategy was, for its time, the expression of democratic and internationalist capitalism, and by 1928 it had produced a general recovery of the economy and a marginalization of extremist parties of left and right. The Nazis got only 2.6 percent of the vote in the Reichstag elections of 1928, and the KPD also lost ground. David Abraham's work (1986), based on his analysis of the internal strategy newsletter of the national industrial cartel, the Reichsverband Deutscher Industrie (RDI), indicated a grudging but growing acceptance by export-oriented big business of political democracy as compatible with its own economic goals. Had the Great Depression not intervened, it seemed likely that democratic capitalism, with an internationalist orientation toward normalized diplomatic and trade relations with the other major Western states, would have consolidated itself. But the economic crisis shattered the still weak legitimacy of the Weimar system, and gave rise to challenges from left and right, two alternative understandings of the crisis and two very different strategies for overcoming the crisis. In the final analysis, the far-right alternative, voiced by the National Socialists, was able to mobilize a mass base of support around the message of national salvation through Hitler's leadership and the destruction of the Weimar democracy. Elites in the military, business, and political sectors, never supporters of democracy, saw in Hitler and his Nazi Party an opportunity to smash Weimar and reorient the political economy, to serve the interests of the military-industrial complex. The political schemers of the established elites (Papen, Hugenburg, Oskar Hindenburg) formed their coalition with the Nazis in the early 1930s, and provided the critical leverage for the seizure of power and the building of the Third Reich. The role of the antidemocratic elites in the final betrayal of Weimar (Kühnl, 1983; Hörster-Philipps, 1983; Schweitzer, 1964) is pretty well documented, but they would never have found an opening if the Nazi Party had not been able to mobilize a very impressive mass base of support (which reached 37 percent of the electorate in the first Reichstag election of 1932, but then showed signs of having peaked, with a decline to 33 percent in the second elections of that year). What were the critical factors that enabled the far-right Nazi alternative to amass its tremendous following, since there was also a competing left alternative to the Weimar system during the collapse of its legitimacy from 1929 to 1933?

Studies of the rise of the Nazi Party from 1928 to 1933 within a competitive multi-party system have highlighted several factors. First of all, the Nazi Party was in some ways a very modern "catch-all" party (a term popularized by the political scientist Otto Kirchheimer and intended to denote democratic parties that were not very ideological but interested in "catching" as many voters as possible on a pragmatic electoralist basis. The Nazis made direct, policy-relevant appeals to virtually all groups (except Jews, of course) in the German population. There were special interest appeals to farmers, to small business, to workers, to military officers, soldiers and veterans, to small-towns and rural areas, as well as big-city residents, to Protestants and Catholics (cf. Hamilton, 1982; Childers, 1983). The Nazi leadership likewise recruited from a broad swath of German society, though it excluded women (cf. Kater, 1983; Nagle, 1983, 1989), so that it was a cross-class mixture of old and new elites, an alternative elite for capitalism in crisis. The Nazi Party, contrary to some claims, did not operate with big-business money in its early years; this money came later, in 1932, in the critical negotiations over building the political coalition to destroy Weimar. The party was able to be largely self-financing, from its own members and from events it staged; it was an independently funded political force, built on much self-sacrifice among its members. It was also extremely active, campaigning continuously to expand its support, not just during elections. Its appeals to various groups were, to be sure, often contradictory, and its street-fighting did turn off some potential supporters. But its energy, noted by observers at the time, was much higher than that of the pro-Weimar parties, or even of the antisystem communist competition. Despite its use of terror and violence against political adversaries, the Nazis were able to cultivate an image among many "respectable" middle-class citizens as a bulwark, maybe the last bulwark, against the communist menace. The Nazi Party was able to decimate the Protestant voter base of the moderate conservative, nationalist and liberal parties, which shrank from 39 percent of the vote in 1928 to less than 10 percent in July of 1932, while the vote for the Nazis soared from 2.6 percent to 37 percent.

By comparison, the far left offered its own class-specific, proletarian internationalist alternative. As espoused by the KPD, this model was tied to the emerging Soviet political economy, which in the Great Depression did present a vision of class solidarity and full employment despite all the Stalinist atrocities, many of which were not fully visible to outsiders in the early 1930s, in the era before the purges. But a possible left alternative, despite its attraction to young, unemployed working-class men, suffered from several strategic disadvantages.

First, the left was irreconcilably split between its Leninist revolutionary (communist) and its democratic evolutionary (social democratic) wings; despite the common Marxist heritage, the split after World War I made cooperation impossible and deadly political opposition probable. The left vision for a different political economy was undoubtedly less credible to its potential audience because it was indeed a house divided. Whereas before World War I international socialism had room for a great variety of movements and parties, the split between Leninist communists and anti-Leninist socialists had reordered the left into two large camps, each with some real areas of strength and weakness. In those industrial nations with some democratic experience and more solid democratic cultures, the social democratic variant had generally

dominated; in countries with lesser or later industrial capitalist development and with little or no experience in democratic politics, the
Leninist variant had much greater opportunities. In Weimar, both variants had some real opportunities and found resonance among a considerable portion of the working class (and generally only among the
working class). Attempts to find a synthesis or a middle ground that
could accommodate the great majority of workers failed; the Independent Social Democratic Party, which had gotten nearly 8 percent of
the vote in the elections to the first democratic parliament in 1919,
faded quickly (similar experiments, for example the Independent Labour
Party in Britain, were also failures in this sense), and left activists had
to choose one camp or the other. In 1928, at the peak of postwar
democratic recovery and consolidation, the two socialist parties (SPD
and KPD) got 40.4 percent of the vote. In July 1932, at the very
height of the Great Depression with 44 percent jobless, the combined
vote of the SPD and KPD was 13.2 million votes or 36 percent of the
total, compared with 37 percent for Hitler's NSDAP (Kühnl, 1983:
103). But the left vote was split, with 21.6 percent for the Social
Democrats and 14.3 percent for the Communists. In the last free election, in November of 1932, as the Nazi vote dropped to 33 percent,
the left's combined vote stayed at 37 percent, but again was totally
divided (20.4 percent SPD and 16.9 percent KPD) between two fiercely
antagonistic parties (cf. Remmling, 1989).

Second, as Richard Hamilton (1982) and Thomas Childers (1986)
have pointed out, the left parties (both SPD and KPD) devoted their
political mobilization almost entirely to the modern working class in
larger industrial cities; they adhered, as good Marxists, to the grand
story of the proletarian class as the engine of social transformation.
This was, of course, part of the attractiveness of Marx's vision—of the
proletariat as the class in society but not of society, the universal class
that could emancipate humankind from its universal suffering. Despite
the early warnings of Eduard Bernstein, who based his evolutionary
socialism in good measure on empirical findings, that the working
class itself was divided and not nearly so conscious of any unity or
solidarity as Marx had hoped, even the moderate Social Democrats
made little effort to gain support among the many other social groups,
which were also potentially open to alternative visions of a future Germany. As the figures cited above show, both SPD and KPD could in
fact garner very substantial voter followings, but they could not go
beyond the upper limits of the secularized working class to achieve a

clear majority unless they actively appealed to other interests and campaigned actively to broaden their base. In particular, they made little effort among rural and small-town people, farmers, small shopkeepers, and the religious community. They did make some efforts among big-city police, but little effort among the military or veterans. In part they were hampered by their own ideological forecasts of working-class consciousness and solidarity, which were not entirely off the mark but were self-limiting in terms of building a coalition for a different society.

A third factor that hurt the left was its lack of national identification with Germany. This was, of course, one of the lessons of World War I, which socialists (with exceptions like Luxemburg and Liebknecht) at the crucial moment of truth had failed to oppose precisely in order to build their patriotic credentials and to overcome the charge of lacking a fatherland (*vaterlandslose Gesellen*). They wanted to avoid repeating that. But at the same time, inattention to feelings of national identity and—for the KPD, the identification with Moscow's interests—left an empty political space for conservatives and nationalists and finally fascists to fill.

Fourth, the left also suffered from a lack of resources. (Although Moscow did provide some aid to the KPD, this was pretty modest and was given only at the disastrous price of strict obedience to the Moscow line.) The SPD did build its own network of auxiliary organizations and food co-ops, and these served to solidify its working-class popular base. But the SPD, even through its years of serving in coalition regimes through the 1920s, did not utilize this time to build ties to those segments of business, banking, and higher civil service which were more open to prodemocratic discourse and to an more internationalist economic course. To be sure, the barriers that would have to have been overcome were formidable, since the social elites of Germany were generally loath to associate themselves with socialists of any variety. Class cleavages were very deep, and cross-class sharing of resources would require a strong commitment from the left to engage selected elements from the upper classes in political dialogue. These efforts were not made, and in the crucial final years of Weimar, the Social Democrats fought for the survival of the republic with dwindling assets and virtually no allies.

In what follows, I am not suggesting that left rethinkers and renewers abandon any principled opposition to their political rivals, nor that they adopt manipulative tactics to pander to all conceivable interests.

I certainly am not suggesting that the left adopt the style of Nazi campaigns or streetfighting or leader-worship or national-patriotism. But I do see ways in which the current left renewal effort might benefit from some of the "lessons" of Weimar, when the left was in competition with a far-right challenger for reaching a mass audience with a "commonsense" understanding of the social situation, and proposing an alternative politics for dealing with that situation.

First and foremost, the left renewal, without being able to impose any political consensus on a new progressive left politics, can try to avoid the kind of intraleft sectarian thinking that leads to (accurate) public perceptions of unseriousness, disconnection from the real world—utopianism or playing at politics—which most people cannot afford. The end of communism should now have removed the classic split between Leninists and anti-Leninists. Much of this left sectarianism has faded with the demise of the small Maoist and Trotskyite sects of the 1970s and early 1980s, or the desertion of some prominent figures to the neocon right; yet there remains an unpleasant tendency in left intellectual circles to view different opinions on key issues (Cuba, crime, welfare, or religion) as signs that political coalitions are impossible, and that the effort should not even be made. More important, in this view, is preserving principled purity, so that one stands for something very clearly and unwaveringly. That is a fair point, but if it impedes broadening the base of a political project that must aim at reaching majority status, then it must be modified to include engaging people whose views are only partially in agreement with one's own, and working together on creating a new "common sense" or common ground on points of disagreement.

In this vein, a renewed left in our times needs both to regain contact with working-class politics and to transcend the "grand story" of the proletariat as the chosen leading actor for historic social transformation. And if the urban working class was not enough in Weimar Germany, it is clearly not enough in contemporary global capitalism. A revitalized left politics needs to build regular and normal contacts with other potential actors, the widest possible range; the new social movements spoke to this need to go beyond the (male) working class, but this also caused some rupture with the working-class movement. This can, in the current rethinking, be overcome. But the new social movements forgot that committed Christian and other religious believers are also a movement, that rural and small-town citizens are also searching for a political voice, that the military and police are not by definition beyond the pale of a possible left-progressive politics. And, in a political culture where democratic values have much greater support among all classes, the business community cannot be totally written off as outside a renewed left politics. Business politics covers a lot of ground, some areas of which could be very helpful for the left, in terms of advocating a policy which makes economic sense and which has some support from groups with resources and access to others, in leading managerial and executive positions who are open to an alternative political economy.

My story here is of a wider conversation on renewing and pursuing a left politics. I think one of the lessons of Weimar Germany (and other episodes) is that the left needs to open itself up, to a wide range of ideas and perspectives, with the fewest hard boundaries, and to make much greater efforts to reach out to audiences once presumed unreachable or forever hostile. My story is, additionally, of a more bottom-up inductive process of rebuilding a left politics and meeting the far right's challenge. The far right has been experimenting during the decline of the Keynesian welfare state consensus, and in my opinion it is now ahead of the left in mounting its own challenge to global liberalism. The far right has its own "commonsense" vision, based on national patriotism, economic protectionism and autarchy, a strong national security state, and rejection of liberal internationalism and foreign entanglements. It has built up a significant mass base of support through selected antiforeigner, antiimmigrant, antiminority appeals. It benefits from the growing distrust of government and of governmental support for global liberalism, and it utilizes theories of elite conspiracies that find an attentive audience. The Internet is absolutely chock-full of conspiracy theories and accusations, so this is not a movement that has been left behind by communications technology. (Hitler also understood the potential and refined the use of radio and mass rallies as instruments of mass mobilization in interwar Germany.)

The left renewal may be able to avoid some of the disadvantages that handicapped the left during the Weimar era, and there is no inherent reason to believe that it will repeat the mistakes of that earlier Gramscian combat for the "commonsense" support of a broad majority. The European and American democracies are much stronger than they were during the interwar period, and although the Keynesian welfare state is eroding more rapidly in the 1990s, this is still an era of more gradual transformation, with more opportunity for open debate and public discourse on a new political consensus. Neither the masses nor the elites are yet ready to abandon political democracy, and as long as a democratic politics is still possible, there is a chance for a revived left politics to build its base and to meet the far-right challenge for the new "commonsense" political consciousness of our times. Yet the bank account of goodwill for democracy is being drawn down each year by the social trauma of economic dislocation and growing social divisions, and eventually the crisis of legitimacy will encompass not only the politics of global liberalism but also the politics of a democratic state. Before that happens, a revitalized left must be strong enough to prevent an antidemocratic coalition of far-right movements and economic, military, and religious elites from undermining democracy in favor of a regime in command of, and willing to employ, the full array of repressive measures.

F. The Renewed Left in a New World Historical Era

The considerations throughout this book on the nature of the renewal process for a left politics have been shaped by my understanding of the new world historical era of our times. My explicit and sometimes implicit argument has been that, as was the case in earlier political renewals of classic value systems, a successful renewal "matches up" with the larger environment from which it evolves. The shaping of a progressive left today, if successful, will follow this pattern. As a final summary, I would like to attempt an overview of what kinds of "matching up" are the key to anticipating (a lesser form of predicting) the emergence of a rethought left politics.

First of all, the crisis of both communism and social democracy has been caused by the emergence of a newly confident and dynamic form of international capitalism, able to overcome the limitations of Keynesian welfare state democracy in the West and communist statism in the East. This global liberalism was certainly anticipated by Marx already in the nineteenth century, but it was not yet the dominant form of capitalism in his time, nor even in Lenin's time, despite their proclamations. There was, for most of the twentieth century, still plenty of political space for a national-level political challenge to national capitalism, which then took precedence over left internationalism, international solidarity and commitment among left political organizations. The heavy concentration on nation-state political strategy, which was characteristic in an era of nationbuilding, is no longer a good match for a renewed left. Now, finally, at the end of the cold war and the end of the Keynesian compromise, there is a globalizing capitalist project, confident (and with reason) of its ability to challenge governments—even the great powers—that attempt to regulate and manage national economies. While some may claim that much of this is "globalony"—propaganda meant to preemptively disarm critics—I find that claim unconvincing and backward-looking. Therefore, in the current world historical era, a future-oriented left politics must itself "match up with" the reality of global liberalism and develop a politics capable of challenging capitalism on an international scale. While a progressive left challenge will still involve politics on the national level, as well as the subnational and international levels, it must build social coalitions that can counterbalance the still rising dominance of globalizing forces responsive now only to transnational capitalist interests. "Delinking" cannot do this; a new isolationism on the left would be no more convincing than isolationism on the right. The universal challenge of a capitalism which has no loyalty to any social or cultural values, and which Marx overanticipated, has finally arrived.

The extension of democratic values, even formal or bourgeois democratic values, over the last half of this century has been breathtaking. In the nineteenth century only a handful of early bourgeois societies were on a democratizing path; in the first half of the twentieth century, weak democracies were overthrown by fascist coalitions spearheaded by strong right-extremist movements and parties, coalitions in which business, military, and church authorities played their infamous roles of open or tacit support. Now the "democracy trend" offers much greater opportunities for a democratic left politics, and for a much less ambiguous commitment of a revitalized left to democratic politics, not just as compromise but as principled means toward constructing the social counterweight to the hegemony of capitalism. Despite the severe limitations of this "democracy trend," and the setbacks that will surely appear in some nations, the current era offers much greater promise for a left politics as the leading advocate of democratic principles, in formal electoral arenas, in human and civil rights, in the treatment of minorities, and in the economy. The left of our time should be the leading advocate of democratic consolidation in the new democracies of Eastern Europe, Latin America, East Asia, and South Africa; the left should be the lead advocate for democratic breakthroughs in China, Mexico, Cuba and Nigeria. Democratization and democratic consolidation as goals of left progressive politics serve to separate the left from the interests of global capital, which would rather exploit

Chinese, Mexican, Nigerian, and Cuban workers who are denied democratic rights. Without the continued spread of democracy, workers will be confronted with the same issues faced by Bernstein and Lenin and Luxemburg; with democratic expansion, more and more workers will have the chance to develop their own political voice, and to add their voices to progressive parties and movements in other democracies, without splitting into antirevolutionary social democrats and antidemocratic revolutionaries.

Another aspect of the extension of democratic values during the last half of this century has been the growing movement for full citizenship rights beyond the organized working class, although one might well view the labor movement as the godfather of civil rights and the new social movements. The inclusion of women and racial and ethnic minorities in the mainstream life of the affluent liberal democracies has often been seen as a political diversion from class politics, and this is often the case, especially when the labor movement and working-class parties were either defensively conservative or painfully slow in supporting rights for women, racial minorities, and gays. The growth of a culture of universal rights for citizens indicates the impossibility (already outlined by Bernstein in his depiction of a divided working class) of retelling a grand tale of the proletariat as the preordained historical agent of the left, and redirects attention to building a diversity of agents of left progressive politics, a diversity that will have to learn to live with important disagreements at the same time as its component groups stay in contact with each other and continue to talk through their differences.

The "monist" vision of a one-class left politics, which inspired millions over the past century and more, is now less plausible than ever. That has some seemingly negative consequences for a renewed left; with no grand tale to tell, how will a left politics inspire activism, self-sacrifice, and devotion to the cause that gave the left its great icons of heroism and principle in the past? With an end to endism, which I have supported, the left cannot offer a grand historical mission in which people can enlist for a lifetime of struggle and sacrifice. Such total devotion as Lenin required for his vanguard cadre, or even as Western socialists relied upon for building the labor movement, is not a good match for a more modest and less historically certain left politics today. Yet perhaps this is an advantage of our era as well; perhaps the democratization within a renewed left is better served by modesty and humility, less certainty about grand theory, less zeal for reaching our "end of history." Leninism aimed at the selective organization and training, apart from the larger society, of only the most committed, those most willing to sacrifice themselves and others for the great cause, which then turned out to be the Leninist party itself. At the end of communism, one benefit for a left renewal today is the historical experience of the terrible costs of such total devotion; it may now be easier than it was in Lenin's time (when he was also heavily criticized by Bernstein and Luxemburg) to avoid this type of total devotion, and to accept much more democratic pluralism within the left coalition. Such internal diversity will always seem more messy and less coherent, less capable of rapid and decisive action; but it may also be far less capable of violence against others and of wrongdoing in the name of some theoretical end of history. Lenin's motto was "better fewer but better" (a unifed cadre party of the most skilled militants), and this position was able to split the left in two for a century. Now a renewed left can say, "better more but less devoted, and more tolerant of each other."

Marxism for the industrial era did give clear indications of agency and consciousness for radical change. More inductive politics and less grand historical pretensions must also raise new questions about which groups and interests are reachable for a renewed left politics. If the answer is unclear, then any renewal effort would be foolish to write off potential allies. I have argued above, in many sections, that old fault lines between left and nonleft must been thrown out as outdated and harmful. The long-standing tradition that viewed religion and the religious as outside the left project, which was seen as strictly secular and antireligious, needs serious revision. Although there were good reasons why the church was seen as an implacable enemy in an earlier political landscape, there are now many reasons to view religious communities as potential allies, and as first-class partners in a revitalized left politics. Much the same openness and bridge building should be applied to rural, suburban and small-town people, who are often neglected by traditional left politics as hostile to big-city labor. Members of the police, prison administrators, and career military people should also not be automatically written off; the changes in the composition of the police and armed forces alone should give grounds for contesting these groups' political leanings and not surrendering them to the right. Finally, a renewing left should bring its message into the greater diversity of the business community, to develop the left-progressive debate also within the ranks of management and business owners, and to avoid the complete isolation of potential allies within the business community, who command some considerable wisdom and access to resources that a left politics can surely use.

All of this must sound very disturbing to many on the left, and it still sounds somewhat strange to me as well; yet I think that global liberalism is also profoundly disturbing to many people in business, in the military and police, and in religious communities, and these people are new potential audiences for a different left, the kind of democratic and pluralistic left I have been describing. The Keynesian era of cross-class cooperation and collaboration, especially in Germany and in continental Europe generally, has already given evidence of this potential. It is one of the positive legacies of the Keynesian era that many business, military, and religious leaders are now solid supporters of a democratic, socially just society. The political orientation of these key groups, which in the interwar period were indeed hostile not only to socialism but to liberal democracy, is now much more contestable. Earlier socialist politics was aimed clearly and unambiguously against them as class enemies; a renewed left politics needs no unnecessary enemies, and it needs to contest virtually every group for support.

Finally, the current world historical era now contains the living memory of Keynesianism and the social market economy, which despite all the right-wing propaganda and the real shortcomings of the democratic welfare state, still resides in the consciousness of huge numbers of people as proof that collective political effort can manage and regulate a market economy for the improvement of people's lives. The great positive legacy of the social compromises made during the cold war is that now people know that laissez-faire capitalism, or free-market capitalism, can be socially bound through democratic politics. The legitimacy of that effort has not been lost on people, and this is profoundly different from the nineteenth and early twentieth centuries. It was possible, for two generations at least, to construct a consensus politics that did not destroy capitalist markets but did restrain capital and did improve the lives of millions of wageearners. This politics created the highest levels of social security, citizens' rights and fulfillment of human needs in history. Although this cold war consensus politics is eroding and cannot simply be rebuilt as before, there is now a part of the "commonsense" that tells people that they are not simply appendages to markets and machines, not just consumers and isolated individuals. The politics of social solidarity was a great success—peace and prosperity and social equity as never before. The ideologues of global liberalism are trying to eradicate this memory and defame all who support it, but the record of this period is so positive for so many that it would take generations to reduce expectations down to pre-World War II levels. People understand only too well that there is no inherent need for great social insecurity and material deprivation, and they will reject an ideology that tells them they must accept anxiety and downward spiraling of expectations as just part of the inevitable godlike workings of capitalism.

These are my confessions of continued commitment to the open admission of regret for past errors and the willingness to reflect on unpleasant realities, written here in the spirit of optimism that the left is experiencing in fact a historic renewal of its practical politics for a better future, a new left politics which will not end all social conflict and will not end history, but which is desperately needed to effectively challenge the dominance of globalizing capitalism. Despite all of the difficulties ahead, I feel a sense of real joy that this process is well under way.

References

Abraham, David (1986). *The Collapse of the Weimar Republic*, 2nd ed., New York: Holmes and Meier.

Beck, Ulrich (1997). " Capitalism Without Work," *Dissent* (Winter) 51–56.

Borosage, Robert (1996). "Buchanan's Challenge: Is Anyone Listening?" *Nation* (March 18) 18–21.

Childers, Thomas (1983). *The Nazi Voter*. Chapel Hill, NC: University of North Carolina Press.

Chirot, Daniel (1994). *How Societies Change*. Thousand Oaks, CA: Pine Forge Press.

Friedman, Thomas (1996). "Revolt of the Wannabes," *New York Times* (February 7) A19.

Gray, John (1996). *Enlightenment's Wake: Politics and Culture at the Close of the Modern Age*. London: Routledge.

Hamilton, Richard (1982). *Who Voted for Hitler?* Princeton, NJ: Princeton University Press.

Heilbrunn, Jacob (1996). "Germany's New Right" *Foreign Affairs* (November–December).

Hofmann, Gunter (1996). "Und die Moral vom Kapital?" *die Zeit* (April 26) 1.

Holt, John, and David Richardson (1970). "Competing Paradigms in Comparative Politics," in Holt and Turner, eds., *The Methodology of Comparative Research*. New York: Free Press.

Hondrich, Karl Otto (1996). "Die Mär vom Ende der Arbeit," *die Zeit* (October 11) 3.

Hörster-Philipps, Ulrike (1983). "Conservative Concepts of Dictatorship in the Final Phase of the Weimar Republic," in I. Wallimann and M. Dobkowski, eds., *Towards the Holocaust*. Westwood, CT: Greenwood Press.

Hunt, Richard (1974). *The Political Ideas of Marx and Engels*. Pittsburgh, PA: University of Pittsburgh Press.

Huntington, Samuel (1996). *The Clash of Civilizations and the Remaking of World Order*. New York: Simon and Schuster.

Kater, Michael (1983). *The Nazi Party*. Cambridge, MA: Harvard University Press.

Kühnl, Reinhard (1983). "The Rise of Fascism in Germany and Its Causes," in I. Wallimann and M. Dobkowski, eds., *Towards the Holocaust*. Westwood, CT: Greenwood Press.

Markovits, Andrei, and Philip Gorski (1993). *The German Left—Red, Green and Beyond* New York: Oxford University Press.

Nagle, John (1977). *System and Succession: The Social Bases of Political Elite Recruitment*. Austin, TX: University of Texas Press.

———— (1983). "Composition and Evolution of the Nazi Elite" in I. Wallimann and M. Dobkowski, eds. *Towards the Holocaust*. Westwood, CN: Greenwood Press.

———— (1989). "The NSDAP: An Alternative Elite for Capitalism in Crisis" in I. Wallimann and M. Dobkowski, eds., *Radical Perspectives on the Rise of Fascism in Germany, 1919–1945*. New York: Monthly Review Press

———— (1991). *Looking at Marx: A Student Manual*. Syracuse, NY: Center for Instructional Development.

———— (1992). "Befreiung vom Kommunismus" *Sozialismus* (November).

Pierson, Christopher (1995). *Socialism After Communism: The New Market Socialism*. Oxford: Polity Press.

Remmling, Günter (1989). "Destruction of the Workers' Mass Movements in Nazi Germany," in I. Wallimann and M. Dobkowski, eds., *Radical Perspectives on the Rise of Fascism in Germany, 1919–1945*. New York: Monthly Review Press.

Rupert, Mark (1995) *Producing Hegemony*. NY: Oxford University Press

———— (1997a). "Globalization and American Common Sense: Struggling to Make Sense of a Post-Hegemonic World," *New Political Economy* 2:1

———— (1997b). "Globalization and the Reconstruction of Common Sense in the U.S.," paper prepared for presentation at the annual meeting of the Interantional Studies Association in Toronto.

Rorty, Richard (1997). "Labor and the Intellectuals," *Dissent* (Winter) 31–34.

Schwab, Klaus and Claude Smadja (1996). "Start Taking the Backlash Against Globalization Seriously," *International Herald Tribune* (February 1) 8.

Schweitzer, Arthur (1964). *Big Business in the Third Reich*. Bloomington: Indiana University Press.

Scialabba, George (1997). "Community or Collapse," *Dissent* (Winter) 132–136.

Soros, George (1997). "The Capitalist Threat," *Atlantic Monthly* (February) 45–58.

Stackl, Erhard (1996). "Grenzen der Globalisierung," *der Standard* (Vienna) (December 27) 2.

Standard (1996). "Abräumen, um den Tisch neu zu decken," *der Standard* (Vienna) (December 24, 25, 26) 4–5.

Wördehoff, Bernhard (1997). "Es war einmal—'Wohlstand für alle'," *die Zeit* (January 24) 6.

Zöchling, Christa (1996). "Faszination Haider," *Profil* 27:52 (December 23) 42–44.

Index

MAJOR CONCEPTS IN POLITICS AND POLITICAL THEORY

This series invites book manuscripts and proposals on major concepts in politics and political theory—justice, equality, virtue, rights, citizenship, power, sovereignty, property, liberty, etc.—in prominent traditions, periods, and thinkers.

Send manuscripts or proposals, with author's vitae to:

Garrett Ward Sheldon
General Editor
Clinch Valley College
of the University of Virginia
College Avenue
Wise, VA 24293